THE ESSENTIALIST VILLAIN

THE ESSENTIALIST VILLAIN

ON LEO BERSANI

MIKKO TUHKANEN

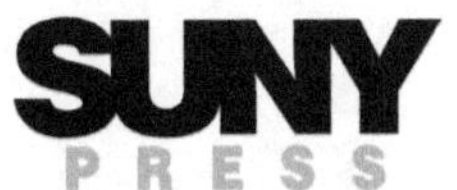

Cover art of Leo Bersani—passport photo, circa 1967—used by permission of Leo Bersani.

Published by State University of New York Press, Albany

For information, contact State University of New York Press, Albany, NY
www.sunypress.edu

Production, Diane Ganeles

Library of Congress Cataloging-in-Publication Data

Name: Tuhkanen, Mikko, author.
Title: The essentialist villain: on Leo Bersani / Mikko Tuhkanen, author
Description: Albany: State University of New York Press [2018].
Identifiers: ISBN 9781438469676 hardcover | ISBN 9781438469683 (ebook) | ISBN 9781438469669 pbk.
Further information is available at the Library of Congress.

10 9 8 7 6 5 4 3 2 1

Contents

Acknowledgments vii

Abbreviations ix

Introduction 1

1 Homomonadology: Proust–Deleuze–Beckett–Blanchot 23

2 Wanting Being: Freud–Laplanche 57

3 Rethinking Redemption: Benjamin–Baudelaire–Nietzsche 85

4 Simultaneity and Sociability: Benjamin–Beckett–Simmel 119

5 Narcissus, a Cosmology: Luther–Freud–Plato–Speculative Astronomy 147

Notes 177

Works Cited 213

Index 239

Acknowledgments

I extend my sincere thanks to Leo Bersani; Tim Dean; Marian Eide; Elizabeth Freeman; Emily Johansen; Andrew Kenyon; E. L. McCallum; David McWhirter; Mary Ann O'Farrell; Peter Rehberg; Nicholas Royle; Jenelle Troxell; the contributors to *Leo Bersani: Queer Theory and Beyond*; and, at *differences*, Elizabeth Weed and the anonymous readers of "Homomonadology."

~

An earlier version of chapter 1 has appeared as "Homomonadology: Leo Bersani's Essentialism," *differences* 25.2 (Summer 2014): 62–100.

Abbreviations

AI Bersani and Ulysse Dutoit, *Arts of Impoverishment: Beckett, Rothko, Resnais* (Cambridge: Harvard UP, 1993).

BB Bersani, *Balzac to Beckett: Center and Circumference in French Fiction* (New York: Oxford UP, 1970).

BF Bersani, *Baudelaire and Freud* (Berkeley: U of California P, 1977).

C Bersani and Ulysse Dutoit, *Caravaggio* (London: BFI, 1999).

CR Bersani, *The Culture of Redemption* (Cambridge: Harvard UP, 1990).

CS Bersani and Ulysse Dutoit, *Caravaggio's Secrets* (Cambridge: MIT P, 1998).

DSM Bersani, *The Death of Stéphane Mallarmé* (Cambridge: Cambridge UP, 1982).

FA Bersani, *A Future for Astyanax: Character and Desire in Literature* (New York: Columbia UP, 1976).

FoB Bersani and Ulysse Dutoit, *Forms of Being: Cinema, Aesthetics, Subjectivity* (London: BFI, 2004).

FrB Bersani, *The Freudian Body: Psychoanalysis and Art* (New York: Columbia UP, 1986).

FV Bersani and Ulysse Dutoit, *The Forms of Violence: Narrative in Assyrian Art and Modern Culture* (New York: Schocken, 1985).

H Bersani, *Homos* (Cambridge: Harvard UP, 1995).

I Bersani and Adam Phillips, *Intimacies* (Chicago: U of Chicago P, 2008).

IRG Bersani, *Is the Rectum a Grave? and Other Essays* (Chicago: U of Chicago P, 2010).

MP Bersani, *Marcel Proust: The Fictions of Life and of Art* (New York: Oxford UP, 1965).

TT Bersani, *Thoughts and Things* (Chicago: U of Chicago P, 2015).

Introduction

This study makes two related claims about Leo Bersani's work: it is *essentialist*; and it is *speculative*. These may, we recognize, read like indictments. In contemporary theory, "essentialism" and "speculativeness" have come to indicate ancient errors of thought that we are supposed to have overcome. For us, "essence" most often names a prosthetic fantasy with which philosophers used to prop up their rickety ontologies, cover over their systems' constitutive incompleteness and instability; contemporary theory has taken as its task the exposure of such sleights-of-hand, the undoing of their treacherous glamor. There are ways to flirt with essentialism: the sin is redeemed, for example, when one's confession is accompanied by an appeal to "strategy." When we declare ourselves "strategic essentialists," we acknowledge the necessary performativity of our onto-political actions, recognize the ethical impurity of our worldly being. Otherwise, we are supposed to have learned from the Continental thinkers of the twentieth century—most important of whom for our context is Jacques Derrida—that claims to essences merely reveal an imperious wish to universalize our inescapably partial perspectives, to evade the ethical implications of our radical immanence.

"Essence" is a familiar ruse particularly in "speculative" thought. If twentieth-century philosophy has done much to delegitimize once-routine claims to essences, the error of "speculation" was pointed out by even earlier commentators. It is particularly in Immanuel Kant's critique of metaphysics and Karl Marx's de-idealization of Hegelian thought that the long hegemony of speculative philosophy came to an end. The critical turn of Kant's philosophy consisted of his outlawing all synthetic *a priori* propositions in metaphysics. Such propositions, according to Kantian epistemology, aim at a realm beyond human experience; they remain, hence, merely speculative. As Kant writes in the 1787 preface to the *Critique of*

Pure Reason, critical philosophy should "*deprive* speculative reason of its pretension to extravagant insight [*der spekulativen Vernunft zugleich ihre Anmaßung überschwenglicher Einsichten* benehme]." Without this dispossession, the raptures of the speculative mind are wont to turn into the unbridled fanaticism of *Schwärmerei*.[1] Marx deploys the same term, *überschwänglich* (effusive, rapturous, exuberant), to abjure German idealism: according to him, Hegel's political philosophy has managed to supply nothing but "abstract extravagant *thinking* on the modern state [*abstrakte überschwengliche* Denken *des modernen Staats*]."[2] If Hegel wanted to render mappable the realm that Kant deemed out of bounds, Marx implies that his philosophy has done nothing but produce political theories of oneiric unrealness, the kinds of idiosyncratic fantasies that Kant warned await for us once we engage in speculations. Marx saw in Hegel a return to the idealist excesses of seventeenth-century metaphysics, the kind of "*wild speculation* [trunkenen Spekulation]" that he and Friedrich Engels identified in the likes of Descartes, Malebranche, Spinoza, and Leibniz.[3] Many Marxist philosophers have since then continued to call out the drunken antics of their speculative predecessors.

We begin to observe Bersani's frequent indifference to such commonplaces of contemporary thought by following the unfolding, ongoing now for half a century, of his oeuvre. We can commence this effort by turning to a recent, brief text. In the preface to the second edition of his first book, *Marcel Proust: Fictions of Life and of Art* (1965; second ed. 2013), Bersani observes that the early study contains, in an unelaborated, virtual form, much of what is to develop, or perhaps to actualize, in his writing about Proust over the course of the next fifty years: "all the later work," he writes, "is, in some way, already included in the first study."[4] This observation, we propose, should be situated in three intellectual-artistic contexts, read alongside three thinkers whose work has been crucial in informing Bersani's thought. It is here that a Bersanian essentialism begins to emerge.

Bersani obligingly draws our attention to the first, and most obvious, of these experimenters. If his work begins with Proust, it not only never leaves the Proustian sphere but also cannot but replicate the peculiar structure of the Proustian novel. Like Proust's, his work, in proceeding from its initial articulation, modifies its earlier stages in a movement of what Bersani is to call "circular mobility" (*DSM* ix) or "circular hermeneutics" (*CR* 15). He evokes Germaine Brée's argument, in *The World of Marcel Proust* (1966), that the "Combray" section—the first couple of hundred pages of *À la recherche du temps perdu*—contains in an embryonic form everything that is to follow in Proust's novel. Each subsequent section constitutes a deepening of the initial figuration. Already in *Marcel Proust,* he calls this "a process of invention and enrichment" (*MP* 6) characteristic of Proust; *À la recherche*'s "idea of growth" consists not of "an accumulation of new experiences, but [of] a re-creation and an *approfondissement* of past experience" (*MP* 83). As he writes later, in this mode the text unfolds in "concentric circles . . . in which each section is a mistaken yet illuminating replication and *approfondissement* of the preceding section" (*CR* 14). Despite numerous disagreements and repudiations, Bersani remains, in important ways, Proustian.

Like Proust's, Bersani's work constitutes a structure in which "[e]ach present is an inaccurate replication—or, as I now like to call it, a re-categorization—of all our pasts."[5] When a thought is "recategorized," it is rendered, as Bersani continues in an interview, "a little more precise, or more expansive. It's as if later versions of certain thoughts keep spiraling out with new additions. It's a strange relation of undoing but not quite undoing what you've thought."[6] What he calls the process of "recategorization" is familiar not only from Proust's but also from the psychoanalytic theorist Jean Laplanche's work. It is in psychoanalysis, and particularly the characteristics of the Freudian thought that Laplanche has elaborated, that we find the second important source for the spiraling-deepening movement—*approfondissement,* recategorization—of the Bersanian oeuvre. Bersani repeatedly draws our attention to the proximity of Proust and Freud. He often posits that Proust is the most psychoanalytic of novelists: "Proust," he writes, ". . . has given us the most incisive and thorough representation of what we might call the psychoanalytic subject" (*IRG* 157).[7] Observing this, he is not speaking of any particular character in *À la recherche.* Rather, it is the novel itself that evinces a psychoanalytic logic. As he continues in the preface, "the spiraling movement of Proust's novel, its development from the central point of 'Combray' into ever widening concentric circles of drama and analysis, confirms Freud's claim, in the first chapter of *Civilization and Its Discontents,* that nothing is ever lost in mental life."[8] What Bersani describes as peculiar to Proust and Freud is readable—if only in ways that require complication—in terms of the temporality of "traumatic repetition," a structure where something in an originary coming-into-being is missed and hence calls for a retrospective—*nachträglich* or *après-coup*—repetition. For psychoanalysis, the X of the present marks the spot of a buried corpse, which we must unearth to discover whom we will have become. Experience becomes accessible through the labor of retrospective re-collection, a series of returns to the scene of the crime, where something crucial, a clue to being's mystery, has remained undiscovered. This something calls the subject with the force of a *fascinating enigma*: an intimate other, from whom we have become estranged in a moment of an originary trauma, holds the key to our being.

Laplanche argues that, because Freud was the progenitor of a revolutionary account of the human subject, he was only partially able to render explicit that which he sought to theorize. Instead, the Freudian text comes to exemplify, to recapitulate, the dynamic of its object: human consciousness. One of the tendencies of anthropogenesis that the Freudian text repeats is the constitutive betrayal of the traumatic scene of origination, a betrayal that necessitates recurrent returns to witness that which has taken place at the (missed) origin. This produces the peculiarly human time of afterwardsness—as Laplanche suggests we translate *Nachträglichkeit*—whose tempo modifies also the twists and turns of Freud's self-betrayals.[9] Laplanche argues that afterwardsness is characterized not so much by circularity as by a spiral compulsion. "A fruitful thought," he writes of the psychoanalytic mode of thinking, "would be the one that could, at least at times, rise from the plane of the circle, and transform its circular movement into a deepening one [*approfondissement*]."[10] If he gives us a "spiral model," spirality in his conceptualizations indicates that "we go back over the same themes but make some progress with them."[11] As Bersani writes in his second book, *Balzac to Beckett: Center and Circumference in French Fiction* (1970), in this involutive movement "a restatement of the past creates new possibilities for the future," a claim that he identifies as a "psychoanalytic assumption" (*BB* 203). Bersani will call this mode of involution "recategorization": differences are introduced to the self, which nevertheless retains what Proust would call its "fundamental notes" (see *MP* 111–21). In Laplanche and Bersani, this description obtains an ontological validity. As Bersani continues in *Thoughts and Things* (2015), "We spiral forward in time, which means that moving forward is indistinguishable from a relooping movement backward. Our futures are relooped, spiraling pasts" (*TT* 69). It is a process where, as Laplanche writes, "I change and am the same."[12]

The claim that Bersani is Proustian and Freudian is at once uncontroversial and in need of elaboration, for throughout his work he insistently, and increasingly, distances himself from both Proust and psychoanalysis. To put it differently, his thought spirals away from Proust and Freud, only to return to them with the gift of their alienated being, contaminating the origin with its perverse truth. This movement of "betrayal" is a characteristic operation in Bersani's thought. One of the ways Bersani betrays Proustian and Freudian thought is by reconsidering them beyond the schemas of privation that he claims are constitutive of their ontologies. In the above description of Laplanche's reading of Freud, for example, Bersani would, particularly in his post-1980s work, question the dominance of the *traumatizing scenario* in the account of consciousness and artistic production. He would propose that the insistence on traumatic origination forces us into a specific model of desire: one that is based on castration. One way to describe Bersani's entire oeuvre is to say that it seeks other modes of our moving-in-the-world than that compelled by an originary lack. Bersani recategorizes this understanding of consciousness through intricate readings of varied aesthetic texts: literature, film, painting, theater, sculpture. Yet, as chapter 1 will suggest, philosophically speaking it is the encounter with Gilles Deleuze's work in the late 1960s and early 1970s that nudges him to complicate psychoanalytic ontology. This is the third context, after Proust and Freud-Laplanche, in which we situate Bersani's work. As our study argues, it is in Deleuzean philosophy—whose paradigmatic disagreements with psychoanalytic thought are well known—that we find a contemporary oeuvre that most closely resonates with Bersani's own thinking (even if its influence works for the most part silently).[13] Bersani reads Deleuze already in the late 1960s; *Balzac to Beckett*, and particularly its final chapters, constitutes a record of this encounter. Bersani here becomes the first Anglo-American critic to engage Deleuzean thought; it is here, too, that his work takes on some of its most distinctive characteristics.[14]

Indeed, while scholarship on Bersani has frequently emphasized his psychoanalytic influences, it is important to note that his ontology takes its initial shape in *Marcel Proust* and *Balzac to Beckett*, some years before his encounter with the "French Freud" in *A Future for Astyanax: Character and Desire in Literature* (1976) and *Baudelaire and Freud* (1977).[15] When Bersani reads Freud, Laplanche, and Jacques Lacan, he does this as a thinker who has already been impressed by not only Proust's but also Deleuze's work. Even though he initially seems less than rapt with Deleuze and Félix Guattari's *Anti-Oedipus: Capitalism and Schizophrenia* (1972)—which he calls one of many "philosophical pastorals of pre-Oedipal desire" (*FA* 7)[16]—Deleuzeanism inflects his thought through his familiarity with such books as *Proust and Signs* (1964; see *BB* 235), *Difference and*

Repetition (1968; see *FA* 325n1),[17] and *Kafka: Toward a Minor Literature* (1975; see *FA* 319n2).

If *Marcel Proust* enfolds everything that Bersani will say about Proust—but enfolds it in a form whose unfolding or actualization is predictable only in retrospect—it is in his few subsequent texts that we find the preliminary articulation of his entire body of work. In terms of his philosophical sources, *Balzac to Beckett* is important in demonstrating Bersani's early reading of Deleuze; the following two books—*A Future for Astyanax* and *Baudelaire and Freud*—evince the entrance of psychoanalytic theory, particularly Freud's and Laplanche's, onto his orbit. We might say, not at all ungenerously, that after this nothing new happens in Bersani's work. By the end of the 1970s, his thought has gained its most distinctive forms, ones that are elaborated—*nachträglich* repeated and betrayed—in his subsequent work. There is, as Bersani notes in the 2013 preface to *Marcel Proust*, "a profound continuity" in his body of work.[18] "I'm not interested in variety very much," he admits in an interview. "People have said to me, 'You already said that twenty years ago.' Well, fine. That simply means that it was an important idea and it's remained an important idea but I've found ways to recategorize it, to play with it in a different way, adding something, changing something. I think that's all very important. I think that's what Proust does."[19]

This self-assessment indicates a distinction between his work and much of what will have developed as poststructuralist theory, influenced by the same generation of (mostly French) thinkers whom Bersani discovers in the late 1960s and early 1970s. Unlike scholars who take their cues from Derrida's deconstructive philosophy, he remains stubbornly disinterested in the discourses of "difference" that proliferate as something like an onto-ethical commonsense in his contemporaries' work. Indeed, he will occasionally argue that such discourses have come to enjoy, by the late 1980s, an uninterrogated hegemony. Rather than "difference," Bersani seeks "essence," the *bête noire* of much of contemporary theory. In this sense, despite its impact on a number of scholarly fields—literary criticism and theory, queer theory, film and visual studies, cultural studies, psychoanalytic theory—Bersani's work has, at least until recently, constituted something of an anomaly in Anglo-American thought. It has been only partially recognizable to the various scholarly fields whose practitioners nevertheless make frequent appeals to his texts. At stake here are what we can call "paradigmatic differences": Bersani has often been read through interpretive lenses that, not always unproductively, distort much of his work.

Driven by the "tort" of *torquere*, "distortion" can always be claimed as a queerly productive reading method. As Pierre Hadot notes, "very often, mistakes and misunderstandings have brought about important evolutions in the history of philosophy. In particular, they have caused new ideas to appear."[20] Nevertheless, our study, in an un-Bersanian gesture of fidelity, seeks to place Bersani's work in the philosophical frame from which it emerges in the 1970s.

Much of the strangeness of Bersani's thought—its influence and inassimilability—has to do with his commitment to ontology. Like the related concept of "essence," "ontology" has become the target of considerable critical energies in contemporary theory. We are frequently told to place existence before being, for any ontological system, we are reminded, proceeds by obfuscating life's actual variety and complexity. As feminism has pointed out, such reduction has traditionally taken place according to criteria where hegemonic particularities are universalized and where other perspectives, such as women's, are rendered partial, inadequate, or, simply, inconceivable.[21] In the context of queer theory, Christopher Castiglia voices a parallel warning when he laments "the conversion of epistemology into ontology, of history into psychic universalism."[22] Paul Gilroy similarly critiques what he calls "the ontological essentialist view," which has allowed the proliferation of nationalist and neonationalist discourses in diaspora politics.[23] When not "strategic," essentialism is politically and ethically dangerous; we are hence called to move away from ontological thinking, its presumed prioritization of being over existence, essence over contingency.

Bersani nevertheless suggests that we haven't quite finished with the question of ontology, or with the ontological concept of "essence." He muses, for example, that "the way in which the Foucauldian suspicion of sexual essences has been picked up by queer theorists has made me almost nostalgic for those very essences" (*IRG* 39). He also writes of feeling like "an essentialist villain" amidst his deconstructive contemporaries (*IRG* 33). Even if he says this jokingly, his queer-theoretical polemic *Homos* (1995) is an effort to promote what we might call "homoessentialism." In this effort, he shares Deleuze's obliviousness to all the admonishments to "forget ontology" that dominated twentieth-century Continental philosophy. As Alain Badiou recalls, Deleuze "liked to say that he had no problem with metaphysics," a striking cavalierishness amidst his philosopher contemporaries.[24] If we can imagine Bersani saying something similar, this is because he begins to think being—inspired, in part, by Deleuze—before ontology's deconstruction by Derrideans in the decades to come. If critical theory in late twentieth century has built an *ethics of difference* by following, to a large extent, the centrifugal trajectory of Derridean dissemination—which Diana Fuss calls "the most rigorous anti-essentialist discourse of all"[25]—from his earliest work onward Bersani remains consistently fascinated by the thought of "essence," a trait that renders his work problematic for the 1980s and 1990s "critique of essentialism."

We can illustrate Bersani's *speculative* orientation by turning to his queer-theoretical work, particularly "Is the Rectum a Grave?" (1987) and *Homos*. These remain his most-cited texts. Indeed, the impact of "Is the Rectum a Grave?" is such that its commanding formulations have to an extent determined our understanding of Bersani's entire oeuvre and, arguably, obfuscated its more idiosyncratic features.

In the essay, Bersani seeks to elucidate the panic unleashed by the AIDS crisis by drawing on his earlier studies on psychoanalysis and art. "There is a big secret about sex," goes the essay's famous opening line: "most people don't like it" (*IRG* 3). This is, as Bersani immediately admits, *pure speculation*: no statistics or polls exist to confirm his claim. Yet the thesis helps explain the vehemence that the spectacle of dying young men unleashed in the cultural imagination. According to Bersani's psychoanalytic reading, "most people" don't "like" sex (or have "a certain *aversion*" to it [*IRG* 4]) because its intensities remind them of what Freud suggests is the incipient human being's originary relationship with the world. Freud wavered between two models with which to depict the infant's earliest, formative experiences. On the one hand, he proposed that the small human's orientation to its surroundings is one of "nonsexual aggressiveness." In this model, objects are puppets whose strings the child imagines pulling in an effort to overcome his lack of control over their presence or absence. Such aggressive fantasies bind the forces of a world where the being that is becoming human is stymied by a protracted stage of defenselessness, having arrived on the scene too early. Yet, alongside this pathos of imagined mastery, another model emerges, one that Laplanche suggests Freud does his best to dismiss because of its radical onto-ethical implications. In such texts as "Instincts and Their Vicissitudes" (1915) and "The Economic Problem of Masochism" (1924), Freud speculates that the infant first meets the world not through efforts of control but by ecstatically yielding to its devastating forces. This surrender—which Freud calls "primary masochism"—may have an evolutionary function: the infant survives overwhelming odds by founding its self on the pleasure of its own annihilation. The aporetic jouissance—aporetic because it indicates the simultaneity of the emergence and the undoing of a self—is subsequently sought and avoided as the most profound human experience.

Bersani proposes that, on this side of death, the experiences of sex and art bring us closest to the constitutive trembling of our being. It is this model that for him explains the fascination that those dying of AIDS exert on the public imagination. It is not only that we consider painful death a fitting punishment for those revealing, and reveling in, the obscene truth of our profoundest pleasures: that we eagerly seek our own annihilation. The sadistic glee elicited by the other's pain also indicates our *masochistic identification* with such suffering. We are captured by these scenes because in witnessing them we are brought close to re-experiencing our originary jouissance. While we spend most of our days avoiding the lure of this undoing—for which Bersani borrows the term *ébranlement* from Laplanche and the Marquis de Sade—we should, instead, follow its call and use it to challenge "the sacrosanct value of selfhood," in whose defense much violence is deployed (*IRG* 30). The gay men Bersani speaks of in "Is the Rectum a Grave?" are exemplars of the *radical passivity*, the will to disappear and fall silent, that he has, in his previous work, identified in varied artistic experimentations. Like Beckett's mud crawlers, gay cruisers are artists of ontological debasement, perilously experimenting with the unpalatable truths of becoming-human.[26]

The force of the argument concerning *ébranlement*—much of it having to do with the thrilling bombast of the essay's rhetoric—is such that the complications with which Bersani immediately supplements his conclusions have been easy to miss. If sex, in its capacity to render the subject unavailable as a seat of power, should become "our primary hygienic practice of nonviolence" (*IRG* 30), the cultivation of shattering can also be done by a subject as a passively sadistic voyeur. As much as Lacan identifies Kantian ethical disinterestedness with the coldness of the Sadean torturer, Bersani implies that it may be in Sade that we find the truth of the psychoanalytic subject that Laplanche outlines for us.[27] It is not only that sex unbinds us into passivity; the subject, seeking the repetition of its pleasurable suicide, can also end up taking the world down with him. The antisocial subject, celebrated by some queer theorists, may turn out to be a suicide bomber. In reading "Is the Rectum a Grave?" one should, then, observe the ways in which the psychoanalytic assumption of an ethical *ébranlement* is immediately—one is tempted to say, always already—recategorized. As the present study will suggest, much of such recategorization takes place through the complication of psychoanalytic ontologies with concepts that resonate with those in a philosophical genealogy whose best-known contemporary representative is Deleuze.

Despite its inability to move beyond an ontology of lack, or to imagine a nonsadistic subjecthood, Bersani never quite lets go of psychoanalysis. What remains compelling in Freud is the speculative daring of his thought, the "extraordinary speculative risk[s]" (*FrB* 99) he courts. Freud pushes his "speculations"—Bersani uses the term insistently—beyond all evidentiary plausibility, aiming at something that, like dreams, can be remembered only as the traces of secondary phenomena, only after they have undergone several rounds of revisions. In *The Freudian Body: Psychoanalysis and Art* (1986), Bersani reads Freud as an artist of collapsing narratives and failed argumentation, someone trying to live by the constitutively muddled logic of his dreams. From the beginning, Freud exhibits a remarkable willingness to " 'lose[] himself' " in "*blocked but productive speculation*" about pleasure, masochism, sublimation, and so forth (*FrB* 102). Rather than learning his lesson from early blunders, he compulsively repeats the failure, as if relishing the pleasure of having his arguments veer out of authorial control. This is what makes reading Freud a little bit like having sex or experiencing art. When Bersani speaks of Freud's oeuvre as a series of "radical speculative movements" that at once invite and defy the turning of his insights into institutionalized practice (*FrB* 3), he means that this speculativeness is originary, "of the root." Freud's work is "radical" because, in an unprecedented way, it yields to the self-defeating, aporetic logic of the entity it describes. Psychoanalytic discourse follows the fate of the human subject, whose deepest nature is the compulsively repeated failure to speak of its traumatized constitution. Psychoanalysis recapitulates this movement: its "revolutionary nature . . . consist[s] in a speculation about its own unreadability" (*FrB* 101). If the Freudian revolution is, as Laplanche puts it, "unfinished," it remains so constitutively.

Bersani identifies this repeated "collapse" as both "speculative" and "aesthetic." The Freudian failure amounts to an "estheticizing movement," he writes (*FrB* 11). He wants to own this as his own mode of thinking: as he observes in an endnote to *The Freudian Body*, his own work, whether or not explicitly addressing Freud, is "informed by a certain type of psychoanalytic speculation" (*FrB* 118n2). In light of this, we are obliged to extend our indictment of Bersani's villainy from the charge of essentialism to that of speculativeness. By this term, we mean to evoke the maligned strand of Western thought called "speculative philosophy." As John Dewey writes, the phrase denotes "[a] form of theorizing which goes beyond verifiable observation and reflection, characterized by loose and venturesome hypotheses."[28] In twentieth-century philosophy, Gerhard Schweppenhäuser observes, "the terms 'speculation' and 'metaphysics' [have] been reduced to insults for attacking mere guesses and weird supernatural ideas"; "there is often a certain reluctance, not to say distaste," notes another expert witness, "with which [the speculative orientation] is treated."[29] While the suspicion concerning the speculative orientation extends at least to what is arguably the rise of modern thought in Martin Luther's theology,[30] it is with German Idealism that "speculation" becomes a coherently deployed concept for the first time.[31] The best-known moment in this modern history of speculative thought is its reining-in by Kant. "A theoretical cognition is *speculative*," he writes in the *Critique of Pure Reason*, "if it pertains to an object or concepts of an object to which one cannot attain in any experience."[32] Instead of the speculative reach for the in-itself, thinking must acknowledge its inherent limitations: only objects that conform to mind's conditions can be thought. This postulation of "correlationism," as Quentin Meillassoux calls it, has been recently taken on by proponents of "speculative realism," who identify in it the unquestioned commonsense that has guided all poststructuralist theorizing. Speculative realists have set themselves the task of overcoming such strict Kantianism, which, according to them, has determined the limits of modern philosophy for generations of thinkers.[33]

Even before speculative realism, of course, the Kantian epistemology has not gone unchallenged. In the 1812 preface to the *Science of Logic*, Hegel laments Kant's "renunciation of speculative thought," the stipulation that "the understanding ought not to go beyond experience, else the cognitive faculty will become a theoretical reason which by itself generates nothing but fantasies of the brain."[34] Like recent speculative realists, Hegel sought to escape Kant's epistemological prisonhouse. He considered his predecessor's refusal to approach things in-themselves a form of philosophical cowardice. The Kantian thinker is a traveler who stays home because he is scared of the arduousness and unpredictability of the journey. In avoiding the speculative, Kant steers clear of "the pathway of *doubt*," "the way of despair [*der Weg des* Zweifels, *der Weg der Verzweifelung*]," which for the Hegelian sojourner is the only way to honor thinking.[35] In ruling out realms of thought rather than earnestly tackling them in their difficulty, critical philosophy is motivated by "the fear of falling into error."[36] Kant becomes "the frightened philosopher."[37]

Instead of relinquishing being to noumenal shadows, Hegel plans for us a journey where "the speculative" emerges as the most advanced mode of thought, superseding the dogmatism of "the understanding" and reconciling the concepts' internal contradictions that "dialectical" thought will have revealed. Hegelian speculativeness is a strictly internal process of reflection, of the mind's turning in on itself—as if to face a mirror (*speculum*)—and working out the strangeness that it encounters there. The speculative subject is characterized by the kind of immanence for which Hegel's system is often celebrated: a movement in which being unfolds self-reflectively, where contradictions in search of solution remain internal to the subject. In the grammatical terms in which Western metaphysics has often been thought, the "predicates" of the speculative being are no longer accidents and contingencies but "inhere" in the subject. In "argumentation" or "ratiocinative thinking" (*das Räsonieren, das räsonierende Denken*), carried out in predicative propositions, the "Subject constitutes the basis to which the content [as accident and predicate] is attached, and upon which the movement runs back and forth."[38] Predicative propositions assume a passive subject, a material, inert self that is given form—stamped, as it were—by the predicates that it receives. For us to be truly thinking, we must renounce this being that passively receives a world of contingent events. In the speculative mode, the status of the subject and the predicate shifts so that the clear distinctions on which empirical propositions rely are dissolved. The predicate no longer functions as a generality attached to a preexisting subject. Rather, this passive subject "perishes" (*geht zugrunde*) as, moving to the realm of speculative thinking, we find that "the Predicate is really the Substance, the Subject has passed over into the Predicate, and, by this very fact, has been sublated."[39] Herbert Marcuse writes: "The speculative judgment does not have a stable and passive subject [like common sense or traditional logic]. Its subject is active and develops itself into its predicates. The predicates are various forms of the subject's existence."[40]

In the speculative proposition, we have, as Rodolphe Gasché continues, "the absolute identity of subject and object": the predicate becomes "the very substance, the essence of the subject. The subject of the ordinary proposition becomes lost in the substantial essence of the predicate in the speculative proposition."[41] Speculative philosophy assumes an *essentialism* of the notion or concept. Ventriloquizing Derrida, we might say that the relation between the subject and the predicate becomes "undecidable" in the speculative proposition: the two are characterized by the peculiar dynamic that Derrida calls "supplementarity." Yet, notwithstanding our deconstructive generosity, the Hegelian speculative remains stubbornly essentialist. In its engagement with things, it "distinguishes their essence from their accidental state of things."[42] As Hegel puts it, undoing the untroubled or inert (*unbewegt*) subject of ratiocination, speculative thought actualizes the "pure self-movements [*reine Selbstbewegungen*]" of concepts.[43] In becoming speculative, thought is lifted out of the world of "material stuff" in which it is mired (*versenkt*); it reaches purity and solitude, the realm of concepts' self-becoming.[44]

As one might imagine, Hegelian speculativeness has not fared well with subsequent thinkers. It should be immediately clear, for example, why none of the representatives of speculative realism embraces Hegelian thought as a possible counterpoint to Kantianism. The Hegelian version of speculativeness remains caught in the kind of subject-centered thinking whose hegemony speculative realists want to bring to an end: it constitutes a "metaphysics that eternalizes the Self or the Mind, turning the latter into the perennial mirror for the manifestation of the entity."[45] While Hegel's revolutionary insight was to render the system of the spirit's becoming radically *immanent*, he was also a staunch *idealist*, that is, a thinker whose worldview was entirely centered on human consciousness. Hegel purports to dissolve the carefully patrolled borders of Kantian epistemology; but his unremitting focus on the knowing subject becomes as destructive an order as Kant's ruling out the in-itself as a legitimate object of thought. Like Kant, Hegel is, above all, an "abstract" thinker, one who, as the term's etymology tells us, gazes at the world from the heights of disembodied solitude. As the rap sheet provided by Louis Althusser reads, Hegelian philosophy is "unreal," "ideal(ist)," "abstract," and—in a word—"speculative."[46]

Many of the following chapters will ascribe a certain "anti-Hegelianism" to Bersani's work, a trait that we propose can be traced in part to his early involvement with Deleuzean philosophy.[47] If, as Elizabeth Grosz posits (herself loosely following Deleuze), Hegel's philosophy affirms an ontology, typical to Western thought, premised on "an economy of scarcity,"[48] Bersani, in contrast, wants us to relinquish our "prejudicial view of lack as constitutive of desire" (*IRG* 138). Relatedly, if twentieth-century philosophy has all but exclusively conceptualized ethics according to a dialectical notion of "otherness," Bersani's early work on aesthetics and philosophy prevents him from joining what he comes to call "the cult of difference" (*IRG* 34) and, instead, pushes him to experimentations with "sameness" or, to use his coinage, "homoness."[49] And if "lack" and "difference" produce in Hegelian thought a subject that "can only be understood in its movement,"[50] Bersani seeks to understand being otherwise, often in terms of passivity and immobility. All this sets his thought in contradistinction to some very Hegelian assumptions. Yet, we now posit that, like Hegel, Bersani is a *speculative thinker*. His onto-ethics/aesthetics echoes the postulations that organize speculative idealism. This does not indicate, however, that Bersani is Hegelian; it reveals, rather, the *Leibnizian* influences—or influences that found a particularly clear articulation in monadology—that inflect both his and Hegel's thinking.

The terrain implied by this ambitious triangulation can be outlined in the following way: In his early work, Hegel considers the monad a potential example of self-determination (*Selbstbestimmung*), of a being that follows its own voice (*Stimme*), actualizes its own destiny (*Bestimmung*). Yet, the contrivance of "preestablished harmony" indicates to him that Gottfried Wilhelm Leibniz's system does not achieve the level of conceptual thinking (*begriffliches Denken*). Supported by the *deus ex machina* of the supreme watchmaker who sets the world in synchrony, the monad falls short of self-positing; determinations in monadology are not, as Hegel concludes in the *Science of Logic*, "raised into speculative Notions [*nicht zu spekulativen Begriffen erhoben sind*]."[51] If Leibniz fails the rigors of speculative thought, Hegel picks up the slack in the *Phenomenology*. There "the speculative proposition" achieves the self-determination that would have been the monad's. Hegel deems his own speculative idealism to have succeeded in becoming the philosophy that Leibniz audaciously, but ineffectually, sought after.

According to Marx and Engels, Hegel, notwithstanding his dismissal of Leibniz, embraced the worldview of seventeenth-century metaphysicians, whose systems assume a disembodied, solitary subject, typical of the speculative tradition. In this view, Hegel revives Western tradition's idealist abstractions, undermining the work of the eighteenth-century French thinkers whose materialism Marx and Engels deemed to have been part of the movement that manifested itself in the revolution that toppled the *ancien régime*.[52] While Marx and Engels also name Descartes, Malebranche, and Spinoza, it is Leibniz who engages in the headiest of modern philosophy's "*wild speculation*." Indeed, when subsequent critics comment on Hegel, they frequently evoke the excesses of his speculative idealism by using Leibnizian terms. Judith Butler, for example, writes that the subject of "speculative metaphysics" is most often "the subject of internal or psychological harmony who is at once—at least potentially—in harmony with the world of objects and others"; such a "unified subject is a theoretical requirement, not only for the moral life, but for the grander effort *to secure a preestablished metaphysical place for the human subject*."[53] More frequently than "preestablished harmony," it is "the monad" that is used as shorthand for speculative assumptions. In these accounts, the Hegelian subject figures as a direct descendent of the Leibnizian monad. Like those of the speculative proposition, the predicates of the monadic subject "correspond to" or "agree with" its being. Nothing that happens to this subject can be an accident or a contingency; every one of its predicates is contained in its concept. Consequently, as much as the Hegelian speculative is marked by "pure self-movement," the monadic subject's being unfolds according to a strictly internal logic. Leibniz writes in the *Monadology*: "the monad's natural changes come from an *internal principle*, since no external cause can influence it internally."[54] Leibniz aims—but, for Hegel, fails—to conceptualize what Hegel in the *Science of Logic* calls the "self-moving soul, the principle of all natural and spiritual life."[55]

Especially after Marx's critique, Leibniz's radicalization of Aristotelian predication—which we will explore in more detail in chapter 1—has often been taken as a moment where Western metaphysics reveals its hidden truth: that it is, in fact, not of sound mind. Too compulsively logical for his—and the metaphysical family's—own good, Leibniz pushes the wrong-headed propositions he has inherited to their ridiculous extremes. Like the nutty relative, the revealer of family secrets, he betrays the idealist aporias undergirding much of classical thought. Monadology constitutes, as critics write, a "fantastic and arbitrary" "fairy-tale"; it is "so obviously false" that the mind boggles why anyone would propose such a system; it deserves a prize as "the most absurd theory of truth that has ever been advanced."[56] For Marx, Leibniz's monadic ontology provides a nicely revealing portrait of the bourgeois weltanschauung, in all its delusional glory. He argues that, contrary to what Leibniz, and then Hegel, assumed, the travails of the human spirit do not unfold centrifugally, beginning with an internal principle that then makes its mark on the outside world; becoming-human should rather be understood as a *centripetal* process, where human "essence" is produced in a network of social relations.[57] As he puts it in the sixth thesis on Feuerbach, "the essence of man is no abstraction inherent in each single individual," but "the ensemble" of relations in which each is embedded.[58] A year earlier, in 1844, he writes, critiquing the Young Hegelians, that "*man* is no abstract being encamped outside the world."[59] The same year—and in the pages of the same publication, the sole issue of *Deutsch-Französische Jahrbücher*—he famously adopts the

Leibnizian monad to trope the bourgeois abstractions against which he polemicizes: in "On the Jewish Question," he likens the abstract individual to the monadic isolate, "withdrawn into himself [*als isolierter auf sich zurückgezogener Monade*]."[60] It is this agent that he will in *Grundrisse* (1939 [1857–58]) call a "Robinson Crusoe," the imperial being at the center of Adam Smith's and David Ricardo's economic theories.[61] For Marx, as for his followers, the monad comes to figure the self-possessed actor of the marketplace who refuses to acknowledge his embeddedness—often his privileged position—in a network of labor relations.

In twentieth-century thought, Marx's gesture to Leibniz is repeated in assessments that find in monadology the apotheosis of Western philosophy's idealist indulgences, its relentless, speculative egocentrism. Explicitly or implicitly, Bertrand Russell, Jacques Derrida, Jean Laplanche, Fredric Jameson, and James Miller borrow from Marx the concept of the "monadically self-reliant agent," rendering it the decontextualized, dehistoricized ipse whose delusions have been codified in metaphysics' authoritative formulations.[62] In his early work, for example, Derrida deconstructs Husserlian phenomenology by directing his Socratic gaze to Husserl's frequent references, especially in the fifth of *Cartesian Meditations* (1931), to Leibnizian metaphysics; he speaks of the transcendental ego as "the egological monad."[63] In largely corresponding ways—and clearly influenced by Derrida—Laplanche argues that the radical rethinking of otherness in the Freudian revolution goes astray when the monadic ego reasserts itself in various guises in psychoanalytic theory.[64] Like Derrida and Laplanche before him, Jameson finds in the monad, again in an echo of Marx, a name for "the bourgeois ego."[65]

Even as the "monadic individual"[66] remains for many a symptomatic representative of classical philosophy's egocentric excesses, it is perhaps the outrageousness of the Leibnizian system that has attracted other writers to explore it as fertile ground for all manner of speculative thought. In its flagrant absurdity—it is "quite unthinkable . . . as a serious project"—monadology remains, as Ian Hacking puts it, "fascinating."[67] For Walter Benjamin, the monad, as the nonextended singularity that "involves" the whole world, figures as a concept with which to think the unpredictability of messianic becoming in contrast to the steady unfolding of dialectical history.[68] For Theodor Adorno, the monad refers to the administered society's "liquidated" individual, whose isolation renders him susceptible to fascism and can be undone only through "solidarity."[69] Yet, at the same time, the independent sphere of art carries a potentiality that, like

Benjamin, Adorno often describes by turning to Leibniz's system. For Deleuze, the monad figures the incorporeal principle of individuation, one that *exceeds* but doesn't *precede* its embodiment in mattered bodies. And, straddling art and philosophy, Samuel Beckett often borrows from what he admires as Leibniz's gallery of "splendid little pictures" to outline the nonrelational being that seeks silence in his texts.[70]

To contextualize Bersani's essentialism and speculativeness, *The Essentialist Villain* situates his oeuvre on this continuum, which stretches, often unnoticed, across the work of twentieth-century thinkers.[71] In Bersani, the monad constitutes what Laplanche calls a "crypto-concept," a concept that, "although it forms the object of no individual article or specific presentation, plays an important role in the structure of the system, even if this role is only a provisional one."[72] The "monad," that is, functions in the Bersanian text in the same way that "*supplément*" does in Rousseau's work or "*plasticité*" in Hegel's. As Catherine Malabou writes in her study on the overlooked centrality of the notion of "plasticity" in Hegelian thought, when we discern the organization of a text around such concepts, "something essential" becomes "suddenly recognizable"; a crypto-concept reveals to the reader "something accidental . . . that [brings her] to the essential."[73]

In large part, the following chapters read the Bersanian oeuvre as a playful echoing of monadology. Apart from observing Bersani's frequent allusions to monads, we can commence by noting the resonance between, on the one hand, Leibniz's depiction of "preestablished harmony" as "the mystery of the universal connection between phenomena"[74] and, on the other, Bersani and Ulysse Dutoit's affirmation of an "essentially mysterious connectedness in the universe" (*FV* 46). For them, this connectedness bespeaks what they call "the total relationality of being" (*AI* 140; see also *CR* 77–78): "*Everything*," they declare, "connects to and within the wholeness of being" (*CS* 99). A similar insistence on the faultless continuity of being characterizes, in Leibniz, the continuum: "all existing things are in intercourse with each other";[75] given "the plenitude of the world," "there is no vacuum in place and time, . . . nor is there a place which is not full."[76] Bersani and Dutoit's argument that "there are no gaps, no empty spaces, in creation" (*CS* 72)—or, as Bersani writes, that "there are no leaps of being" (*FA* 327n2)—may be understood in the context of Leibniz's *lex continuitatis*: "*nature never makes leaps*,"[77] a principle that was subsequently adopted in the natural sciences by Carl Linneaus and Charles Darwin. Bersani's ontology, as it develops through a series of readings over the course of his work, bears a Leibnizian character.

Our turning to Leibniz, and his "apparently bizarre metaphysics,"[78] is motivated by the sense in which, in terms of Bersani's work, monadology is included in what Henri Bergson would call "ontological memory," a field of the virtual whose potential is reduced by our (necessary) focus on the immediate present and the immediately present. We propose to relinquish for a moment our "pragmatic" engagement with what is directly recognizable in Bersani and dilate our focus by tracing the genealogy of his thought, through various sources, to monadology. This détente allows us to highlight the oddity that Bersanian ontology has constituted in contemporary critical theory. The intention is not to identify Bersani's system with Leibniz's, if this gesture would mean the uncovering of a solid blueprint that the former's work faithfully reproduces. Leibniz's name, it should be noted, gets merely a couple of references in Bersani's extensive oeuvre.[79] For us, "Leibniz" designates not an author or a doctrine but what Derrida calls "the name of a problem," a framework that, often in undetected ways, informs the articulation of a discourse.[80]

It is in this intellectual context that Hegel and Bersani share the orientation of their Leibnizianism. If Hegel's speculative subject gives us "the development of a simple interiority,"[81] Bersani seeks in monadism a principle of the subject's relation to the world that would differ from the form of otherness or difference whose often unacknowledged hegemony he discerns organizing the thought of Freud, Proust, Laplanche, Benjamin, and Butler. If monadology's role in Bersani's thought has not been noted in the by-now voluminous scholarship on his work, such elision may be the result of the paradigmatic incompatibility—perhaps, in Leibniz's terms, incompossibility—of theoretical perspectives.[82] The gravitation of Bersani's philosophy toward this indivisible singularity announces the grounding difference between his work and the commonplaces of contemporary Anglo-American cultural and critical theory that has taken its cues from Derrida's early texts.

When we call Bersani a "speculative" thinker, we should, however, carefully detail the charge. In *Thoughts and Things*, Bersani briefly discusses the work of Lawrence Krauss (we'll return to this moment at the end of our study). Krauss is one of the most recent—and most controversial—contributors to what has been called "speculative astronomy," a field for which the work of the pre-Socratic philosopher Anaximander is often cited as foundational. If speculative astronomy deals with "hypothetical objects," describable only on the evidence of the effects they have on other, "observational" objects, it shares its method with the speculative philosophy whose hypothetical object has traditionally been God or Being. The observable functions, as St. Bonaventure put it, as an obscure mirror (*speculum*) where traces (*vestigia*) of divinity can be apprehended.[83] In this sense, Bersani is *not* a speculative thinker. Without fail, his onto-ethics/aesthetics limits itself to an observational object: the work of art. For him, artworks are not "representational" in the sense that observable phenomena are for speculative philosophy or speculative astronomy: they do not indirectly express divinity or tell us about the unrecoverable conditions of the universe. In an endnote appended to *Caravaggio's Secrets*, he writes with Dutoit that "the aesthetic" can be considered "the concretizing or sensualizing of the metaphysical" (*CS* 110n9). He echoes this point when he asserts in a later interview that art "bring[s] being into the phenomenological."[84] Yet we must note that what is here termed "being" or "the metaphysical" is not distinct from that in which it can be observed. "The work of art," Bersani and Dutoit continue in the endnote, "is the site where the world reappears—*and* appears for the first time—as the 'correspondences' (to use a Baudelairean term) that design, and perceptibly fail to design, the always mobile unity of phenomena" (*CS* 110n9). In Bersani's work, "art" constitutes the field of "experience" that speculative thought, in its abstractions, is often said to bypass. It is through varied experimentations in the "ontological laboratories" (*CS* 59, 63) of literature, philosophy, and the visual arts that Bersani extracts and (re)formulates an onto-ethics/aesthetics where, as in the aesthetic theory of Charles Baudelaire, the world's (re)appearing is understood as an *aesthetic event*.

In *The Freudian Body*, Bersani suggests that, when this emergence takes place beyond what we recognize as art, we must extend our conception of "the aesthetic." (Freud's work, for example, evinces this "estheticizing movement"; we should, therefore, approach it as we would an artwork.) Indeed, thinking of the aesthetic as "art" is a way to demarcate and domesticate this dynamic, to "territorialize," as Deleuze would say, its forces. In much the same way that, as Freud suggests, we routinely neutralize our singular death-orientation by externalizing it as aggressiveness, restricting the experience of the aesthetic to the field of art is one of the ways in which we have learned to escape the jouissance of our becoming. Bersani's gesture of deterritorialization is to suggest the potential everydayness of this event. This is what he implies when he asks, in the endnote in *Caravaggio's Secrets*, "[A]re there definable conditions under which the real qualifies as 'art'?" (*CS* 110n9). His work can be understood as an effort to articulate such conditions, whereby our lives could begin to function as art, to participate in the "estheticizing movement" that also marks Freud's speculative theory of hominization. We can unlearn, he suggests, our extant modes of being in the world; we can be retrained in the *aestheticization of our lives*. This retraining entails what Bersani, borrowing the term from Beckett, often calls "impoverishment": we must undo the habits by which we have marked our territory, plugged into—made ourselves recognizable to—the world. In ways that we will consider in the following chapters, this program shares a considerable deal not only with the onto-ethics of the later Foucault but also, for example, with Georg Simmel's *Lebensphilosophie*.

Yet, even if Bersani does not deal with "hypothetical objects," he remains, like Hegel, a speculative thinker. This is because his onto-ethics shares with Hegelian idealism—and Leibnizian monadology—the effort to think being strictly in terms of *an internal principle*, of what Hegel calls "the speculative proposition." Marx indicated the folly of this enterprise. For him, and critics following him, Hegel's insistence on this internal logic constitutes his breakthrough and his tragic error. His emphasis on the dialectic as a process that unfolds in the solving and dissolving of its internal contradictions allowed the conceptualization of history as an immanent process, purged of all otherworldly alibis (including the preestablished harmony). Instead of resorting to the interventions of transcendent otherness, we realize that "what seems to happen outside of [substance], to be an activity directed against it, is really its own doing."[85] This argument has had enormously enabling consequences in subsequent, and particularly twentieth-century, conceptualizations of history, politics, and becoming.[86] Yet as in all great tragedies, the Hegelian system's triumph is inextricable from a devastating hamartia. If Hegel's thought owes its remarkable force to the immanence of the speculative movement, this internal logic has also rendered the Hegelian sojourner a figure for an imperial self. While some recent commentators—most notably, Catherine Malabou and Jean-Luc Nancy—have observed the "shakiness" of Hegel's system (indicated, for both Malabou and Nancy, in the "plasticity" of the unity in which the speculative construction is supposed to have found its telos),[87] most readers, influenced by Marx, have considered the Hegelian subject the philosophical version of the bourgeois agent of the "Robinsonades" of late eighteenth-century economic theories: Robinson Crusoe in his imperial, monadic solitude.

The precise limits of the analogy between Bersani's and Hegel's onto-ethics need to be traced out more carefully than we can do here.

What remains clear, however, is that for Bersani, as for Hegel, the speculative dynamic constitutes the highest principle of becoming. For Bersani, Freud, as we have noted, is a "speculative thinker" insofar as his work evinces an "estheticizing movement." The "aesthetic" force of the Freudian text consists of the tortuous hesitations, backtrackings, and self-contradictions—the endless *ébranlement*—by which psychoanalytic theory (not describes but) recapitulates the originary trembling that marks the human subject's emergence. In his early (1970s and 1980s) texts, Bersani gleans this argument from Laplanche. In his later work, he comes to suggest that psychoanalytic thought is limited by its anthropocentrism. Like practically all post-Kantian theories, psychoanalysis assumes the human subject as its frame of reference, the measure of all things. Moving from Freud and Laplanche to varied works of art—and the occasional philosophical text—Bersani comes to propose that the "estheticizing movement" may not be exclusive, or may be indifferent, to the human. In this way, his work anticipates—while proceeding in a different direction than—the more recent arguments of speculative realism.

The Essentialist Villain explores the ways in which Bersani, beginning in the mid-1960s, extracts and develops an onto-ethics/aesthetics of being and becoming from his engagement with literature, art, and philosophy. While he insists that his primary allegiance is to aesthetic texts—as he puts it in an interview, he considers himself neither "a professional philosopher" nor "a theoretician"[88]—our study focuses on the unfolding of his work primarily in philosophical terms. By tracing his philosophical genealogy, we seek to parole his work from what Proust calls "the safe custody of names," to undo some of the persistent appellations through which we have come to grasp his relevance to our work.[89] The chapters track the unfolding—recategorization—of the oeuvre chronologically, beginning, in chapter 1, with his encounter with Proust-Deleuze and Beckett-Blanchot in *Balzac to Beckett*. At this moment, we are introduced to the "fundamental notes" that Bersani's subsequent texts go on to fugue. Chapter 2 moves to his later 1970s texts, where we witness his work's complication with psychoanalytic theory, with Freud and Laplanche. Chapters 3 and 4 focus on a turning point in the oeuvre: the shift in emphasis that takes place between the early 1990s texts *The Culture of Redemption* (1990) and *Arts of Impoverishment: Beckett, Rothko, Resnais* (1993). These texts should be read together, for in between them occurs the move from what Bersani sometimes calls "the psychoanalytic subject" to "the aesthetic subject." In many ways echoing Foucault's and Pierre Hadot's work, he argues that the latter mode of being has been neglected, indeed suppressed, by modern thought. He locates the beginning of the modern episteme in Descartes, one of the seventeenth-century thinkers whose metaphysics Marx and Engels charge Hegel of reviving and developing into his speculative idealism. In chapters 4 and 5, we contextualize Bersani's work in modern philosophy, but also extend this field to Martin Luther's theology. It is in Lutheran individualism that the modern era begins. It is also in Luther that we find one of the earliest condemnations of what we call "speculative narcissism," whose features both Hegel and Bersani exhibit. The concluding chapter traces the development, over the course of some forty years, of the concept of "narcissism" into something of a cosmology, an onto-ethics/aesthetics whose different forms in the Bersanian oeuvre our study will have outlined.

1

Homomonadology

Proust–Deleuze–Beckett–Blanchot

Published five years after his first book, *Balzac to Beckett: Center and Circumference in French Fiction* (1970) marks an important early moment in Leo Bersani's trajectory. It is here that through the work of Marcel Proust and Samuel Beckett, as well as Gilles Deleuze's and Maurice Blanchot's commentaries on the two writers, his thought begins to follow a track shared by few contemporary commentators: in all his subsequent work, Bersani insists on the thought of *being*, that is, ontology, in a way that, notwithstanding the recent expansion in scholarship on Deleuze's, Alain Badiou's, and Jean-Luc Nancy's thought, has been nearly inadmissible in Anglo-American critical theory of the past thirty years.[1] That he never leaves this field of thought is suggested by the title of his and Ulysse Dutoit's 2004 book: as they announce here, theirs remains a concern with "forms of being," a phrase that has the added benefit of drawing our attention to the role of *aesthetics* in the articulation of Bersani's speculative ontology. Much of his later, better-known work remains to an extent unreadable if one does not contextualize its articulations in the moves that take place in the 1970s texts; this is particularly true of the second book.

To trace this trajectory, we begin this chapter with an outline of the encounter between French modernist literature and poststructuralist philosophy that Bersani stages in *Balzac to Beckett*. *Balzac to Beckett* is framed through an appeal to what would soon become the canonical formulations of poststructuralism in Jacques Derrida's "Structure, Sign, and Play in the Discourse of Human Sciences" and *Of Grammatology*, both published in 1967 (and translated into English in 1970 and 1976, respectively).[2] We suggest that the concept of "centrifugality," whose operations Bersani discerns in numerous literary texts, is a rendering of Derridean dissemination: the literary texts Bersani focuses on both illustrate the appeal of essentialist thinking—of what Derrida refers to as the "presences" propping Western metaphysical systems—and exemplify the "fugitive" movement away from the stability of centers. Yet no sooner has Bersani invited the reader to appreciate the centrifugal forces of ever-proliferating differences than he makes what—from the perspective of "différantial" thinking—cannot but seem a relapse onto speculative philosophy in the form of a counterintuitive (re)turn to the idea of "the centripetal." This move away from the philosophy of *différance* becomes a return to an essentialism of sorts: *Balzac to Beckett* finishes with an encounter between Proust and Beckett—an encounter that also, and crucially, engages Deleuze and Blanchot—where the questions of "center" and "essence" are reconsidered.

For Bersani, sexuality becomes a privileged experience of being's centripetal drive. Yet when he insists on "the inherently solipsistic nature of sexuality" (*CR* 37), he is not exactly contradicting the perhaps more familiar arguments about "the centrifugal force of sex."[3] Like Michel Tournier, who calls sex "that eternal breaker up of isolation," "the centrifugal force that drives you out of doors,"[4] Bersani suggests that we are profoundly moved, or perturbed, by the intensities Freud designates as sexual. But the forms of relation that sexuality weaves constitute a very specific kind of fugue. The sexual is a privileged example of "the ecstatic suffering of pure ébranlement" (*CR* 38) or what Adam Phillips, Bersani's recent collaborator, recalls an analysand naming "the ecstasy of solitude."[5] The seeming contradiction of the centrifugality of ecstasy and the centripetality of solitude is characteristic of what we propose to call Bersanian "homomonadology." We indulge in coinage to indicate some of the peculiarities of Bersani's thought in the context of both critical theory and queer thought, peculiarities that can be rendered in the idiom of Leibnizian metaphysics. Gottfried Wilhelm Leibniz's monadology has the advantage—or, as Bertrand Russell writes in his classic critique of Leibnizian metaphysics, the inconsistency—of combining nonrelatedness with connectedness.[6] Monads are characterized at once by radical disconnect—they have no external relations, that is, no predicates except those which their essences involve—and by universal concomitance, the *mise en abyme* of infinite mirroring.[7] The "unity" or "one[ness]" that the Greek term *monas* suggests[8] is that of both the singular, windowless monad and the field of "preestablished harmony." The paradox of Leibnizian thought—where singularity is combined with radical relatedness—necessitates, for example, that we reconsider appeals to Bersani's work in the controversies around queer theory's "antisocial thesis." Insofar as Bersanian thought is to play a role here, the futurelessness of the antisocial mode must be complicated by the Leibnizian *lex continuitatis*, a oneness that, to Russell's ostentatious incomprehension, does not coincide with monism.

This chapter outlines Bersani's reading of French modernism in *Balzac to Beckett*, and then situates his observations in the larger philosophical field organized around twentieth-century mobilizations of monadology. We finish by revisiting, from the homomonadic vantage point, Bersani's queer-theoretical polemic *Homos* (1995). Twenty-five years apart, *Balzac to Beckett* and *Homos* conclude in analogous ways. If in his 1970 study Bersani turns to Beckett to negotiate the problems that he detects in *À la recherche du temps perdu*, "The Gay Outlaw," the final chapter of *Homos*, repeats this trajectory, albeit replacing Beckett with Jean Genet as Proust's interlocutor (a trajectory that, incidentally, repeats Blanchot's similar move from Beckett to Genet).[9] Bersani's aim in *Homos* is to challenge extant forms of queer theorizing—largely influenced by Judith Butler's concept of performativity—and to reformulate the lessons drawn from his earlier engagements with literature and philosophy into a queer theory. Recategorizing the speculative arguments first floated in *Balzac to Beckett*, Bersani discovers that he has in fact always already been speaking of a queer onto-ethics/aesthetics.

Proust–Deleuze, Beckett–Blanchot: *Balzac to Beckett*

If Proust and Beckett are for Bersani two of the most fecund petri dishes in art's "ontological laboratories" (*CS* 59, 63), jointly they may suggest something about the fundamental shape of his oeuvre. What arguably attract Bersani in Proust and Beckett are two forms of modernist literary experimentation productively at odds with one another. One the one hand, we have the Proustian art of textual and descriptive proliferation, his "fully saturated style"; Roland Barthes calls *À la recherche du temps perdu* the last novel to "master the planetary breadth of the world, the complexity of its problems, of its structures."[10] The Beckettian aesthetic, on the other hand, seems diametrically opposed to the Proustian saturation; it evinces a paradoxical ambition to reduce its performances to silence, to make its vehicle disappear. Energized by the tension between these tendencies—Proust's proliferations and Beckett's impoverishments[11]—Bersani, over the years and numerous texts, develops an onto-aesthetics that is at once Proustian and Beckettian. Acting as catalysts of sorts in the literary laboratory, Deleuze's and Blanchot's philosophies, including but also exceeding their commentaries on the two writers, speed the crystallization of Bersanian ontology.

What gives Bersani pause in *À la recherche* is the way in which the textual detail, inscribing a potentially inexhaustible repertoire of experiences, is put in motion only for the text to discern in its profligacy something Proust calls the interrelated, if not identical, "essences" of objects and experiences. "In Proust," Bersani observes in his first book, the 1965 monograph on *À la recherche*, "to have wide experience means to be in a position to realize the fundamental sameness in what appear to be the most diverse experiences" (*MP* 165). It is particularly art that reveals the essence, or essences, that go unnoted in experience. While trying to express a new thought or affect in his work, a composer, if he is to remain an artist, cannot but create in a way that divulges "profound similarities" behind various forms and that lets a concealed essence—"the unknown colourings of an inestimable, unsuspected universe"—shimmer through in the expression.[12]

One might expect an argument for a "fundamental sameness" organizing a variety of phenomenal expressions to rile a critic like Bersani, who is obviously impressed by the emergent voices that were soon to be canonized as the groundbreaking texts of poststructuralism and deconstruction. This expectation finds confirmation in the opening of the subsequent study, *Balzac to Beckett*, where he gives an appreciative nod to the reorganization of the literary-critical field through Derrida's and Michel Foucault's recent work. While Foucault reemerges as a crucial component in later Bersani, particularly his queer-theoretical work, much of *Balzac to Beckett*—its consideration of the antinomies of language and stable selves, its initial privileging of "centrifugal" as opposed to "centripetal" texts—seems guided by the deconstructive ethos of *différance* and dissemination offered by Derrida in "Structure, Sign, and Play" and *Of Grammatology* (the latter of which Bersani references in *Balzac to Beckett*'s opening section). Proust's "fundamental sameness" readily becomes an example of Western thought's tendency to organize its systems around what Derrida calls the "fundamental ground"—the self-presences of speech, being, identity, and so forth.[13] For Bersani, French modernist literature experiments with the undoing of such stabilities. We recognize the logic of supplementarity in his description of literature's differential repetitions that undermine the authority of the origin: "the centrifugal movement . . . is most authentically liberating when it creates a discontinuity between its own satellites and a center to which the satellites seem no longer attracted. Each satellite, as it were, throws off other satellites further and further from the orbit of the original planet. The extensions and diversity of circumferential points would not only subvert the meaning at the center; at the extreme, it would silence all interpretation and make the critic continue the novel by inventing his own life" (*BB* 19). Indeed, much of *Balzac to Beckett* proceeds along eminently Derridean lines as it constructs a genealogy of writers—Balzac, Stendahl, Flaubert—whose texts evince a "centrifugal" drive away from essentializing notions of the self. In Bersani's later texts, the term occasionally occurs in this precise sense. In *The Culture of Redemption*, for example, Bersani characterizes psychoanalytic theory as "centrifugal" because Freud postulates that whatever we might have thought as the "original" object of libidinal energy is always already lost in the proliferative movements of the drive (*CR* 30). As psychoanalysis conceives of them, objects are like the "satellites" in whose centrifugal multiplication Bersani, in *Balzac to Beckett*, sees the loss of the original "planet."

The deployment of the "centrifugal" in psychiatry and musicology suggests the term's utility as a synonym for the "play" that, according to Derrida, Western metaphysics works to immobilize. As the *Oxford English Dictionary* recounts, a "fugue state" refers to a "flight"—from the Latin *fugere*—away from "one's own identity," a pathological loss of the subject's experience of self-sameness. This usage points to psychiatry's participation in the Western discourses that ground themselves in identity to "orient, balance, and organize the structure," here, the structure that is the human subject.[14] This web of denotation also neatly discloses these discourses' normative force, suggesting the *lawlessness* of such "fugitive" states: to enter the fugue is to transgress or betray the very center of one's being, to flee, as it were, the plantation.

Put in musicological terms, "fuguing" entails the polyphonic complication of the "subject"—a given melody—by contrapuntal melodies or "countersubjects" (*OED*). As a process of repetition and differentiation, the flight from the center that the (centri)fugal names evokes deconstructive logic, and Bersani, although perhaps the first, would not be the only critic to identify in dissemination a centrifugal force. Writing in 1993, Richard Harland, for example, refers to "the centrifugal movement of dissemination."[15] A recent biographer, David Mikics suggests that this aspect of deconstruction is expressed stylistically, calling the composition of Derrida's early texts "centrifugal," in contradistinction to the traditional mode of argumentation and demonstration in philosophical texts.[16] And Julia Kristeva, in *Strangers to Ourselves* (1988), and particularly its first chapter, "Toccata and Fugue for the Foreigner," deploys the term to describe the condition of the foreigner and the philosopher, precisely because of the fugue's artful de-emphasis of origins. For her, the musical form of the fugue suggests the "perpetual motion" of a "harrowing otherness," which refuses to ground itself on fundamentals: "The foreigner, precisely—like a philosopher at work—does not give the same weight to 'origins' as common sense does."[17] That (the Algerian-born) Derrida might be one of the philosophers she has in mind is suggested by her description of the foreigner-philosopher as someone who "has been brought up, relieved, disseminated, inscribed in an original play developed, without goal, without boundary, without end."[18]

If one discerns Derrida's influence in Bersani's notion of centrifugality, nothing would appear more foreign to such a disseminative drive than the reduction of a world of inexhaustible variety to the seeming immobility of "essences," such as one finds in Proust. Yet it is with Proust and, later, Beckett that the (retrospectively) predictable trajectory of deconstructive reading veers off course. It is also at this juncture that, rather than Derrida's, two important philosophical voices begin to exert a pull on Bersani's understanding of French modernism: Deleuze's and Blanchot's.

In *Balzac to Beckett*'s penultimate chapter, Proust provides a turning point in the study's narrative of French modernism because his work is, paradoxically, both centrifugal and centripetal. Dazzling the reader with "an abundance of self-diffusing metaphors," Marcel "enact[s] the self along such a variety of surfaces that it tends to disappear in its own enriching diffusions" (*BB* 11, 5); yet the Proustian "self's admirable talent for diversifying and multiplying its fictions" is inextricable from "the astonishing magnetism which draws the most diversified experience into an expanding but always recognizable individual psychology" (*BB* 239, 234). Proust's theory of art, Bersani notes, obeys centrifugal and centripetal principles: "two very different things appeal to the Proustian narrator: the fragmentary nature of major artistic productions in the nineteenth century, and the notion that great art, by definition, has a 'vital' unity and completeness which critical recognition [such as Marcel's] can make explicit but does not create. . . . [T]he latter expresses a nostalgic view of the relation of art to the world and the self" (*BB* 196). This doubleness demands that Bersani complicate the argument he has been unfolding so far, and he does this by turning to Deleuze's reading of *À la recherche* in *Proust and Signs* (1964). Deleuze asks us to regard the descriptions from *Albertine disparue*—the contrapuntal repetitions of Albertine in Andrée and others, whose centrifugality the volume's original title, *La fugitive*, suggests—as one of a string of examples where the experiences of love, jealousy, and art unfold as series of *singularities*. Borrowing the term from *À la recherche*, Deleuze refers to these as "essences." He attributes to Proust's "peculiar, volatile essence"[19] the characteristics of *the monad*, an entity that perceives the world from a particular perspective. "Proust is Leibnizian," he asserts: "the essences are veritable monads, each defined by the viewpoint itself referring to an ultimate quality at the heart of the monad."[20] The monadic essence is a singular viewpoint that individuates but neither preexists nor is reducible to the subject.[21] As Bersani, explicitly borrowing from *Proust and Signs*, writes in *Balzac to Beckett*, and repeats verbatim in *A Future for Astyanax: Character and Desire in Literature* (1976), the monad constitutes an "individuality of a point of view embodied in but not dependent on the existence of an individual person" (*BB* 235; *FA* 256).[22]

Deleuze is not alone in his assessment of Proust's "Leibnizianism"; Derrida, a year before the publication of *Proust and Signs*, discerns in narratives such as Proust's echoes of the metaphysics among whose classic articulations he situates Leibniz's system. In the early essay "Force and Signification" (1963), he suggests that the Proustian text is tellingly appropriable by the kinds of structuralist readings whose teleological certainties deconstruction and poststructuralism will disrupt. Notably, he identifies in structuralism—his primary example is Jean Rousset's study *Forme et Signification: Essais sur les structures littéraires de Corneille à Claudel* (1962), and especially its chapter on Proust—an ambition similar to Leibniz's effort to uncover continuities and connections in all phenomena: Rousset "is . . . Leibnizian," he writes: "he seems to think that, confronted with a literary work, one should always be able to find a line, no matter how complex, that accounts for the unity, the totality of its movement, and all the points it must traverse."[23] For Derrida, structuralism (and, by implication, Proust) repeats the Western ontotheology exemplified by Leibniz's law of continuity. Such a structuring ambition renders one blind to whatever does not fit into one's perspective: "everything not intelligible in the light of a 'preestablished' teleological framework, and not visible in its simultaneity, is reducible to the inconsequentiality of accident or dross."[24] If structuralism repeats, while claiming to have transcended, logocentrism,[25] Derrida suggests that it is the Leibnizian inflection of structuralist thought such as Rousset's that reveals its ontotheological orientation, what he elsewhere calls "[s]tructuralist totalitarianism."[26]

In his description of Proust as "Leibnizian," Deleuze may be responding to Derrida's argument about the crypto-Leibnizianism of structuralist literary theory. (We can note the exact repetition by Deleuze of the syntax of Derrida's declarative: Rousset/Proust "is Leibnizian," followed by a colon.) If so, he does this to give Proust's Leibnizianism an assessment that radically departs from Derrida's condemnation of structuralism. He finds in Proust an occasion to explore further the ontology whose theorists he locates around this time also in Friedrich Nietzsche (*Nietzsche and Philosophy* [1962]) and Henri Bergson (*Bergsonism* [1966]). The contrast between Derrida's and Deleuze's evaluations of Proust's monadism throws into sharp relief the turning point that *Balzac to Beckett* marks in Bersani's thought: instead of embracing Derrida's reading of Proust and Leibniz as exemplars of familiar metaphysical assumptions, Bersani opts for Deleuze's affirmation of Proustian-Leibnizian ontology as a moment in an alternate philosophical genealogy. His turn to Deleuze's "brilliant[] analy[sis]" (*BB* 235)—the same phrase is used in *Balzac to Beckett*'s opening to reference *Of Grammatology* (*BB* 4)—of *À la recherche* enables him, first, to claim ontological thinking as a viable critical practice and, second, to move toward conceptualizing difference in terms of *nonrelatedness*. Constantin Boundas points to Deleuze as one of only two ontologists—Emmanuel Levinas being the other—in poststructuralist philosophy.[27] Already in 1954, Deleuze declares that "philosophy, if it means anything, can only be ontology."[28] This emphasis he is never to relinquish: as Badiou observes some fifty years later, "Deleuze purely and simply identifies philosophy with ontology."[29] The enabling presence of Deleuze's thought in the early texts, in other words, allows Bersani to insist on the ontological dimension that, with a kind of an untimely persistence, characterizes his work from *Balzac to Beckett* onward. To be more precise, through Deleuze Bersani locates in monadism the potentiality for an ontology of unrelated, singular beings. In this, his brief discussion of *Proust and Signs* constitutes a significant turning point. In all of Bersani's subsequent work, Proustian-Deleuzean monadology allows the thought of singularity to proceed.

Yet if Bersani extracts the notion of singularity from Leibniz–Proust–Deleuze, the argument does not conclude here but is further routed—as the book's title suggests—through Beckett and, concomitantly, Blanchot, whose gloss on Beckett's onto-aesthetics, in *Le livre à venir* (1959), inflects Bersani's reading.[30] If *Balzac to Beckett*'s early chapters suggest that the centrifugal texts of modernism disenable all "reactionary nostalgias for centers of reality before all expression" (*BB* 21), Bersani, prompted by Beckett, executes a move that we will find repeated numerous times in his subsequent work: he proposes that we may have abandoned a concept—here, the "center"—too readily, without adequately unfolding its potential. What henceforth draws Bersani's attention is the centripetal gravitation toward nonexpressiveness in Beckett: "In Beckett, th[e] centrifugal aspiration is reversed, and in place of an effort to diffuse the self so that its liberty will not be crippled by a center of easily recognizable pressures and designs we have an attempt to block all inventiveness and freedom and to return to the most extreme monotony of being" (*BB* 310). As Bersani continues in his conclusion, the trajectory from Balzac to Beckett that the study's title names ultimately moves from the centrifugal to the centripetal: "Whereas Balzac both struggles to move away from a paralyzing center of being and also dramatizes a coherent psychological definition of that center, Beckett's work is an attempt to approach a center of being which all definition violates" (*BB* 328).

No less than Proust's, Beckett's work may be read as an experiment in monadology. While Bersani, in the early study, does not explicitly mention Beckett's numerous allusions to Leibniz—which others have documented[31]—the two modernists' monadological bent renders their art readily available laboratories for joint experimentation. For Bersani, monadology comes to function as a connecting tissue, a point of attraction, or a site of friction between the Proustian and Beckettian worlds as, moving from Deleuze's reading of Proustian metaphysics, he completes the centripetal (re)turn by finishing his study with Beckett-Blanchot. Bersani is here drawn—and draws our attention—to the resonance and friction between Deleuze's and Blanchot's philosophies. With Beckett and Blanchot, he recasts the Proustian–Deleuzean essence—the nonrelated, singular monad—in terms of the kind of "stillness" or "silence" that Beckett's and Blanchot's texts grind toward. Early on in *Balzac to Beckett*, he observes that, in the examples of literature he traces, "there is an ideal of silence inspired by the yearning for a center of being behind *all* centers" (*BB*

21); this is "the silence of which the universe is made" that, for example, the narrator of *Molloy*'s second section discerns "beyond the [world's] fatuous clamour."[32]

If art's ontological laboratories allow Bersani's experimentation with Proustian–Deleuzean essences, with the move to Beckett and Blanchot the monadic self becomes an unnamable point of condensation, reduction, and failure. In his early commentary on Proust's literary practice, Beckett writes: "The only fertile research is excavatory, immersive, a contraction of the spirit, a descent. The artist is active, but negatively, shrinking from the nullity of extra-circumferential phenomena, drawn in to the core of the eddy."[33] To speak of literature, Blanchot subsequently echoes, must be a movement of "descending . . . to a point where only impersonal neutrality seems to speak."[34] Given his familiarity with monadology, we can propose that what Beckett refers to as the "core" is a version of what Leibniz, too, calls the "core [*Kern*]" of each monad, its indivisible, nonextended essence.[35] According to Leibniz, essences cannot be destroyed by "natural means," that is, without the intervention of divine annihilation:[36] they are "indivisible, ingenerable, and incorruptible."[37] With the death of the body—the undoing of the individuated organism—the essence "can, so to speak, draw itself into an invisible center."[38] Calling this core, this essence, "an individuating viewpoint superior to the individuals themselves," Deleuze renders it a version of what he elsewhere calls the force of "actualization."[39] Like a virtual potential, the monadic essence "is not individual," that is, neither a preformed possibility waiting to be realized nor, in Judith Butler's terms, a body seeking to "matter"; rather, essence is "a principle of individuation" that "remains superior to the person who assumes it."[40]

This onto-ethical argument, first formulated in the laboratories of Proustian and Beckettian texts, is further unfolded twenty years later when, in *Arts of Impoverishment: Beckett, Rothko, Resnais* (1993), Bersani and Dutoit return to Beckett, attracted by the "metaphysical speculation" of his work (*AI* 64).[41] Moving through Beckett's entire oeuvre, they render explicit the Leibnizian orientation of their reading with their numerous allusions to monadism.[42] The reorganization of the Proustian essence via the Beckettian monad, already evident in *Balzac to Beckett*, takes place here too: Bersani and Dutoit rethink Leibniz's singular being in terms of the kind of "failure" of expression that Beckett considers the lot of art. As he asserts in conversation with Georges Duthuit, "to be an artist is to fail, as no other dare fail."[43] But as Beckett's famous decree to "go on"[44] suggests, such ethics of failure also entails the call for a continued failure to continue, or to fail, or to fail to continue, or to continue to fail. Painters, as Beckett observes to Duthuit, experiment with the nonexpressiveness of being—"there is nothing to express, nothing with which to express, nothing from which to express, no power to express, no desire to express"—by heeding the simultaneous "obligation to express."[45] This "obligation" is the impossible injunction that Beckett's unnamable narrator calls his being "obliged to speak," his "ha[ving] to speak of things of which [he] cannot speak."[46]

The frictional space between the Proustian–Deleuzean theory of actualization and the Beckettian–Blanchotian insistence on expressive failure is the site of becoming for Bersani's onto-ethical/aesthetic system. If Deleuze's onto-ethics, especially in its Bergsonian moments, emphasize life's ceaseless proliferation, with Beckett–Blanchot this *élan vital* turns into being's resistance to articulation, its self-annihilating loyalty to inert nonbeing—the effort, as the Unnamable puts it, to "[o]vercome . . . the fatal leaning towards expressiveness."[47] Put in another way, Beckett's experimentations necessitate Bersani's simultaneous adherence to and divergence from the assumptions of the tradition whose persistence in Western thought Arthur Lovejoy identifies in his classic history-of-ideas study *The Great Chain of Being* (1936). As Lovejoy shows, this influential philosophico-theological line of thought posits "the necessary plenitude and continuity of the chain of being," as well as its correlate, maximal actualization: "there is in the absolute essence a real necessity of the real existence of all possible things to the maximal possible degree of diversity."[48] One of this tradition's important moments can be found in Leibniz, for whom the best of possible worlds is one in which "the greatest amount of essence of possibility is brought into existence."[49] Bersani shares the tradition's investment in an ontology of continuous allness—as does, at least occasionally, Beckett: "in reality we are one and all from the unthinkable first to the no less unthinkable last glued together in a vast imbrication of flesh without breach or fissure."[50] But Bersani relinquishes the emanationist proposition of full expression, of being's "pouring itself forth without limit," as Giordano Bruno puts it.[51] Instead, he replaces the principle of ceaseless generation with the principle of *impoverishment*. Beckett calls this being's or expression's "impoverishment," its drive to "shrivel and shrivel";[52] in his later work, he refers to it as language's "leastening," its moving toward an "unlessenable least."[53] The thinkers in Lovejoy's genealogy advocate emanationism, *exigentia existentiae*, because God cannot be thought of as an entity enviously holding being back from actualization; Beckett's ontology, on the contrary, posits a niggardly, jealous being, one whose "stinginess" or "ontological miserliness" Bersani notes already in the early essay "No Exit for Beckett" (1966).[54] In this ontology, as he often repeats, "individuation is a metaphysical error or crime" (*AI* 140), a "criminal separation" (*DSM* 81).

Yet the indeterminate "murmur" of being, never done in its failed adherence to silence, marks a further gravitation toward Deleuzean production: the immobility of which Beckett speaks "is not repose, not the dignity of silence, for it is what still speaks when everything has been said."[55] That is, if Bersanian ethics seems to advocate only withdrawal and failure (as many a queer-theoretical commentator has implied), it is important to note that Beckett's falling-silent constitutes a stillness that, as Blanchot writes, "cannot be silenced":[56] it forms an immobility that coincides with a failure where one is driven to "[f]ail better."[57] The grinding-down of the Beckettian expression is, thus, also a becoming, "the incessant, the interminable";[58] it coincides with the barely discernable "murmur" in Beckett's texts, the sourceless solicitation that Molloy calls "that rumour rising at birth and even earlier, What shall I do? What shall I do?"[59] Channeling Blanchot, Bersani and Dutoit suggest that Beckett's is an experimentation with "a kind of failure that is somehow compatible with the failure to fall silent and even with the diversification of expressive moments" (*AI* 17). That this proliferative failure informs Bersani's thinking throughout his career indicates that, as much as Bersani is (correctly) cited as a thinker of aporia and immobility, his is, perhaps primarily, an ontology of becoming. In *Balzac to Beckett*, he seeks in, for example, Flaubert's work ways of thinking "the possible" and "the new" (*BB* 272). This is not a "naïve" moment in a thinker's early work, but an emphasis characteristic of Bersani's project. Whatever their differences, the resonances between his and Deleuze's systems should attune us to this largely neglected aspect of Bersani's oeuvre.

Radicalizing Predication: After *Balzac to Beckett*

Bersani's continued engagement with ontology is enabled by his project's having taken shape before the deconstruction of metaphysics turned into a commonplace, arguably the very ground from which theory in the social sciences and the humanities most often proceeds, in the Anglo-American academy of the post-1970s. Indeed, from the perspective of contemporary critical theory, Bersani's ontology—at least until very recently—may have appeared as a kind of a remnant, a leftover from earlier stages in critical practices: useless and atrophied, it stubbornly but precariously sticks to a body otherwise sufficiently adapted to the contemporary world. As an ungainly protuberance of sorts, ontology in the Bersanian body may cause embarrassment and prohibit some movement, but it can be, and has been, politely ignored, particularly since the rest of the body remains eminently supple in our critical practices.

Bersani is aware of the oddity of his oeuvre in contemporary criticism. Assessing his contribution to queer theory—most explicitly formulated in *Homos*—he notes in 1996 that, compared to the "invigoratingly centrifugal queer studies," his work must make him seem like "an essentialist villain" (*IRG* 33). As opposed to the "centrifugal" drive of (queer) antiessentialism, his thinking moves *centripetally*, becoming, by implication, *essentialist*. One of the roots of the queer theory whose judgment Bersani ventriloquizes reaches to the essentialist-constructivist debates of the 1970s and 1980s, in which feminist thought played a crucial role.[60] The critique of essentialism sought to expose the hegemonic consolidation of hierarchies in the name of universalizing ontologies, where certain forms of being are consecrated as immortal and unchanging essences while others get relegated to the realm of transience and accident. "Essentialist arguments," as Diana Fuss writes, "frequently make recourse to an ontology which stands outside the sphere of cultural influence and historical change."[61] Among Western philosophy's primary strategies in this effort has been the appeal to the logic of Aristotelian predication. What is the substratum—the essence or, in grammatical terms, the subject—around which predicates, as the accidents that befall being, cohere? The subject-essence, as Aristotle writes in *Metaphysics*, must remain unaffected by such contingencies: he demands that we "dismiss accidental being" and ground ontology on something more permanent.[62] He seeks the solution in grammar, which posits a nameable subject as the ground onto which various and sundry predicates are subsequently attached. The utility of deconstruction for the efforts to critique the logic of predication resides in its demonstration that predicates *supplement* the grammatical subject, in the sense in which Derrida uses the term in and after his reading of Rousseau: they are the parasites that in fact constitute the subject's evanescent being. According to deconstructive logic, neither the subject nor the predicates are primary;

theirs is an "undecidable" relation. The self-sameness of the subject is but a phantom called forth by predicative difference.

This deconstructive logic has aided the undoing of the "untroubled solidities" of gender essentialism.[63] If feminist thought, most notably perhaps in Simone de Beauvoir and Gayle Rubin, had dislodged gender from sex, in *Gender Trouble* Butler suggests that the sex-gender composite accomplishes but a false revolution. She proposes that gender traits must be seen as the predicative supplements to the putative subject of the sexed material body. Feminist antiessentialisms such as Butler's constitute some of twentieth-century Western philosophy's exemplary articulations, insofar as the latter have sought to reorganize the relation that pertains in classical metaphysics between, on the one hand, the subject, essence, or cogito and, on the other, contingency, difference, or otherness. In varied but complementary ways, this reconceptualization informs the ethical imaginaries of such divergent thinkers as Levinas, Derrida, and Laplanche. Bersani's oeuvre similarly entails a rethinking of ontology, but, beginning with *Balzac to Beckett*, his work appeals to an alternate philosophical genealogy than the one that orients, for example, Derridean deconstruction and Laplanchean psychoanalysis. Indeed, Bersani suggests that, by the last decades of the century, "centrifugal" theories of being—where the subject becomes unlocatable as it is subsumed by its predicates—have become something like habitualized responses to the challenge of otherness; they have congealed into what he calls a "cult of difference," a regime that "supports the dominant mode of relations" (*IRG* 34). His targets here, as in *Homos*, are theories of difference that have taken their cues from deconstruction, such as those promulgating the allegedly subversive repetitions or reappropriations of discursive power, associated most immediately with Butler's work. Compared with the impact of such extensively explored theories as peformativity, the potential of the genealogy whose articulations *Balzac to Beckett* locates in the encounter of Proust–Deleuze and Beckett–Blanchot remains largely unactualized; what I have called Bersani's essentialism—his homomonadology—comprises a series of experimentations soliciting this potential.

If "the hegemony of this relational regime" (*IRG* 150) is bolstered by the prioritization of difference, monadology's utility for breaking its spell becomes evident when we recall the peculiar asperity of Leibnizian logic: the fact that it posits only internal relations. As Russell puts it, Leibniz "endeavoured to reduce [all relational propositions] to the subject-predicate logic."[64] Leibniz's metaphysical argument that the universe is comprised of self-enclosed, "windowless" (or "doorless") monads lacking external causal connections—"nothing happens to the substance except out of its own being and in virtue of its own laws"[65]—is helped along by his reconceptualization of philosophy's classic formulation of subject-predicate logic, but one that burrows in a diametrically opposed direction to that of deconstruction. In developing his conception of substance in distinction to Cartesian dualism and Spinozian monism, Leibniz in effect radicalizes Aristotelian predication. He posits a *complete concept* for every substance: a substance is not only the subject of its predicates, the substratum of sundry contingencies; more radically—or, as some commentators have noted, crazily—the subject "involves" *all* its predicates, without becoming their sum. Consequently, whatever befalls a subject—the sin Adam commits, the decision Caesar makes on the Rubicon, the journey one takes to a conference—constitutes a predicate entailed in the subject's essence: as Leibniz declares to Antoine Arnauld, "the individual concept of a substance involves all that will ever happen to it."[66] Leibnizian substances are Aristotelian categories pushed to their "delirious" extreme: each substance becomes a concept. Discussing Deleuze's reading of Leibniz, Daniel W. Smith writes: "At a certain point . . . the process of conceptual specification must stop; one reaches the final species (*infima species*), which groups together a plurality of individuals. Leibniz, however, . . . does not stop. Instead, he attempts to push the concept to the level of the individual itself; in Leibniz, 'Adam' and 'Caesar' are concepts, and not simply proper names." In Leibniz, we consequently have "an almost hallucinatory conceptual creation."[67] Such delirium results not from Leibniz's abandonment of the logic of predication but from his having pushed it to its aporetic extreme. This makes him something of an essentialist villain of Western philosophy. Exposing what really goes on in the metaphysical family's closet, he renders explicit, with a kind of suicidal self-parody, the absurdist logic of Western essentialism. He follows his predecessors' practices too eagerly and spoils the show by revealing how the trick is pulled off.

Like monadology, the ontology Bersani finds in Beckett proceeds by eliminating all (extrinsic) relations: the Beckettian monad is conceptualized in terms of "an identity wholly independent of relational definitions" (*AI* 51). If the term *identity* gives us pause here, it is because it is deployed in the context of a philosophical tradition that has not become the academic commonplace that the Hegelian conceptualization of dialectical differences has. With it, Bersani and Dutoit approximate what Deleuze's avowedly non-Hegelian thinking designates as differences that do not emerge from a network of relations, but, rather, constitute singular, nonrelational points of becoming—for example, Leibniz's incompossibilities, Nietzsche's active forces, or Duns Scotus's haecceities. Bersani moves on a trajectory parallel to Deleuze's when, in texts following *Balzac to Beckett*, he begins to track artistic and theoretical experimentations with unrelatedness.[68]

We can follow this trajectory by noting Bersani's use, in *A Future for Astyanax*, of the term "individuality" to designate essences that would constitute entities of "true singleness" (*FA* 181). These entities emerge in Arthur Rimbaud's work, which gives us "a succession of unrelated, briefly illuminated scenes" with "no continuity" (*FA* 243, 241). Evoking monadology, as usual, without naming Leibniz, Bersani writes that Rimbaud postulates "a world without relationships, one in which each thing is enclosed within itself" (*FA* 242). The theater of cruelty similarly constitutes an onto-ethical testing ground for singularity: Antonin Artaud's work exhibits a "passionate antipathy toward all derivation" (*FA* 267). In the following book, *Baudelaire and Freud*, the possibility of "true singleness" is evoked in terms of "a particularity so radical as to resist any generalizing enterprise" (*BF* 20). Bersani regards Charles Baudelaire's and, again, Rimbaud's work as laboratories of such "radical particularity": Baudelaire's moves toward "[a] notion of a particularity which, as it were, goes nowhere, which is not a 'part' of anything" (*BF* 20); similarly, "[i]n his most radical work, Rimbaud is testing the possibility of a poetic utterance devoid of all structural references, an entirely new utterance without depth and with no past" (*BF* 51). In a review article published, like *Baudelaire and Freud*, in 1977, Bersani enlists Henry James, too, as a practitioner in the art of "the unrelated self";[69] and in *Arts of Impoverishment*, Beckett becomes an experimenter in solipsistic singularity *par excellence*: Bersani and Dutoit write that Beckett "is arguing for nothing less than a total break with the past," producing "work[s] of art cut off from all cultural inheritance" (*AI* 18, 19). In this way, his texts enact "a contagious destruction of relations," aiming at "creating solipsistic chaos" (*AI* 24).

We find in monadology a philosophical articulation of such isolation and discontinuity. The quirkiness of Leibniz's system is registered in Russell's famously exasperated depiction of monadology as an "arbitrary" and "fantastic" construction, a confusion that results from Leibniz's adherence to the logic of predication.[70] For Russell, the proposal that substance, as a complete concept, involves all its predicates without becoming their sum exposes the disabling aporia of any metaphysics that appeals to grammatical logic. He suggests that Leibniz's argument against conceptualizing substance as the sum of its predicates stems from the necessity of positing an ontological entity that remains the same throughout the series of predicated states: substance needs to be understood as "the substratum in which predicates inhere. . . . [T]here would be no ground for opposing subjects to predicates, if subjects were nothing but collections of predicates."[71] Yet because of Leibniz's idealist tendencies, the argumentation falls apart: "the substance remains, apart from its predicates, wholly destitute of meaning," Russell writes; and a substance "destitute of meaning" cannot be "logically employed" in metaphysics.[72]

Blanchot, of course, has a term for the nonrelational condition that Russell considers illogical: partially developing it through his reading of Beckett, he calls it, after Paul Valéry, "essential solitude."[73] Solitude in its "essence"—here we have "Blanchotian essentialism"—does not refer to the blocked traffic between subjects; rather, it constitutes a phenomenon anterior to the derivation of being(s), that is, prior to predication as the articulation of the "I" from whose perspective the "you" and other others become designateable. Rather than the separation of the "I" from the "you," essential solitude names an experience where the "I" fails to depart from or gravitates, centripetally we might say, toward what Blanchot calls *Quelqu'un*, "Someone." Capitalizing this term, Blanchot suggests its status as an impersonal proper name. Departing from Someone's company, the "I" emerges in the process of individuation that Bersani considers an "ontological fall, or sin" (*FoB* 67), "a crime against Being" (*CR* 93); its possibility coincides with a separation that at once constitutes otherness and detaches one from the company of solitude, "the solitude of that which expresses nothing except the word *being*."[74] Even though it is logically anterior to predication—referring to "the pre-conceptual singularity of things as they were before their destruction by words"[75]—essential solitude, as Blanchot suggests, can be approximated only through language, through the "word" that misnames its silent ontology.

Lessness and Allness

Beckett appears to affirm Russell's assessment of the absurdist potential of Leibniz's "arbitrary" system: with what seems like a nod to the *Critical Exposition*, he turns the monads' "pre-established harmony" into "a pre-established arbitrary."[76] Given his recurring thematic of beings' radical isolation, the elimination of all extrinsic relations in Leibnizian logic would have appealed to him.[77] But he, and then Bersani, draws from monadology different lessons than the representatives of the emanationist tradition, among whom Lovejoy situates Leibniz. If the drawing of individuating boundaries constitutes "a crime against Being," Beckettian ethics continues the philosophical tradition of *antinatalism*. In this tradition, individuation marks, as Nietzsche writes in an early commentary on Greek philosophy, "insolent apostasy from the primeval one-ness of all things"; its thinkers conceptualize "coming-to-be as though it were an illegitimate emancipation from eternal being, a wrong for which destruction is the only penance."[78] In *The Birth of Tragedy* (1872/1886), he quotes Silenius's advocacy of refusing birth and, since that error has already been committed, a precipitate death.[79] The antinatalist position—whose most important predecessor in early Nietzsche is Arthur Schopenhauer—continues in Beckett's onto-ethics/aesthetics of impoverishment, whose voice we listen to in the "feeble murmur seeming to apologize for not being dead," "this long sin against the silence that enfolds us."[80]

As a self-proclaimed representative of vitalism—"Everything I've written is vitalistic, at least I hope it is"[81]—Deleuze might seem an odd fit with this tradition. Yet there are moments when he promotes the kind of maximal eradications of relations to which Beckett, echoing Schopenhauer, appeals as an ethical imperative. One such moment is his consideration of *the tick*, prompted by Jakob von Uexküll's work.[82] What fascinates Deleuze in *ixodes ricinus* is its ability to withdraw from an already impoverished life into a state of near-virtuality. The tick is plugged into the world with few affects, able to survive almost indefinitely in a state of a coma-like suspension. In it, one can observe as depersonalized or anonymous a mode of existence as possible: a minimally individuated life. For Deleuze, affects (or, in the terms we have used above, predicates) that individuate being also mark the territorialization of life's impersonal potential. The predicates that supplement the subject parasite it as so many personalizing traits: they situate the emergent subject in the world, rendering being namable, re-cognizable. This process dissipates the virtual force for which Deleuze often borrows Bergson's term *élan vital*. The tick has a remarkable ability to access the impersonal *élan* that embodied lives territorialize: becoming a subject without predicates—a body without organs—it can withdraw from *life* into *a* life.[83]

"This retreat from the actual," writes Bersani, "creates a freedom that might be defined as a kind of being to which no predicate can be attached" (*TT* 66). Here, in the recent text *Thoughts and Things*, he is not speaking of ticks; his subject is Jean-Luc Godard's cinema. Like Beckett before him, Godard provides for Bersani a counterexample to Proust's centrifugal, expansive onto-aesthetics. If *Balzac to Beckett* contrasts Proust's proliferative art with Beckett's impoverishing of expression, in his latest work Bersani observes the divergent deployment of "analogies" in Proust's and Godard's art. According to him, as we've noted, Proust dazzles us by revealing, through hidden analogies and similitudes, a "fundamental sameness" in the seemingly disparate entities that populate his novel. In *À la recherche*, varied objects are fragments of being that, if situated properly, should, like matching pieces of a puzzle, allow us to make full sense of the world. The promise that objects will contribute to the world's completion, its becoming fully readable, endows them with an enigmatic quality, the sense that they are secreting something of vital importance behind their dissimulated appearance. This enigmatic splendor solicits desire. Proust's lovers are captured by the semblances behind which, they think, truth resides: they are fascinated by each beloved's "secret self, behind the veil of eyes and flesh";[84] they seek the "essence" of a love object, an essence whose revelation would allow the lover not only to understand the other but to comprehend his own being. Moving toward the world thus becomes a process of coercing the object into surrendering its secrets so that one can not only see its place amidst other objects, but also move closer, piece by piece, to solving the world's riddle. Bersani calls Proust's novel "an epistemological detective story" (*DSM* 41; see also *CR* 114): by organizing the varied clues and red herrings into a cohesive narrative, we ideally strengthen our grasp of—and finally comprehend—the world and our place in it.

Godard, too, thinks in similitudes and correspondences. Yet his method of comparison is different from the one we find in *À la recherche*. Bersani suggests that, while Proust maps the world centrifugally—*enriching* reality by ever-proliferating analogies—Godard's, much like Beckett's, witnessing of being takes place in a centripetal movement of *impoverishment*. As an example, he points to the relation between *Passion* (1982) and *Scenario* (1982), the latter of which is an account of the construction of a scene from the former film. He suggests that the short film—released some months after the feature-length work—is something like *Passion*'s undoing, its withdrawal from the world: it is "as if Godard's time had become a reel he could unwind—that is, not a time from a scenario to a finished film, but rather from the film that has been made to its tentative form that must have preceded but now follows it" (*IRG* 165). Developmental chronology is reversed: we move from the "finished" statement to its embryonic form. Yet dispossessing the artwork of its expressive richness simultaneously moves it from the actual to the potential. "The Godardian movement backwards," Bersani writes, "far from negativizing or simply erasing the finished being it leaves, actually expands it by potentializing it. Partially derealized being is virtual being" (*IRG* 165). A being's scope is enhanced when its realized variety is diminished. In its withdrawal from actuality, being becomes virtual. In its becoming-virtual, it accesses the potential that has had to be relinquished at the moment of appearance or figuration. According to Bersani, Godard films being's destitution, its retraction from an actualized form back to a state of mere potentiality, where the artwork has not yet been narrowed in terms of what it may become.

Godard's experimentations bet on the proposition that "lessness is the condition of allness" (*IRG* 70; see also *FoB* 165). Like numerous other formulations by Bersani, this paradigmatic statement—it encapsulates Bersanian onto-ethics/aesthetics in its entirety—can be translated into Leibnizian idiom. The exasperation Russell and others have expressed about Leibniz has to do with the eccentric ramifications of his radical theory of predication. Involving all its predicates, the nonextended monad is not only solipsistic—without relations—but also, and at the same time, *all-related*: since it entails all possible attributes, it must encompass the world in its totality. As Daniel Smith writes, "once Leibniz says that the predicate 'crossing the Rubicon' is included in the notion of Cesar, he cannot stop; he is forced to include the totality of the world in Cesar's concept. This is because 'crossing the Rubicon' has multiple causes and multiple effects, such as the establishment of the Roman Empire and the death of Jesus; it stretches to infinity backward and forward by the double play of causes and effects."[85] Hence we have what Smith calls "the fantastic Leibnizian concept of *expression*: the notion of the subject expresses the totality of the world. Each of us, in our concept, expresses or contains the entirety of the world."[86] Each noncommunicating, self-enclosed substance partakes in "preestablished harmony," reflecting the entire universe and, consequently, *corresponding* or *agreeing with* every other substance: the monad, writes Leibniz, "expresses the whole universe, according to a certain aspect."[87] The withdrawal from actuality, the undoing of expressed being, that we find in *Passion* and *Scenario* constitutes an artistic experimentation with the reactivation of universal correspondence. This movement aims at "an essential being prior to, and removed from, the conditions of all realized being" (*AI* 49). By such self-impoverishment or self-subtraction we approach, as in Leibniz's metaphysics, "the total relationality of being" (*AI* 140).

Godard's cinema exemplifies what both Bersani and Deleuze consider an ethical injunction: beings' impoverishment by their disengagement from attributes, a (centripetal) "retreat from the actual" (*TT* 66), a becoming of "a body without attributes" (*IRG* 61)—a phrase that should evoke for us Deleuze's "body without organs." This dynamic informs what we have tentatively called Beckett's, and now Bersani's, antinatalism: in expression, being loses some of its capacity to *resonate*—to replicate sonically (re-*sonāre*)—with (or in) the world. As it is deprived of attributes (or affects or predicates), an individuated being becomes *sonant* again, that is, regains the radical fluctuancy that makes music the most Dionysian, most nonplastic, of arts for Nietzsche. Risking phonocentrism, we might say that deactualizing being becomes re-sonant, shifts from the *figural* (what Derrida would call "writing") to the *sonic*. Along with Beckett's and Godard's, Stéphane Mallarmé's work offers Bersani a counterexample to the Proustian riches. Rather than the Proustian fugue, in Mallarmé "the self undergoes an ontological regression in poetry," what we have called the monad's centrifugal withdrawal: "it recedes into virtuality and becomes a play of fictions" (*DSM* 42). Mallarmé writes that each "soul," in its singularity, constitutes a "rhythmic knot" (qtd. in *DSM* 42). Bersani writes: "The individuality expressed in [Mallarmé's] poetry is an event of linguistic inflection rather than of psychological depth. . . . The 'rhythmic knot' in individuals is not a psychic enigma. Rather, psychic enigmas are, so to speak, the demusicalization of that knot, its reduction to the status of reportable fact, or movable currency" (*DSM* 42). Mallarmé's poetry becomes for Bersani a privileged occasion of *sonicate art*.

Deleuze, too, finds in music the drift from impoverishment to allness, characteristic of Bersani's homomonadology. For him, Uexküll's biophilosophy suggests monadic sameness as an ontological principle. According to Uexküll, the world is organized into differentiated spatialities and temporalities that constitute a field of noncommunicating beings. As Giorgio Agamben writes in his genealogy of philosophy's biopolitics, for Uexküll "a unitary world does not exist, just as a space and a time that are equal for all living things do not exist. The fly, the dragonfly, and the bee that we observe flying next to us on a sunny day do not move in the same world as the one in which we observe them, nor do they share with us—or with each other—the same time and the same space."[88] However, if, as several commentators have noted, Uexküll's world is distinctly Leibnizian,[89] this is not only because each being constitutes a monadic "bubble" but also because of the compositional harmony, the *accord*—"intensity, resonance, musical harmony"[90]—of such noncommunicating vessels. Apart from the famous tick, Uexküll's favorite examples include the spider and the fly, two bodies sealed in their worlds and affects, blind to one another, whose disparate "melodies" are nevertheless perfectly orchestrated into an encounter. With his fondness for musical tropes, Uexküll suggests that we understand the animal's "primal image" (*Urbild*) also as "a primal melody" or "score."[91] For him, the fly and the spider provide examples of the natural world's "contrapuntal" complication:[92] the encounter of monadic substances is orchestrated, in other words, as a *fugue*. Yet this fugue is crucially different from that which we find in Proust's "Albertine cycle": it does not posit a "subject" (for the narrator, Albertine) that would retain its priority as "the dominant colour" or "tone" in the sequence comprised by subsequent "countersubjects" (Andrée and others).[93] Rather, the fugue in Uexküll unfolds *in between* the monadic subjects: with the encounter of the spider and the fly as "melodies in counterpoint," there occurs "the constitution of a new plane."[94]

Deleuze implicitly engages such animal symphonics in *Proust and Signs*: he finishes the description of Proust's fugitive universe with a silent allusion to Uekülls work. Locating in Proust a Leibnizian world of noncommunicating entities ("a schizoid universe of closed vessels, of cellular regions") and pointing out "the insistence with which Proust presents the narrator as incapable of seeing, of perceiving, of remembering, of understanding . . . , etc.," he suggests we consider *À la recherche*'s narrator a spider whose body without organs has no way to relate to its objects except through its coordination via the primal score.[95] Like Proust, Uexküll, too, becomes Leibnizian: "Leibniz was the first to raise the problem of a communication resulting from sealed parts or from what does not communicate" in his combining of monadic solitude and universal concomitance.[96] The Proustian search unfolds as an encounter between noncommunicating bodies, an encounter whose dynamics and productions are not inherent in either of the encountering bodies but operate on "a new plane": the *recherche* thereby constitutes the Deleuzean fugue, flight, or becoming as a movement "which is not common to the two [encountering bodies], . . . but something which is between the two, outside the two, and which flows in another direction."[97]

Prompted by Uexküll, Deleuze proposes an onto-ethical imperative of being's becoming-monadic, of its deterritorializing retreat, tick-like, from the world. It is only by unplugging its attributes—unlearning its mode of existence—that actualized being can access the virtuality spent in expression. The centripetal withdrawal repotentializes being; in unplugging, being becomes resonant, responsive to frequencies beyond the range of its actualized self. The same principle—of being's "shriveling" or "leastening"—organizes Beckett's thought. Bersani brings Deleuze and Beckett in contact already in *Balzac to Beckett*; in the following decades, he continues to unfold the implications of this encounter. In the 1970 study, he writes of Beckett's effort to "draw[] . . . creation back into its uncreated source": "If the ultimate Beckett 'home' contains the entire universe, it is only in the sense that the inhabitant of that home has not yet lost the possibility of being everything and everywhere by being born into a particular body and a particular place in the universe" (*BB* 324). Prompted by Beckett, Blanchot, too, speculates about the ethical necessity of impoverishing being. It is this onto-ethical background, having cohered over several decades in Bersani's work on theory, literature, and art, that informs his quarrel with what had by the early 1990s emerged as the scholarly field of queer theory.

From Centrifugal to Centripetal Queer Theory

In *Homos*, Bersani not only critically addresses some of queer thought's recent formulations but also sketches another orientation for the newly emergent field. He does this by engaging the French modernist texts familiar from his earlier studies. To use the term he evokes in the later work, he *recategorizes* his earlier insights in the context of queer thought. The queer theory that he offers builds on, and remains to an extent obscure without knowledge of, the onto-ethics/aesthetics he has formulated since the first book, in 1965, on Marcel Proust. In *Balzac to Beckett*, he makes the case for reading much of French modernist literature, including Proust, as instances of centrifugal art, before locating a centripetal turn in Beckett's works. As we have noted, in a lecture from 1996, collected in *Is the Rectum a Grave? and Other Essays* (2010), he identifies in queer theory an "invigoratingly centrifugal" practice (*IRG* 33). The terminological repetition in the 1970 and 1996 texts is no accident, for Bersani wants to replace the mode of queer theorizing most in vogue at the time with one that would take its cues from the "centripetal" onto-ethics/aesthetics that he has elaborated with the help of Beckett and others.

In the 1996 commentary, Bersani goes on to out himself as an "essentialist villain," mistakenly invited to a cocktail party of "centrifugal" queer theorists. The party whose protocols he disrupts is held at Judith Butler's house. The queer thinkers he comes out to are mostly scholars whose work has been inspired by Butler's influential 1990 study, *Gender Trouble: Feminism and the Subversion of Identity*. This is the *Ur*-text for what Bersani takes as contemporary thought's unwitting allegiance to, and support of, the "cult of difference" that continues to determine society's extant mode of relationality. Although perhaps familiar, the philosophical genealogy that prompts Bersani's resistance may be worth a brief revisit. Butler's concept of performativity bears the strong mark of her earliest influences, particularly Hegelian thought. In her political thinking, Butler relies on Hegel's idea of dialectics, the spirit's sojourn where every dialectical stage is riven by internal contradictions, which force the journey's continuation. Like numerous other twentieth-century readers of Hegel—whose work Butler explored in her dissertation, published as *Subjects of Desire: Hegelian Reflections in Twentieth-Century France* (1987)—she adopts the Hegelian model, but dispossesses it of its teleological frame. As she writes in an early essay, the becoming (*Werden*) that she gleans from Hegel is deprived of the movement's conclusion in what Johann Gottlieb Fichte called its "synthesis." Hers is a "decapitated" dialectic, a theory for the "post-teleological age."[98]

At the end of *Subjects of Desire*, Butler forges a model that will produce the concept of performativity in her next study, *Gender Trouble*, and whose ramifications she will elaborate in all her subsequent work. In the concluding chapter, she engages three twentieth-century thinkers in a kind of a dialectical endgame, where the thesis (Lacan) and antithesis (Deleuze) yield a theoretical synthesis, one that she identifies with Foucault's work. Butler deems Lacan's theory of subject formation too constraining in its universalizing understanding of the symbolic order; rendering paternal prohibition an uncontestable law, it naturalizes what she will call, in *Gender Trouble*, "the heterosexual matrix." Deleuze, on the other hand, posits a subject who can access, through forces of becoming unconstrained by any prohibitions, "an elusive and tantalizing 'beyond' to culturally instituted desire" and find there "the promise of liberation."[99] It is Foucault's thought that emerges as the culmination of Butler's theoretical dialectic. Synthesizing the Lacanian notion of the simultaneous inescapability and productivity of the incest prohibition with the Deleuzean thought of the ceaselessly disruptive outside, Butler argues for a strategic position internal to power "that subverts and proliferates th[e] law from within the terms of culture itself."[100] For her, Foucault manages to conceptualize both the cultural immanence of desire (which Deleuze does not do) while at the same time opening a way to undo prohibition from within its own domain (a possibility that is preempted in Lacan). As the happy medium between Lacan and Deleuze, Foucault thus "offer[s] a normative framework which entails a subversive struggle with existing prohibitions, a thoroughly cultural program which disavows any appeal to a desire that has a natural or metaphysical structure said to exist either prior or posterior to linguistic or cultural laws."[101]

When Butler identifies in Foucault a politically usable method of "subver[sion] and proliferat[ion]," she is thinking of the strategy he calls "'reverse' discourse."[102] His best-known example of reverse discourse concerns the seizing of the unintended opportunities afforded by the emergence, at the end of the nineteenth century, of "homosexuality" as a pathologized identity category. As an example of this realignment, such scholars as Lillian Faderman have shown that the final quarter of the century saw the reassessment of women's romantic friendships, previously a largely unproblematic part of affective life in the middle-class private sphere, as sexually deviant.[103] While Foucault finds much to admire in such work—he gives an appreciative nod to Faderman's groundbreaking book, *Surpassing the Love of Men: Romantic Friendship and Love Between Women from the Renaissance to the Present* (1981), in an interview[104]—he also suggests that, rather than lamenting, as Faderman often does, the elimination of the affective potential that nineteenth-century women found in friendships, we should recognize and learn from the counterdiscursive practices of various queer folk after homosexuality's "invention." As Foucault famously notes in the first volume of *The History of Sexuality*, it is by appropriating the idiom of medical discourses that "homosexuality began to speak in its own behalf, to demand that its legitimacy and 'naturality' be acknowledged."[105] His lesson concerns subjects' ability to mobilize the side effects of the discursive proliferation by power-knowledge apparatuses. Extracting from this the concept of performativity, Butler also finds an analogy to Foucauldian discursive mobilization in Derrida's concept of "iteration," whose deconstructive lessons—performative iterations are nothing but the groundless work of *différance*—help her counter criticism about her theory's voluntarist assumptions.[106] Her synthesis of Foucault and Derrida allows a rigorous antiessentialism: the Butlerian subject becomes a groundless accumulation of performative iterations, an entity of discursive construction whose continuity is guaranteed only by the repetition of such speech acts. While the subject is coerced to this performative repetition under the threat of her survival, a necessary time lag intervenes between iterative moments. In this temporal gap resides the freedom of the subject, who can, through a labor of considerable difficulty and danger, repeat her formative injunctions differently, thereby inflecting her being toward new possibilities. Here takes place "a repetition of the law into hyperbole, a rearticulation of the law against the authority of the one who delivers it"; the performative iteration "produces a set of consequences that exceed and confound what appears to be the disciplining intention motivating the law."[107]

In the first volume to *The History of Sexuality*, Foucault characterizes the production of categories of deviance by eighteenth- and nineteenth-century medical discourses as "a centrifugal movement."[108] He argues that, during the time span he studies, we witness the gradual disappearance of the normative model of heterosexuality as the standard according to which instances of deviance were assessed. The medical gaze increasingly focused on the expanding catalogue of deviant bodies and desires, all the while losing the heterosexual couple as the point of reference for these accounts. One way to understand the strategies of "performativity" and "reverse discourse," insofar as they concern sexual politics, is to see in them an intentional exacerbation of this movement away from the definitional center of normative heterosexuality. Deconstruction radicalizes this proposition: had Derrida addressed Foucault's claim about medical discourses' "centrifugal" flight from the norm, he would have proposed that the norm of "the heterosexual couple" in fact emerges as a mirage conjured up, *après-coup*, by the ever-expansive catalogues of deviance.[109] What Foucault calls "a centrifugal movement" obeys the logic of *Nachträglichkeit*, of afterwardsness, the temporal structure of dissemination. Basing her thought on the Hegelian dialectic, and supplementing it with Foucault's genealogy and Derrida's deconstruction, Butler develops the idea of performativity along these lines: she gives us a "centrifugal" queer theory.

Centrifugal queer theory, such as we find in Butler, is anticipated in Bersani's early description of French literary modernism in *Balzac to Beckett*. Much like Butlerian performativity, Bersani's argument about the "centrifugal" thrust in texts by Balzac, Stendahl, Proust, and others is supported by Derridean deconstruction. Bersani implicitly acknowledges this parallel when, in order to address queer theory's promise and limits, he concludes *Homos* by repeating the trajectory of his 1970 study. As much as his discussion of centrifugal French fiction in *Balzac to Beckett* culminates with a reading of *À la recherche*, in "The Gay Outlaw" he turns to Proust to describe contemporary queer thought. As the artist and thinker of the centrifugal *par excellence*, Proust again functions as foil for a writer in whose work Bersani identifies more interesting onto-ethical lessons, ones that take us beyond the centrifugal dynamics of the Proustian world. This time the artist is not Beckett (nor, as it will later be, Godard); instead, Bersani engages Jean Genet's texts. Beckett and Genet, he proposes, share a considerable deal. He sees in Genet's "cult of waste" an extension of Beckett's "cult of failure": "Genet," he writes, "is much like Beckett who, in his determination to fail, would have to be in sympathy with Genet's scatological aesthetic" (*H* 181). But here texts like *Funeral Rites* (1953) also take us further. While Genet, particularly with his ethics of "betrayal," comes to represent the centripetal imperative Beckett has figured, Bersani identifies in his work something beyond the contraction toward impoverished being. After a rigorous ascesis of unlearning being's extant habits, an ecstatic fugue can commence.

"The Gay Outlaw" opens with the promise of the Proustian world as Bersani gives us a dizzyingly complex account of the theory of "inversion" described in the opening pages of *Cities of the Plain*. Creatively experimenting with—or ontologizing—the discourses of nineteenth-century sexology and racial sciences, Proust seems to propose the impossibility of homosexual relations. For him, inverts, with their mismatched desires and bodies, fail in their *rapport sexuel*: they are incapable of forging anything but entirely fantasized connections to each other. What Bersani finds appealing in *À la recherche*'s tortuous delineation of transsexed attractions is Proust's spectacular failure to put forward a psychologically viable theory of desire, that is, an account that would assume coherent or legible individuals as its agents.[110] Instead, Proust pushes the incipient disciplines of sexology and psychiatry into epistemological overdrive from whose agitated production—a centrifugal movement—it is not possible to rescue any operative account of sexuality's relation to bodies or pleasures.

While Bersani appreciates Proust's experiment of driving the biopolitical discourses into the territory of the comedic grotesque, however, "the Proustian dance of essences is only provisionally liberating" (*H* 144). This is because the kind of excessive and wayward, and perhaps a little insane, descriptions that we witness in *Cities of the Plain* remain tethered to the discourses from which they borrow. Taking Proust as an (unlikely) example of a practitioner of reverse discourse and performativity, Bersani insists that, for all their inventiveness, for all their subversions and proliferations, such strategies amount to what Nietzsche calls slavish, reactive practices:

however brilliant and creative and insubordinate, their performers only ever call themselves by derivatives of the names bequeathed to them by their masters. Indeed, in its Hegelian immanentism, performativity postulates that such names are our only resource; paradigmatically, performativity's dialectical framework rules out all other possibilities than those which are always already inscribed in the dialectic.

If Proust figures as a progenitor to the queer theory that Bersani wants to contest, Genet continues the onto-ethical experimentations that are identified with Beckett's work in *Balzac to Beckett*, *Arts of Impoverishment*, and other studies. Beckett's art advocates being's centripetal impoverishment; Genet's, a radical self-betrayal. "*Betrayal*," as Bersani puts it in one of his famously punchy opening lines, "*is an ethical necessity*" (*H* 151).[111] What attracts him in, for example, *Funeral Rites* is something he calls "nonrelational betrayal" (*H* 162). Its examples are found in scenes of pointless, nonproductive disowning of revolutionary or affective loyalties—the repugnant, inexplicable betrayals of one's allies and lovers that cannot be resolved by appeals to either sacrificial or psychologizing rationalities (a person is destroyed for the benefit of a greater good; the betrayal is a symptom of an individual pathology). We must, he writes elsewhere, "betray the relational modes sanctified by the dominant culture" (*IRG* 60). This betrayal is not a message to the betrayed other, a retaliatory response to previous events defining the relational dynamics (and hence a solicitation for counteractions). Instead, Bersani wants to imagine a betrayal without an object, one that, refusing all dialectical economies, would constitute *an active force*.

Among other endeavors, Bersani's onto-ethics of centripetality, impoverishment, and betrayal seeks to undo the mapping, the territorialization, of human potentialities by the biopolitical discourses whose rise, as Foucault argues, gave birth to the modern homosexual at the end of the nineteenth century. Bersani alludes to these discourses when he writes, in *The Death of Stéphane Mallarmé* (1982), of the ways in which the imposition of "psychological depth" and "psychic enigmas" in poetry leads to the "demusicalization" of individualities (*DSM* 42).[112] The discourses of psychiatry and sexology assign the individual attributes that anchor it in the world, rendering it legible and recognizable. Bersani wants these attributes betrayed; he seeks the restoration of what Nietzsche would call being's *musicality*. This task cannot be accomplished through the cumulative work of resignification—"the centrifugal multiplication of words and gestures," as he, repeating our keyword, phrases it in a recent discussion of Genet (*TT*

20)—that performativity prioritizes (and whose funnily grotesque version we have in *Cities of the Plain*). Rather, through the ever-widening and increasingly detailed definitions, vocabularies, and theories, the singularity that Bersani calls "individuality" is rendered progressively namable (and, hence, nonmusical). Even if such names make no claims to representing an unchanging essence, they individuate being in psychological personhood, whose secret depths we are trained to read and desire.

The self-loss that, as Bersani postulates in his theory of *ébranlement*, one supposedly experiences in the sexual can provide an occasion for training oneself to live with less of the self, for finding pleasure not in the self's enrichment but in its dismantling. If this withdrawal from the world takes place through betrayal, as Genet suggests, queer theory has, according to Bersani, failed to adequately carry out its labor: "Nothing we [queers] have imagined so far sufficiently betrays the relational orders under which much of humanity continues to be oppressed" (*IRG* 51). We have failed to unplug ourselves from the extant world, failed to refuse the attributes that name our essence. We have not become sufficiently poor in being.

Bersani closes "Is the Rectum a Grave?" by suggesting that the sexual jouissance that shatters the self can be cultivated into "a mode of ascesis" (*IRG* 30). The term "ascesis" is meant to indicate his alternative to the practices of "subversive parodies" (*IRG* 12) that, before they became identified with Butler's signature concept of "performativity," were lauded by Jeffrey Weeks and Richard Dyer in their mid-1980s discussions of "gay macho" cultures. Weeks had argued that the deployment of traditional masculine styles in gay men's pick-up choreographies "gnaws at the roots of a male heterosexual identity."[113] For Bersani, such claims to political radicalness not only overstate the effects of what he sees as gay macho's "worshipful tribute" to straight masculinity (*IRG* 13), but also obfuscate homosexual men's affective investment in questionable norms. Straight culture does not tremble at the sight of the leather queen; moreover, claiming cruisy gay men as combatants in what Weeks calls a "semiotic guerilla warfare" carries more than a whiff of self-flattery.[114] Gay macho is imbued with "wholly nonsubversive intentions" (*IRG* 13). Formulated as commentary on Weeks and Dyer, this argument returns in the critique of Butler in *Homos*: "resignification cannot destroy," Bersani reiterates in 1995; "it merely presents to the dominant culture spectacles of politically impotent disrespect. . . . It is . . . extremely doubtful that resignification, or redeployment, or hyperbolic miming, will ever overthrow anything. These mimetic activities are too closely imbricated in the norms they continue.

As long as the cues for subversion are provided by the objects to be subverted, reappropriation may be delayed but is inevitable: reappropriation, and reidealization" (*H* 51). Instead of the centrifugal practices of parody and performativity—their "reverse discourse"—a different starting point must be found for queer theory's contestations with the norm.

When Bersani speaks of "ascesis" in 1987, he is evoking the project that Foucault, to the bewilderment of many of his readers, had initiated during the last years of his life. Abandoning his initial plan for a study of "the history of sexuality" in six volumes,[115] he unexpectedly turned to a description of the ancient ethics of *askēsis*, "the cultivation of the self," that he found in the texts of Plato, Plutarch, Seneca, and others. He anticipates this project in an interview in the early 1980s. We must proceed to an "ascesis," which, he says, "is the work that one performs on oneself in order to transform oneself or make the self appear which, happily, one never attains."[116] In the famous interview—"Friendship as a Way of Life," originally published in the French gay journal *Gai Pied* in April 1981—he discusses the role that the habits, extant and potential, of modern homosexuality may have for our rethinking of ethical life. He calls for the development of "a homosexual ascesis," a practice that "would make us work on ourselves and invent—I do not say discover—a manner of being that is still improbable."[117] In citing "a mode of ascesis" as an alternative to the parodic repetitions that Weeks and Dyer—and, soon thereafter, Butler—theorize as queer practice, Bersani proposes that we turn to the work Foucault produced in the 1980s and that was left unfinished because of his early death.[118]

If Foucault himself identifies a "centrifugal movement" in the creative proliferations of the "reverse discourses" he theorizes in the 1970s, his later work moves toward practices that comprise the kind of impoverishment or "self-subtract[ion]" (*IRG* 48) whose potential Bersani has developed since his early encounter with Beckett. One of the sources for this shift can be identified in the ancient texts to which Foucault turned to reinvent his project. As Arnold Davidson points out, the Greek philosopher Plotinus likened the ethical work required of citizens to artistic practices: the aim was to create the self as a work of art. Plotinus's model for what Foucault, in the second volume of *The History of Sexuality*, calls "an aesthetics of existence"[119] was not painting—which was thought to constitute "an art of addition"—but sculpture, the "art of taking away." "Since the statue already exists in the block of marble," Davidson describes the logic, "it is sufficient to take away what is superfluous in order to make the statue appear." The care of the self that Foucault draws from the Greek manuals can thus be understood as "the sculpting of oneself as a statue, the scraping away of what is superfluous and extraneous to oneself."[120] The subject whom Bersani poses as an alternative to the performative being similarly chips away at the crust of his being; shedding his habits, he seeks to impoverish his existence into a work of art.

Yet it is not sufficient to say that the sole or ultimate aim of the ascetic's work—his scraping away at his self—is the self's reduction. Neither in Foucault's sources nor in Bersani does the withdrawal from the various ways in which one has existed, and found pleasure in existing, in the world constitute the entire narrative arc. As Davidson points out, the observations of Foucault's contemporaries in the field of classics suggest some implications of his unfinished work beyond the ethics of impoverishment. These studies indicate that the classics Foucault discussed embrace a cosmology whose potential relevance to his "aesthetics of existence" has remained largely unaddressed. Drawing from Pierre Hadot's studies—with which Foucault was familiar—Davidson notes that programs such as Seneca's assumed that the proper "cultivation" of the self can precipitate "a cosmic consciousness, a consciousness of being part of the cosmic whole."[121] Modern thought is likely to misrecognize the aim of the self-management promulgated by Seneca as that of "individual autonomy"; but what ancient ethics/ascetics seeks is, rather, the self's articulation in the larger terms of a cosmic onto-ethics: "one of the most distinctive features of that care of the self studied by Foucault . . . is its indissociable link with this cosmic consciousness; one philosophical aim of this care of the self is to transform oneself so that one places oneself in the perspective of the cosmic."[122] In the ascetic practices Foucault sought to outline, the self's reduction into a work of art is followed by, or perhaps coincides with, a disseminative movement into the universe.

We find a correlative to the contractive-expansive movement of the ancient "aesthetics of existence" in Bersani's oeuvre. Even though Bersani, first in his early discussion, in *Balzac to Beckett*, of French modernist experimentations and then in his critique of queer theory in "Is the Rectum a Grave?" and *Homos*, prompts us, against all deconstructive wisdom, to halt the centrifugal flight from "essences," the impoverishing movement toward an unactualized center of being is itself always implicated in an elaboration of what he calls, adopting the term from Baudelaire, "correspondence of forms." Thus we have studies like *The Forms of Violence: Narrative in Assyrian Art and Modern Culture* (1985) and *Caravaggio's*

Secrets (1998), where the term "centrifugal" reemerges, this time to indicate not the limits of escape in nineteenth-century modernist fiction nor the wrong turn queer theory has taken with dialectical thinking, but *an onto-ethical exigency*. In the analysis of Assyrian art in *The Forms of Violence*, Bersani and Dutoit deploy the term to mark the seduction of the spectator's gaze away from the brutal narratives that constitute the artworks' explicit subject. The Assyrian artists pay ostentatious homage to rulers' and armies' prowess in their confrontations with beasts and men by constructing compelling narratives that culminate in moments of carnage. Yet amidst the fascinating violence something else takes place, a distractive invitation that enables an ethical disengagement with such narrative violence. Apart from focusing the viewer's attention on the centers of action in the reliefs' hunting and battle scenes, the Assyrian sculptors also draw the spectator's eye along a series of repeating forms that join disparate, noncommunicating entities—the human and the nonhuman, the sentient and the inanimate—into varied aesthetic forms. The reliefs thus solicit a form of attention that, rather than being motivated by, and looking forward to, the denouements of narratives, is oddly disinterested in the sequencing of the violent events that are being celebrated. Inviting a "visual mobility . . . created by insistent but inexact repetition," this movement proceeds with an "explosive centrifugal force" (*FV* 98), which now enables an ethical orientation.

Similarly, in their 1998 book Bersani and Dutoit attribute to Caravaggio's art a mobilization of spectatorial attention that is strictly analogous to the distraction of the viewer's concentration on the Assyrian battle scenes' violent centers by the pleasurable experience of formal repetitions in the tableaux. As much as the ancient artists obediently glorify the Assyrian armies' gory exploits, Caravaggio is at great pains to render in inviting detail his models' sex appeal. Yet Bersani and Dutoit propose that, in his later work, he increasingly betrays the models' eroticism, whose captivating force is analogous to the reliefs' compelling violence. Caravaggio does this by directing the spectator's attention to the "nonerotic sensuality" (*CS* 79) of repeating arrangements that, in a "centrifugal" movement, extend the male bodies onto other forms and surfaces. As opposed to the highlighting of the boy's genitals and buttocks in *Victorious Cupid*, such later paintings as *St. John Baptist with a Ram* deemphasize the model's sexual attractiveness and, instead, invite the viewer's gaze to follow "a series of fanlike structures opening outward, away from the youth's body": the scene "opens out, centrifugally, in various directions, countering the centripetal pull of the youth's gaze" (*CS* 81). The image retains its "centripetal movement" (*CS* 97) through the boy's commanding gaze, but this momentum is embedded in the "centrifugal sensuality" (*CS* 88) of repeating arrangements, whether of human or nonhuman forms.

Without noting its original appearance in *Balzac to Beckett*, Bersani thus uses our keyword in a series of texts, particularly in the analyses of visual arts in his collaborations with Dutoit. Alluding to their argument, in *The Forms of Violence*, about the Assyrian reliefs' "nonunifying centrifugal mobility" (*AI* 138), Bersani and Dutoit, in *Arts of Impoverishment*, find examples of this movement in Alain Resnais's cinema. They call *Muriel* (1963) "a wholly centrifugal film," whose action is "constantly rushing away from a narrative center never firmly established in the first place" (*AI* 190). They write that Resnais repeatedly stages examples of a "hysterically centrifugal movement that [his] characters' efforts to narrativize their past fail to counter" (*AI* 199; see also 191, 197, 204). In *Forms of Being*, they similarly find the shifting between the centrifugal and the centripetal illustrated in Godard's films (*FoB* 61–63, 65). In all of these examples, centrifugal connectedness occurs after the ascetic labor, the impoverishment, of a centripetal withdrawal. The spectator gains access to the centrifugal pleasures in Caravaggio's art only after having learned to become unresponsive to the commanding appeal of the models' sexiness. Suggesting that the loosening of sexuality's spell constitutes the self's impoverishment, Bersani follows Foucault, who argues that it is primarily sexuality that has territorialized the modern self with significance. Sexuality constitutes a crucial component in "the hermeneutics of the self": the moderns are trained to regard sexuality as constitutive of "their deep identity. Sexuality is . . . a manifestation of what is the most secret in our individuality."[123] It is through the world's enigmatic significance that we orient ourselves; by becoming unresponsive to its sexiness, we can *dis*orient ourselves in the world. It is only after such ascetic practice—whose varied forms Bersani has outlined since his first encounter, in the mid-1960s, with Beckett—that the reinvention of relationality can proceed. The centripetal is the condition of the centrifugal.

In Bersani, as in the classical sources of Foucault's ethics texts, the self's reduction is supplemented by a movement analogous to the ancient exercises of "dilating the self beyond the self."[124] A version of this "cosmic consciousness" always inheres in Bersani's call for the self's impoverishment. That the inextricability of the centripetal and the centrifugal is, to different degrees of emphasis, a constant feature of his thought renders obvious the incompleteness of most queer-theoretical readings of his work. The solipsism of *ébranlement*, which is often mobilized as the psychoanalytic ground for positing "the antisocial thesis," must be doubled in the expansive movement of the centrifugal, of *correspondances*.[125] The double movement is evident in *Homos*, which concludes with a reading of Genet's *Funeral Rites* that emphasizes the extension of relationality's betrayal into a centrifugal escape, a fuguing of what remains of the desiccated self. This is at stake for Bersani in the scene where the young German soldier Erik buggers the French Nazi collaborator Riton on a Paris rooftop. If the two men have turned away from each other, theirs is a narcissistic disconnect and solitude; they do not constitute an intimate "oval," the ideal of coupleness that, contrary to what Bersani indicates elsewhere, should not be confused with the (homo)monad.[126] Theirs is the kind of monadic disconnect that this chapter has observed elsewhere in Bersani's work. Yet this solitude simultaneously constitutes, per Leibnizian delirium, a mode of universal concomitance. In the terms developed in Bersani's other studies, what Erik and Riton find in the world is comparable to the formal correspondences that enable an alternative pleasure to that of narrative violence in Assyrian art; and to the centrifugal expansion of forms and surfaces that competes for the viewer's attention with the fascination of Caravaggio's sexy boys.

The example of Erik and Riton tells us that—as Bersani asserts in a recent interview, in what he says is a paraphrase of Foucault—"all truly revolutionary action must begin with a change in the relations between people. And that takes time."[127] The "time" that the reconfiguration of relationality takes is the time of the centripetal withdrawal, of unlearning the enjoyments we take in each other's personalities, in each other's rich complexity. Without this disengagement, we are stuck in a "dialectical progression" (*H* 175), the kind of call-and-response on which Butler's theory of performativity relies. Bersani suggests that we turn to art for instruction. Genet, for example, models for us a betrayal of the assumptions that organize our "culture's *episteme*: the injunction to find ourselves, and each other, in the sexual" (*H* 165). There will be losses: "Our complex views of intersubjectivity, nourished by an intricate consciousness of desire, have the effect of channeling our imagination of human relations into the narrow domain of the private. To give up that consciousness, which fascinates us, would be a great loss" (*H* 123). What "fascinates" is the enigma of otherness, the call that, issuing from outside, tantalizes us with the truth of our being. Bersani's onto-ethics/aesthetics is a project of learning to turn a deaf ear to this call, to refuse one's vocation of exploring our significant differences.

2

Wanting Being

Freud–Laplanche

In his *Introductory Lectures on Psychoanalysis* (1916–1917 [1915–1917]), Freud famously posits psychoanalysis in the genealogy of discourses that have undermined the human subject's claims to agency, exceptionality, and self-knowledge. From the pantheon of modernity's architects, he singles out Copernicus and Darwin, whose sciences challenged "the *naïve* self-love of men" through a double decentering: the eviction of the earth from the heart of cosmos and the demotion of the human subject from his "supposedly privileged place in creation."[1] As he continues elsewhere, psychoanalysis dealt a third, "*psychological* blow to men's narcissism," after the "*cosmological*" and "*biological*" insults of heliocentric and evolutionary theories.[2]

Like his mentor Jacques Lacan before him, Jean Laplanche accepts Freud's claims for psychoanalysis's revolutionary potential: the Copernican undoing of *geo*centrism's narcissistic illusion is repeated in the Freudian devastation of human *ego*centrism.[3] Freud's work provides an unprecedented decentering of Western thought's categories: his early clinical experiences with hysterics revealed that the other *precedes* the subject—that the subject is solicited into becoming by the world. Yet the psychoanalytic revolution, according to Laplanche, remains an unfinished coup: no sooner had Freud disempowered the human subject's narcissism than he reestablished a center around which the subject could securely revolve. The history of psychoanalysis, that is, offers "a testimony both to the fundamental nature of the Copernican revolution and to the impossibility of sustaining its radicality consistently and to the end."[4] In Freud, we find a "double history of innovation and going-astray," of a Copernican revolution and its Ptolemaic betrayal[5]—a betrayal to which Laplanche frequently alludes as the yielding of Freudian thought to narcissistic monadism.

After *Balzac to Beckett: Center and Circumference in French Fiction* (1970), Leo Bersani's 1970s work is marked primarily by his encounter with psychoanalytic theory, particularly that of Freud and Laplanche. Psychoanalysis enters his orbit in *A Future for Astyanax: Character and Desire in Literature* (1976), whose opening chapters draw from Freud and whose final chapter includes, in an endnote, his first reference to Laplanche. The endnote, briefly glossing Laplanche's account of "the genesis of sexuality" and "shattering" in *Life and Death in Psychoanalysis* (1970), concludes with a promise to engage the French psychoanalytic theorist more thoroughly in a subsequent work (*FA* 332n2). This takes place a year later in *Baudelaire and Freud* (1977), whose sixth and seventh chapters consolidate the importance of psychoanalysis for Bersani's thinking. It is here that psychoanalysis begins to supplement the theory of homomonadology, which had emerged in *Balzac to Beckett* from Proust–Deleuze and Beckett–Blanchot. The following studies, *The Death of Stéphane Mallarmé* (1982) and *The Freudian Body: Psychoanalysis and Art* (1986), establish the framing of psychoanalysis through which Bersani continues to elaborate his onto-ethics/aesthetics.[6]

But the encounter with Laplanche in *A Future for Astyanax* and *Baudelaire and Freud* coincides with an immediate divergence: Bersani at once embraces and rejects Laplanchean theory. His intensive relation to Laplanche[7] pivots, we propose, on the question of the *monad*, that is, the thought of the "essence" whose initial articulation in *Balzac to Beckett* we traced in the previous chapter. The theory of seduction and translation that Laplanche extracts from Freud assumes incompatible premises to the argument about the singular essence that we find in Bersani. Laplanche insists over and again that, as the being that psychoanalysis explicitly engages, the human organism or the infant is *never* a self-enclosed entity—never a monad—but always already in complex ways related to and infiltrated by the world. Writing in 1970, he argues that a text such as "Formulations on the Two Principles of Mental Functioning" (1911) erroneously postulates what he calls "the biological monad" at the beginning of life, a concept that presupposes "the evolution of the human psyche starting from a kind of *hypothetical initial state in which the organism would form a closed unit* in relation to its surroundings."[8] This is a complaint that he never relinquishes. Some twenty years after *Life and Death in Psychoanalysis*, he writes: "The idea of an organism initially closed in upon itself, and only then opening itself to the object (or constructing it, even?)[,] is one of the modalities of *biological idealism or solipsism* that so many theorists of psychoanalysis have imprudently adopted."[9] After its prodigious beginning, psychoanalysis falls back on the conceptualization of "man closed in on himself, a Ptolemaic system"; Freud gives up his own revolution by yielding to "a monadological, auto-centered conception" of the human subject.[10]

With his frequent references to monadism, Laplanche indicates what he considers Western thought's inability to deal with otherness. "Western philosophy," he writes, ". . . has always stumbled over the problem of the other." Idealism is the logical conclusion to the way in which "the otherness of the external world has always appeared doubtful, problematic, having to be deduced solely from the evidence of subjectivity." In Western thought, we find but "the endless re-appearance of a way of posing problems, together with an account of origins, in which access to reality and to the recognition of the other is secondary, derivative in relation to a single, primary testimony—that of the ego."[11] As his references to the history of philosophy imply, in rejecting psychoanalytic monadology Laplanche participates in the rethinking, or deconstruction, of classical metaphysics, which, ever since Plato and Aristotle, has prioritized essence as the self-same, bounded entity that needs to be given before the thought of relation can proceed. In such metaphysics, any being worthy of the name must be defined only in itself, not through its relations: the essence, as the subject of predication, is in no need of any particular attributes. If Bertrand Russell calls classical metaphysics' reliance on predication a symptom of philosophy's "infantile" illness,[12] for Laplanche monadology evinces the kind of "*naïve*" narcissism that Freud deems heliocentric, evolutionary, and psychoanalytic theories to have disrupted.

In his deconstructive reading, Laplanche argues that Freudian thought entails the prioritization of the other, and the concomitant undoing of idealist conceptualization of the ipse. While focusing on Lacanian thought, Diana Fuss's commentary—that "next to deconstruction, psychoanalysis is generally the discourse most strongly identified as sufficiently able to repudiate metaphysical idealism and its reliance upon essentialism"—is equally applicable to Laplanche's work.[13] Rather than regarding the subject as a starting point, Freud's 1890s theory of seduction—of which more below—conceptualizes becoming in terms of a solicitation that issues from the other: the human subject is called into becoming through the primal estrangement that takes place with the enigmatic signifier's failed translation. The name for this estrangement is *sexuality*, a term that psychoanalysis invests with an idiosyncratic meaning. Psychoanalytically speaking, only humans have sexuality, for sexuality refers to the subject's straying off, under the spell of the enigmatic signifier, from the straight path of need to the tortuous road of desire. Like Julia Kristeva, Laplanche suggests that the human subject, whose emergence is strictly coincident with that of sexuality, is a stranger to herself, the uncanny other of *l'inquiétante étrangeté*.

Bersani agrees that Freud's early work revolutionizes the subject's relation to otherness under the sign of sexuality; but he stops short of accepting the argument according to which the monadic thesis amounts to the elimination of this radical notion of otherness, and the return of the ego as the center of the human universe. Here we find the intensive moment, the simultaneous encounter and divergence, between Bersani and Laplanche. Bersani recognizes the brilliance of Laplanche's reading of Freud, the exceptional clarity with which it pinpoints the singular force in the psychoanalytic notion of sexuality. Yet instead of moving along with Laplanche's argument, he wants us to slow down and dwell on the question of the (monadic) ego: "But what, exactly, is the ego?" he asks in *The Freudian Body* (*FrB* 93). Similarly, he persists, what do we mean when we speak of narcissism? The answers we get from the two theorists differ in crucial ways; it is this divergence that informs Laplanche's rejection and Bersani's affirmation of what might be called *monadological psychoanalysis*.

If, for Laplanche, Freud betrays the primacy of the other in his reprioritization of the monadic organism, Bersani, in contradistinction, claims that the idea of human *nonrelatedness*—we might say, the monadism of the homo—is one of the discoveries from whose logical inferences Freud and his followers were quick to recoil. Bersanian onto-ethics/aesthetics, formulated under the sway of Marcel Proust's and Samuel Beckett's Leibnizianism, insists on what Laplanche deems the wrongheaded, even dangerous postulation of monadism. While for Laplanche Freud betrays the revolution by reinstating the entity that he had, perhaps unwittingly, deposed—the entity that the history of philosophy has called, among other appellations, the cogito and the transcendental ego—Bersani suggests that Freud's failure consists of his inability or refusal to *properly name* this very entity. Freud flees not the question of the other but that of the same.

If Laplanche attacks the metaphysical notions of *ousía* and the subject, the comparison between him and Bersani suggests that the latter's ontology aligns with classical metaphysics' prioritization of essence, the "individual." But, his trajectory having been inflected via the literary-philosophical laboratories one finds in *Balzac to Beckett*, Bersani wagers that we do not yet know what we mean when we speak of the "individual." Deleuzean and Beckettian experimentations suggest to him that Laplanche fails to distinguish the discrete concepts that have been erroneously—but perhaps inescapably—posited under the same name, a proposition that parallels Martin Heidegger's argument about the muddling of philosophical categories in their translation from Greek to Latin.[14]

While Laplanche thus considers monadism a vehicle for the imperial ego's return, Bersani sees in the theory of object relations, as it develops in later Freud, an escape from the implications of monadic solitude. He summarizes his views in 1990: "The history of Freud's thought—and, to a large extent, of psychoanalysis itself—is the history of the repression of the psychoanalytic definition of the sexual. . . . Fearful of an intrinsic indifference to others in human sexuality, Freud managed to reinterpret *his theory of primary narcissism* as he formulated it so that narcissistic pleasure itself would appear as a derivative of object relations" (*CR* 45, emphasis added). The *unrelated* here functions as a synonym for *singular*: in his encounter with psychoanalysis, Bersani continues his conceptualization of monadism as a form of singularity. While "unrelatedness" signals for Laplanche the betrayal of Freud's revolution in thinking otherness, Bersani suggests that the monadic moments in psychoanalytic theorizing in fact point the way to the radicalization of our understanding of relatedness. If Laplanche considers the monad an insane phantasm where the tendencies inherent in classical metaphysics are made embarrassingly legible, Bersani takes up monadology, as it is worked out in Proust, Deleuze, Beckett, and Laplanche—among others—as an occasion to speculate about new ways of thinking about the onto-ethics/aesthetics of relatedness.

While the beginnings of this trajectory are already evident in his engagement with Proust–Deleuze and Beckett–Blanchot, Bersani elaborates his view of psychoanalysis as a philosophy of singularity in texts such as *A Future for Astyanax*, *Baudelaire and Freud*, *The Death of Stéphane Mallarmé*, and *The Freudian Body*. The question of *primary narcissism* emerges as the pivot around which turns his disagreement with Laplanche.

Betraying the Revolution

Laplanche pinpoints the counterrevolutionary moment in Freud's abandonment of the seduction theory, announced in his 1897 letter to Wilhelm Fliess.[15] In his clinic, Freud had clocked in a surprising number of patients, particularly adolescent girls, whose neurotic symptoms he had traced to scenes of sexual seduction by their adult relatives. Freud soon begins to doubt the veracity of his patients' claims: as he, palpably disturbed, writes to Fliess, "surely such widespread perversions against children are not very probable."[16] For Erich Fromm and Jeffrey Masson, this refusal to accept the implications of his clinical observations—the stunning frequency of child abuse in Viennese families—amounted to a cover-up that discloses the doctor's bourgeois and patriarchal allegiances, his willingness to dismiss the truth of his patients' experience for the benefit of professional recognition.[17] Laplanche, on the other hand, suggests that the letter to Fliess marks a turning point to a wrong path in psychoanalytic theory, not because Freud here wills himself blind to the physical abuse of his adolescent patients, but because the logic that informs his incredulity rests on *a pre-psychoanalytic understanding of sexuality*. Freud dismisses his patients' claims to having been molested by their parents because, not yet having deprivileged the genital zone's significance, a deprivileging whose most authoritative articulation we will find in *Three Essays on the Theory of Sexuality* (1905), he regards sexual seduction as an operation that necessarily involves the stimulation of the child's genitals. In an often-quoted footnote added in 1915 to the *Three Essays*, Freud recalls his realization of the necessity to "ascribe the quality of erotogenicity to all parts of the body and to all the internal organs."[18] Yet, in the same text, he also conceptualizes childhood seduction as an event that would prematurely usher the child into sexuality by "teach[ing] him, in highly emotional circumstances, how to obtain satisfaction from his genital zones, a satisfaction which he is then usually obliged to repeat again and again by masturbation."[19] This understanding of seduction allows him to conclude that, in such earlier texts as "The Aetiology of Hysteria" (1896) (published a year before Freud wrote his letter to Fliess), he had "overrated the importance of seduction in comparison with the factors of sexual constitution and development."[20] Here Freud himself succumbs to "a confusion between 'sexual' and 'genital'":[21] if every surface, every organ, is a potential erotogenic zone, why would seduction require that the infant's genitals be stimulated? Freud, according to Laplanche, mistakenly opts for a "restricted" theory of seduction—where some children have the misfortune of being abused by perverted or "unscrupulous" caretakers[22]—rather than recognizing seduction as a universal phenomenon. Given the "fundamental postulate" that "the entire body is initially a potential erotogenic zone," Laplanche asks: "[H]ow should we see the gesture of touching the child's big toe? Is this a seduction or not? Under what conditions is it a seduction?"[23]

For Laplanche, we must see seduction as a "*universal and originary situation*" of "being human and becoming human."[24] The seduction in question needs to be considered "real" not in the sense of what Freud calls "material reality" nor what he terms "psychical reality." The seduction in question, that is, does not correspond to what might commonly be understood as a real event in the human child's history, nor is it a question of her having fantasized the scene; the seduction is neither an actual incident nor a false memory. Freud's error was to accept this binary: "Freud . . . remains trapped in a single opposition—that between material and subjective reality: between what are called 'facts' and what are called 'fantasies,' the latter held to be purely subjective imaginings."[25] Rather, Laplanche situates the seduction on the level of "a *third domain of reality*."[26] This reality is established by the peculiar character of what he calls *interhuman communication*: an exchange between beings who are subjects of the unconscious.[27] The communication here is one where the circulating messages are opaque to both participants, the sender and the addressee. This exchange, riddled with impasses, constitutes the Laplanchean variant of anthropogenesis, becoming-human.[28] The infant is called, or seduced, into being by the enigmatic messages (vocalizations, gestures, caresses) originating in the other (the adult caretaker). This call impels a work of translation that would "metabolize" the message. Yet the translation can never be completed since the sender of the messages, also a subject of the unconscious, is not in possession of their meaning: the seductive signifier is unreadable both to the transmitter and the recipient. The unconscious is the result in the addressee of the repression of the inassimilable remainder of the enigmatic messages, the "waste-matter" that is left over from the process of their translation.[29] This, in turn, is what drives becoming-human: hominization names the emergence of sexuality through the untranslatable and consequently repressed enigmatic signifiers.[30] The implantation of the unconscious marks the moment of going-astray (*fourvoiement*) of the instinct, its perversion onto the trajectory of the drive.

For Laplanche, Freud's original postulate of seduction, taken as a "general theory," enables a radical decentering of the subject in that, rather than beginning with the ego, it posits hominization as a process prioritizing the enigma of the other, yet an other who is enigmatic to herself. To highlight this, Laplanche makes a distinction between an *enigma* and a *riddle*, both of which are translations of *das Rätsel* in Freud. He observes that Freud uses *Rätsel*—which James Strachey renders alternately as "puzzle" or "riddle"[31]—to refer to the force with which sexuality enthralls the child. As Freud's subheading in the *Three Essays* puts it, sexuality presents the child with "The Riddle of the Sphinx [*Das Rätsel der Sphinx*]";[32] elsewhere Freud speaks of "the facts and riddles [*Rätsel*] of sexual life."[33] But "riddle" may not adequately indicate the otherness Freud encounters: "An enigma, like a riddle, is proposed to the subject by another subject," Laplanche writes. "But the solution of a riddle in theory is completely in the conscious possession of the one who poses it, and thus it is entirely resolved by the answer. An enigma, on the contrary, can only be proposed by someone who does not master the answer, because his message is a compromise-formation in which his unconscious takes part."[34] Whereas a "riddle" denotes mysteries that can be unraveled—whose keys, albeit perhaps difficult to locate, lie somewhere—an "enigma" remains opaque, *undurchschaubar*: transmitted in primary seduction, it confounds not only the message's recipient but also its sender. An enigma can be issued only by a subject of the unconscious; unlike the riddle's, its answer is possessed by no one. Thus Laplanche speaks of "the enigma of the Sphinx: you cannot think that she already knew the answer to her enigma, because the enigma was such a problem for her that when it was solved by Oedipus she killed herself as it was something unbearable to her, revealing to her something of her unconscious."[35]

According to Laplanche, one of the consequences of seduction theory's abortion is Freud's articulation, after 1920, of the second topography: the triad of the id, the superego, and the ego. This shift amounts to "the abandonment of a theory of human sexuality as exogenous, intersubjective, and intrusive" and the reconceptualization of sexuality as endogenous, phylogenetic, and *centered*.[36] In the form of the id, the unconscious becomes the inherited locus of the human being, not the alien presence, the enigmatic, traumatically implanted *das Andere*. In the letter to Fliess, Freud recognizes that his rejection of the seduction theory leads to "the factor of a hereditary disposition regain[ing] a sphere of influence from which [he] had made it [his] task to dislodge it"—"the id," he writes in

The Ego and the Id (1923), ". . . is capable of being inherited."[37] According to Laplanche, in such texts as "Formulations on the Two Principles of Mental Functioning" and *The Ego and the Id*, "Freud lapses back . . . into a conception of the human individual constructed around a primal kernel, which would be the unconscious—a necessarily innate, biological, instinctual kernel. The unconscious would thus be at the center of the individual. . . . Far from being an alien inside me, the unconscious would be my foundation, my starting-point."[38] As a "*biologising*," "*endogenous*," and "*genetic*" concept,[39] the "phylogenetic hypothesis" is one of Freud's "'naïveties.'"[40] Laplanche and Pontalis use the term in quotation marks, signaling that the phylogenetic remapping of the unconscious in the form of the id is a moment where Freud succumbs to what he himself calls "the *naïve* self-love of man."[41]

Laplanche sees this narcissistic closure, this domestication of otherness, not only in the move to the second topography but also, and concomitantly, in Freud's shift to the argument according to which "primary narcissism" constitutes the subject's originary stage of existence. In the entry "Primary Narcissism, Secondary Narcissism" in *The Language of Psychoanalysis* (1967), Laplanche and Pontalis write that in the texts of 1910–1915, Freud considers primary narcissism emerging in conjunction with the ego, that is, between the stages of autoerotism and object-love; despite its name, it is not the organism's primal stage but follows the earlier phase of autoerotism.[42] As they argue in the entry devoted to the subject, autoerotism itself should not be understood as the human animal's originary condition: "although it is possible to describe auto-erotism as objectless, this is by no means because this state occurs prior to any relationship with an object, nor yet because with its advent all objects cease to be present in the search for satisfaction. The sexual instinct now detaches itself from the non-sexual functions (e.g., nutrition) upon which it has theretofore depended anaclitically and which have laid down its aim and object."[43] Autoerotism does not describe the organism's original nonrelatedness to the surrounding world. Rather, human sexuality is autoerotic because it is marked by its divergence, its going-astray, from a chronologically earlier condition, that of instinctual life, the vital order. In this earlier (and earliest) stage, the organism is, as Laplanche writes three years later, "directly plugged into external reality."[44] Thus, while the organism becomes-human at the moment of its perversion—the moment "when sexuality draws away from its natural object, finds itself delivered over to phantasy and this very process is constituted *qua* sexuality"[45]—at no stage does it constitute a "biological monad."[46] As Laplanche and Pontalis propose elsewhere, it is "easy to demonstrate, with much clinical detail, the variety and complexity of the links which, from the beginning, relate the infant to the outer world and, particularly to its mother."[47] It is only with its seduction by the enigmatic messages that the human child turns in upon itself, plunging into a world of fantasies—but even then, its inward gaze meets only the enigma of otherness.

Around 1915, however, Freud begins to readjusts this schema—which for Laplanche contains the seeds of the revolution—to allow the possibility of an originary monadism: he begins to deploy "the term 'primary narcissism' to mean rather a first state of life, prior even to the formation of the ego, which is *epitomised by life in the womb*."[48] By the time of *Group Psychology and the Analysis of the Ego* (1921), "Freud has come to maintain an absolute opposition between a first (objectless) narcissistic state and object-relations," that is, between "primary narcissism" and "secondary narcissism" ("the formation of the ego through identification with other person").[49] "*Primary narcissism*," Laplanche later pronounces, "is one of Freud's most deceptive notions" because it allows monadism's possibility, which Freud's early work had rejected. The monad—Laplanche repeatedly deploys this term—"would not be defined by a cathexis of the ego, since it would be even prior to the differentiation of an ego, but by a kind of stagnation in place of libidinal energy in a biological unit conceived of as not having any objects."[50] This shift signals the Freudian subject's rescue from the decentered world, his reconsolidation in the familiar ground of the Ptolemaic universe: the narcissistic self turns out to be the self-same body around which everything else supposedly orbits.[51]

The references to monadism carry considerable conceptual weight in Laplanche's texts. The monadic tendencies in psychoanalysis designate the moments where Freud strays off the singular path that the original theory of seduction had opened. With this wrong turn, psychoanalysis begins to approximate more traditional philosophical ways of conceptualizing the rational, self-possessed human subject. Laplanche, whose specialization in psychoanalytic theory was preceded by his studies in philosophy,[52] implies that the post-1915 reconceptualizations of primary narcissism as an originary state and the unconscious as the id align psychoanalysis with *idealist* trends in the history of philosophy—with the argument, as Proust describes it, "that the outer world does not exist, and that it is in ourselves that we develop our life."[53] The prototype for the primary-narcissistic state of being is best figured, as Laplanche and Pontalis note in *The Language of*

Psychoanalysis, by "life in the womb," or, as they continue in another entry, by sleep: "The primitive state, now [with the second topography] called primary narcissism, is supposed to be characterised by the total absence of any relationship to the outside world . . . ; intra-uterine existence is taken to be its prototypical form, while sleep is deemed a more or less successful imitation of that ideal model."[54] In *Life and Death in Psychoanalysis* and *New Foundations for Psychoanalysis* (1987), Laplanche similarly sees the moment of the psychoanalytic revolution's overturning in Freud's offering us "the image of a primal state, closed in upon itself, the prototype of the state of sleep and of dreaming"; idealist psychoanalysis figures the beginning of life as "a purely narcissistic state, with sleep as its prototype."[55]

Leibnizian philosophy readily yields for Laplanche a language with which to describe such idealism. Beginning with Russell's turn-of-the-century critique, twentieth-century thinkers have frequently considered Leibniz's system the apotheosis of Western philosophy's idealism. Monadism postulates, as Christia Mercer writes, that "for each perceiving mind, the world exists as an elaborately constructed appearance whose source is the perceiving mind itself."[56] In contemporary thought, it is not only for Laplanche that Leibniz figures as one of idealism's most important, or radical, proponents. Arthur Lovejoy regards "the metaphysics of Leibniz [as] a form of idealism";[57] and Russell's assessment of monadology as "fantastic" similarly amounts to an objection to its idealism as the philosophical trend with which Russell broke at the turn of the century, the time of his writing the *Critical Exposition*. For Russell, the tortuous—and self-serving—formulations of Leibniz's philosophy led him to "a kind of Berkeleian theory."[58] Leibniz himself recognized monadology's proximity to idealist philosophies: in his annotated copy of George Berkeley's *Principles of Human Knowledge* (1710), he notes "the similarity between his own doctrine of mind—which held that individual substances encompassed within themselves causal powers—and Berkeley's commitment to minds as substances."[59]

The charge of philosophical idealism carries familiar political implications. Laplanche suggests that the narcissistic monad becomes a Freudian version of the Robinsonade: "This is the last word in Crusoesque enterprises," he writes, "by which I mean the attempt to reconstruct the world of culture on the basis of the endogenous resources of the solitary baby Robinson."[60] He echoes numerous other commentators in considering the monad the apotheosis of entrepreneurial individualism, "the bourgeois ego, or monad," in all the sociohistorical implications that this term carries.[61] With the implicit allusion to Marx's reference to Daniel Defoe in *Grundrisse*,[62]

Laplanche's critique is aimed at what Theodor Adorno calls "the bourgeois philosophy of idealism."[63] Laplanche follows Louis Althusser in adding Marx to Freud's list of modernity's revolutionaries;[64] this suggests that his own work of resuscitating radical psychoanalysis may be considered analogous to the Marxist revision of Hegelian dialectics. Both Laplanche and Marx argue that their predecessors' revolutionary and indispensable thought founders on idealism. As much as Laplanche critiques the way in which post-1915 psychoanalysis begins to resemble "the most delusional systems of the great idealists, Berkeley, Fichte, or even Hegel,"[65] the Marxist project entails the de-idealization of Hegelian dialectics. As Friedrich Engels writes, Hegel's "conception of history was essentially idealistic"; Marx's dialectical materialism revolutionized the idea of the individual by embodying spirit's becoming in the proletariat's negotiations with the material conditions of capitalist economy.[66] Laplanche's primary narcissist—"the 'primitive monad'"[67]—is the psychoanalytic manifestation of the "individual and isolated" subject of David Ricardo's and Adam Smith's economic theories, frequently embodied in Defoe's shipwreck-turned-entrepreneur.

At best, Freud breaks the spell of idealism: Laplanche writes that Freud's early thought is marked by the "*fundamental realism*" of the 1895 "Project" and the "realist attitude" of dream theory.[68] The realist Freud not only asserts the priority of the world to perception but also posits the traumatizing infiltration of this world—in the form of enigmatic otherness—as the condition of the human subject's coming-into-being. In doing so, he undoes philosophy's ipsocentrism. With the second topography—especially the introduction of the phylogenetic id—and the reconfiguration of primary narcissism, the psychoanalytic revolution is nevertheless thwarted: what becomes "a monadological project and an instance of biological idealism" constitutes a betrayal of Freud's momentous move from the ego to the other, from essence to relation, from the dream of a self-sustaining being to the other's traumatizing priority.[69] With the abandonment of the seduction theory, the emergence of the second topography, and the reassessment of primary narcissism, Freud gets caught up in "the contortions typical of all idealism . . . in their attempts to recover what they have lost."[70] While Laplanche is increasingly sympathetic with Freud's all-too-human inability to think otherness,[71] he consistently considers the turn from realism to idealism an ethical failure.

Bersani, too, speaks of "Freudian realism" (*FrB* 119n4) and the "realist Freud,"[72] but his assessment of such tendencies in psychoanalysis differs, one might say diametrically, from Laplanche's. According to him, Freud's realism signals the territorialization of the most radical aspects of psychoanalysis. For both Laplanche and Bersani, monadological psychoanalysis allows "a dream of wholly unrelated being";[73] but while for Laplanche this indicates the kind of oneiric idealism from whose delusions the early Freud stirs us after Enlightenment philosophy's failure to do so, Bersani insists on tarrying with this dream as the possibility of a radical psychoanalytic ontology. At the center of this disagreement is the status of primary narcissism. Speaking in 1967, Laplanche and Pontalis caution that the post-1915 model of primary narcissism "incur[s] two risks. First, there is a danger of running counter to experience by asserting that the newborn baby is without any perceptual outlet on to the external world"—i.e., we conceptualize the infant as a windowless monad. "Secondly, we may find ourselves re-opening the door—and in the naïvest way—to a version of the idealist fallacy [*l'aporie idéaliste*] made all the more flagrant by being expressed in 'biological' language: just how are we supposed to picture the transition from a monad shut in upon itself to a progressive discovery of the object?"[74] As the original French formulation indicates, the idealist monad constitutes the *aporetic point*, *l'aporie idéaliste*, in psychoanalytic theory. The "naïvest" mistake of entertaining monadism indicates the resuscitation of what Freud, in the *Introductory Lectures*, calls "the *naïve* self-love of men."[75] Yielding to the Möbius-logic of its own etymology, the revolution morphs from a *coup d'état* to the circular return of the previous regime.

For Bersani, this very "aporia" signals that something remains unthought in what Laplanche rejects as psychoanalytic theory's idealist monadism. His previous engagement with Proust–Deleuze and Blanchot–Beckett pushes him into the conceptual abyss of monadological psychoanalysis. Given the thought of *aporetic essence* that emerges in the final chapters of *Balzac to Beckett*, he demands that we be more specific about the terms of our diagnoses. What exactly do we address when we speak of primary narcissism? What precisely is the monadic self under whose spell psychoanalysis falls circa 1915? What virtual potentialities might be obfuscated in the recognition of the narcissistic monad as a reincarnation of *ousía*, the self-identical essence that has grounded Western thought? Might we have misconceptualized primary narcissism in an analogous way to the one in which Western metaphysics, according to Heidegger, has labored under the mistranslation of the Greek *hypokeimenon*?

Primary Narcissism, Revisited

Bersani's encounter with and departure from Laplanche happens in the twinkling of an eye. The initial contact, in the last chapter of *A Future for Astyanax,* is followed by the more explicit and sustained engagement in *Baudelaire and Freud.* Yet in the latter study Bersani also carefully registers a point of divergence from Laplanchean psychoanalysis—a complication that one detects, in hindsight, also informing the revisions that *A Future for Astyanax* proposes to the psychoanalytic understanding of desire. For both theorists, the late 1910s and the early 1920s—particularly the articulation of the death drive in *Beyond the Pleasure Principle* and the second topography in *The Ego and the Id*—mark an important turning point in Freudian theory. The second topography (whose ruinous effects Laplanche emphasizes) and the death drive (whose ramifications occupy Bersani's attention) entail shifts in Freud from which they draw radically divergent inferences. Whereas Laplanche considers the modifications of the early 1920s the final nail in the coffin of *étrangèreté*, for Bersani they move us toward a useful, indeed imperative rethinking of essence and otherness. Both agree, however, that the adjustments allow the articulation of monadological psychoanalysis: while Laplanche sees in the "*monadological* character"[76] of post-1915 psychoanalysis the ruination of any ethically viable conceptualization of otherness, Bersani proceeds to formulate an ethics based on *the singularity of the nonrelated monad.* Here one detects the pull that Bersani's homomonadism—his earlier work on Proust–Deleuze and Beckett–Blanchot—exerts on his reading of Freud and Laplanche.

In its final chapter, "Persons in Pieces," *A Future for Astyanax* closes with an account of narcissistic fantasies that largely agrees with (and anticipates) Laplanche's critique of the Ptolemaic move in psychoanalysis, which, recentering the world around the narcissistic monad, allows the elimination of this world's principle of *dis*organization in enigmatic otherness. Desire proceeds along a narrative whose aim is to obtain, and negate, the other(ness) that, as absence, drives the desiring subject. In the terms that Laplanche develops in his later work, the alien-ness of the other is reinscribed as a story whose denouement is reached with the eradication of otherness in its complete translation—inscription without a residue to be repressed—into meaning. But as the center of the universe, the subject turns into a black hole that swallows up everything, including itself, into a realm of undifferentiation. Desire seeks "the annihilation of the world" (*FA* 286); and the subject ends up consuming itself: "death is the happy condition for a total possession" (*FA* 287). Bersani frequently repeats this observation in his later work. In 2004, he writes with Ulysse Dutoit: "To satisfy the drives we must die to the world; the 'death instinct' pursues a fantasy-ecstasy given by fantasy-objects, and in so doing it removes us from life itself. The death drive can be satisfied only by the violence that annihilates it" (*FoB* 115).

This very brief discussion should signal Bersani's implicit observance, in his critique, of a *particular understanding* of desire. This orientation is announced in "Murderous Lovers," the introductory chapter to *A Future for Astyanax*, which explicitly establishes the paradigm that informs the analyses that follow. "Desire is an activity within a lack," Bersani writes in the introduction; "it is an appetite stimulated by an absence" (*FA* 10). Already here, he is quick to indicate the ethical problem, explored in subsequent chapters, in this formulation of desire: "the logic of our desiring fantasies leads ultimately to *the annihilation of all otherness*. In order for plenitude to replace absence, the world we desire must replace the world we perceive. Desire is intrinsically violent both because it spontaneously assumes *this annihilation of everything alien to it*, and because its fantasies include a rageful recognition of the world's capacity to resist and survive our desires" (*FA* 13, emphases added). The repeated term *annihilation* should guide us to the relevant chapters in our histories of philosophy: it suggests we follow this genealogy of desire, via its critique in Gilles Deleuze and Félix Guattari's *Anti-Oedipus* (1972),[77] to Hegelian thought, where the movement of becoming (*Werden*) consists in the annihilation of difference along the dialectical process of negation. As Daniel Smith and Elizabeth Grosz note, the conceptualization of desire as moved by loss stretches from Plato to Hegel to Marx and, importantly, to Freud,[78] where its violent paradox—felt as the persistent pressure of lacking—is lived in the vicissitudes of *love and hate* that psychoanalysis calls *ambivalence* or, after Lacan, *aggressiveness* (*l'agressivité*).[79] Desire in its Platonic-Hegelian mode is figured "as both a lack and a potential devastation of the world" (*FA* 291); "the relation between the totalitarian project of omnipotence and the radical experience, in desire, of a lack" remains inescapable (*FA* 288).

This problematization of desire's paradigms, whose incipient formulation one finds in *Balzac to Beckett*, informs Bersani's simultaneous embrace of and divergence from Laplanchean psychoanalysis, and particularly the assessment of primary narcissism. In "Desire and Death," chapter 7 of *Baudelaire and Freud*, Bersani notes the insightfulness of Laplanche's commentary on Freud's postulations in "Instincts and Their

Vicissitudes" (1915) and "The Economic Problem of Masochism" (1924). He writes that this reading, which Laplanche provides in *Life and Death in Psychoanalysis*, "leads to some startling conclusions concerning the relation between masochism and the genesis of human sexuality" (*BF* 76n). The originality of Laplanche's argument consists of his demonstrating that sexuality, as reconceptualized by Freud, must be understood as constitutively masochistic. Laplanche is led to this conclusion in his reading of the oddly muddled chronology of ego-constitution in Freud's texts. In "Instincts and Their Vicissitudes," Freud postulates that the human being is initially oriented toward the world through attempted mastery, carried out in the form of "nonsexual sadism," which he considers the infant's way of controlling external stimuli. The attempt at an active control of the world gives way to a stage of suffering: the self becomes the object of mastery, while the aim (*Ziel*) of the drive turns passive. This is followed by a third stage, which, as Freud writes, is "commonly termed masochism": another being enters the drive's trajectory, but this time as an active participant—the master rather than, as was the case in the first stage, the object of mastery—while the self remains the recipient of punishing attentions. The third stage thus returns us to the first one but with the roles reversed: "[T]he passive ego [has placed] itself back in phantasy in its first role, which has now in fact been taken over by the extraneous subject."[80] Laplanche argues that, in sketching this chronology, Freud characteristically misses the implications of his own paradigm-shifting insights: as with the abandonment of the theory of seduction, Freud is led down a wrong path because he cannot, or refuses to, heed the psychoanalytic understanding of sexuality's specificity in the human domain. He neglects the fact that "nonsexual sadism" is properly *outside the domain of psychoanalytic thought*, for it precedes the moment of sexuality's emergence; sexuality comes into being, and the work of psychoanalysis begins, only at a subsequent stage, the moment when need veers off, in the prematurely born organism, onto the labile paths of desire. He writes that what Freud calls the "sadistic child" should in fact be called the "aggressive child," for the term "sadism" indicates sexualization—that is, *hominization*—which has not yet happened.[81] Beginning with Freud and epitomized by Kleinians, psychoanalytic theorists are guilty of "an unjustified conflation of sadism and aggressiveness."[82] Consequently, what is indicated in "Instincts and Their Vicissitudes" as the "masochistic" stage becomes *the scene of the subject's emergence*: the moment of the organism's becoming-human. With these corrections to Freud's vocabulary, Laplanche notes, we are compelled to observe "the priority of the masochistic moment in the genesis of the sadomasochistic drive insofar as the latter is a sexual drive."[83] He concludes: "sexuality emerges only with the turning round [*sic*] upon the self, thus with masochism, so that, within *the field of sexuality*, masochism is already considered as primary"; and the field of sexuality, as Laplanche insists, is the field of the human in psychoanalytic theory.[84]

Bersani follows Laplanche in formulating the subject's emergence in terms of a masochistic jouissance for which the distinction between pain and pleasure is irrelevant—a jouissance synonymous with sexuality, which, as he repeats in numerous texts, may function as a survival mechanism for the prematurely differentiated human organism.[85] He closely echoes Laplanche in noting that, in "Instincts and Their Vicissitudes," Freud seems to hypothesize "two quite different kinds of sadism existing simultaneously once the infliction of pain has become an instinctual aim: an 'original,' nonsexual sadism which seeks to master the world, and a derived, sexual sadism which is actually a pleasurable fantasy-identification with the intense (sexualized) pain of the victim" (*BF* 79). Bersani agrees that, when we follow the Freudian logic, we in fact find that hominization occurs only at masochism. This argument emerges already in the final chapter of *A Future for Astyanax*, where Bersani, again alluding to Laplanche's reading of Freud, proposes that properly sadistic pleasures—that is, those of sexual sadism—rest on prior, masochistic jouissance. Sadistic pleasures are but the remembered excitements of masochistic intensities: "pain is a perturbation [*ébranlement*] like any other perturbation"[86]—such as the sundry sources of sexual pleasure (train travel, intellectual work, a good theater piece) Freud discusses in the *Three Essays*.[87] Here we find what Bersani later calls "the masochistic ontology of the sexual": "sexuality is indissociable from masochism" (*FrB* 60, 61).

For Laplanche and Bersani, masochism needs to be considered the primal moment in anthropogenesis, the emergence of the sexual. Bersani will make more of this observation than Laplanche. While the latter's focus, after *Life and Death in Psychoanalysis*, turns to the theory of the enigmatic signifier, Bersani develops the question of hominizing masochism into the cornerstone of his theory of *ébranlement*. For him, becoming-human is initiated by the traumatizing intrusion of the outside—of the other—where the self is constituted in its *ébranlement*, a term that, as Bersani and Dutoit later note, also appears in the Marquis de Sade's writings.[88] If here, at the intersection of Laplanche and Sade, emerges the concept of "shattering," let us also note the hesitation that stalls Bersani's argumentation at this juncture in *Baudelaire and Freud*. Having followed Laplanche so far, Bersani pauses for a footnote and a paragraph break. In the note, he instructs us that he is about to part "in important ways" from Laplanche's company. The divergence, he specifies, concerns "the relation between 'nonsexual sadism' . . . and primary masochism" (*BF* 79n). The quotation marks around "nonsexual sadism" suggest not only the source of the phrase in Freud but also a resistance to the concept on Bersani's part; the phrase "primary masochism" is not similarly disidentified with. In quoting the phrase, Bersani alludes to Laplanche's argument that for psychoanalysis there can be no such thing as a "nonsexual" anything: the psychoanalytic field *is* the field of sexuality. For both Laplanche and Bersani, *in the realm of psychoanalytic thought* nonsexual sadism is a nonsensical concept. To claim anything else is to violate the integrity of psychoanalysis by forcing its postulations into the nonpsychoanalytic realm.[89]

But Bersani goes further than Laplanche, and in this departs from the latter's company. He radicalizes the argument that, strictly speaking, nonsexual sadism is beyond psychoanalytic ontology. When we aim at hominization's origins, he suggests, primary masochism is the farthest we get, with or without psychoanalysis's help. Despite arguing that "nonsexual sadism" is beyond the psychoanalytic field, Laplanche, on the other hand, gives a certain *reality* to this concept: it designates the initial stage of the being that will become-human, even if psychoanalysis has nothing to say about this being. Importantly for us, this suggestion is analogous to Laplanche's argument that before becoming-human—before sexualization—the infant is "plugged into" the vital order, the realm of needs. Like "primary narcissism," "primary masochism" names a secondary order of affect for Laplanche. As he writes, we may be able to postulate the infant's nonsexual being only in terms of an "abstraction."[90] In both cases, Bersani pushes the *deconstructive tendencies* evident in Laplanche's thinking to their aporetic conclusions: nothing like the vital order is available to the infant at the beginning; the incipiently human being is always already undone, shattered, disconnected—that is, monadic.

Bersani, then, insists on thinking not only primary masochism but also, in a parallel way, primary narcissism as the aporetic essence, *l'aporie idéaliste*, of the shattered subject. This constitutes his departure, in *Baudelaire and Freud*, from Laplanchean theory. Both Laplanche and Bersani designate the primal narcissist as a monadic being; but while for Laplanche this concept marks the yielding of Freudian theory to self-same essence, whose most radicalized articulations he finds in idealist philosophy, Bersani, having engaged, in *Balzac to Beckett*, several thinkers' work on Leibnizian philosophy, sees in the monad a possibility to think desire otherwise. He suggests that it is only with the primary narcissist as a self-enclosed monad that we depart from the hegemonic—that is, *dialectical*—conceptualizations of desire and otherness. In his subsequent studies, he tests the ethical ramifications—and limits—of Laplanchean psychoanalysis.

Toward Monadological Psychoanalysis

The stakes in Bersani's break from Laplanchean otherness become clear in *The Death of Stéphane Mallarmé*, a work squeezed between the explicitly psychoanalytic studies *Baudelaire and Freud* and *The Freudian Body*. While psychoanalysis is hardly mentioned in this opuscule—Laplanche's name is absent, and Freud and Lacan get one reference each (*DSM* 84, 27)—the book's argument about the ethics of literary criticism evinces the influence of the theoretical texts Bersani had encountered in his previous works. With his study of Mallarmé and *mallarmistes*, Bersani continues to think about (the limits of) the ethics of otherness that we find in Laplanchean psychoanalysis.

Bersani prefaces the study by contrasting his readerly method to that of traditional literary scholarship, the form of "critical interpretation" that, according to him, "penetrates and illuminates texts which it thereby rescues from their own *enigmatic density*" (*DSM* vii, emphasis added). This school of thought deems the literary text in need of an *interpreter*, a trained mediator who, adequately transposing literary discourse into comprehensible language, relieves the text of its solipsism, its inability to communicate its messages. Interpretation tackles the text's "enigma" as a pathology: it approaches its object "as if [the literary text] were sick, as if it were *deficient in narrativity*" (*DSM* vii); like a body unable to complete its natural range of movements in space and time, the text needs to be delivered from its incommunicative silence, compensated for its stunted abilities. But its solipsism is also a form of intransigence: the text needs to be not only prosthetically supplemented but, like a difficult customer or willful child, "straightened out" (*DSM* vii). Orthopedic criticism undoes the text's "enigmatic density" by "substitut[ing] syntactic and narrative coherence for the syntactic and narrative 'puzzles' of a poem or essay" (*DSM* vii).

One detects echoes of Laplanchean idiom in this brief description. Taking the form of an "enigma" and a "puzzle," the literary text exerts a fascination like that which Laplanche assigns to "the enigmatic signifier": the text calls out to the reader, much like the caretaker who unwittingly seduces the child by compelling her with the promise of secret knowledge. Bersani suggests that art's appeal rests on its ability to echo the calls constitutive of the human subject, calls that "are seductive because they are opaque, because they convey something enigmatic."[91] The mode of criticism he targets in *The Death of Stéphane Mallarmé* is a response to literature's alluring interpretability, an effort to trace the secret genealogies of meaning dissimulated by the text's aesthetic surfaces. The critic's vocation recapitulates the infant's seduction by otherness; Mallarmé's "seductive unreadability" (*DSM* ix) lures us like enigmatic signifiers.[92] The interpretive desire is moved by a "nostalgia" for transparent meaning: seeking to domesticate the otherness of art,[93] literary criticism repeats desire's frenzied efforts to repair the desiring self's lack by undoing and assimilating the other's riddles. Criticism, like desire, ultimately seeks its own obsolescence, the kind of stasis that, according to Freud, is the aim of *Todestrieb*. Bersani frequently calls this momentum, which wants to "rescue" its objects from the disability of their otherness, "redemptive": a "pastoral" mode of seeking lost being that is inseparable from a "suicidal violence," from an effort to disarticulate beings' individuated forms in a climactic denouement.[94] For Bersani, this form of narrativity organizes our culture's representations, the stories with which we render ourselves and the world meaningful.

Even when critics provide "straightened" accounts of literature's tortuous designs, interpretation is concluded only to be found, like desire itself, lacking. The riddles of literature, and art in general, have the capacity to reinitiate the audience's attention, and a new round of reading unfolds further the text's "enigmatic density," with the renewed hope of untangling its knots and reaching the stasis of complete transparency. Criticism thus functions as an analogue to the dialectic of desire that psychoanalysis arguably inherits from Western philosophies. This dialectic gives us a movement that aims to appease the subject's hunger for lost being. The other captures the subject—for example, the critic—with the promise of total legibility, a moment that would both vindicate and render obsolete his paranoid vigilance. If Hegel's is the most influential version of this paradigm, from his 1970s texts onward Bersani works toward alternatives to its commanding formulations. When he writes, in *The Death of Stéphane Mallarmé*, that reparative criticism aims at "an annihilating elucidation" of the literary text (*DSM* vii), we are returned to his initial encounter with psychoanalytic theory in *A Future for Astyanax*, where the term "annihilation" names the operations of desire-as-lack. Bersani most frequently identifies this mode of desire with the Proustian narrator. Marcel's becoming, his *recherche*, unfolds as the interdependent articulations of desire and lack. His is a consciousness seduced by the secret meanings it intuits behind sundry phenomena. Albertine appears to him as an "enigma," brimming with "that unknown life which permeates her and which we aspire to possess in her."[95] Like the literary critics Bersani speaks of, Marcel seeks to "'solve' the mystery of otherness" (*CS* 68), to unriddle the other. This appropriative dynamic is evident in the narrator's aesthetic theory: Marcel declares that "we do not possess a picture because it hangs in our dining-room if we are incapable of understanding it [*le comprendre*]."[96] Bersani calls this form of aesthetics "critical imperialism" (*DSM* vii).[97] He discerns annihilating desire in literary scholarship that aims to coerce the text into yielding its secrets. This criticism is also the scholarly counterpart to the "adaptive" therapy that, by revealing the individual traumas codified in the analysand's unconscious, hopes to eliminate their crippling effects. Here we find what John Forrester calls psychoanalysis's "breathtakingly imperialistic requirement to reveal all."[98]

For Laplanche, it is this ethical failure in conceptualizing desire as a force of incorporating and annihilating the other that, when we undo Freud's self-betrayal, psychoanalysis potentially addresses. He resolves the ethical problem of the incorporative-annihilating tension between the ego and the other with the theory of the untranslatable enigma, the perennially opaque other of *der Andere*, who materialize the primary other of one's own unknowability (*das Andere* of the unconscious). Implicitly, Bersani tests this very hypothesis in the study of Mallarmé: in psychoanalysis, and particularly its Laplanchean variant, we may find a mode of desiring attention that does not seek in its objects the lost key to the subject's self, the riddle that promises the self's completion in providing the missing code. In an idiom that he borrows from Laplanche, he postulates that the theory of the enigmatic signifier may enable a shift from the "textual imperialism" that has dogged literary criticism to another mode of reading. Assuming something like Laplanche's Law of "theoretico-genesis," he suggests that the two forms of criticism are responses to—recapitulations of—"two types of difficulty in modern writing" (*DSM* 60). Literary criticism recapitulates the movement of its object, as much as, according to Laplanche, psychoanalytic theory cannot but repeat the "logic" of the human subject.[99]

The first of these two modes entails the complexity of texts like *Ulysses* (1922) and *Finnegans Wake* (1939), which compel the reader to unravel their intricate webs of allusions, a labor that promises to reward her with the coherent sense plotted by a literary genius. Joyce is Bersani's primary example of solvable riddles, the critical focus on which "result[s] in the interpretive centering of highly valued texts, a centering which reinforces traditional cultural hierarchies and privileges" (*DSM* 60). As Bersani continues in *The Culture of Redemption*, *Ulysses* demands to be read "with an excruciatingly close attention and a nearly superhuman memory. It asks that we be nothing but the exegetical machine necessary to complete its sense." This form of difficulty aims at "the final elucidation of [the text's] sense, the day when all the connections will have been discovered" (*CR* 175). The "will have been" couches reading in the future perfect (or, to use the French-inflected translation prevalent in poststructuralist theory, the future anterior) tense: it orients the story's disjointed materials into a narrative whose denouement, as in a good murder mystery, reveals the function of the seemingly random clues—including the red herrings—that have puzzled the reader. It promises the world's future totalization.

If *Ulysses* lures us with riddles, a different form of opacity is exemplified by the Mallarméan text. Unlike Joyce's, Mallarmé's obscurity does not impel the reader to laboriously excavate the text's genealogies of meaning; rather, his work unfolds with, and his reader needs, "an extreme mobility of attention" (*DSM* 60)—not the "nearly superhuman memory" required to put together the Joycean puzzle, but *a susceptibility to being distracted*. For Bersani, the author himself exemplifies this mode. Moving forgetfully from poetry to fashion pieces to the Easter egg inscriptions he presented his friends, Mallarmé's oeuvre consists of an "extraordinary diversity of literary projects": "No single compositional activity seems to have occupied or *held* Mallarmé as *Ulysses* and *Finnegans Wake* held and centered Joyce" (*DSM* 46). The Mallarméan text is too flighty, too easily sidetracked, to yield to the imperialist "occupation" that holds sway over the author (and, consequently, the reader) of *Ulysses*. Joycean difficulty is the difficulty of the unconscious whose relentlessly guarded, censored, and dissimulated contents can, with enough therapeutic attention, be discovered. Mallarmé's texts, on the other hand, are contentless: "far from hiding any secret meanings," Bersani writes in an implicitly Laplanchean mode, "his difficulty is peculiarly empty" (*DSM* ix). In this mode, the literary text resembles the Laplanchean unconscious, made up of the untranslatable leftovers of enigmatic messages.

Published five years after *Baudelaire and Freud*, Bersani's first full-fledged encounter with psychoanalysis, the Mallarmé study thus tests Laplanche's (and more generally, psychoanalysis's) usefulness in disentangling ourselves from the "critical imperialism" that mistakes art's "enigmas" for "riddles" that call out to be solved. Does the enigmatic, and enigmatically empty, signifier enable one to relinquish his exclusive attention on the other's secrets and address the otherness within oneself? For Laplanche, what appears as the other's enthralling and threatening alterity is but a repetition of the subject's own unfamiliarity, his uncanny strangeness to himself. In thus rethinking otherness, Laplanche's work may disallow the use of psychoanalysis as an instrument of power-knowledge that would share its modes of operation not only with what Foucault calls "confessional" psychology but also with what Édouard Glissant and others have identified as the epistemological dynamics of (neo)imperialism. If we are able to grant the enigmas of the other (the unconscious, the work of art, the human other) their radically irresolvable or opaque status, we may be able to access a desire that does not suicidally drive toward the possession of otherness: "in esthetic terms the parallel to uncharted sexual desire would, I think, be a mobilizing of forms which makes them radically, permanently unreadable" (*DSM* 60).

According to Laplanche, psychoanalytic ethics should promote "*the reversal of the problem of access to the other into that of the priority of the other*";[100] in the realm of aesthetics, enigmatic art would analogously undo the primacy of the desiring gaze that seeks in the world a cure for its own incompleteness, for the blind spots that it knows to riddle its field of vision. Bersani tries out such ethico-aesthetic formulations when, in an extremely dense couple pages that insistently, and silently, evoke Laplanche, he takes up Henry James's texts as laboratories for experimentation with desire, both annihilating and enigmatic. He identifies in *The Golden Bowl*'s Maggie Verver two crucially different aesthetic modes: "She (and, through her, James) vacillates between a view of art best represented in the novel by her father (a view in which forms are collected, centralized and immobilized in museums)"—a description in which we should recognize the Joycean aesthetic effect that, as Bersani writes in the following paragraph, "result[s] in the interpretive centering of highly valued texts"—"and a notion of art as improvised, even aleatory 'mobile syntheses'" (*DSM* 59). To illustrate the latter, he finds in Maggie an embodiment of the enigmatic signifier, whose emptiness seduces the observer-reader into desiring interpretation. Her "silent, statue-like presence" solicits in the novel's other characters an "interpretative scramble" for the meaning of her unreadable stillness; "her enigmatic, withheld sense" renders her "an unpenetrable work of art" (*DSM* 59).

Bersani suggests we juxtapose Maggie's seductive interpretability to the coerciveness of Joycean labor; but while, in her unreadability, she is an enigma, and not a riddle, her presence has effects that are not readily distinguishable from those of annihilating desire. If "everyone around her is reduced to frantic conjectures" about her meaning (*DSM* 59), her appeal is the kind that also impels dialectical formulations of otherness. She commands a *fascinated attention*: "Her *imperialistic control* over the other figures in the novel is, most directly, the result of their mistaken belief that they can possess her sense; they are victimized by their own yearnings for settled interpretations" (*DSM* 59, emphasis added). Like "annihilation," the term "fascination" (which occurs, let us note, twice in the immediately preceding discussion of Mallarmé [*DSM* 58]) suggests the suicidally aggressive nature of desire: the subject not only seeks to assimilate the other but, like a bird paralyzed by the serpent's gaze, will itself be devoured. As Proust writes, fascinating magic leaves one "fe[eling] transfixed, as a small bird might do on catching a sight of a snake"; it immobilizes one with "the strange and unexpected forms of an approaching death."[101] As Bersani notes in his subsequent commentary on *The Golden Bowl* in *The Freudian Body*, this is also true of Maggie: as "an *unreadable text*," "[s]he *fascinates* the other characters" (*FrB* 84, emphases in original).

But can "fascination" constitute a mode of ethical perception? There is a totalization of violence in its enchantment: while Maggie is the object of their devouring desire, her enigma exerts an "imperialistic control" over Amerigo, Charlotte, Mr. Verver, and the Assinghams.[102] Like the bird glamored by the serpent's gaze, it is the fascinated subject who will be devoured. This is precisely the structure of annihilating desire that Bersani had detailed with tangible ambivalence in *A Future for Astyanax*: the desiring subject, wanting the other, will be eclipsed in the annihilating synthesis. Bersani thus concludes that *enigmatic desire, like its annihilating counterpart, captures the subject with the force of devouring fascination*: if the dialectic entails "the 'desiring' destruction of objects in order to possess them internally" (*FrB* 87), the final synthesis in desire's movement will also undo the desiring entity itself in the apocalypse of its completion.

What Bersani calls James's "vacillat[ion]" between two modes of desiring perception (embodied in Mr. Verver and Maggie) is no less his own. In his commentary on *The Golden Bowl*, he can't quite settle on an assessment of enigmatic desire's ethical status. Does the enigma allow, as Laplanchean theory suggests, the reconfiguration of otherness such that the narrative violence of the dialectic is obviated, or is the enigma too readily transformed into the kinds of puzzles that exert on the subject a fascinating pull toward catastrophic syntheses? *The Golden Bowl* indicates to Bersani that the distinction between the "enigma" and the "riddle" is not as tenable as Laplanche needs it to be. The impenetrable enigma readily collapses into—may finally be indistinguishable in its effects from—the riddle. The subject is conceptualized as knowable, and psychoanalysis begins its service as one of the discourses of modern disciplinary society.

Wantless

Laplanche and Bersani find in Freudian theory an instructive way to displace Western philosophy's schematizations of the self and the other. For both, the early articulations from which Freud soon backtracked point to a crucial reconceptualization of the ethics of otherness. Both wish to undo forms of desire that yield the self a priority over the other, who in turn becomes the object of the self's devouring, annihilating appetite. For Laplanche, the solution to the ethical dilemma posed by annihilative desire is to prioritize "enigmatic" otherness. The desiring entity cannot become the self-contained monad, for this entity is split by otherness whose enigma cannot ever be completely metabolized. It is only in the delusions of Western philosophy, radicalized in idealism, that the monadic ego has managed to colonize the subject.

For Bersani, however, this solution is inadequate: even when otherness becomes enigmatic we are still operating with a mode of desire where the other designates a lack, an absence, a loss—a source of "paranoid fascination" (*IRG* 92). Our language betrays the primacy of desire's conceptualization in terms of privation. When we speak our desire, we speak, after all, of our *wants*: "I want you." "Wanting" designates an orientation where the object is deemed missing from the desiring self. This mode of desire locks subjects in a tight dialectic of circulating wants, where he who wants wants the want returned in the desiring gaze: "I want you, but I want you to want me too." Marvin Gaye might as well be singing of Proustian desire; we might catch Marcel whispering, "I give you all the love I want in return," to the ear of the imprisoned, sleeping Albertine.[103]

Starting with *A Future for Astyanax*, *Baudelaire and Freud*, and *The Death of Stéphane Mallarmé*, Bersani hesitates with, and then departs from, Laplanchean theory. He does this primarily because he considers desire's grounding in privation problematic. His ambivalence is informed by ethical considerations: it is unclear to him whether psychoanalysis can provide an account of the subject's desiring relation to the world that would revise the violently oppositional and incorporative assumptions and practices that he has observed also in Proust, where declarations of desire are always versions of "*Tu me manque*." Instead of "the Proustian equation of desire with lack" (*H* 133)—or, say, the Lacanian *manque-à-être*—he seeks an understanding of the world where, in Herbert Spencer's words, "nothing wants."[104] If psychoanalysis is indebted to a theory of desire whose most influential formulation may be Hegelian dialectics, it frames the self and the other in terms of oppositions that can be overcome only in an annihilative synthesis.

In terms of immediate philosophical influences, the conflicting accounts of monadological psychoanalysis in Laplanche and Bersani can be explained by the respective organizations of their work according to traditions instantiated in Derrida's and Deleuze's philosophies. One finds an analogy to Laplanche's and Bersani's differences in Peter Hallward's critique of Deleuze in *Out of This World: Deleuze and the Philosophy of Creation* (2006). Identifying what he considers one of Deleuze's most dangerous idiosyncrasies vis-à-vis most of his contemporaries, Hallward notes the elimination, in Deleuzean thought, of "the most precious sacred cow of contemporary philosophy—*the other*." In Deleuze, "a liberating return to the immediate and the impersonal will requires elimination of the other. Nothing is more foreign to Deleuze than an unconditional concern for the other qua other."[105] Hallward appends an endnote to his critique: he points out that Laplanche's emphasis on the constitutive role of the seductive other for the processes of becoming-human renders his work an exemplary counterpoint to the Deleuze's "world without others."[106] Having suggested the partially joint genealogy of, and consequently the resonance between, Deleuze's and Bersani's philosophies, we propose that what Hallward observes as the point of conflict between Deleuze and "contemporary philosophy"—the status of otherness—is applicable to the divergence of Laplanche's and Bersani's systems. That is, *the elimination of the other* constitutes one of the grounding moves of Bersanian thought. It is because of this that Leibnizian monadism—derived from Proust–Deleuze and Beckett–Blanchot—remains central to Bersani. Concomitantly, Bersani's insistence that we not see, like Laplanche does, post-1915 primary narcissism as a return to classical metaphysics' ipsocentrism is motivated by his effort to rethink desire in ways that would actualize an alternate genealogy of the subject's relation to the world. Bersani is attracted to the psychoanalytic account of the enigmatic other; yet his previous work in *Balzac to Beckett* suggests to him the limits of such reconceptualizations. In *A Future for Astyanax*, *Baudelaire and Freud*, *The Death of Stéphane Mallarmé*, and *The Freudian Body*—his 1970s and 1980s studies on psychoanalysis and aesthetics—he tests the limits of psychoanalysis and seeks to reconfigure desire *otherwise than as a mode of lack*; here the singularity of the monad, whose psychoanalytic manifestation is the primary narcissist, is the vehicle for such reconceptualization. As the aporetic entity that is at once singular and connected, nonrelational and totalized, the monad allows one to think desire in a way that does not anchor it in privation. In this way, Bersani offers an interpretation of Leibnizian metaphysics that differs in crucial ways from not only Laplanche's but also those of other thinkers—for example, Adorno, Derrida, and Jameson—whose anecdotal reading of monadology has been influenced by Marx's comments in "On the Jewish Question."

For Leibniz, there is, indeed, nothing beyond substance: "The complete or perfect concept of an individual substance contains all of its predicates, past, present, and future"; hence, "[e]*very individual substance contains in its perfect concept the whole universe*, and everything existing in it, past, present, and future."[107] Nothing lacks—nothing wants—in the monad; in its wantlessness, it cannot be fascinated by anything that it would not already involve in its being. Monadology—homomonadology—suggests to Bersani a way to think about the world where desiring movement is not determined by constitutive wants; for him, the fact that monads have no external relations means that, offering us a world without lack, Leibnizian thought allows us to experiment with modes of relatedness whose potential has been obfuscated by hegemonic ways of thinking difference.

3

Rethinking Redemption

Benjamin–Baudelaire–Nietzsche

Having begun his career of writing as a critic of modernist art—initially literature but then expanding to other genres—Leo Bersani soon finds himself confronted with some definitional questions regarding his scholarly field. By the end of the 1970s, the theoretical premises of his thought, explored in the previous chapters, push him to address the ways in which modernism or, more expansively, modernity has been formulated by nineteenth- and twentieth-century commentators, whether artists, philosophers, or critics. In the next fifteen years, much of his critical energies are spent redefining "modernity" by situating its problematic in the frame of the onto-ethics/aesthetics that his 1970s work has begun to yield. Beginning with the essay "The Other Freud" (1978) until the Ulysse Dutoit collaboration *Arts of Impoverishment: Beckett, Rothko, Resnais* (1993), a major emphasis of his work falls on the ramifications that this frame has for his scholarly field. More specifically, Bersani seeks the implications of homomonadic singularity—the thought of being that neither emerges in dialectical relations nor can be identified with the notion of "substance" in classical metaphysics—for one's understanding of modern art and culture. In a string of texts—"The Other Freud," *The Forms of Violence: Narrative in Assyrian Art and Modern Culture* (1985), *The Culture of Redemption* (1990), and *Arts of Impoverishment*—he works toward an alternate genealogy of modernity to the one he considers premised on annihilative ontologies of being and becoming.

For Bersani, such ontologies are frequently inscribed in *pastoral narratives*, that is, representations of modern existence as damaged or fallen. These define modernity negatively, in terms of the loss of "premodern" stability and tradition. In "The Other Freud," he suggests that, framed thus, modernity's artistic and theoretical self-representations call us to an immobilized, mournful contemplation of our injured being. Constitutive of the pastoral imagination, the yearning for a lost wholeness leads to "our fascination with"—our captivation by and mimetic identification with—"the spectacles of alienation, anxiety, and violence in modern art." Bersani problematizes "the pastoral view of alienation as a peculiarly modern loss of cultural wholeness and harmony" because alienation assumes the circuitry of desire whose aim, as he had observed in *A Future for Astyanax: Character and Desire in Literature* (1976), is being's completion through a suicidal undoing of difference.[1] Theories that understand modernity in terms of a force isomorphic with Platonic-Hegelian desire—whose aim is "for plenitude to replace absence" (*FA* 13)—trap the critic in a model where otherness can only be the object of an aggressively appropriative movement. It is on this theoretical basis that, as Bersani and Dutoit continue in *The Forms of Violence*, we must problematize "the myth of modern art as a 'crisis,' as a response to massive cultural dislocations which have, perhaps permanently, and *tragically*, unsettled the moral and esthetic orders of Western humanism. From this perspective, even the most sympathetic response to modern painting or literature is indistinguishable from a sense of loss: modern men and women have been cut off, alienated from the possibilities of cultural harmony and wholeness" (*FV* vii–viii, emphasis added). We have been habituated to approach modernist art as compensatory expression for our damaged existence, expression that seeks to undo modern alienation, even when it melancholically acknowledges the futility of this endeavor. Premised on an ontology of lack, such expression yields "tragic" narratives of impossible desires where one remains in thrall of that which has been irretrievably lost; as Daniel Smith, too, writes, the ontology of lack "presents us with a 'tragic' vision of humanity: as humans, we are incomplete and riddled with deficiencies, and ontological desire is the sign of our incompleteness, our 'lack of being.'"[2] "Lack is judged to be omnipresent," Bersani and Dutoit continue in a discussion of Jacques Lacan's work: "what desire lacks is also missing from the world, not as something lost but, more tragically, as something that was never, that never could be, in the world" (*FoB* 115).

Bersani's search for an alternative genealogy of modernity culminates in two early-1990s texts: *The Culture of Redemption* and *Arts of Impoverishment*. In the former, Bersani offers a series of readings that explore the ways in which representations of modernity have been organized as stories of loss oriented toward a "redemptive" denouement, a climactic moment that obeys the logic of annihilative desire's apocalyptic fulfillment. In *Arts of Impoverishment*, he and Dutoit discuss three *auteurs*—Samuel Beckett, Mark Rothko, and Alain Resnais—in whose work they identify a search for an alternative to the narrative logic in which the self and the other are positioned in a dialectic of injury and healing, deprivation and fullness, difference and overcoming.[3] This early-1990s moment in Bersani is significant enough of a turning point that we propose to explore its details in this and the subsequent chapter. The present chapter focuses on Bersani's engagement with three theorists of modernity in "Boundaries of Time and Being: Benjamin, Baudelaire, Nietzsche," the third chapter of *The Culture of Redemption*. The subsequent chapter, "Simultaneity and Sociability," moves to "Inhibited Reading," the opening chapter of the Dutoit collaboration. These chapters in *The Culture of Redemption* and *Arts of Impoverishment*, we propose, are implicitly linked and should be read together. They jointly elaborate the concept of modernity on the basis of Bersani's previous work. They also effect a shift that Bersani comes to emphasize in his subsequent work: what he calls the move from "the psychoanalytic subject" to "the aesthetic subject."

In *The Culture of Redemption*, the targets of Bersani's ethical critique are representations of modernity as constituted by a sense of loss; this loss is not only irrecuperable but, more radically, unrepresentable. The deracinated modern is a melancholic creature, a brooder, in his inability to remember and, hence, mourn the losses that have given birth to the catastrophic present. Despite various diagnoses of what precipitated modernity's alienations (epistemic breaks, forced migrations, colonial expansionism, the Industrial Revolution, the rise of capitalism), what seems distinctive of our modernity is the fact that its emergence constitutes an *inapprehensible catastrophe*, that it "is understood not merely as a break with the past but as an inability to understand the past. . . . Modern consciousness, in short, is irremediably cut off from other ways in which human beings have understood their modernity, their comparatively limited break with their own past. This is the apocalyptic nature of our modernity" (*CR* 48). It is this that, as he continues, gives our modernity "an incomparable aura:

that of being spiritually stranded, uniquely special in its radical break with traditional values and modes of consciousness" (*CR* 47–48).

The phrase "incomparable aura" indicates Bersani's debt to Walter Benjamin's work on the modern subject's pensive or melancholic—*grüblerisch*—contemplation of history's ruins.[4] While Bersani leaves the phrase unattributed, it comes from Benjamin's 1936 essay on Nikolai Leskov. Benjamin closes his meditation on the eradication of the art of storytelling in modern life by arguing that, since the eighteenth century, "the incomparable aura that surrounds the storyteller [*die unvergleichliche Stimmung . . . um den Erzähler*]" has been eclipsed by the rise of the novelistic genre.[5] The latter, even though emerging from the same source as storytelling, is a symptom of modernity in its inability to convey anything but "information," its entrapment of the reading subject in the kind of alienating solipsism that numerous theorists have suggested plagues modernity.

Storytelling, in other words, is one of the "auratic" arts that, as Benjamin argues in the contemporaneous essay "The Work of Art in the Age of Mechanical Reproduction" (1936), have died with the proliferation of various nineteenth-century technologies, most notably photography and film. With the mass technologies that emerge with the Industrial Revolution and capitalism, modern forms of art have lost the stamp of "authenticity" that attached to earlier formations: "what withers [*verkümmert*] in the age of the technological reproducibility of the work of art is the latter's aura [*Aura*]."[6] With infinite, accurate repeatability, one loses "the here and now of the work of art—its unique existence in a particular place."[7] If art is stripped of its "cult value," it ceases to function as a mechanism that translates the momentary sensation—what Benjamin calls *Erlebnis*—into the wholeness of *Erfahrung*.[8] The work's authenticating signature is lost; the artifact no longer "bears the trace of the potter's hand."[9] Artisanry has been usurped by mechanical reproduction. Correspondingly, as the speed of urban life shocks the subject's receptive apparatus into paralysis, experience undergoes an "atrophy [*Verkümmerung*]"[10] as the continuum of *Erfahrung* is broken up: "Nothing distinguishes the ancient man from the modern man so much as the former's absorption in a cosmic experience scarcely known to later periods."[11] For Benjamin, the universal can be reached only in the particular; the accelerated technologies of modernity fail to produce the unique auras that previously attached to works of art.

For Bersani, Benjamin's account functions as an exemplary case of a "redemptive" configuration of modernity/modernism, a counterpoint to the onto-ethics/aesthetics he seeks to develop. In *The Culture of Redemption*, he spends a mere fifteen pages considering Benjaminian thought as a particularly flagrant example of the annihilative logic that he has more ambivalently identified in Proust and psychoanalysis. Furthermore, unlike the frequently critiqued but always reappearing Proust, Freud, and Laplanche, the German-Jewish philosopher is never again mentioned in Bersani's subsequent work. Yet, while the rejection of Benjamin is unequivocal, his philosophy constitutes a more central interlocutor than the brevity of this engagement would suggest.

There are two ways in which we can locate Benjamin in Bersani, ways that this and the following chapter will respectively explore. First, Benjaminian understanding of modernity provides the very frame for Bersani's critique in *The Culture of Redemption*. The term "redemption" itself can be traced to Benjamin's formative sources, including the forms of Jewish mysticism on which his friend Gershom Scholem went on to produce famous studies. The term's centrality in Benjamin is highlighted by Richard Wolin, whose study *Walter Benjamin: An Aesthetic of Redemption* (1982) constitutes an important source for Bersani. As Wolin writes, Benjamin is "the 'philosopher of redemption'": "It is a relentless desire for redemption which represents the inner drive behind the entirety of Benjamin's theoretical *oeuvre*."[12] Benjaminian modernity consists of a traumatizing break from the "premodern" mode of life, in which Benjamin sees, according to Wolin, a "continuum of experience where time has the character of a meaningfully ordered, organic sequence of events, and where even the phenomenon of death fits meaningfully within this sequence."[13] Wolin goes on to note the "considerable nostalgia in his tone when [Benjamin] speaks wistfully of the decline of the integrated fabric of experience which was characteristic of communal social life."[14] The "overly rigid and potentially misleading" distinction between the modern and the premodern, however, relents in Benjamin's subsequent work, for example "On Some Motifs in Baudelaire," where, Wolin argues, Benjamin has relinquished the earlier, naïve concept of the past: "No longer does Benjamin abstractly seek to counterpose an idyllic past to the decadent present. Instead, he attempts to work through the dilemmas of modern social life in a more immanent fashion."[15]

Bersani does not share Wolin's observation about the shifts in Benjamin's thinking; rather, Benjamin persists for him as a theorist of redemptive annihilation. The importance of Benjamin's philosophy as a counterexample against which Bersani defines his understanding of modernity is evident in the echoes of Benjamin one detects in Bersani's texts that do not mention his proper name. When Bersani writes in a 1989 encyclopedia article about our habitual tendency to view art as "an annihilating and redemptive replication of experience," Benjamin is his silent interlocutor.[16] Similarly, we can discern traces of Benjamin in his description, in the prologue to *The Culture of Redemption*, of the object of his scrutiny: "A crucial assumption in the culture of redemption is that a certain type of repetition of experience in art repairs inherently damaged or valueless experience. Experience may be overwhelming, practically impossible to absorb"—here we have the "shock experience" that, as Benjamin writes in "On Some Motifs in Baudelaire," has prevented the translation of *Erlebnis* into the continuum of *Erfahrung*—"but it is assumed . . . that the work of art has the authority to master the presumed raw material of experience in a manner that uniquely gives value to, perhaps even redeems, that material" (*CR* 1). That it is Benjamin who is hiding behind the passive voice of "it is assumed" becomes clear when Bersani goes on to speak of "[t]he catastrophes of history" (*CR* 1) for which redemptive art compensates.

The second point to be made about Benjamin's role for Bersani concerns a curious omission in the latter's commentary. After all, Benjamin, much like Proust, Beckett, Deleuze, and Laplanche, provides yet another example of a twentieth-century thinker who finds in Leibnizian metaphysics a speculative language with which to express post-Enlightenment ontologies. Beginning with his early work—most notably, the failed *Habilitationsschrift*, written in 1924–25 and published in 1928 as *Ursprung des deutschen Trauerspiels*—monadology constitutes a crucial component in Benjamin's analysis of modernity, persisting in his writings through his encounter with dialectical materialism in Georg Lukács, Theodor Adorno, and Bertolt Brecht, until his final works in "On the Concept of History" and the fragments of *The Arcades Project*. While several of the Benjamin texts cited in "Boundaries of Time and Being" include allusions to Leibniz and monads, Bersani declines to address this point of contact between Benjamin and his other sources.[17] In its silences, Bersani's commentary on Benjamin thus echoes his encounter with psychoanalysis. As we argued above, Bersani and Laplanche share Leibnizian metaphysics as a crucial frame of articulation: the monad provides an intensive point of encounter and departure between Bersanian onto-ethics and Laplanchean psychoanalysis. Yet Bersani never notes monadology's importance in Laplanche. Similarly with Benjamin: Bersani elides the recurring Leibnizian references in the latter's work. Yet his dispute with Benjamin's philosophy can be articulated in terms of their differing readings of monadology, a point that our next chapter will pursue.

This chapter tracks the further elaboration of Bersanian homomonadology by unfolding the argument about the onto-ethics/aesthetics that Bersani, in "Boundaries of Time and Being," develops in contrast to Benjamin's theory of modernity. After his brief critique of Benjamin, he proceeds to consider Charles Baudelaire and Friedrich Nietzsche, two thinkers of modernity who constitute important sources for Benjamin (and whom, Bersani implies, he misreads).[18] He extracts from Baudelaire and Nietzsche an alternative account of modernity's ontology, one in which expression does not aim at "the petrifying translation of life into truth."[19] As Baudelaire writes, "The exclusive taste for the True . . . oppresses and stifles the taste for the Beautiful. Where one should see nothing but Beauty . . . , our public looks only for Truth."[20] For Bersani, Baudelaire's aesthetics offers a counterpoint to the Proustian model of art, where the artist, through "an annihilating salvation" of life, "discovers and expresses a preexistent truth" (*CR* 11). Similarly, what attracts him in Nietzsche is the polemic against "the *art of metaphysical comfort*" that Nietzsche sees in the expressions of Romanticism and Christianity.[21] It is in art that modernity's ontology is experimentally given existence.

Bersani follows Benjamin's tracks to Baudelaire and Nietzsche to actualize what remains unseen in the two thinkers from the perspective of redemptive philosophy. We, in turn, follow the path he indicates further by turning to texts by Baudelaire and Nietzsche that Bersani does not address. Our aim in doing this is to further elaborate Bersani's onto-ethics/aesthetics. Bersani turns to the theory of "idealization" in Baudelaire; its counterpart in the early Nietzsche is the dynamism between the Dionysian and Apollonian aspects of art. Crucially, as Bersani cannot but note, Nietzsche calls both the Apollonian and the Dionysian *redemptive* forces. It is this theory of redemption, of *Erlösung*, that comes uncomfortably close to Bersani's theory of shattering, the subject's undoing in impersonal ecstasy. To elaborate in detail what Nietzsche means by redemption, we move from *The Birth of Tragedy*, on which Bersani focuses, to the four "untimely meditations." If Nietzsche forces us to reconsider redemption as a concept whose utility may exceed the redemptive modality Bersani finds in Benjamin, it also brings us back to psychoanalysis, where, as Laplanche frequently points out, terms derivative of *Lösung* and *lösen*—undoing, untying, loosening—play a crucial role.

Scattering Being

As Jürgen Habermas writes, Benjamin's thought "brought together motifs that ordinarily run at cross purposes."[22] Habermas, and Wolin after him, argues that throughout his work Benjamin continues to toggle between radically disparate influences: rather than denouncing messianic philosophy after the encounter with Marxist thought in Lukács's *History and Class Consciousness* (1923), conversations with Max Horkheimer and Adorno, and his friendship with Asja Lacis, Benjamin's oeuvre entails, in Scholem's phrase, an "intimate interweaving of mystical-cosmic and Marxist insights."[23] He was fond of asserting that the theoretical prolegomena to his *Trauerspiel* study was unreadable for anyone not versed in the Kabbalah (as the examiners of his *Habilitationsschrift* turned out to be).[24] Scholem reports his friend's pronouncement in 1916: "'If I ever have a philosophy of my own . . . it somehow will be a philosophy of Judaism.'"[25] He may become more discrete about the importance of mystic influences after the 1920s; yet, as he suggests in one of his final pieces,[26] with the shift from such early texts as "On Language as Such and on the Language of Man" (1916) to the dialectical analyses of "The Work of Art in the Age of Mechanical Reproduction," the unsightly dwarf of theology merely withdraws inside the puppet of historical materialism, where it continues to pull the strings.[27]

The implications of such thinly veiled mysticism irk Bersani. Benjamin's work amounts to, as he not too delicately puts it, a "postlapsarian dirge" (*CR* 53). As the reference to the myth of the Fall suggests, what renders Benjamin a particularly flagrant example of redemptive modernism is his explicitly theological bent. Benjamin's modernity leaves us fascinated with loss: the shattering of *Erfahrung* into *Erlebnis*, the replacement of communal storytelling with solitary novel-reading, the disappearance of auratic arts and the rise of mechanical reproduction. Benjamin reframes this violence in a redemptive narrative oriented toward what Habermas calls "unmutilated experience."[28] For Bersani, Benjamin's persistent attraction to theological formulations indicates that his influential philosophy must be read as a privileged example of theories that rely on, and breathe new life into, the pastoral-transcendent myths of our culture. Benjaminian modernity postulates "the fall from the grace of *Erfahrung*" (*CR* 53). Premising his thought partially on Jewish cosmology, Benjamin conceptualizes modernity—history itself—in terms of a catastrophic loss that provides the hermeneutic frame for all subsequent phenomena. He embraces "the messianic idea" in Judaism, which, as Scholem observes, is at once "restorative and utopian": restorative because it seeks the actualization, perhaps for the first time, of the dismembered, catastrophically lost past; utopian because this past will return in the form of an apocalyptic future event.[29]

Messianism's eschatological nostalgia renders Benjamin's methodology and metaphysics *annihilative* in the sense in which Bersani uses the term in *A Future for Astyanax*. Because of his lapsarian assumptions, Benjamin's diasporic ontology[30] constitutes an economy where identities seek their completion through the reassimilation of mythically lost being. Benjamin, in other words, premises his ontology on the thought of lack, "an irreparable loss,"[31] which Bersani, beginning with *A Future for Astyanax*, finds orienting the psychoanalytic theory of desire. Similarly, the aim of cataloguing the disjointed *Erlebnisse* of modern life is their redemptive annihilation: "[I]n Benjamin we find the traits most deeply characteristic of [redemptive] culture: the scrupulous registering of experience in order to annihilate it, and the magical and nihilistic belief that immersion in the most minute details of a material content will not only reduce that content but simultaneously unveil its hidden redemptive double" (*CR* 54). For Bersani, Benjamin continues the genealogy of Western thought where desire seeks the extinction of the individuations produced by primordial separation. In *The Culture of Redemption*, he thus proposes an explanation for the compulsive appeal of annihilation: we remain enthralled by what he calls "narrative violence" because its death-driven stories promise a rescue from alienated *Erlebnis*. We assent to violence because of its redemptive, salvational potential.

Bersani seeks to demonstrate the tendentiousness of Benjamin's thought by turning to two of his most important sources, Baudelaire and Nietzsche. For Benjamin, Baudelaire is the chronicler of transitions whose losses and shocks characterize modernity. Wolin writes that Baudelaire's importance for Benjamin stems from the French writer's having "stood at the crossroads of traditional and modern societies. . . . Because he stood so to speak on the cusp between two historical eras, witnessing the extirpation by modern industrial capitalism of the last vestiges of traditional life, Baudelaire was ideally situated to chronicle this important process of transition."[32] Françoise Meltzer agrees: Baudelaire sees two worlds, "the Paris before Hausmann, and the Paris during and after its redevelopment; France before the revolution of 1848, and France in the increasingly triumphant capitalist culture that followed; the death throes of the ancien régime with its unraveling social fabric, and the preening bourgeoisie with its nouveau riche self-satisfaction that touted social utilitarianism and 'good works' to repress political guilt and crass mercantilism."[33] Baudelaire's thought, like the forms of dandyism that it frequently observes, draws its energies from "periods of transition."[34]

For Benjamin, Baudelaire's poetry bespeaks "something irretrievably lost."[35] But Benjamin, according to Bersani, misreads the French writer. Bersani argues that Baudelaire, unlike Benjamin, does not prioritize contemporary formations of modernity as qualitatively different from the "nowness" of other eras' experiences: "Baudelaire—all the signs of nostalgic remembrance notwithstanding—did not think of his own time as having effected a radical break with the past through revolutionary changes in the very structure of human experience" (*CR* 65). If for Benjamin the contemporary present, whether understood in the context of nineteenth-century upheavals or earlier diasporic legacies, is unprecedented in its peculiar forms of dispossession, in Baudelaire "[t]he present is . . . both an all-important and an empty category; its value is not in what it contains, but in its presentness" (*CR* 66). No "incomparable aura" enhances nineteenth-century modernity in Baudelaire. What, then, does Bersani find in Baudelaire that Benjamin misses?

On Speculative Beauty

If Bersani is repelled by the dualities that organize Benjaminian thought (premodern/modern; *Erfahrung/Chockerlebnis*), Baudelaire's aesthetic theory nevertheless boasts equally binary concepts. Of these, Bersani notes the dichotomy between art's "eternal" aspects and their materialization in "the relative" or "the ephemeral." As Baudelaire writes in "The Painter of Modern Life" (1863), his essay on Constantin Guys, beauty "always and inevitably contains [these] two elements": "one element that is eternal, invariable and exceedingly difficult to assess, and . . . another element that is relative and a product of circumstance."[36] It is only in its "relative" form, or historical instantiation, that "the eternal" in art becomes consumable: while the former "is, so to speak[,] the amusing, stimulating, appetizing icing on the divine cake," the latter, noumena-like, remains "beyond our powers of appreciation; unadapted and unsuitable to human nature."[37] Even if, as Bersani insists, Baudelaire does not subscribe to the idea, embraced by Benjamin, of modernity's traumatizing uniqueness—Baudelaire "erases from the concept of modernity the Benjaminian connotations of rupture and loss" (*CR* 66)—his ontology of art proceeds from premises that, in some respects, don't immediately strike one as incompatible with Benjamin's: expressing what one critic calls "[t]he fundamental duality of Baudelaire's universe,"[38] neither are the eternal and the relative readily distinguishable from Western theological models.

Especially since Bersani is writing at a moment of deconstructionist hegemony in the fields of literary theory relevant to his own work, we may be surprised by the counterintuitive insistence with which he refuses to relinquish a term as heavily burdened with the discursive histories of theology and metaphysics as "the eternal." But this is not, as we have suggested, an unprecedented move in his oeuvre: the counterpart to the Baudelairean "eternal" in Bersani's earlier work is the concept of "essence," equally weighted with the metaphysical significance laboriously unpacked by "antiessentialists" of various kinds. Bersani proposes that we not assume "the eternal" or "the essence" to be, and hence abandon them as, *fully articulated concepts*, but let them unfold further in ways that draw out their unactualized potential.

He begins this work by suggesting that Baudelaire's texts perform the disappearing act of the eternal: in Baudelaire, the dichotomy of the eternal/the relative "nearly collapses under the excessive weight of one of its terms" (*CR* 64). This near-collapse is precipitated by the prioritization of the relative at the expense of the eternal, a prioritization that, importantly, does not so much eliminate as make unlocatable the latter term. It is as if Baudelaire's "excessive" focus on the subordinate term—the proliferation of illustrative examples—breeds doubt as to whether the eternal remains an operative concept apart from its manifestations, or whether it is rendered completely dependent on the local varieties of the relative: "What we see in art is 'the relative, circumstantial element'; the 'eternal element' would appear to be more of a theoretical assumption—or perhaps a theoretical necessity—than a determinable aspect of works of art themselves" (*CR* 64).[39] Baudelaire's style, Bersani similarly suggests, destabilizes "the religious ground" of the argument, "caress[ing]" the ideas such that their solidity "soften[s]" into the pleasures of expression: "a certain preciosity of rhetoric . . . places us at some distance from [the] ideas" in Baudelaire's critical writings (*CR* 64). The dandified pleasures of Baudelairean style obscure the weighty subject matter: "The argument risks becoming elegantly dilettantish under the light but repeated pressure of a coaxing voice calling attention to the moves of its argument" (*CR* 64).

One finds another example of "the curiously collapsing and telescoping opposites of Baudelaire's universe" in "On the Ideal and the Model," the section of "The Salon of 1846" to which Bersani subsequently turns.[40] As he writes, the terms indicated in the section title substitute for "the eternal" and "the relative": "The relation of the ideal to the particular is analogous to that of the eternal to the transitory. The ideal and the eternal are the veiled presence of what the particular or the transitory lacks; they are the form the circumstantial takes in aspiring to be different from itself" (*CR* 67). The ideal names the "unique harmony" of the individual whom the artist has taken as his model.[41] Art is the work of undoing the model by forcing its further complication toward the remembered forms of its ideal. This is why, as Baudelaire frequently writes, artistic representation cannot amount to skillful copying ("exact imitation spoils a memory");[42] what is needed is the forgetting of the model's forms by re-collecting that which was sacrificed for representation to emerge.

Baudelaire calls this process of artistic remembering—the model's self-differentiation—"idealization." It is with the concepts of the ideal and idealization that, as Michel Brix writes, Baudelaire's aesthetic theory at once approximates and breaks from Platonism.[43] Although reminiscent of it, the Baudelairean concept of Beauty does not coincide with the ideality of Platonic Forms, the divine origins to whose eternal perfection—to whose Truth—their earthly approximations aspire. Baudelaire announces this in the opening of his essay on Guys as he declares his "opposition to the theory of a beauty that is single and absolute."[44] Instead, the "unique harmony" that for him constitutes the ideal is, first, specific to an individual and, second, a unique aggregation of *correspondences*. The singular harmonies that idealization seeks must guide the painter's work, as Baudelaire suggests when he cites the eighteenth-century philosopher and physiognomist Johann Kaspar Lavater, who produced guides for artists on how to appropriately match different elements in representation. For Baudelaire, idealization in painting must be informed by such correspondences: as he writes, following Lavater, a particular hand "demands" a certain kind of foot; a skin type "produces" a matching hair.[45] Lavater may have got the details wrong, but the idea, Baudelaire insists, is correct. The artist's task is to seduce an unactualized harmony out of his model. Art re-calls the ideal into visibility by combining forms that "agree together [*qui jurent de* figurer *ensemble*]"; this agreement expresses individuals' "proper natures [*caractère*]."[46] Its task is to evoke correspondences.

Rendering visible such correspondences, idealization produces the effect of beauty: "*The beautiful is the effect of our discovering the nonrepresented in the represented*" (*CR* 67). Idealization entails the forgetting of the model and the remembering of an unactualized ideal. It is a principle of de-composition and re-membering: the artistic imagination "decomposes all creation, and with the raw materials accumulated and disposed in accordance with rules whose origins one cannot find save in the furthest depths of the soul, it creates a new world, it produces the sensation of newness."[47] Beauty is the artist's *avocation*: it calls forth figures that distract the gaze from models' extant shapes. The undoing of the model in idealization, Baudelaire continues, may be discernible only in art: "I am not claiming that there are as many fundamental ideals as there are individuals, for a mould gives several impressions; but in the painter's soul there are just as many ideals as individuals, because a portrait is *a model complicated by an artist*."[48] Art is an ontological laboratory, as Bersani will say: it "imitates that for which there is no model outside art" (*AI* 100). Art experiments with ideal, singular beings that exist nowhere in nature.

Baudelaire's rejection of Platonism—his displacement of Truth with Beauty—similarly informs his revisions of the eighteenth-century Romantic and theological concept of *correspondances*. The famous term is not of Baudelaire's coinage: the sources for his theory include not only the Romantic understanding of synesthesia but also Emanuel Swedenborg's theology. Like Platonism, which postulates mattered life's vertical aspiration to eternal Forms, Swedenborg sees in correspondences a transcendent movement toward divinity. In Baudelaire, on the other hand, the term "correspondences" "does not have any religious connotation."[49] His theory of idealization—the mutual gravitation of family resemblances—assumes a *horizontal* movement that traces beings' unactualized connections. "The secularization and aestheticization of Swedenborgianism,"[50] Baudelaire's move from vertical to horizontal correspondences repeats the break from Platonism in his aesthetic theory; and while textual evidence abounds of his persistent appeals to vertical correspondences, Bersani echoes the majority of critics in locating his originality in the way in which his poetics, much more consistently than his theoretical statements, prioritizes the immanent world of horizontal correspondences to ideals like Platonic Forms.

As Bersani writes, Baudelaire's theory of correspondences implies that "an individual, or an individual trait, always tends to be in the space between its own material presence and those other material presences which it both remembers and toward which it projects correspondences" (*CR* 68). If Platonic and Swedenborgian correspondences move vertically, the relative in Baudelaire "aspir[es] to be different from itself" along a horizontal glide (*CR* 67). The ontological distinctions that Bersani seeks in Baudelaire's aesthetics should be clear: while the mobility of vertical correspondences is "primarily transcendental" (*CR* 75), in horizontal correspondence the individual becomes different from itself by extending nonhierarchically, rhizomatically, immanently. If vertical correspondences assume transcendence, horizontal relations constitute "a finite universe in which all objects are continuously moving toward and away from one another" (*CR* 75). "The spectacle of nature," agrees Brix, "finds equivalents in a supernatural world, but *surnaturel* for Baudelaire is not synonymous with *céleste* or *divin*."[51]

In the immanent world of horizontal correspondences, the ideal is not an external object to be approximated; rather, Baudelairean idealization assumes an involutive movement, one that takes place through memory. Art, Baudelaire writes, "is a kind of mnemotechny of the beautiful."[52] Beauty is remembered; it is the calling forth of family resemblances: "in memory the artist creates the terms for correspondences, which means that he sees each part of his model's body in relation other parts" (*CR* 68). Rather than Lavater's taxonomies, Baudelaire advocates *naïveté* as the method or affective mode that enables the artist to access individual harmonies.[53] The artist remembers naively, nonanalytically: "The Imagination is an almost divine faculty which perceives at once, quite without resort to philosophic methods, the intimate and secret connections between things, *correspondences* and analogies."[54]

Idealization is an appetite, "the deathless appetite for beauty [*l'immortel appétit du beau*] [that] has always found its satisfaction."[55] Baudelaire speaks of the artist's perennial yearning for beautiful forms; but he also alludes to beauty itself as an immortal appetition, the hunger *for*, but also *of*, ideal forms, a hunger that, as he adds, never fails to be satisfied. If Bersani invites us to think psychoanalytically—he synthesizes Baudelaire and Laplanche—we can extend his reading by recognizing the proximity of Baudelairean idealization to what psychoanalysis calls "the drive." In Laplanche's terms, the drive is the name for the straying (*fourvoyé*) organism's compulsive movement toward its annihilation in jouissance; following Laplanche, Bersani conceptualizes it as the undoing of individuated forms at the moment of an ecstatic fusion with otherness. Bersani comes close to identifying Baudelaire's idealization with the drive when he writes: "The Baudelairean aesthetic is inseparable from Baudelairean erotics, and in both jouissance is identical to the masochistic pleasure of self-shattering" (*CR* 72). We find in Baudelaire's aesthetic theory the force of becoming-in-undoing that for Laplanche comprises hominization, the infant's shattering when called by sexuality's unbearable enigma. The intensiveness of this enigma precipitates the incipient being's defiguration, the redrawing of boundaries in masochistic jouissance. Jouissance coaxes us to life by the pleasure of a deadly undoing; in Baudelaire, the name for this jouissance is *the aesthetic*.

Bersani, then, thinks Baudelairean aesthetics psychoanalytically, but in terms of a psychoanalytic theory that is itself inflected via the onto-ethics/aesthetics that we have called homomonadic. When he writes that, "[i]n the finite universe of horizontal correspondences, there are no unrelated terms," but only "the order of total relationality" (*CR* 77–78), his proposition can be understood in the light of Leibniz's *lex continuitatis*. Drawn from Baudelairean aesthetic theory, his conclusion that "[a]n individual body is completed or idealized (the two are synonymous here) to the extent that it is dematerialized by relations entirely internal to its own structure" (*CR* 68) is similarly readable as a Leibnizian-inflected theory of becoming in which "the monad's natural changes come from an *internal principle*."[56] Idealization constitutes not a movement toward an external form but an approximation of an imperfectly completed internal figuration, like the form of actualization that Deleuze in *Proust and Signs* ascribes to the Leibnizian monad. In the terms we explored in our introduction, Baudelaire gives us a *speculative* theory of the aesthetic.

If the ideal and the eternal name that which "the particular or the transitory *lacks*" (*CR* 67, emphasis added), the eternal is not exactly something that has been lost in the fallen world of modernity; it does not designate an absence. Rather, it names the incompletion of the relative, not in terms of an externalized loss but in terms of an unfinishedness, of a virtual that hasn't been fully actualized—what Baudelaire calls "the deathless appetite for/of beauty." Formulating his aesthetic dualism some years before the study on Guys, Baudelaire writes in "The Salon of 1846": "All forms of beauty, like all possible phenomena, contain an element of the eternal and an element of the transitory—of the absolute and of the particular. Absolute and eternal beauty does not exist, or rather it is only an abstraction creamed from the general surface of different beauties."[57] As in "The Painter of Modern Life," Baudelaire conceptualizes beauty on a model of *appetition*: beauty, expression of the eternal, is the "crème," the excess product of material manifestations of the eternal; the eternal becomes consumable only in the form of a luxurious waste product of the relative.

With the theory of beautiful edibles in Baudelaire, we return to Bersani's concern with otherness in his previous studies. The model of desire that he detects in psychoanalysis is a model of consuming the other. In the schema of lack, otherness is the object of one's appetite that must be metabolized to keep the self going. But Bersani suggests that, with its rhetoric of eating, Baudelaire's aesthetic theory gives us something else: what one consumes is not the other but a remembered part of one's self—not difference but sameness. Lovers and poets "rediscover the nonself *within* the self. It is in themselves that their insatiable appetite for otherness is satisfied; in art and love, *the self is penetrated by the alien nature of its own contents*, by a world it now remembers having contained" (*CR* 74, second emphasis added). The self seeks its undoing in the nonself with which it continues to correspond or harmonize; Bersani calls this an *ecstatic* undoing, a phrase that he frequently uses in his work. He writes of Baudelaire: "The nonself in which a particular self seeks ecstatically to be obliterated is the internally inscribed history of the self's relations with the world" (*CR* 74).

As an illustration of such sensuous aesthetics, Bersani cites Baudelaire's example of an artist-friend's childhood memory, a recollection of the erotic attention with which the child would observe the scene of his father dressing: he "would gaze, in wonderment mixed with delight, at the muscles of the arms, the graduated shades of faint pink and yellow of the skin, and the bluish network of veins. The picture of life's outward appearances was already filling the child [*le pénétrait*] with deep respect, and laying hold of his very brain. Already he was obsessed and possessed by the contemplation of form."[58] If this is a scene of an artist's awakening, Baudelaire suggests that aesthetic pleasure captures the child in a dangerously receptive posture: his "penetration" by the paternal tableau at once vivifies and immobilizes him; his becomes a "fixed and animally ecstatic gaze," passively taking in the body he assumes to become.[59] What not only arrests and narrows the child's gaze but also renders it inhuman—"animally ecstatic"—may be the intimations of death revealed in the close-up of the father's body: the pinks and yellows and blues that comprise the father's corporeality suggest something of the queasy fragility of his embodiment, the ready corruptibility of the muscle, the skin, the veins, or their dissolution into purely aesthetic forms. With his homoerotic gaze, the child's is what Bersani calls a "penetrated aesthetic consciousness" (*CR* 80). For Bersani, Baudelaire's retelling of the artist-friend's memory evokes the Laplanchean schema of hominizing *ébranlement*, the other's enigmatic solicitation that shakes the subject into wakefulness. As much as the Laplanchean infant discerns in the other's messages coded truths about himself, in the childhood memory we find the subject immobilized as if in front of a mirror: the child observes in the father his future self, his doppelgänger-to-come.

But if the child gazing at the father is in thrall of death, the movement he witnesses is at the same time that which Baudelaire calls idealization. The disintegration of the father's body into aesthetic forms anticipates the dissolution of the model toward the ideal that the artist the child will have become elicits. And if, further, the child is drawn toward the father as if toward his future doppelgänger, this doubleness is not one whose forms are emerging, ready-made, from behind the veils of repression; rather, its beauty is carved out by the idealizing movement. It is in this way that, with Baudelairean idealization, Bersani aims at an onto-aesthetics not based on an economy of lack, as Benjamin's appears to him.

Having begun to rethink the ontology of modernity he finds in Benjamin through Baudelaire, Bersani, in the third chapter of *The Culture of Redemption*, proceeds to Nietzsche, another crucial source for Benjamin. While Baudelaire, the paradigmatic French modernist, figures centrally in Bersani, "Boundaries of Time and Being" is the only text in which he at length draws from the Germanic tradition's diagnostician of modernity's ills. Yet like Benjamin, who never reappears in Bersani's oeuvre, Nietzsche provides a crucial vehicle for his formulations of onto-ethics/aesthetics. If Benjamin is the redemptive philosopher *par excellence*, in Nietzsche's work Bersani finds a critique of redemption that matches his own in its vehemence. As Nietzsche writes in his tract on Richard Wagner, "The need for *redemption*" is "the quintessence of all Christian needs . . . : it is the most painful affirmation of decadence."[60] Redemption constitutes a symptom of the life-negating torpor and slavishness that he diagnoses in nineteenth-century European cultures. The self in need of redemption is "*haïssable*" for its inability to embrace affirmation, to pronounce "a triumphant Yes . . . to *oneself*," to live in "self-affirmation, self-glorification of life."[61]

But if Bersani identifies in Nietzschean thought a particularly explicit critique of *Erlösung*, we should note that Nietzsche's work is not simply antiredemptive. Instead, already in *The Birth of Tragedy*, we find *more than one mode* of redemption; in his later work, and particularly in *Thus Spoke Zarathustra* (1891), he pursues a non-Christian formulation of redemption, which he identifies, as he does in his first book, with the figure of Dionysus. As Keith Ansell Pearson writes, "At the center of [*Thus Spoke Zarathustra*] is a new teaching of redemption. . . . In contrast to the English word 'redemption[,]' which suggests the payment of a debt, the German word *Erlösung* is connected with solution (*Lösung*) and dissolution (*Auflösung*), and thus names a setting free."[62] In what follows, we trace the emergence of this double redemption in Nietzsche's earlier work, *The Birth of Tragedy* and the four "untimely meditations." Nietzsche's splitting of redemption into two—briefly noted in "Boundaries of Time and Being"—has some crucial ramifications for our reading of Bersani. Despite what he suggest in his polemical moments, Bersani, like Nietzsche, works with(in) the concept, complicating the easy divisions on which the ideologies they oppose rely. Yielding to the appeal of considering Bersani an antiredemptive thinker without addressing the complication of the concept would lead to an error analogous to the common reflex of divorcing his thought on "solitude" and "shattering" from the persistent emphases on "correspondences" and "communication" in his work. Nietzschean *Erlösung* allows us, furthermore, to cast another look at Laplanche's psychoanalytic ontology.

Nietzsche's Two Redemptions

Bersani's turn from Baudelaire to Nietzsche in "Boundaries of Being and Time" is motivated by two considerations. First, although less explicitly than Baudelaire's, Nietzsche's thought influences Benjamin's delineation of European modernity. As much as Benjamin is critical of the atrophying of mechanized modern life, Nietzsche, in *The Birth of Tragedy*, speaks of "the desolation and exhaustion of contemporary culture."[63] Like Benjamin after him, he is critical of the toll industrialized modernity takes on us: "life is made sick," he writes in a later text, "by this dehumanizing and mechanical grinding of gears, the 'impersonality' of the laborer, the false economy of the 'division of labor.'"[64] Similarly, Benjamin's complaint about the novel as modernity's symptom shares a considerable deal with Nietzsche's critique of nineteenth-century German education in the second untimely meditation, "On the Utility and Liability of History for Life" (1874). Such resonances are evident in Benjamin's earliest work, where he criticizes "the degeneration of study into the heading up of information."[65] For him, the emergence of the novel bespeaks an alienation from communal and communicable *Erfahrung*, the replacement of the "intelligence" conveyed by stories with the "information" offered by modern print media, novels, and newspapers.[66] Benjamin's lament echoes Nietzsche's critique of the way in which German *Bildung*, rather than cultivating life, stymies it with the mere accumulation of positivist knowledge. Storytelling, on the other hand, has characteristics that Nietzsche would call *unzeitgemäß*. Its enigmatically open messages have the capacity to reactivate in an untimely manner: a story "is like those seeds of grain that have lain for centuries in the airtight chambers of the pyramids and have retained their germinative power to this day."[67] Contrary to such untimeliness, the information peddled by print media is valid only in "the moment in which it [is] new";[68] it is fully adapted to, and extinct after, the present moment.

Second, Baudelaire and Nietzsche offer analogous philosophies of modernity in that theirs are not mere diagnoses of their historical moments, the shifts brought about in industrializing, revolutionary Europe. Like Benjamin after them, Baudelaire and Nietzsche make *onto-aesthetic claims* in which Bersani discerns elaborations of the forms of thought he has been engaging since *Balzac to Beckett: Center and Circumference in French Fiction* (1970). Bersani considers *The Birth of Tragedy* "a brilliant if at times confused philosophical condensation of the problems we have been considering [with Benjamin and Baudelaire], more specifically the relation between the individual (both in the sense of a nonpsychological, relational *individuel* established by correspondences and in that of a constituted self) and the redemptive claims of art" (*CR* 87). In "Boundaries of Time and Being," Bersani aligns Nietzsche's early reading of the Dionysian and Apollonian dynamics of Greek tragedy with Baudelaire's aesthetic theory: according to him, both think the aesthetics of being—to cite Nietzsche, "aesthetical metaphysics"[69]—amidst the turmoil of nineteenth-century revolutionary Europe. Yet the brevity of the discussion of Nietzsche can obfuscate his contribution to Bersanian onto-ethics/aesthetics. Where Baudelaire is a constant point of orientation in Bersani's work, notwithstanding brief allusions in some later texts Nietzsche's presence is confined to "Boundaries of Time and Being." Yet we find in Nietzsche an attack on Platonism that parallels Baudelaire's. If Baudelaire separates "beauty" from "truth" by horizontalizing correspondences, Nietzsche's does the same work of reducing "truth" to "appearance" (*Schein*, *Erscheinung*) by framing onto-aesthetics in the interplay of Dionysian and Apollonian redemptions.[70] We will consider the ramifications of this pivotal moment in the tradition of German aesthetics in this and the following chapter.

In *The Birth of Tragedy*, Nietzsche's famous dyad of the Apollonian and the Dionysian is, for Bersani, a rearticulation of the dualities one finds in Baudelairean aesthetic theory. While Apollo is the god of plastic, representational art—of meaning and visible forms—in Dionysus we have a primal force undoing distinct individuals: he is the god of intoxication and ecstasy. Nietzsche sees Apollo "as the transfiguring genius of the *principium individuationis* through which alone the redemption in illusion [*Erlösung im Scheine*] is truly to be obtained"; with Dionysus, "the spell of individuation is broken."[71] Or, as Bersani writes, the concept of Apollonian *principium individuationis*, borrowed from Arthur Schopenhauer,[72] embodies "the impulse to articulation . . . central to all art" (*CR* 95); this principle is relentlessly supplemented by its undoing in the Dionysian tendency "to collapse difference back into the primordial unity" (*CR* 91). Bersani invites us to regard the Dionysian pull toward undifferentiation as analogous to what Baudelaire calls idealization, driven by the force of artistic naïveté. As much as Apollonian forms are undone in the frenzy of Dionysian intoxication, Baudelaire writes that the defiguring of the model in idealization is accomplished in states of deliria: drunkenness, dreams, opium haze. It is in such moments that the artist can "remember" the correspondences suppressed by cohering representation. The child enthralled by the father's body and the artist share their readiness for getting high. "For the child everything is *new*," Baudelaire writes; "he is always *drunk* [ivre]."[73] He suggests we consider Edgar Allan Poe's alcoholism evidence of the fact that, as the "mnemotechny of the beautiful," art frequently requires experimentation with hallucinogenics. Unfocusing the subject's gaze from life's realized forms, these allow him to recall the virtual. "Poe's drunkenness [*l'ivrognerie*] was a mnemonic device," Baudelaire writes,

> a deliberate method of work, drastic and fatal, no doubt, but suited to his passionate nature. Poe taught himself to drink, just as a careful man of letters makes a deliberate practice of filling his notebooks with notes. He could not resist the desire to return to the marvelous or terrifying visions, the subtle conceptions, which he had encountered in a previous storm; they were old acquaintances which peremptorily called to him, and in order to renew relations with them he took the most perilous but the straightest road. One part of what delights us today was the cause of his death.[74]

As much as Baudelaire considers Poe's drinking a dangerous artistic practice that allowed him to remember the ideal forms that art evokes, Dionysus, Nietzsche writes, offers "the narcotic draught" that discoheres the self.[75] Intoxicants enhance one's "immoderate taste for beautiful forms"; they enable access to the "intoxicated reality" of art.[76] It is in such states that we reach Dionysian ecstasy, the movement whereby "the *moi* becomes the *non-moi* without ever really leaving itself" (*CR* 71).

Apollo releases being from what Nietzsche in the 1886 preface to *The Birth of Tragedy* calls its "overfullness." Nietzsche assigns this redemptive power to the artist-god, who, in creating, "frees himself from the *distress* of fullness and *overfullness* and from the *affliction* of the contradictions compressed in his soul."[77] In figuring—drawing (out)—being, Apollo redeems it from the undifferentiation of Dionysian primal unity; as Nietzsche writes, "the redeeming vision [*der erlösenden Vision*]" of Apollonian art consists in its being "the apotheosis of the *principium individuationis*."[78] By cutting up—or cutting into—being, the Apollonian principle "saves" or "rescues" us from "the distress of nonidentity," from "an always potential oneness of being" (*CR* 95). In this mode, art is the decompression of being into figuration, the unfolding of an infinite density: its Apollonian mode works toward the "demotion of appearance to the level of mere appearance [*Depotenzieren des Scheins zum Schein*]."[79] Apollonian individuation loosens or untangles the dense knot of Dasein, punctuates its faultless being. At the same time, being, in order to appear, must relinquish some of its latent force: Apollo "de-potentializes" the Dionysian virtual. As "the 'shining one,' the deity of light [*der 'Scheinende,' die Lichtgottheit*]," Apollo filters out some of the unbearable brightness (*Schein*) of Dionysian luster.[80]

It is not surprising that, following Nietzsche, Bersani should point to Apollonian individuation as an instantiation of "redemption." Cutting into the "primordial" connectedness of being, Apollo draws a line and redeems beings from their overproximity. This redemption may ultimately serve the kinds of "authoritative identities" (*CR* 3) whose construction depends on figured beings' separation from their others; Bersani speaks of "the redemptive illusion of the individual" (*CR* 100). Less easily assimilable is the fact that, for Nietzsche, the Dionysian, too, constitutes a redemptive mode. Bersani cites a passage from *The Birth of Tragedy* that identifies the superiority of "objective" to "subjective" art in the former's ability to complicate Apollonian expression with Dionysian forces: "[W]e know the subjective artist only as the poor artist," Nietzsche declares, "and through the entire range of art we demand first of all the conquest of the subjective, redemption [*Erlösung*] from the 'ego,' and the silencing of the individual will and desire."[81] "Redemption from the 'ego'"—*Erlösung vom "Ich"*—appears a strikingly unidiomatic phrase in Bersani's language. His work entails an unrelenting critique of modern culture's redemptive ethos, the way in which singular phenomena are departicularized by being embedded in universalizing narratives of lost (and hence potentially recuperable) wholeness of being, like Aristophanes's myth of the divine trauma visited upon humankind. Whether in the context of nineteenth-century biopolitics, psychoanalytic narratives of sexuality, or the conceptualization of art in terms of fascinating riddles, the redemption that concerns Bersani obeys, to put it in Nietzschean terms, an Apollonian force divorced from its Dionysian undertow. As he writes in the prologue to *The Culture of Redemption*, the "redemptive aesthetic [is] based on the negation of life" (*CR* 2), a formulation where, anticipating the third chapter's turn to *The Birth of Tragedy*, "life" denotes the Nietzschean affirmation of the eternal return, the immanent infinity of becoming, thwarted by the slavish dialectics of difference.

In *The Birth of Tragedy*, Dionysian ecstasy nevertheless becomes "redemptive" in its ability to dismantle ego-figurations by plunging them into being's "mysterious primordial unity."[82] The "Apollonian redemption through mere appearance [*Erlösung im Scheine*]" is coupled with a Dionysian form of redemption, that is, "the shattering of the individual and his fusion with primal being [*das Zerbrechen des Individuums und sein Einswerden mit dem Ursein*]"; Dionysus seeks "to destroy the individual and redeem him by a mystic feeling of oneness [*das Individuum zu vernichten und durch eine mystische Einheitsempfindung zu erlösen sucht*]."[83] The Apollonian and the Dionysian offer two forms of *Erlösung*; redemption is "a two-way street" (*CR* 93, 100) for Nietzsche, who repeats and develops this line of thought in his later work. Thus, prompted by Nietzsche, Bersani reconsiders the onto-ethical question of redemption. He notes the dilemma that Nietzsche's doubled concept poses to him: "Most startlingly from the perspective of my argument about the authority of art in a culture of redemption, *The Birth of Tragedy* simultaneously attacks that culture and raises the possibility of a metaphysical legitimizing of an aesthetic of redemption" (*CR* 87). No longer can we rely on orienting ourselves in Bersani by considering redemption as the ethical failure *par excellence*, the crime of categorization in which we lose sight of both beings' singularities and their boundary-violating correspondences. The redemption we habitually recognize as Bersanian must be supplemented with its Dionysian counterpart, which is nothing but a *shattering*, *das Zerbrechen*, of the ego, the undoing of its boundedness. It is at the very moment of articulating his rejection of redemptive onto-ethics in *The Culture of Redemption* that Bersani is pushed to complicate the critique by implicitly considering two modes of redemption.

Bersani does not cite Nietzsche's subsequent moves in rethinking redemption, but we can follow them here, especially as they take place in the four "untimely meditations," published in the four years—from 1873 to 1876—after the study of Greek tragedy. These texts illustrate the paradigmatic tendencies in Nietzsche's thought whose incipient forms in *The Birth of Tragedy* attract Bersani. In philosophical terms, the primary point of attraction is Nietzsche's resistance to theories of being and becoming whose most authoritative articulation in the nineteenth century, no less than in more recent eras, was provided by Hegel. Looking back at *The Birth of Tragedy* in 1888, Nietzsche disdainfully notes Hegelian accents in his discussion of Greek theater.[84] In all subsequent works, including the untimely meditations, his conceptualizations of redemption are inflected by his critique of the master of German Idealism, an antagonism shared, if implicitly, by Bersani. While the latter's problematization of Hegelianism develops from his reading, initially in *Balzac to Beckett* and *A Future for Astyanax*, of literary texts, psychoanalysis, and Deleuzean philosophy, in his meditations Nietzsche objects to Hegelian influences because he discerns in them a dangerous catalyst of nineteenth-century German culture's ailments, what he calls in *The Birth of Tragedy* the cultivation of the Socratic "theoretical man" at the expense of Hellenic culture's artful, life-affirming naïveté. While, in the first meditation, he calls Hegelian thinkers "the vilest of all the corrupters of German [language],"[85] the objections rest not only on aesthetic grounds. In the second installment, "On the Utility and Liability of History for Life," he asserts that Hegelian influence exacerbates modern Germany's historical illness, the relentlessly backward-looking Zeitgeist inscribed in the nation's educational system:

> I do not believe that there was any dangerous deviation or turn in German cultivation in this century that did not become more dangerous due to the enormous and still spreading influence of this philosophy—Hegelian philosophy. In truth, the belief that one is the lateborn offspring of prior ages is paralyzing and upsetting, but it must seem horrible and destructive when one day, in a brazen inversion, such a belief deifies this lateborn offspring as the true meaning and purpose of all previous historical events, when his knowing wretchedness is identified with the culmination of world history.[86]

Nietzsche objects to the Hegelian conceptualization of history as a dialectical process because in it the past overdetermines that which exists today, immobilizing the present and evacuating it of its inventive potential. Even worse for him is the antiquarian pride that dialectics cultivates in the paralytic wretch that is the Hegelian "now": the assumption that one's existence constitutes the height of history's inevitable development. Such historically oriented human being believes in the redemptive force of "process," that is, of dialectical becoming, in which history unfolds with a teleological certainty, resolving in *Aufhebung*. Quoting from Eduard von Hartmann's *Philosophy of the Unconscious* (1869)—for him, a case study of Hegel's moribund influence—Nietzsche notes that in this thought, exemplified also by Christianity, "it is process alone that can lead to redemption [*zur Erlösung führen kann*]."[87] Like Christianity, dialectics is redemptive (*erlösend*) in that it purports to unravel or solve (*lösen*) what Schopenhauer calls the riddle of the world, *das Welträtsel*; this process provides the "[m]eaning and solution of each and every riddle of becoming [*Sinn und Lösung aller Werde-Rätsel überhaupt*]."[88]

Among other forms of progressivism, Nietzsche's critique can be directed at evolutionary Marxism, whose belief in the inevitability of revolution is later critiqued by Benjamin. This reading points to the Hegelian self-assurance in Marx's vision of communism as "the riddle of history solved," one that "knows itself to be this solution [*Er ist das aufgelöste Rätsel der Geschichte und weiß sich als diese Lösung*]."[89] In this view, the proletarian revolution provides the redemption from and the solution to the varied antagonistic relations (between subjects; between the subject and nature) that riddle modern human beings; such antagonisms are inevitably resolved in the dialectical process. In narrativizing history's forces into the dialectic, evolutionary Marxism belongs to what Nietzsche calls "the cynical canon," where history is written in the imperative case: "[T]hings had to evolve in precisely the way they did, and the human being could not have become any different from human beings today, since it is futile to rebel against this 'must.'"[90] The strict causality of the dialectic allows "no alternative to our present,"[91] no escape from the relentless historical logic of Hegelian *Werden*, a point that Foucault, too, makes in "Nietzsche, Genealogy, History" (1971), his "Dear John" letter to Hegel. Consequently, as Deleuze writes in *Nietzsche and Philosophy* (1962), "the whole of the dialectic moves within the limits of reactive forces," that is, "it evolves entirely within the nihilistic perspective."[92]

But the thought of redemption is not exhausted by the cynicism of the dialectical process: if Nietzsche rejects the world's redemption in the Hegelian Absolute—because here the present becomes an always calculable continuation of the dialectic's unfolding, its "perfectibility"—he also works toward an alternate theory of *Erlösung*, one that would affirm the singular potential of every "now" (*Jetztzeit*). In opposition to the paralyzed mind of the historical being, he posits "the suprahistorical human being, who does not seek salvation in a process, but for whom instead the world is complete and has arrived at its culmination in every individual moment."[93] The suprahistorical being—anti-Hegelian in its abandonment of progress toward the Absolute—can access the redemptive potential of each moment disembedded from dialectical relations. History is cut up into discontinuous moments, whose potentiality is thereby unchained from their subordination to a progressivist narrative.[94]

With its radical ability to jettison history, the suprahistorical being is vulnerable to what Nietzsche calls "nausea" or "disgust" ("*Ekel*").[95] The term *Ekel*, important for subsequent existentialist thought, occurs already in *The Birth of Tragedy*, where it signals the terrifying clarity of Dionysian intoxication. If Apollo is "the god of individuation and of just boundaries," "the rapture of the Dionysian state with its annihilation of the ordinary bounds and limits of existence [*Vernichtung der gewöhnlichen Schranken und Grenzen des Daseins*] contains, while it lasts, a *lethargic* element in which all personal experiences of the past become immersed. This chasm of oblivion separates the worlds of everyday reality and of Dionysian reality. But as soon as this everyday reality re-enters consciousness, it is experienced as such, with nausea [*Ekel*]: an ascetic, will-negating mood is the fruit of these states."[96] The danger in becoming suprahistorical is twofold: either the ungrounded being seeks Christianity's aid for locating meaning—"Christianity was from the beginning, essentially and fundamentally, life's nausea and disgust with life"—or the suprahistorical being becomes a paralyzed, brooding Hamlet, the paradigmatic existentialist: "Conscious of the truth he has once seen man now sees everywhere only the horror or absurdity of existence"; he is engulfed by a "nausea [that] inhibits action."[97]

But if Christianity offers a cure for the Dionysian hangover, in art Nietzsche finds another vehicle for the "discharge of the nausea of absurdity."[98] Whatever he later renounces of his arguments in *The Birth of Tragedy*, the concept of art's metaphysical function remains constant for his project. He restates the argument in the third meditation, dedicated to Schopenhauer. Following Goethe, he writes that philosophy and art have a "metaphysical purpose" for nature; they make accessible that which remains obfuscated "in the tumultuousness of [nature's] own becoming."[99]

Nietzsche continues in an idiom that resonates with the Dionysian language of *The Birth of Tragedy*:

> nature ultimately needs the saint, whose ego has entirely melted away [*das Ich ganz zusammengeschmolzen ist*] and whose life of suffering is no longer—or almost no longer—felt individually, but only as the deepest feeling of equality, communion, and oneness with all living things; the saint, in whom that miracle of transformation occurs that the game of becoming never hits upon, that ultimate and supreme becoming human [*Menschwerdung*] toward which all of nature presses and drives onward for its own salvation [*hindrängt und -treibt, zu ihrer Erlösung von sich selbst*]. There can be no doubt that all of us are related and connected to this saint, just as we are related to the philosopher and the artist. There are moments and, as it were, sparks of the brightest, most ardent fire in whose light we no longer understand the word "I."[100]

Art's redemptive potential is crucially different from that of Christianity (or, as Benjamin will add, evolutionary Marxism): whereas the latter cures nausea with the promise of salvation in a covenanted future, art, exacerbating the Dionysian undoing of the self, provides something of a homeopathic remedy. In this context, the above translation calls for an adjustment. Rather than seeking "its own salvation," nature drives—*hindrängt, hintreibt*—toward redemption *from itself* in art: *zu ihrer Erlösung von sich selbst.* If nature exhibits a "pressing need for redemption [*erlösungsbedürftigen Drange*],"[101] it *undoes itself* in appearance, unbinds the figures that shackle it to its current forms, pushes becoming into a Dionysian frenzy. This is precisely the Dionysian *Erlösung vom "Ich,"* which forces Bersani to complicate his reading of redemption in his discussion of *The Birth of Tragedy*. "In the Nietzschean aesthetic," he writes, ". . . redemption should probably be understood as a kind of release of being rather than as a moral rehabilitation" (*CR* 98).

Bersani doesn't cite the untimely meditations, but let us ventriloquize: Nietzsche's postulation of a redemptive becoming-human (*Menschwerdung*) in art both echoes Baudelaire's aesthetic theory and anticipates the ontological schema of Freudian-Laplanchean psychoanalysis. Bersani describes Nietzschean redemption in language that he gleans from Baudelairean idealization when he writes that "being consists of mobile fusions and correspondences—or, in other terms, that being is not reducible to identities" (*CR* 99). Similarly, in the onto-ethics of both Nietzsche and Laplanche, becoming is understood as the dangerous repetition of an originary shattering (*ébranlement*, *Zerbrechen*). For Nietzsche, *Menschwerdung* is coincident with the undoing—or a collapse, a melting (*zusammenschmelzen*)—of the "I" into a primal unity, but also its rescue from Apollonian forms. He writes *zusammenschmelzen*, not *schmelzen*: the ego disappears, melts, into something like an internal "togetherness" or "oneness," the Dionysian *Ur-Einen* that he discusses in *The Birth of Tragedy*. Its undoing consists of a centripetal movement.[102]

From the Bersanian perspective, Nietzsche's terms for the forces behind *Menschwerdung* invite further analogies with psychoanalytic thought: the individual's undoing moves with something like pressure or drive. But before we identify the Nietzschean *Drang* or *Trieb*, *hindrängen* or *hintreiben*, with what we most immediately understand as the Freudian death drive, we should turn, finally, to the fourth meditation, "Richard Wagner in Bayreuth" (1876). In this text, Nietzsche introduces some crucial distinctions to the redemptive drive. Depending on its constitution, being seeks redemption in either *nothingness* or *difference*. He writes: "Now, only what is natural, not what is unnatural, can ever experience true satisfactions or deliverance [*Erlösungen*]. The only thing left for what is unnatural once it has arrived at consciousness of itself is the yearning for nothingness; by contrast, what is natural desires to be transformed through love. The former does *not* want to be; the latter wants to be *different*."[103] The "natural" here designates a being characterized by its ability to move toward that which is singular, untimely, yet-to-come in the phenomenal world: the existent Nietzsche will call *Übermensch*. That these lines anticipate his later work on the Overman can be gauged in passages from the Schopenhauer meditation that, like the Wagner essay, call "love" the affect characteristic of a being that anticipates the becoming of the *Übermensch*. In the earlier essay, Nietzsche sees the value of education in the extent to which it cultivates in the individual the readiness for a sacrifice not for the common good or the State but for the unique, superior "specimen," which he calls "great, redeeming human beings [*großen erlösenden Menschen*]."[104] He writes: "the goal of any species' evolution is that point at which it reaches its limit and begins the transition to a higher species; its goal is not a large number of specimens and their well-being, nor is it those specimens that are the last to evolve. On the contrary, its goal is precisely those seemingly scattered and random existences that arise here and there under favorable conditions."[105] It is love—in the Wagner essay, the affect of the natural—that orients being to becoming: "only in love does the soul not only gain a clear, analytical, and contemptuous perspective on itself, but also that desire to look beyond itself and to search with all its might for a higher self that lies hidden somewhere."[106] The contemptuous glance at oneself does not annihilate the self so much as seek what is internally different in *das Ich*.

If what Nietzsche calls the "unnatural"—which for him is the numerical majority, the herd—moves with "the will to nothingness,"[107] the "natural" wills difference. Since one of the themes that runs through the four meditations is the critique of Hegel, what Nietzsche here means by difference is something other than that which emerges dialectically, through negation. Neither is it the difference that awaits our re-cognition in the native land of lost origins. Rather, turning back to Baudelaire, we may suggest that Nietzschean onto-aesthetics concerns the kind of difference that fascinates the child in the paternal tableau: even when the gaze that wills difference turns toward something like an origin—the father—what arrests it there is the unraveling of the self into an aesthetic form of what the self will have been.

We find, then, Baudelairean idealization reconfigured in Nietzschean redemption-into-difference: both suggest the undoing of the actualized individual by a horizontal move toward corresponding differences. As Bersani writes apropos Baudelaire's onto-aesthetics, "the ideality of all being . . . is outside all particular being. In aspiring to a state of completeness, creatures . . . reach toward the ultimate difference-from-themselves that is self-effacement" (*CR* 70). As the approximation of the "unique harmony" of *individuel*, idealization constitutes a process in which the individual is pulled apart: it entails a movement of undoing visible forms in their gravitation toward ideality, like the father in Baudelaire's tableau. An individual "corresponds to others not on the basis of similarities or of complementarity but in self-erasure, in *fusion* with others" (*CR* 70). This fusion is what Nietzsche, in *The Birth of Tragedy*, calls Dionysian redemption; for Bersani, this "Dionysian liberation from the fetters of the individual [*die dionysische* Lösung *von den Fesseln des Individuums*]" coincides with Baudelairean idealization.[108]

Laplanche's Undoing

Variously modified, the German term for "redemption" repeats across Nietzsche's oeuvre—*Erlösung*, *Auflösung*, *Ablösung*, and so forth—to the extent that, as one of his translators puts it, the playful aesthetics of Nietzsche's German orients his thought: one "sometimes . . . has the feeling that the potential of the German language for making new words by adding or changing prefixes actually determined the direction of Nietzsche's thought—that the conceit dictated the conception, so to speak."[109] If this is true, the Nietzschean text is composed and de-composed along an associative chain which carries thought into constellations determined not so much by conscious logic as by something like the force of submerged etymological histories: words unravel and recombine like elements in a chemical process; reacting to the presence of other components, they dissolve to form new compounds that re-collect a past that may not ever have been fully actualized.

The relation of language and thought exemplified by Nietzsche's "etymological puns"[110] anticipates the model that emerges as Freud's methodology in *die Traumdeutung*: that of free association. The aim of free association is to decompose conscious thought, its signifying chains, into its constitutive elements, which in isolation fail to signify, to make sense, in the existing frames of logic. That free association enables the disintegration of compounds is suggested by the Greek term for "analysis": *ἀναλύειν*, to undo or loosen. Laplanche often discusses this term, central for psychoanalysis. As he writes, the work of analysis consists of, precisely, such unraveling: "psychoanalysis, along the chains of free association, analyses—that is to say, it breaks down material and reduces it to discrete components."[111] It is a mode of "decomposition": "It ana-lyses, that is, it dissolves"; it is a form of "analytic unbinding."[112] "To interpret in psychoanalysis," he continues, "is first of all to radically dismantle and lay out flat the organization of the manifest 'text.'"[113] In this context, as Laplanche notes, we must also distinguish between psychoanalysis and psychotherapy. While the latter "seeks to rebind, to reassemble, to synthesise," psychoanalysis, working against "the ego's natural tendency toward synthesis," searches for "the means of dissociating, of unbinding [délier] the ties that uphold conscious discourse, our personality (our ego), our symptoms, the ideologies that orient how we tell ourselves our own histories."[114] If this untying (*dé-lier*) of the subject can go as far as precipitating *delirium*, analysis can perhaps be seen as facilitating in the analysand the kind of risky artistic creation that for Poe, Baudelaire, and Nietzsche required states of deliria, where the artist, relinquishing her fascinated attention on what exist, can begin to *see things*.

Laplanche draws our attention to repetition in Freud's work of the same cluster of terms that recurs in Nietzsche's: "Terms formed with *lösen*," he writes, "occur very often in Freud, and are moreover extremely difficult to translate"; time and again we find Freud evoking his clinical practice as the work of "*Lösung*: analysis, solution and resolution, dissolution; a term which unfortunately cannot be translated into French, with all its compounds (*Auflösung, Erlösung, Ablösung* . . .)."[115] *Lösung*, then, emerges as the *very name* for the Freudian methodology, the precise German translation for *ἀναλύειν*: "*Αναλύειν* [analuein] . . . is very exactly *auf/lösen*, to dissolve, to ana/lyse: what it refers to is a resolution which operates by 'going back over' (*auf- ἀνα*), that is by drawing near the elementary or the originary."[116] Laplanche suggests that "'[p]sycho-analysis' could have been named by Freud, if he had not wished to choose a Greek term, *Seelen-Auflösung*: disentangling, dissolution or resolution of souls"; *Lösung* and *Auflösung* give us "the very model of psychoanalysis: unweaving so that a new fabric can be woven, disentangling to allow the formation of new knots."[117] If illness is the undoing of the subject, analysis offers a homeopathic remedy, as Thomas Mann suggests in *The Magic Mountain* (1924): Hans Castorp finds himself in "the dissolute company of the sick [*in ungebundener Krankengesellschaft*]" and witnesses in Berghof "the redemptive effects of analysis [*der erlösenden Wirkung der Analyse*]."[118] If the "unbound" ill—the German term denotes primarily freedom—find redemption in psychoanalytic treatment, it is not that of their re-binding or re-cathexis but, rather, a further, or a different kind of, unraveling.

Bersani's ethical complaint about psychoanalysis is that it is not primarily the "soul"—the psychoanalytic subject—that finds itself unraveling in its encounter with the enigmatic signifier; solicited by the enigma, the subject, rather, undoes the object to locate the secret knowledge about his being that it seems to contain. Is there a way to rethink psychoanalysis beyond this mode of violence that it describes and, as Bersani implies, justifies? In *Caravaggio's Secrets* (1998), Bersani and Dutoit turn, once again, to Proust to exemplify psychoanalytic theory, but also to locate where psychoanalysis—and Proust—exceeds its manifest intentions. In Proust and psychoanalysis, as they write, "[w]e are in a relational system entirely dominated by secrets and knowledge. And what is taken to be a successful unveiling of the secret is in fact the establishment, by the subject, of a new relation to himself" (*CS* 67). Proustian appetition—Marcel's desire to consume the objects he wants—becomes the prototype for the subject's relation to the world that psychoanalysis postulates. Bersani and Dutoit turn to a famous scene in *À la recherche* where Marcel's gaze is arrested by a field of buttercups:

> the buttercups grew past numbering on this spot which they had chosen for their games among the grass, standing singly, in couples, in whole companies, yellow as the yolk of eggs, and glowing with an added lustre, I felt, because, being powerless to consummate with my palate the pleasure which the sight of them never failed to give me, I would let it accumulate as my eyes ranged over their gilded expanse, until it had acquired the strength to create in my mind a fresh example of absolute, unproductive beauty [*jusqu'à ce qu'il devînt assez puissant pour produire de l'inutile beauté*].[119]

The visual pleasure of the flowers immediately evokes consumable matter, egg yolks, which stimulates Marcel's appetite. As Bersani notes in an earlier discussion of this scene, Marcel seeks "the satisfaction, on a non-physical level, of a desire to assimilate" (*MP* 36). The scene constitutes one of the numerous moments where Proust's narrator wants to "'solve' the mystery of otherness by digesting it" (*CS* 68). The riddles of enigmatic signifiers are "solved"—the quotation marks around the term suggest not only its metaphoric function, but also its status as a borrowed concept (from Laplanche)—by their incorporation and digestive dis-solution: they become part of the subject's being, while also producing unmetabolizable waste matter. The passage bespeaks Marcel's "fantasy of knowing by eating" (*MP* 37). In this way, psychoanalysis "perpetuate[s] the myth of a detached subject intent on understanding what is different from it. The reality behind that myth is a sadistic subject intent on preserving its own integrity, its own presumed autonomy, and . . . destroying what is different from it" (*CS* 69). The subject's "sadism" consists of its repetitive undoing of objects, like the actions of a curious child who pulls his toys apart to know what makes them "tick." Elsewhere, Bersani identifies in Dennis Cooper's fiction—with its depictions of the "cold and brutal ripping open of bodies as a means of knowing the other" (*IRG* 34)—a culmination of this mode of desiring otherness, emblematic of Proustian and Laplanchean ontologies.

Can we rethink the subject's relation to the world otherwise than in terms of the unrelenting fascination exerted by signifying enigmas? As Bersani frequently asks, can we conceptualize "a nonsadistic type of movement" (*AI* 147), "a *non*sadistic relation to external reality" (*CS* 69; see also *AI* 6; *TT* 1)? *Masochism* might most immediately suggest a different mode of relatedness. If the subject called into being by the enigmatic signifier is a sadistic one, it is in shattering, of course, that we find a subject masochistically undone; while the sadistic subject dis-solves its object, the masochistic subject of *ébranlement* unravels in the intensities of the outside world. But while in his earlier work—culminating most notably in the essay "Is the Rectum a Grave?" (1987)—Bersani highlights the ethical potential of shattered subjects, by the time of writing *Caravaggio's Secrets* he has come to doubt the ethics of *ébranlement*. Two years after the Dutoit collaboration, he asserts: "Masochism is not a viable alternative to mastery, either practically or theoretically" (*IRG* 110). The masochistic subject remains a psychoanalytically defined being; what Bersani and Dutoit seek in *Caravaggio's Secret* are the outlines of what Bersani will call "the aesthetic subject."

To suggest what this subject might be, we can return to the Baudelairean-Nietzschean onto-ethics/aesthetics of "Boundaries of Time and Being." In this context, the verb "to solve," rather than borrowed from Laplanche, becomes a translation of "*lösen*" in Nietzsche. Proceeding from a new slant, Bersani and Dutoit return to Proust's buttercup scene to tease out a different mode of onto-ethics/aesthetics: "the passage," they write, "proposes a genealogy of art that, for the most part, remains implicit, theoretically unexplored" in Proust's novel, a mode that exceeds or escapes the subject's "appropriative relation to the world" (*CS* 69). Marcel, having compared the flowers to egg yolks, continues: the buttercups are "glowing with an added lustre, I felt, because, being powerless to consummate with my palate the pleasure which the sight of them never failed to give me, I would let it accumulate as my eyes ranged over their golden expanse, until it became potent enough to produce an effect of absolute, purposeless beauty" (the translation is Bersani and Dutoit's). Marcel is unable to consume the flowers, even after the initial metonymic invitation to see them as egg yolks. Instead, they arrest him in an experience of "absolute, purposeless beauty" such as wouldn't appear—such as would be constitutively impossible—in one's seduction by enigmatic signifiers (what remains purposeless in enigmatic summons is repressed). This mode of beauty becomes "a form of connectedness" (*CS* 70) different from that which the enigmatic signifier solicits. What we have in the buttercups passage is not, as it initially seemed, another example of the appeasement of Marcel's ravenous appetite. The subject doesn't "solve" the object by incorporating it. Rather, the movement becomes that of *lösen* in Nietzsche's account of double redemption: of being delivered into the web of correspondences whose movement Apollo had happily, but momentarily, arrested.

As we reconfigure the source of the quoted word, "solve," the "beauty" that Bersani and Dutoit observe in the scene from Proust becomes identical to the "idealization" that Bersani, in "Boundaries of Time and Being," finds developed in Baudelaire and reconfigured in Nietzsche. As much as Baudelairean aesthetics relies on horizontal correspondences, Proust's undeveloped ontological theory postulates beauty as "a mode of relationality, a manifestation of the subject's implication in the world" (*CS* 70). Such links are indicated by Bersani and Dutoit's deployment of terms central to the onto-ethics/aesthetics sketched in Bersani's earlier discussion of Baudelaire and Nietzsche: "Through his pleasure," they write, Marcel "'corresponds' with and to that which is at once different and identical to himself—a segment of the world's appearance" (*CS* 71). "Appearance" here evokes Nietzschean *Erscheinung* (which Walter Kaufman translates as "appearance," but which can also mean a "ghost" or a "specter"), as much as the verb "to correspond," in quotation marks, refers us to Bersani's discussion of Baudelairean *correspondances* in "Boundaries of Time and Being."[120] According to Bersani and Dutoit, then, Proust proposes two modes of art, one that they identify with Laplanche, the other with Baudelaire–Nietzsche: "art as appropriating the secrets of truth and beauty without which the subject is incomplete, and art as the demonstration of an active insertion into the movement of being" (*CS* 72). The first theory assumes a subject fascinated by, and dis-solving, enigmatic signifiers; the other a subject "inserted" into the world through "correspondences," a subject like that of Baudelairean idealization. The latter suggests a mode of *Er/lösung* where being is, as Nietzsche writes, *redeemed into difference*. If we can find this form of redemption in the psychoanalytic account of *Seelen-Auf/Erlösung*, Laplanche's theory of seduction would enable a relational movement that "demolishes the very distinction between subject and object which sustains [Proustian-psychoanalytic] appetite" (*CS* 72).

Despite Bersani's explicit rejection of redemptive ideologies, redemption itself, as a concept, is marked by its self-difference. When the concept, in its majoritarian form—such as we find it, according to Bersani, in Benjamin—is placed in the minoritarian context of Baudelaire's and Nietzsche's aesthetic theories, it dissolves into a new form. The dissolution (*Auflösung*) that redemption denotes consists of two movements. First, it comes to designate the kind of undoing that Bersani approximates with his concept of "shattering." *Erlösung* is the untying of the knot that actualized being constitutes, the being whose emergence antinatalists lament as the bungling of noumenal perfection into the travesty of phenomena.

Second, *Erlösung* marks, in the Baudelairean and Nietzschean context, the reorganization into difference of that which has been shattered. This mode of redemption expresses the conjoined concepts of the psychoanalytic subject and the aesthetic subject. As Bersani writes, "Ideally conducted, analysis can lead to the dissolution of the self—that is, to the loss of the very grounds of self-knowledge. Psychoanalysis could undo the subjectivity necessary to a psychological philosophy of knowledge" (*IRG* 161). Nietzsche suggests that this undoing, this *Auflösung*, becomes a redemption-into-difference: conceptualized thus, "psychoanalytic treatment . . . would be an exercise in the depersonalizing of both analyst and analysand, in the creation of a new, third subjectivity to which no individual name can be attached, a subjectivity in which the two find themselves corresponding—*co-responding*—in the transindividual being which, they have discovered, 'belongs' to neither of them, but which they share. . . . We can call such an exchange an experience of impersonal intimacy" (*IRG* 161–62, emphasis added). Thinking across Nietzsche, Baudelaire, and Laplanche, Bersani redefines the onto-ethics/aesthetics suggested by the concept of shattering. Joining Nietzsche and Baudelaire in "Boundaries of Time and Being," he seeks to rethink *ébranlement* by slowing down the totalizing undoing of figured beings that Nietzsche calls their *Zusammenschmelzung* into the movement of idealization, which for Baudelaire suggests figures' unraveling across horizontal *correspondances*. Freud calls this process that of *Auflösung* (or *Entbindung*) and Laplanche *délier*. Read with Nietzsche and Baudelaire, psychoanalysis can become redemptive (*erlösend*) in the sense that it facilitates "depersonalization," that is, the release of the tension that holds the subject in place, and, at the same time, teaches subjects to move toward one another, as if (co)responding to a joint *summons* in which they recognize the echoes of a shared, impersonal *Stimmung*.

4

Simultaneity and Sociability

Benjamin–Beckett–Simmel

The tradition of Western thought has frequently—perhaps, unfailingly—described the processes of becoming, including those of anthropogenesis, in terms of *calls*, calls whose implications, in turn, become foundational for these philosophies' ethical imaginations. In Christianity, God's calling constitutes an irrevocable event, one for the believer to heed unwaveringly: each should "abide in that calling wherein he was called [*Jeder bleibe in der Berufung, in der er berufen wurde*]" (1 Cor. 7.20). Martin Luther—whose Reformation many consider to have precipitated Western modernity—affirms Paul's advice to the Corinthians, embracing the idea of a singular, unchangeable vocation (*Berufung*) in which each person is summoned to a particular office.[1] In Luther, "man is ultimately a hearer, someone who is seized, claimed, and subject to judgement, and . . . for this reason his existential being depends upon which word reaches and touches his inmost being."[2] If Luther forged *Berufung* into the central concept of his revolution, Martin Heidegger, beginning with the early drafts of *Being and Time*, engaged his namesake's theology to think the calling in which Dasein finds its orientation toward authenticity. Yet there will be no prizes for guessing, not for a contemporary reader, that the story immediately goes awry, that the Christian (or Dasein) loses her way even before she sets upon the narrow road to godliness and authenticity. Pointing to the symptomatic collapse, in the Protestant discourse of "vocation," of the distinction between *Beruf* and *Berufung*, Max Weber found in the call for inwardness, as the subject's inexpressible, incalculable intimacy with God, a ruse for the production and maintenance of industrial modernity's docile workforce.[3] A somewhat less appreciated thinker, one of Weber's contemporaries claimed that the call that turns the temporal stasis of beastly being into the out-of-jointness of human becoming—as the anthropocentric narrative goes—is also, always, a deadly deception, too efficiently distracting the hominizing subject from the present moment, the "now" of survival. Edgar Rice Burroughs suggests in *Tarzan of the Apes* (1912) that the dead father's books, beguiling the ape-boy from the natural "vocations" of his adoptive mother's tribe, do not constitute in any unproblematic way the redemptive solicitation of which Luther spoke (and to which, about a decade after Burroughs, Heidegger would return). They become, more ominously, the son's "fascinating avocation."[4] Reaching Tarzan, the call to become one's authentic, human self is parasited by the prefix *a-*, which morphs one's "vocation" (from the Latin *vox* and *vocare*) into a "distraction" that, as the *Oxford English Dictionary* puts it, "has the effect of calling away or withdrawing one from an occupation." Simultaneously the call to become-human is turned into the deadly seduction of an evil eye (*fascinum*) with which serpents are said to paralyze their prey before devouring them alive. In a characteristically tragic outcome, the lure of learning will lead the hominizing, civilizing subject to miss the mark (*hamartanein*) of human potential and become, as Burroughs knowingly puts it, a "queer animal."[5] This queered being—the term's contemporary sense emerges in the last quarter of the nineteenth century in the interlinked discourses of racial sciences and sexology—is embodied in *Tarzan of the Apes* in the tragicomedy of two overcivilized, degenerate male subjects, psychotically out of joint with the urgent reality of the moment, absent-mindedly straying into the jaws of death on a West African beach.[6] While the novel allegorizes in Tarzan's character Western civilization's rescue from this queer passivity and self-absenting, his education, as a calling-away, is contaminated from the start by the demonic forces that mark the concept of "fascination."[7] *Tarzan of the Apes* suggests that if "[t]he philosophical and religious texts of the European tradition know only a world that follows a call, a world called forth and called on to do something, in which everything has a vocation and everything is addressed as that which it is,"[8] such summonses are indistinguishable from deadly fascinations where the processes of becoming are led astray, corrupted, queered.

We find variations of such aporetic accounts of calling in Jean Laplanche and Samuel Beckett. In Laplanche, the call takes the form of the enigmatic signifier, the mysterious message that awakens the infant from its saturable state, summoning it to desire. With Jean-Bertrand Pontalis, he writes of the child's stirring into *response-ability* by parental solicitations: "hearing, when it occurs, breaks the continuity of an undifferentiated perceptual field and at the same time is a sign (the noise waited for and heard in the night) which puts the subject in the position of having to answer to something."[9] The anthropogenetic seduction to sexuality takes place as the fascinated infant begins translating the other's enigmatic dispatches. The work of translation implants a "foreign body" in the child, one that, obscure like cultural myths of origins, demands to be re-called and endlessly interpreted. In this way, the process of translating the untranslatable—the infant's unyielding fascination with the ventriloquized messages—constitutes the human "'vocation.'"[10] With the quotation marks, Laplanche signals that his onto-ethics borrows from and revises the tradition of the anthropogenetic ethics that stretches at least to the rethinking of the "individual" during the Lutheran Reformation. For Laplanche, anthropogenesis amounts to the sexualization of the child: it constitutes a going-astray or swerving (*fourvoiement*) from the infant's prior occupation with need. More accurately, then, the work of translation is not a *vocation* but—like Tarzan's efforts to decipher the writing in the primers left behind by his human parents—an *avocation*, a distractive, secondary call that produces the human subject by seducing him away from his "proper" (but, as psychoanalysis tells us, inaccessible) occupations, those concerning the vital function (Laplanche) and the exigencies of life (Freud). In Laplanche, as in numerous other Western philosophical systems, *work hominizes*: the calls from the enigmatic other *occupy* the subject, who attunes to their frequencies; this occupation—this labor—is synonymous with the subject's constitution.[11]

We are by now familiar with the issues Leo Bersani has with this account. He considers psychoanalytic ontology one of our culture's most authoritative—if productively muddled—narratives prioritizing the subject's grounding in epistemophilia. The Freudian text (and its literary counterpart, the Proustian narrative) constitutes something of a user's manual for extant ways of desiring. As Laplanche shows, the psychoanalytic subject becomes-human as it follows the call that promises to reveal the secret knowledge behind the other's enigma. If anthropogenesis coincides with the infant's seduction into sexuality, in this model we become-human in our search for knowledge. Bersani suggests that psychoanalysis ventriloquizes typically Enlightenment conceptualizations: he borrows from Michel Foucault the phrase "the Cartesian moment" to indicate the historical turn that for him consolidated the epistemophilially oriented being in Enlightenment modernity. By this he means the shift from the practices of *epimeleia heautou*, the care of the self, to a regime where subjectivity was defined in its relation to knowledge. The Cartesian moment designates "the moment when knowledge and knowledge alone—in detriment of spirituality [e.g., the care of the self]—became the subject's path to truth" (*IRG* 154).[12]

While Bersani recurrently returns to Freud, Laplanche, and Proust—suggesting that their potentiality may not have been exhausted—he also searches for other sources with which to explore other ways of being in the world. He comments in 2003: "[I]t is doubtful that psychoanalysis can help us to define an other order of pleasure. How, then, might we best approach the mode of being that makes that pleasure available to us?" (*IRG* 65). Attempting to deprivilege what has become his signature concept—that of psychic shattering in the intensities of the sexual—he seeks something that would take us "'beyond [the] *jouissance*'" of *ébranlement* (*IRG* 65). He locates this "beyond" of sexuality, psychoanalytically conceived, in *the aesthetic*: from the experimentation with the psychoanalytic subject we move to "the cultivation of the aesthetic subject" (*IRG* 66).[13]

Although the connection is never rendered explicit in his work, Bersani finds in Beckett an account of becoming-human—of what we will call the *(a)vocative ethics* of hominization—that allows him to rethink Laplanche's theory of anthropogenetic going-astray. It is not difficult to discern similarities between the Laplanchean subject, who emerges as a response to the other's mysterious call, and the tortured narrative consciousnesses of the Beckettian text. The latter frequently surface as the speakers, recipients, or echoers of the calls and solicitations that break being's solitude and silence (most famously, the voices of the "they" that invade and stir the Unnamable to discourse).[14] Similarly, as much as Laplanche considers the labor of solving the other's messages the human (a)vocation, Beckett, in an early theoretical statement, describes artistic creation in terms of the artist's "expressive vocation."[15] Like the Unnamable's efforts at silence, this calling is one that seeks its own extirpation in an "impoverished" art, an art that would be "too proud for the farce of giving and receiving." Later exemplars of narrative consciousness such as the Unnamable illustrate this work in which, as Beckett continues, responding to the call should be to fail "as no other dare fail," to seek the silence unbroken by intrusive solicitations.[16]

What Bersani finds in Beckett, then, is an alternative to Laplanche's theory of the human subject's seduction onto its path of becoming: because "each of us is made into a human subject—socialized—by the voices we hear" (*AI* 62), it is important, "[i]f we want to change the nature of our community, . . . to rethink our originary call into it—how human organisms are made into human subjects" (*IRG* 176). As Bersani and Dutoit put it, we need to move beyond "the narrow environment that first called us into the world" (*CS* 64). What Bersani calls the transition from the psychoanalytic subject to the aesthetic subject concerns this effort to think of other ways of becoming-human and of our consequent being-there.

Our task here is to chart this shift, which becomes exceptionally visible between "Boundaries of Time and Being"—the third chapter of *The Culture of Redemption* (1990)—and "Inhibited Reading," the opening chapter, on Beckett, of the Dutoit collaboration *Arts of Impoverishment: Beckett, Rothko, Resnais* (1993). However brief, Bersani's engagement with Walter Benjamin's philosophy in "Boundaries of Time and Being"—which we explored in the previous chapter—pushes him to render explicit the transition. Monadology offers both Benjamin and Bersani ways to conceptualize becoming unmoored from the modes of causality and teleology whose most influential formulations they find in Hegelian philosophy. Benjamin's concept of "now-time" emerges from Nietzsche's early work, which also informs Bersani's speculations about the time of the *at once* in *The Culture of Redemption* and *Arts of Impoverishment*.[17] Both concepts are spoken in Leibnizian idiom: from the early 1920s on, the monad becomes Benjamin's recurrent figure for *Jetztzeit*, for the dialectical image at a standstill; the Leibnizian concept similarly inflects Bersani's early commentaries on Proust and Deleuze, culminating in the analysis of Beckett in "Inhibited Reading." As much as Benjamin seeks to think history otherwise than through the steady narratives of progress that he discerns framing nineteenth-century positivism, Bersani wants to disrupt the teleological trajectories of *wanting being* that he, from *A Future for Astyanax* onward, locates in our culture's most authoritative theories of desire. In their rejection of conceptualizations of becoming whose most prominent occasion takes place in Hegel, they proceed in analogous trajectories. As previous chapters have suggested, Bersani's early work can be read as a series of investigations into literary and visual-art experimentations with "singularity" and "discontinuity," that is, with unrepeatable newness. Benjamin similarly seeks to excavate "the absolute novelty borne by each moment," novelty that the dialectic would harness within its teleology.[18] Bersani shares Benjamin's opposition to conceptualizations of history that, as Foucault writes in his manifesto of Nietzschean historiography, "dissolv[e] the singular event into an ideal continuity"; instead, both thinkers insist on "the singularity of events outside any monotonous finality."[19] This singularity is articulated in both Bersani and Benjamin in Leibnizian language.

The shift in emphasis in Bersani's work that takes place between "Boundaries of Time and Being" and "Inhibited Reading" pivots on the question of *time*. Bersani renders explicit the move from the psychoanalytic to the aesthetic subject when he discovers the proximity between, if not the overlap of, the temporal mode in which he thinks *ébranlement*—we will call it the time of the *at once*—and the monadic time of simultaneity that Benjamin's messianic historiography seeks. The temporal (near-)coincidence with messianism draws out new aspects of Bersani's onto-ethics/aesthetics. Ever since "Is the Rectum a Grave?" (1987), we have been familiar with the ethics of *shattering* in his work: the undoing of the imperious ego in the radical passivity of ecstatic jouissance. In his later texts, it is a form of connectedness that can be called *chattering*, however, that emerges as an ethical mode *par excellence*. If Benjamin, in his early exegesis of Genesis, calls the bourgeois subject of modernity "the prattling man, the sinner [*der geschwätzige Mensch, der Sündige*],"[20] Bersani becomes increasingly interested in the curiously appealing emptiness of "talk" as a practice in what he will call, echoing Georg Simmel, "sociability." "Sociability" demands the kind of centripetal impoverishment that we saw outlined in *Balzac to Beckett: Center and Circumference in French Fiction* (1970). It is, again, Beckett who provides the best examples. The comedy of his texts consists of the kind of impoverished sociability where, in the absence of psychological individuals, we have the likes of Estragon and Vladimir "blathering about nothing in particular."[21] This movement of "leastening," of the subject's unplugging from the social circuits that have constituted her, is also theorized by Simmel in his early twentieth-century work.

Having spent the previous chapter with "Boundaries of Time and Being," we begin by exploring "Inhibited Reading," where Bersani and Dutoit's analysis proceeds as an account of Beckett's trial-and-error experimentations with monadology. We will then return to *The Culture of Redemption*'s chapter on Benjamin, Baudelaire, and Nietzsche to detail the shift in emphasis that occurs between the 1990 and 1993 texts. On the way we'll briefly dip into two larger philosophical contexts that Bersani's work brushes against: one, the philosophy of "appearance" from Plato to Nietzsche; the other, Kabbalistic theology. Despite these rather ambitious tangents, the main objective of this chapter is to follow Bersani as he proceeds from "shattering" to "chattering," from psychoanalysis to the aesthetic. We propose that this reconfiguration, as it happens in "Inhibited Reading" (but also, if less obviously, in "Boundaries of Time and Being"), reveals an allergic reaction of sorts that Bersani has to Benjaminian philosophy. Some of his earlier formulations now seem too close to Benjamin's, who also deploys Leibnizian categories to think history and becoming. Echoing his neglect to note the references to Leibniz in Laplanchean psychoanalysis—where monadic thought always designates the "idealist aporia" in Western philosophy's ipsocentrism[22]—Bersani refuses to observe Benjamin's habit of couching his redemptive philosophy in Leibnizian terminology. If Laplanche's programmatic rejection of monadology—we can speculate—irritates Bersani enough for him to continue elaborating monadism as a virtual resource for rethinking psychoanalysis, Benjamin's *embrace* of Leibniz nudges him in the opposite direction: to betray his earlier propositions spoken in Leibnizian language, and, in the process, to lay increasing emphasis on what he will call "the aesthetic subject." Since we are focused here not on doing justice to Benjamin, but on detailing the turning point that the encounter with his philosophy constitutes for Bersani's thought, we largely adopt, in what follows, the tone that marks Bersani's reading of Benjaminian thought. Yet our remaining with Benjamin over two chapters should indicate that the issue of possible overlaps between his and Bersani's philosophies remains an open question.

Time of the Aesthetic

Even if its repeated collapse or undoing is "the constitutive sign of psychoanalytic thinking" (*FrB* 9)—a sign that indicates the "speculative" nature of Freud's thought—it is in Beckett that Bersani identifies more productive and far-reaching experimentations with the onto-ethics/aesthetics of failure. "Perhaps the most serious reproach we can make against Samuel Beckett," he and Dutoit open their discussion in *Arts of Impoverishment*, "is that he has failed to fail" (*AI* 11). To speak of Beckett is to account for "the forms [failure] takes throughout his work" (*AI* 11), forms that, Bersani and Dutoit indicate, constitute Beckett's monadology. Beckettian "forms of failure" are strictly synonymous with what Bersani and Dutoit in the title of a subsequent book will call "forms of being." If ontology is an aesthetics, Beckettian ethics concerns the *figuration* of being in beings, driven by the force of individuation that, while an irresistible solicitation, constitutes an ethical failure to remain *untraceable*, that is, still with being, with what Beckett, in his first published short story, calls its "terrifying silent immobility."[23] Bersani proposes that the drawing of individuating boundaries must be thought of as "a metaphysical error or crime" (*AI* 140). This antinatalist position is the philosophical counterpart to Beckett's onto-ethics/aesthetics of impoverishment, whose voice we listen to in the "feeble murmur seeming to apologize for not being dead," "this long sin against the silence that enfolds us."[24]

Like antinatalists, Beckett experiments with "[t]he prospect of an essential being prior to, and removed from, the conditions of all realized being" (*AI* 49). This formulation evinces Bersani's early engagement with Gilles Deleuze and Maurice Blanchot: "essential being" names the synthesis of, on the one hand, the monadic virtuality that Deleuze finds in Proust and, on the other, Blanchot's "essential solitude," the solitude that, as "the pre-conceptual singularity of being,"[25] is not the result of a withdrawal from relations but, "prelinguistic[ally]," precedes "the relational status of grammatical identities" (*AI* 51). This is, for example, Sula's solitude, "a loneliness so profound the word itself had no meaning. For loneliness assumed the absence of other people, and the solitude she found in that desperate terrain had never admitted the possibility of other people."[26]

Put in Leibniz's terms, especially those highlighted in Bertrand Russell's turn-of-the-century study, essential solitude is monadic insofar as the monad is a subject in which all possible predicates are enveloped. This is the being that, as Bersani writes in an early review article, Beckett's 1950s fiction aims at: "to get rid of all the things 'that stick out' from some mysterious core of being—everything from bodily protuberances to fictional characters and anecdotes and, finally, verbal inventiveness itself."[27] While Blanchot develops the concept of "essential solitude" most extensively in *The Space of Literature*, its early formulations take place already in his engagement with *The Unnamable* in *The Book to Come*.[28] Like Beckett's, Blanchot's onto-ethics/aesthetics is marked by being's "refusal to come into the world."[29] In this, it repeats the Unnamable's quest for "a self that has somehow succeeded in failing to live and has thus saved itself from being dissipated and betrayed by expression" (*AI* 50), an unlived or unfigured being for which the nonrelational, nonextended monad provides a ready trope.

The Unnamable, Beckett's narrative consciousness, aims at the monadic core of being, the silence that expression betrays. The singularity of the monad as the nonrelational individual "dissipates" in networks where identities are carved out dialectically. One of the names Bersani gives to such relational entities is *personality*: "Personality," he writes in a discussion of D. H. Lawrence, "is the trap in which the individual gets lost. It is the sign of the self's inability to remain alone, an alluring invitation to self-destroying fusions" (*FA* 174). The monadic "individual" is seduced—(al)lured—from its isolation into a relationship that adulterates its singularity. We can gloss this psychoanalytically: "lure" is the term with which Jacques Lacan designates *the immobilizing fascinations of the imaginary*, the constitution of the infant's ego through the narcissistic misrecognition of the self and the other.[30] While Lacan most famously figures such imaginary entrapments in terms of the subject's visual identification with gestalt apparitions—the mirror stage being the primary example—etymologically the "lure" also denotes an auditory seduction, "[t]he cry of a falconer recalling his hawk" (*OED*); and Lacan in an early seminar delineates the process as the fledgling's acceptance of a call that pulls it to the human realm: "it is when the call [*l'appel*] is made that dependency relations establish themselves in the subject."[31] It is through a similar solicitation that, according to Laplanche, the infant becomes-human, that is, a subject of the unconscious: the puzzling messages (vocal or haptic) with which the caretaker unknowingly addresses the small animal to seduce the latter onto the trail of desire. Following their call, the child goes astray from the straight path indicated by the "vital function"—that is, need—and becomes perversely driven after what Laplanche names the irresolvable enigma of desire. For Beckett, this is a failure of monadic solitude: "they'll have said who I am," laments the Unnamable, "and I'll have heard."[32]

While the Unnamable bravely refuses all such solicitations, this model of resistance, as Bersani and Dutoit continue, is plagued by a paradox: the Unnamable's attempts to thwart figuration are marked by "the anomaly of that resistance taking place in a language whose very use signifies the defeat of any such resistance" (*AI* 50). The blankness or muteness of being can be indexed only in the ink that blights the page, the words that break the silence. If *The Unnamable* constitutes a catalogue of repeated bids at reaching the stillness or silence of a perfectly failed being, the work itself amounts to a record of failed attempts to complete the movement to fail. The drive to fail—to reach "the peace of a sameness from which the individuating event has all but disappeared, the peace of the undifferentiated" (*AI* 139)—leaves in its wake figures that comprise both the crime and its evidence. However swift the annihilation, it always comes too late to undo the mistakenly individuated being; attempts to reach pure nonbeing coincide with solitude's failure. As the Unnamable puts it, "The search for the means to put an end to things, an end to speech, is what enables the discourse to continue."[33]

Bersani and Dutoit speak of this irresolvable paradox in the Unnamable's onto-ethics in *temporal* terms: "To articulate th[e essential, prelinguistic] self," they observe, "would be to dissipate it *at once*; it is not slowly eroded by relational impurities, but is cataclysmically annihilated by the very beginning of articulation" (*AI* 51, emphasis in original). "*At once*": the predication of the (essentially) solitary being coincides, in an intensive moment of simultaneity, with the monad's abolition in expression. It is at this moment that the reading of Beckett in *Arts of Impoverishment* echoes with some precision Bersani's earlier commentary in "Boundaries of Time and Being." Apart from "Inhibited Reading," the phrase *at once*—italics and all—appears in the third chapter of *The Culture of Redemption*: an endnote appended to the discussion of Baudelairean aesthetics anticipates Bersani and Dutoit's depiction of the temporality of the Unnamable's "cataclysmic" failure. Finding in Baudelaire's account of "idealization" echoes of what psychoanalysis would name the self's "narcissistic jouissance" (*CR* 74), Bersani, digressing into the endnote, writes that "in primary narcissism ego boundaries are *at once* constituted, 'cathected,' and exploded" (*CR* 220n29, emphasis in original). The undoing of Beckett's nonrelational monad takes place in the same intensive *Augenblick* of *at once* as that in which the egoic boundaries are drawn and erased in primary narcissism. Beckett's monad, in its immediate failure, is a rearticulation of Freud's theory of primary narcissism, "the simultaneous constitution and shattering of ego boundaries" in *ébranlement* (*CR* 73).

Across "Boundaries of Time and Being" and "Inhibited Reading," Bersani proposes a series of convergences: the *at once* of the unnamable being's predication-and-undoing returns us to the theory of shattering, which itself rephrases—recategorizes—Baudelaire's theory of aesthetics. Describing the latter "in Freudian terms," Bersani writes: "The external stimuli that gravely, and erotically, 'shake' us are those that reactivate—faster than they can be mastered—memory traces of other stimuli. The nonself in which a particular self seeks ecstatically to be obliterated is the internally inscribed history of the self's relations with the world" (*CR* 74). The reference to our overwhelming by stimuli evokes the lesson of originary masochism, which Laplanche—whose term "*ébranler*" is here translated as "to 'shake'"—draws from Freud's account of ego constitution. The subject later seeks to relive this constitutive jouissance, the ecstatic scattering into the world that precipitates becoming-human. Bersani proposes we read these Freudian speculations, made explicit by Laplanche, as versions of Baudelaire's account of art's capacity to *re-call*—summon to actuality—potentialities whose forgetting, or remaining virtual, has been the price for figuration's possibility. The calling of the "particular self" by the "nonself" initiates a horizontal gliding: the actualized self's defiguration consists of its movement toward family resemblances, indicating what the self may (have) become. Art shakes loose the lines that have immobilized the model. As Baudelaire and Nietzsche indicate, the speed of the process is such that, rather than masterfully calculated, it must be driven by an intuition that drunkenness or *naïveté* facilitates.

Immediately before *The Culture of Redemption* and *Arts of Impoverishment*, Bersani had elaborated this onto-ethics/aesthetics in *The Freudian Body: Psychoanalysis and Art* (1986). There he proposes that Freud's speculations are important not so much for what they say as for the performance of their repeated stumbling into incoherence. It is in this movement of "theoretical collapse"—where "arguments are *at once* elaborated and disformulated" (*CR* 3, emphasis added),[34] "*at once* elaborated and subverted" (*FrB* 64, emphasis added)—that we find the psychoanalytic specificity of the Freudian text.[35] Bersani implies that Freud's theoretizations obey the "law of theoretico-genesis," Laplanche's analogue of Ernst Haeckel's law of recapitulation. In their impossibility, Freud's arguments repeat the disorientation of the human subject at its catastrophic emergence. Freud cannot but contract the compulsions of hominization—"it is impossible to describe this process without being implicated in it" (*FrB* 65)—where the human is constituted in its undoing. It is this ready volatility, marked by the time of the *at once*, that renders psychoanalytic theorizing an example of *aesthetics*. A work of art, or one that evinces an "estheticizing movement" (*FrB* 11), replicates, and thereby reminds us of, the unspeakable jouissance that the infant survives by finding masochistic pleasure in the intensities of the self's undoing. Art lures us with this disorienting excitement, which is supposed to have rendered us monads, that is, cut us off from all others and, simultaneously, placed us, in pieces, in the world. We come into being as we are shattered by our unbearable encounter with that which we are to separate ourselves from. The two movements are strictly simultaneous: our shattering is our becoming; the *at once* marks the ontology of becoming-human.[36]

Benjamin has a term for the continuity that the *at once* challenges: he calls it "empty time," by which he means the time of Enlightenment "perfectibility" or that of dialectical teleology. In "empty time," history drones on, the emergent emptied out of all potential for surprise of newness. Benjamin contests the spatialization of time in chronology by adopting the time of an intensive, monadic Now, in his efforts to fuse Jewish messianism and dialectical materialism. Despite the monadological frame of his own work, Bersani leaves unnoted the fact that Leibnizian metaphysics provides the solder for the operation. Leibniz's concept of the monad helps Benjamin elaborate the idiosyncratic synthesis that is his philosophy; but monadology's ready appropriability to his uses has some important ramifications for the emphases in Bersani's work.

Monadic Time

Whatever Nietzsche came to repudiate in *The Birth of Tragedy*, his later understanding of history resonates with his reading of the Apollonian and Dionysian onto-aesthetics of Greek tragedy. He proposes we see the Apollonian moment as the necessary "demotion" or "de-potentializing" (*Depotenzieren*) of being's infinite density in (and by) "mere appearance" (*Schein*).[37] Apollo "redeems" being from its Dionysian "overfullness" by cutting into it with figures. Being drawn, such figures necessarily prevent the actualization of others and, hence, determine future possibilities of representation. In this way, figuration initiates historical causality, whose promotion into the iron law of the dialectic by Hegelian philosophy Nietzsche abhorred as a symptom of European modernity's slavishness. He sought the shedding of the Apollonian chains that his contemporaries had consented to wearing as the price for their redemption from history's unpredictability, its Dionysian potential. What was needed, according to him, was another redemption, this time a Dionysian one, one that would release the present moment from its overdetermination by the dialectic.

Like Foucault after him, Benjamin, in his political philosophy, took his cues from Nietzsche's efforts to release history from its Hegelian bondage, particularly as it concerned the elimination of the potential of *Jetztzeit*.[38] He wanted to resuscitate the maligned now-time, to rescue its singularity from being dissolved in Hegelian-progressivist thought. He refused classical Marxism's understanding of history as a chain of inevitability that would, with dialectical certainty, lead to the covenanted future of a proletarian society.[39] Instead, his ambition was to arrive at "a historical materialism which has annihilated within itself the idea of progress," one whose "founding concept is not progress but actualization."[40] To reconfigure historical materialism, he conceptualized the present as a minefield whose hidden treasures, if stumbled upon, would decimate all maps of the past, all plans for the future. As he writes, that which is hidden in plain sight in the present can "blast open the continuum of history," undo the designs in which we have confined the actualization of that which inheres in the past.[41] Because, at the monad's detonation, the shrapnel's trajectories cannot be calculated, now-time is "not a transition," not a moment in historical chronology, but a "small gateway in time through which Messiah might enter."[42] Influenced by Jewish mysticism—and, in part, Lutheran theology[43]—Benjamin understood the resuscitation of now-time's potential in terms of parousia, the messianic arrival that renders all history, at once, accessible.

Benjamin often elaborated his history of philosophy, as a fusion of historical materialism and Jewish messianism, in the idiom of Leibniz's metaphysics—a tendency to which Bersani remains curiously blind. Leibnizianism uncannily marks his earliest texts—uncannily because, if biographical sources are to be trusted, these were written before his actual encounter with Leibniz's philosophy. Monadology enters his sphere of influence in the late 1910s and early 1920s, via Hermann Cohen's and Heinz Heimsoeth's work.[44] The monad is mentioned in a published text for the first time in "The Concept of Criticism in German Romanticism" (1920 [1919]); in the preface to his *Habilitationsschrift* on the German tragic drama (1928 [1924–25]) he includes a brief but crucial commentary on monadology.[45] From this moment on, the monad, as Paula Schwebel writes, comes to function as "the unique and total expression of his main philosophical point."[46] In such posthumously published works as "On the Concept of History" and the *Arcades* fragments, Leibnizian metaphysics provides Benjamin an idiom in which to couch his messianic-materialist philosophy of becoming. Rolf Tiedemann writes that the "early notion of a monadological truth [as articulated in the *Trauerspiel* study] . . . presides at every phase of the *Passagen-Werk* and remains valid even in the theses 'On the Concept of History.'"[47]

Even though Benjamin had not encountered Leibniz's philosophy at the time, we can hear anticipatory echoes, reverberating with his future work, in the early, posthumously published essay "On Language as Such and on the Language of Man" (1916). In this text, he offers his reading of Genesis, according to which language as we experience it is a weak echo of Adam's capacity to name things with an intensive precision. The loss of Eden "marks the birth of the *human word*, in which name no longer lives intact."[48] The Adamic name "wither[s]" after the fall—like art's "aura" has "wither[ed]" with the intrusion of modern technologies, like genuine experience (*Erfahrung*) "atroph[ies]" in industrial modernity.[49] In withered expression, "the word has an accidental relation to its object": "it is a sign for the things (or knowledge of them) agreed by some convention." Benjamin identifies such fallen forms of naming with "the bourgeois conception of language."[50] The appearance of nineteenth-century political terminology in biblical exegesis may jar, but by calling postlapsarian language "bourgeois," Benjamin ties the narrative he finds in Genesis to his theory of modernity. The French Revolution recapitulates the diasporic moment; the fall into time is replayed in the undoing of the *ancien régime*; Adamic language degenerates into the "prattle [*Geschwätz*]" of bourgeois expression.[51] Language in the bourgeois world obeys—to use the term anachronistically—the law of *différance*, while in Adamic expression names hit the mark, coinciding with things' singularity.[52]

What Benjamin calls Adamic language can be conceptualized monadically: proper names, fully coinciding with that which they designate, imply a Leibnizian ontology. As Daniel Tiffany observes, the concept of the name in the early essay should be proleptically understood as "the verbal counterpart of the monad."[53] Like the grammatical subject of the monad, Adamic names leave behind no residue of contingent predicates; everything is enveloped in names' being, while each being is seamlessly connected to every other. While Benjamin's trajectory would warrant a more detailed account than can be provided here, what remains crucial to note is the fact that Leibnizian monadology helps him in his joint elaboration of messianism and historical materialism, particularly as a critique of progressivist conceptualizations of history. From the early 1920s until such late texts as "On the Concept of History" and the *Arcades* fragments, the concept of the monad recurs in his efforts to endow materialist historiography with unforeseeability and newness. *Jetztzeit* names the potential for a messianic moment in which history, or being, becomes accessible in its entirety, in which the future is not restrained by the causality whose logic Hegelian dialectics rendered hegemonic for European historiography. The task of historical materialism, Benjamin writes, is "to discover in the analysis of the small individual moment the crystal of the total event."[54] The historian looks in the world's ephemera for artifacts that—like Nietzsche's music—have not been drained of their potential to re-sonate with history in new, unexpected ways. When disembedded from their surroundings, such objects or moments are revealed to contain much more than that which a given historical frame has rendered visible. Indeed, the monad, as crystallized now-time, "comprises the entire history of mankind in a tremendous abbreviation."[55] The monad makes the totality of the past, in infinite density, available to the materialist historian. The task of the historian is to precipitate the repetition of this moment, "a messianic arrest of happening" by locating events or artifacts that contain the past in monadic contraction.[56] The messiah is biding his time in the modern world's ruins.

Having adopted the idea that becoming-human begins in the shattering of primary narcissism from Freud and Laplanche, and then elaborated its implications with the likes of Nietzsche, Baudelaire, and Beckett, Bersani's speculative ontology enters, in "Boundaries of Time and Being," the proximity of a tradition, embraced by Benjamin, that stretches to the Kabbalah.[57] Indeed, some of Bersani's sources circulate varied versions of the creation myths of this tradition. In the 1888 preface to *The Birth of Tragedy*, Nietzsche, for example, alludes to the "de-potentializing" of being in Apollonian figuration as the work of the artist-god, who, in creating, releases himself from "*overfullness*" and "the *affliction* of the contradictions compressed in his soul."[58] In an editor's footnote, Walter Kaufman suggests that the allusion here is to a section from Heinrich Heine's "Schöpfungslieder" (1844) where the call to creation undoes the unrelieved sameness of God's solitude.[59] God explains his reasons for creating the world:

> "I'm willing to confess it:
> I felt the call [*Beruf*] within me. Yes, it
> Burned through my soul like a thrusting blade.
>
> "A sickness is surely the basic ground
> On which creative drive has depended;
> Creating, I could be healed and mended,
> Creating, I could be well and sound."[60]

Solitary and all-encompassing, God is a being of indifferent oneness. Precipitated by the sickness of monadic intensity, he responds to an internal call (*Beruf*) that unravels his infinitely contracted being. Creation originates in divine calling, felt as a pressure (*Drang*), where, as in the Kabbalistic myth, difference enters the world when the sameness of being is cut into or exploded. Evoking Heine, Nietzsche suggests we read this as a myth of aesthetic ontology: the aesthetic is the moment of being's redemption from the "*affliction*" of Dionysian sameness. God becomes something of a cutter, releasing the unbearable tension of his crazed, overcrowded mind by carving figures into his flesh.

Importantly for us, Freud, too, turns to the last two stanzas of "Schöpfungslieder" in addressing the problem of primary narcissism. Discussing the infant's originary lack of object cathexes in "On Narcissism: An Introduction" (1914), he imagines the baby's departure from primary narcissism in terms of "the psychogenesis of the Creation" as described by Heine.[61] He asks why the libido ever attaches to others rather than remain confined in the undifferentiated universe of primary narcissism: "[T]his necessity," he answers, "arises when the cathexis of the ego with libido exceeds a certain amount. A strong egoism is a protection against falling ill, but in the last resort we must begin to love in order not to fall ill, and we are bound to fall ill if, in consequence of frustration, we are unable to love."[62] As in Heine, self-referential completeness must be broken in order for being not to fall ill. Freud calls the orientation toward otherness "love." In a moment that Laplanche—for whom the theory of primary narcissism is nonsensical since it cannot account for the eventual genesis of relations—would deem an echo of Western thought's idealist delusions, Freud suggests with Heine that primary narcissism is broken not by the discovery but by the *creation* of otherness. As the unfolding of primary narcissism into relationality, "love" is the mechanism in which the other is created, much like the Apollonian artist undoes "overfullness" by destroying being's sameness in figuration.

To Fail Better

The Culture of Redemption culminates in its third chapter, the last one to be written for the study and, as Bersani writes in the book's prologue, "something like the conceptual center of the work" (*CR* 2). In this chapter, Bersani names Benjamin as the arch-villain of redemptive ontologies. Yet he also discovers that, despite his rejection of Benjamin, that which he has found most problematic in messianic materialism parasites also his own thought, in the guise of Leibnizian ontology. The name of the problem is the monadic *at once*. The time of the *at once* differs, of course, from that of simultaneity: it allows the kind of minimal opening that Derrida, in a moment characteristic of his early work, finds cleaving Husserl's *Augenblick* into afterwardsness, a demonstration of the sleight of hand that Derrida discovers enabling all claims to essences by Western metaphysics. Yet Benjamin's argument for monadic simultaneity suggests to Bersani the dangerous—or perhaps just embarrassing—proximity of the onto-ethics/aesthetics of the *at once* to the redemptive philosophies exemplified by Benjaminian messianism: his work begins to harmonize with what he calls Benjamin's "postlapsarian dirge" (*CR* 53).

Consequently, returning to the *at once* of the "aestheticizing movement" he has located in Freud, Baudelaire, and Nietzsche, he and Dutoit suggest in "Inhibited Reading" that the Unnamable's paradox—the effort to achieve silence via a vehicle inimical to the very project—is symptomatic. With its time of the *at once*, the trilogy culminating in *The Unnamable* constitutes something of a dead end, or a badly conceptualized experiment: in aiming at being beyond language, the 1950s narratives, despite "their magnificent originality and complexity, are perhaps somewhat naïve in their assumptions about the sympathy that literature can provide to a straightforward defense of prelinguistic essential being" (*AI* 51). If *The Unnamable* "seems to believe in the ontology that it also mocks" (*AI* 51), this ontological faith, without the self-disparagement, similarly characterizes Benjamin's materialist messianism. It is at this moment that Bersani diverges from, or pushes further, the trajectory he had followed in "Boundaries of Time and Being": "Inhibited Reading" suggests that Beckett's subsequent work moves on from the *at once* that characterizes the antinatalist ontology of the Unnamable's efforts to escape speech into monadic silence.

Regarding *The Unnamable* as "the most poignant example of Beckett's failing to fail, of the inevitable 'presencing' of occasions and relations in art," Bersani and Dutoit argue that, in his later work, "a crucial shift takes place": the narrative consciousness abandons the efforts, such as the Unnamable's, to figure the monadic perspective and moves to "the point of view of those who would make the Unnamable speak" (*AI* 51–52). Henceforth, Beckett's narratives unfold as the record of solicitations by which the monadic being is "tortured into speaking" (*AI* 56): "the self-contained monad becomes the object of [the narrative consciousness's] persecutorial attention" (*AI* 52). We no longer inhabit the perspective of the would-be monadic being—in which we find the Unnamable—but that of the voices that prod and solicit their others to emerge from the indifferent and undifferentiated peace of their monadic solitude.

This work of "extorting" (*AI* 52–54) or "torturing" (*AI* 56, 58, 62–63) or "tormenting" (*AI* 57, 62) speech from the other—Bersani and Dutoit's terms share an etymology—echoes the scene in which the subject was first called into being. What Beckett illustrates, according to Bersani and Dutoit, is the way in which we repeat, in our "torturing" of others, our own solicitation into speech. "To be tortured out of monadic self-containment into a self-identifying speech is to *become* the brutally authoritative voice that summons others into speech," they write. "We address others in the mode in which we first listened to others, a listening continuously repeated within the consciousness as the enabling structure and model of our speaking. Implicit in all dialogue is a project of mastering the other through the extortion of self-exposing speech. Thus we enter and maintain linguistic intersubjectivity in a reign of terror" (*AI* 63). It is as if the narrative consciousness of Beckett's post-1950s work needles its others into being with the "tortured jealousy" that marks, as Bersani writes in his first book, Proust's narrator (*MP* 80). As in the case of Benjamin's allusion to the "bourgeois" nature of postlapsarian language, Bersani and Dutoit's reference to extant intersubjectivity as "a reign of terror" suggests, perhaps, a historicizing reading of their ontological claims: in modernity, becoming is lived as a process that violently turns against the instigators of its revolutions.

Here we find, then, something like a Beckettian version of hominization, where an intrusive call solicits the incipiently human into anthropogenetic becoming. If social existence is lived "in conformity with the deep structure of reciprocal torment that originally made the social possible" (*AI* 63), it is ethically imperative, as Bersani and Dutoit write some years later, to think about the ways in which "the infant's being" is "call[ed] forth . . . as an independent subjectivity" in "this originary soliciting of the human subject" (*CS* 40). Their observations entail an ethico-pedagogical program: we must learn how to reinitiate our calling-into-being in different ways, perhaps avoiding the "reign of terror" in which we currently emerge as humans and precipitate others' becoming.

It is not difficult to discern the target of Bersani and Dutoit's reading of Beckett: what Beckett exemplifies, according to them, are the terroristic solicitations that psychoanalysis, particularly in its Laplanchean mode, has postulated as paradigmatic for human communication. Human communication's "reciprocal torment" consists of the interrogative work that is elicited by the enigmatic signifier, the secrets that the subject assumes the other to hide and that she unknowingly transmits to those who come after her. These are the secrets, the enigmas, that propel the Proustian search. As Bersani writes in his early work, the lives of the women Marcel desires seem "full of secrets to [him], essentially erotic secrets" (*MP* 58). Consequently, Proust's narrator "often sees people as puzzles to be solved" (*MP* 60), where the work of "solving"—or, as we put it in the previous chapter, dis-solving—designates the other's undoing on the rack of sexual interrogation. Marcel's imprisonment of Albertine is an example of the violence of such interrogative techniques; Bersani later suggests that Dennis Cooper's fiction brings this relation to otherness to its logical conclusion (*IRG* 34).

To become-human is to be queered out of monadic solitude. Voices break our slumber, tormenting and torturing and extorting us with varied solicitations. "To be tortured is the precondition for being humanized," Bersani and Dutoit write. ". . . The torture consists in the fact that as soon as we begin to listen to voices we can't help hearing an injunction to speak" (*AI* 62). Even if they don't have Eve Kosofsky Sedgwick in mind,[63] Bersani and Dutoit are teasing us, we think, with an etymological pun. As Sedgwick notes in the foreword to *Tendencies*—her collection of queer-theoretical essays published, like *Arts of Impoverishment*, in 1993—the term "queer" emerges, like "athwart" and the German *quer* (transverse), from the Latin *torquere*, to twist.[64] It is from this root that we also get, of course, "torture," or the German *quälen* and *Quälerei*. The tortuousness of human existence is the grounding postulation of psychoanalytic theory. Laplanche's close reading of Freud, most notably in *Life and Death in Psychoanalysis* (1970), emphasizes this aspect: hominization occurs when the infant, enigmatically solicited by others (*der Andere*), veers off the blocked path of need and strays into desire. Becoming-human, as Laplanche puts it, constitutes a *fourvoiement*, going-astray—a queering. If Luther admonished each to remain faithful to his vocation as revealed in God's calling (*Berufung*), for Laplanchean psychoanalysis the work of translating the world's messages becomes the human *(a)vocation*. "Sexuality" is the name psychoanalysis gives to the (a)vocative path of becoming-human. That all such paths, onto which the failed animal flees for its life, diverge from "nature" means that the human is by definition a perverted being—a "queer animal."[65] Thinking human becoming requires the (a)vocational ethics of a queer theory.

In *Arts of Impoverishment*, Bersani and Dutoit suggest that torture may be inescapable; but the precise mode of our queering, they further propose, requires careful thought. They write that with the move to such later texts as the 1980s *Nohow On* trilogy, we witness yet a further shift in Beckett's imagination. In the texts that immediately follow the 1950s trilogy, such as *How It Is* (1961), Beckett stages scenes of origination in which the human subject's painful emergence finds its rationale, or is justified, in the continuity of the inaugurating terror. Bersani and Dutoit propose: "*How It Is* diagrams a type of being (the being that is human) structured as the unending repetition of its own origination. As if the deepest structure of being could never be anything but that: the beginning again of its own beginnings" (*AI* 59). If we take this reading as a recategorization of Bersani's earlier work on psychoanalytic theory, we can rephrase it as follows: consciousness survives its devastating emergence through the torment of voices by finding (masochistic) pleasure in the intensity of the moment; echoes of this pleasure are subsequently sought in restaging the torture in scenes where the subject doles out the terror to its others. Both Laplanche and Beckett evoke this scenario, *but with a crucial difference*: in *How It Is*, Beckett *examines* the "grim regime of justice" (*AI* 65) where the shattering violence that initiates becoming-human is justified by its repetitions; psychoanalysis offers this schema as *the* structure of intersubjectivity.

In Beckett's later work, human ontology is otherwise imagined. Others are not summoned to the scene to get their turn on the rack; they are solicited, rather, for company. In *Company* (1980), the circulation of voices "exists *for the sake of* the relations it establishes" (*AI* 65), not for the revelation of enigmatic secrets or the pleasure of re-calling one's own torment. It is in later Beckett, Bersani and Dutoit propose, that we witness a move whereby the torture that constitutes "sociality" unexpectedly produces modes of togetherness they call "sociability" (*AI* 65). Although the latter term remains in the background in *Arts of Impoverishment*, its importance is suggested not only by the publication of the chapter section in question in essay form under the title "Beckett's Sociability" (1992),[66] but also, ten years later, the concept's reemergence and elaboration in Bersani's essay "Sociability and Cruising" (2002) (*IRG* 45–62).

Sociable Lessness

In "Sociability and Cruising," Bersani detours through Georg Simmel's sociology to explore sociability, that is, the kinds of possibilities of togetherness with which, he and Dutoit argue in *Arts of Impoverishment*, Beckett experiments in his later work. In "The Sociology of Sociability" ("Soziologie der Geselligkeit") (1911),[67] Simmel theorizes modes of association that emerge alongside but remain distinct from profit-driven relationships:

forms of connectedness that are not motivated by the purposeful activities characteristic of group life, but, rather, come about as their byproducts. When members of groups come together on varied occasions, an "impulse to sociability" begins to speak in them, as if vicariously borrowing the occasions of motivated association. This impulse parasites the opportunities for interpersonal contact necessitated by individual and group survival, but, like "art and play," goes on to abandon such purposefulness, emptying out the activity of its content, delighting in the forms themselves. In this way, one can observe, in occasions of sociability, "the pure essence of association," as it has been "distil[led]" from social life.[68]

Without explicitly saying so, Bersani is drawn to Simmel because he identifies in "sociability" an effort to describe what he frequently calls, after Foucault, "new relational modes" (*IRG* 59; *H* 77–83). The parasitism of sociability, that is, may provide an occasion to tap into the "affective and relational virtualities" whose actualization Foucault sought in homosocial friendships.[69] As much as the same-sex friendships that interest Foucault are made possible by, but contain potential in excess of, the gender-segregated spaces of, say, the armed forces or correctional facilities, Simmel's sociability is enabled by linkages unintentionally forged in group life.

What interested Foucault, and remains important for Bersani, is to imagine contexts in which the modern subject could lose some of the individualizing traits that have made him who he is (most crucially, those through which the *dispositif* of sexuality individuates subjects). Bersani recognizes an analogous argument in Simmel, for whom the subject, in order to access *Geselligkeit*, must relinquish some of the relations that have not only plugged him into the social world but constituted him in the first place. One of the ways in which Simmel's work has been important for sociology is his conceptualization of an "individual" as an assemblage of varied relations, a node in the multidimensional web of sociality, amidst ceaseless becoming.[70] In entering a scene of sociability, this *networked being* becomes less than she used to be; for sociability to thrive, its subjects must withdraw from their fully constituted selves, must consent to relinquish the connections that have enriched their lives. If sociability proceeds by abstracting its agent from the subject whose varied attributes make him recognizable, this being is present in Bersani's work before his engagement with Simmel. What Bersani in 1976 calls a "creature without relation" (*FA* 205) is one of its many incarnations; another is the "impoverished" individual whose shape begins to emerge, in *Balzac to Beckett*, as a counterpoint to the infinite richness of the Proustian subject. In the terms we used in chapter 1, sociability necessitates this individual's centripetal withdrawal from the meaningfulness with which society has endowed it. In language that is already familiar to us, Bersani writes in 2002 that the *gesellig* subject is a "self-subtracted being" (*IRG* 48), an agent of *lessness*, who discovers in sociability "the particular pleasure gained from the restriction of the personal: the pleasure of the associative process itself, of a pure relationality which, beyond or before the satisfaction of particular needs or interests, may be at once the ground, the motive and the goal of all relations" (*IRG* 46). In *Geselligkeit*, in other words, he finds a sociological description of the modes of becoming he has called impoverished, subtracted, monadic, radically passive: "an individuality unencumbered by selfhood" (*TT* 88).

Benjamin, too, presents us with a "withered" (*verkümmert*) subject, but this is a being whose Adamic precision has dissipated into bourgeois chatter. The argument in "On Language as Such"—that the emergence of modernity repeats humankind's fall into "the abyss of prattle [*Abgrund des Geschwätzes*]"[71]—sounds a familiar theme: the modern world is marked by vacuity, by the proliferation of empty enjoyments, by the replacement of authentic artworks with the culture industry's mass-produced pleasures. For Marx, ideology blows hot air on which the market operates: the capitalist "searches for means to spur [workers] on to consumption, to give his wares new charms, to inspire them with new needs by constant chatter, etc. [*sucht er daher alle Mittel auf, um sie zum Konsum anzuspornen, neue Reize seinen Waren zu geben, neue Bedürfnisse ihnen anzuschwatzen etc.*]."[72] Keeping her in line, chattering and fascinated, with the excitement and allure of new consumer goods, capitalism renders the subject of modernity "a mere receptive organ of the market, an imitator of arbitrarily chosen ideas and styles."[73] Heidegger grants that "idle talk" is inescapably the way in which Dasein operates in the world, but it is in *Gerede* that Dasein also loses its way: "when Da-sein maintains itself in idle talk, it is—as being-in-the-world—cut off from the primary and primordially genuine relations of being toward the world, toward *Mitda-sein*, toward being-in itself."[74] Benjamin gives this critique a biblical-mythic bent: modernity is where Adamic language has dissipated into the referentlessness of chatter.

The (a)vocative ethics of psychoanalytic theory modifies this metaphysical tradition. The psychoanalytically trained ear listens keenly to the nattering and gossip that Luther, Benjamin, and Heidegger deem empty, superfluous, and sinful. Enigmatic signifiers are carried on the frequencies of everyday life, in whose psychopathologies Freud found a treasure trove of overlooked riches. The strangeness of Freud's method consisted of his invitation that we ramble on, deny thought a destination and a final cause, diverge onto minor pathways, dither with the insignificant. "'Come in, talk, and say silly things,'" goes the Freudian invitation. "'That is how we will reach the core of your being.'"[75] For psychoanalysis, we are at our most revealing when we prattle away. While Bersani embraces the call to chatter, he wants us to think of this "core of being" in other ways than through the hidden "meanings" that psychoanalysis has often found in the "silly things" people do and say. This is where psychoanalysis, for him, has turned into a disciplinary project: the assumption of coded messages behind everyday prattle indicates the role of the Freudian science in implanting interiority in the modern subject.

Especially in his post-1980s work, Bersani moves to rethink the place that the representatives of (a)vocative ethics have traditionally given to the distractive noise they call "chatter" (*Geschwätz*, *Gerede*, *snak*). What would it mean to be called to a shared world not by divine dispatches (Luther) or self-authenticating summonses (Heidegger) or fascinating enigmas (Laplanche) but by, say, "the superficial chatter of the *salon*" (*IRG* 48)? What forms of desiring would be enabled were we to relinquish vertical aspirations to deific vocations and, instead, cultivate a horizontal orientation to the "human babble [*menschen geschwez*]" whose wastefulness Luther never ceases to denounce?[76] Complicating the tradition that he finds reformulated in Benjamin's messianic militancy, Bersani locates in Beckett artistic experimentations with alternative modes of becoming. In his later texts, Beckett moves from what Bersani and Dutoit claim is the ontological dead end of *The Unnamable* onto other approaches to thinking being, ones that *Arts of Impoverishment* names "sociability." Like the summons that, issued in "the fundamental anthropological situation" of becoming-human,[77] leads the Laplanchean subject astray, sociable talk diverts individuals from their purposeful relations, replacing profit with pleasures. Illustrated in, for example, Beckett and Henry James, sociability binds people together, but the rapport that is created is not marked by the effort to "translate" whatever messages circulate between the self and the other. Already in *A Future for Astyanax*, Bersani writes that, in James's work, "intelligent chatter reveal[s] the impersonal nature of what makes talk *purely interesting*. . . . [L]anguage . . . continues to chatter on its own steam" (*FA* 141). Jamesian chatter confounds psychological realism's project of making subjects visible and identifiable, a project that James is often considered to have initiated. In James, as in Beckett, communication is not motivated by a search for enigmatic depths, for there are no such depths to sound: as Bersani, commenting on *Waiting for Godot* in 1990, writes: "the strategies of continuing talk survive the absence of psychological subjects" (*CR* 169).

Art of Chatter

While nothing like a break takes place, the trajectory of Bersani's thought noticeably bends between *The Culture of Redemption* and *Arts of Impoverishment*, a redirection caused, we have suggested, by his encounter with Benjamin. Because the onto-ethical postulations of messianic materialism resonate with too-familiar tones, the principle of "shattering" that Bersani has prioritized in his previous work—a tendency culminating in *The Freudian Body* and "Is the Rectum a Grave?"—begins to give way to another onto-ethical mode of becoming. After 1990, the emphasis in Bersani shifts from the ethics of *ébranlement* to that of *Geschwätz*, from *shattering* to *chattering*. While Benjamin, echoing Luther (and such later Luther commentators as Kierkegaard and Heidegger), sees in *Geschwätz* the degeneration of language into the hollowness of bourgeois (or fallen) communication, Bersani takes up and develops the concept of sociability—a work that has begun some years, indeed decades, earlier—in contrast to what he considers the glaringly traditional account of a lapsarian world in Benjamin's work, but also the extortionist tendencies he discerns in the Laplanchean subject. For him, "chattering" does not operate on the participants' mutual extraction of knowledge about each other, but the performance of a connectivity devoid of enigmatic significance. The intimacy one finds in sociability "is not hiding anything."[78] Unlike the shattering encounters of the psychoanalytic subject, the sociability of chattering is not driven by the attractions of the inscrutable, the desire to translate the other's messages. Instead, there is a "happy lack of depth" in such exchanges.[79]

No epistemological injunctions infect the chatter of sociability; unlike *wanting beings*, chatterers are not primarily interested in their partners' personalities or idiosyncrasies or anxieties or traumas. We are often told that queers, like gossipy women, are particularly adept at such empty intercourse. The (unreliable, closeted) narrator of James Baldwin's novel *Giovanni's Room* (1956) looks around the Parisian demimonde and observes, with distaste, "the narcotics of chatter" with whose help vacuous queens seek to escape their unexamined fear and hurt.[80] He is horrified at what he takes as the subculture's impersonality, the lack of genuinely affective connections between the men he meets. As much as Benjamin sees in modern life's empty banter evidence of our fallenness, Jacques, an older gay man in Baldwin's novel, observes to David: "'Nobody can stay in the garden of Eden.'" The queer demimonde is an exemplar of people's alienated existence in the postlapsarian world, often, as in Benjamin and Baldwin, further defined as a life of modern urbanity. Newcomers to the scene seem like "freshly fallen angel[s]," and, as their troubles mount, Giovanni, David's lover, begs him: "'*Ne me laisse pas tomber, je t'en prie.*'"[81]

A postlapsarian imagination marks many of the descriptions, like Baldwin's, of modern alienation, disconnect, and melancholy, all of which are symptomized in the subject's desperate clinging to hysterical, empty chatter. What Luther calls "human babble" prevents the person's hard look at what really ails him (for Luther, his godlessness; for Baldwin, the unprocessed depredations of diasporic modernity). If homosexuality is deemed a telling sign of contemporary world's ills, queers are individuals whom the vise of modernity has twisted into solitary beings, in whom meaningful discourse has been "perverted to the non-committal chatter [*Geschwätz*] of a private *Weltanschauung*."[82] Adorno frequently calls such modern isolation monadic, especially when he is speaking of homosexuality as a symptom of (fascist) modernity.[83] The moderns, as he writes with Horkheimer, are confined to "the windowless monadic fortress of their own person."[84] If, as Marx notes, ideology bewitches people with endless "chatter" about new goods and wares, the pleasures of consumerism leave subjects in the solitary confinement of their jouissance: "They are monads, each abandoning himself to the pleasure—at the expense of all others."[85] With its pleasures of sameness, modern monadism disenables all "solidarity."[86]

Like Adorno, Bersani sees the homo as a monad, but only as a homomonad experimenting with the artistry of (a)vocations, of the call-and-response of sociability. Bersani considers gay bathhouses possible sites for experimentation with a desireless movement in a nonenigmatic world. "Cruising is sexual sociability," he writes in "Sociability and Cruising"; it may yield "a training in impersonal intimacy" (*IRG* 57, 60). "Impersonal intimacy" designates a movement where we are not lured by the hidden depths—the "personalities"—of other people, which we would then seek to translate into more familiar languages. Anonymous sex becomes a case in point. In terms of the onto-ethics/aesthetics we have termed homomonadic, bathhouses can be sites for the kind of subjective impoverishment whose artistry Bersani discerns in Beckett. As he writes, "in cruising . . . we leave our selves behind"; in our ethical experimentations, we would do well to take advantage of "the opportunity anonymous sex offers its practitioners of shedding much of the personality that individuates them psychologically" (*IRG* 60).[87] This becomes the centripetal withdrawal whose necessity both Bersani and Simmel emphasize. As sites of such impoverishment, scenes of cruising are inhabited by minimally individuated bodies, bodies "without attributes" (*IRG* 61). Such bodies participate in the centripetal-centrifugal rhythms we explored in chapter 1.

In order for us to counter our lifelong training in enigmatics, chattering demands work, an *artfulness*. Simmel confirms this. The term *Geschwätz* does not appear in "The Sociology of Sociability," the essay Bersani cites in "Sociability and Cruising." It does show up, however, in a chapter in *Grundfragen der Soziologie* (1917) where Simmel rehearses many of the points of the 1911 text. In "Sociability: An Example of Pure, or Formal, Sociology" ("Die Geselligkeit: Beispiel der reinen oder formalen Soziologie"), Simmel writes that, with sociability, "talk becomes its own purpose; but not in the naturalistic sense that would make it mere chatter [*aber nicht im naturalistischen Sinne, wie im Geschwätz*], but as the *art* of conversation that has its own, artistic laws. In purely sociable conversation, the topic is merely the indispensable medium through which the lively exchange of speech itself unfolds its attractions."[88] We are mistaken, Simmel insists, if we think sociability consists of *Geschwätz*, "mere chatter"; not all scenes of talk yield the pleasures of *Geselligkeit*. It is not, he echoes in the 1911 essay, "that the content of sociable conversation is a matter of indifference; it must be interesting, gripping, even significant—only it is not the purpose of the conversation that these qualities should square with objective results, which stand by definition outside the conversation."[89] It is necessary to develop "artistic laws" specific to the genre of sociability in which one operates. The modes of calling-and-responding will be different from the bar to the classroom to the *salon* to the late-night truckstop.

If the sociable subject emerges only after an individual has unplugged herself from the relations whose network Simmel spent most of his career mapping, this becoming demands a work of considerable difficulty and rigor. It requires, Bersani often notes, a commitment to an *ascesis*: "Considering all the interests and passions we lay aside in order to enjoy sociability, we might speak of sociability as an ascetic conduct" (*IRG* 48). One's withdrawal from social relation requires a stringent practice: "we have had to work in order to achieve the grace of blindness and immobility," of "perceptual impoverishment" (*AI* 136, 137); "a lot," as Bersani notes elsewhere, "has to be renounced."[90] This practice can be thought, as Bersani sometimes does, in connection with the ascetics whose necessity as a mode of self-becoming Foucault began to outline in the 1980s. If this ascesis requires work, the losses one experiences at the desiccation of our enigmatically significant world may not be trivial. In a moment we already quoted in chapter 1, Bersani writes: "Our complex views of intersubjectivity, nourished by an intricate consciousness of desire, have the effect of channeling our imagination of human relations into the narrow domain of the private. To give up that consciousness, which fascinates us, would be a great loss. . . . It would be immeasurably sad to lose the richness of our Proustian perceptions, to settle (if that is even possible) for an intersubjectivity cleansed of all fantasmatic curiosity" (*H* 123–24). Monadic impoverishment doesn't come to us "naturally"; its practices have to be intentionally, often arduously, nurtured. We must learn to distract ourselves from the "fascinating" pleasures that enigmatics offers. Those who experiment with anonymous encounters may not be able to replace their "significant others"—as we tellingly call them—with other kinds of company. Gay men have often negotiated this difficulty, this danger, of queer sociability by experimenting with the institution of "open relationships," where one gets to have the pleasures of a "partner" or "husband," but also the kinds of contacts that for Simmel and Bersani constitute nonsignifying sociability.

The patterns—forms of being—that remain as beautiful husks beyond all social motivation must become objects of our *cultivation*: Bersani and Dutoit speak of "the kinds of talk, of sociability, we have still to invent for relational regimes no longer dependent on identitarian myths" (*FoB* 9). Sociability is constituted of voices that, rather than tempting us with secrets about *who we are*, summon us to join, or try out, various *ways of being*. We can, as Bersani writes in *The Culture of Redemption*, "invent a motive for reading unsustained by a promise of epistemological gain" (*CR* 15). Art, its "ontological laboratories," is one realm in which such invention of and training in new mobilities takes place. Despite having more than once declared psychoanalysis an exhausted resource for ethical work, Bersani also notes that, as demonstrated by Patrice Leconte's film *Intimate Strangers* (2004), analytic discourse and practice may yet provide occasions for "a re-thinking . . . of how we conduct dialogue" (*I* 125). We might institute a mode of "Freudian talk therapy" (*IRG* 156) where analysis does not rely on depth psychology but becomes the kind of chattering, the kind of nonsignifying sociability, that Bersani finds in Beckett, Mallarmé, Almódovar, and Rohmer. Similarly, what for many signal the off-putting pathologies expressed in anonymous sex—a disinterestedness in persons, the use of others as props in the *mise-en-scène* of one's idiosyncratic fantasies—can train one in contact with a world shorn of signifying absences. The tortured souls of *How It Is*, *Company*, and *Ill Seen Ill Said*, Bersani oddly suggests, would find themselves on familiar ground in gay bathhouses. Their example can help us learn how to listen for, in "the [world's] fatuous clamour,"[91] not hidden, meaningful messages but perhaps familiar rhythms that can synchronize our movements with unexpected partners. Bersanian onto-ethics/aesthetics asks us to practice the chatter of sociability that, undetermined by the epistemological emphasis that orients the most familiar modes of our being together, would enable us to respond to the calls that tug at us.

5

Narcissus, a Cosmology

Luther–Freud–Plato–Speculative Astronomy

While Martin Luther opened modernity as he sought to unburden himself of the endless demands of the Pope's bottomless coffers, what he found—and founded—was but another economy of radical uncertainty, one that set him trembling in his efforts to measure the adequacy of his responses to God's call. The call (*κλῆσις*, *Berufung*) elicits anxiety because it always comes from an unassailably enigmatic other, always from beyond an unbridgeable gap between the self and the nonself. The modern other is paradigmatically the other of an unprocessed—*unprocesseable*—trauma, one whose endlessly disorienting solicitation prevents the subject from graduating to ethical exemplarity, the security of having one's debts conclusively paid. The other's inscrutability keeps us moving, tortured with the spiritual terror Luther calls *Anfechtung*. What seems like a deterrent to ethical laziness is also an ontological exigency, for in the onto-ethical system of *wanting being*, organized around constitutive lack, any solution to the other's riddle—a fully adequate response to the call—would amount to the world's dis-solution. Like every other drive, *κλῆσις* is a death drive: insofar as it always calls us back, *après-coup*, to the self's missed origin, it tempts the subject with the promise of catastrophic completion. Hence emerges the balancing act of psychoanalytic ethics, which stipulates that the subject simultaneously not *give up on* and not *give into* her desire (*cédé sur son désir*).[1] In psychoanalysis and elsewhere, the modern other, calling from beyond the cut of trauma, fascinates us with the deadly offer to render the world transparent, and it is our ethical task to take in yet turn away from the obscene spectacle, to remain on this side of the dark mirror.

Narcissus is frequently the figure for our failure to heed the other's enigmatic call. Instead of responding to the other's "creative and dialogic" address, Narcissus chooses deadening sameness. "By opting for monologue," the Lutheran theologian Johannes Schwanke writes, "Narcissus refuses to encounter the other. His creative, other-related communication breaks off, or rather submits to a will that focuses exclusively on its own reflection."[2] Schwanke notes that this all-too-human temptation to exterminate difference, to silence the other's voice, has found an occasion to realize itself in recent scientific developments: "The warning against self-reflective self-absorption and a monologuing existence, which the ancients connected with this myth, has been confirmed in a surprisingly literal way. Creating a reflection of the human self through cloning seems within reach."[3] The Lutheran is not alone in making the connection between narcissism and the science of cloning. The psychoanalyst Adam Phillips similarly notes: "Psychoanalysis calls the simulation of sameness narcissism, which it *tends to treat* as the saboteur of development; Narcissus wanted to be the same as himself, the same as the image of himself, a distinction he didn't have it in himself to make. From a psychoanalytic point of view, successful psychic cloning . . . is a denial of difference and dependence. . . . The art of self-cloning is an attempt to stop time by killing desire. Replicating myself I keep finding nothing else."[4] In desire-killing narcissism, the subject, captured by his imago, is unable to face the encounters with difference that, as both Lutheranism and psychoanalysis tell us, allow the subject to develop, to become itself by becoming different from what it is. If "desire" has been our name for becoming, narcissism prevents its movement of differentiation: "the (narcissistic) solution of creating absolute sameness—the clone—unconsciously kills desire."[5]

In speaking of clones, Phillips and Schwanke are referring to the sheep Dolly, the first animal to be cloned, in 1997. Appropriately, "clone" is also the name for a gay male style of masculinity, usually associated with post-Stonewall cultures of the 1970s United States, particularly on the West Coast. In response to representations of effeminate homosexuals in American culture, clones stylized their bodies as hyperbolically masculine, constructing a desirable image of the gay male subject. But, as would be fitting in the cultural context that concerns us here, their liveries of masculinity also rendered these subjects suspiciously *inhuman*. Gay clones, as Richard Meyer writes, "fashioned [their] appearance upon depersonalized, endlessly reproducible images of ideal masculinity. . . . [Clones prize] the surface of desirable sameness over the depths of humanist subjectivity."[6] When the protagonist of Michael Rumaker's *A Day and a Night at the Baths* (1979) enters the cubicle of "a Christopher Street clone" in a New York gay sauna, he is shaken by a feeling that the man may not be fully human. Fighting his disturbing hunch, he puts an "open palm lightly on [the man's] chest for a moment": "There was a definite heartbeat."[7] If the heart designates here human interiority, the evidence of its presence rescues the protagonist from the uncanny impression that, in facing the clone, he is dealing with something other than a human being.

If the clone, as Meyer writes, chooses surface over "the depths of humanist subjectivity," he courts dehumanization, for it is, as Michel Foucault has shown, interiority that marks human specificity in Western modernity. The "humanist subjectivity" Meyer locates as the antithesis of gay clones' superficiality names a historically specific concept. Its rise is often claimed to have coincided with that of the epistemophilic era whose initiatory point Foucault calls "the Cartesian moment." In our present context, we can stretch its emergence to the Reformation a century earlier, with Luther becoming, as Theodor Adorno puts it, "the inventor of inwardness."[8] Clones betray this onto-ethical system: in their replicative sameness, they disregard the singular, and singularizing, call that is constitutive of the modern subject. Their evident desire for repetition goes against modern theories of hominization and cultural becoming, which, without fail, have relied on the thought of *difference* as that which allows life's salubrious elaboration. We can see this in as varied places as Arthur de Gobineau's nineteenth-century racial theories (where civilizations arise through the incorporation of tribal differences),[9] late nineteenth- and early twentieth-century depictions of American democracy,[10] and Walter Ong's account, influenced by Jacques Derrida's deconstructive theory of *différance*, of the psychic ramifications of literacy.[11] Without difference, becoming cannot be imagined, and the homosexual, seeking sameness, is one, perhaps the primary, modern embodiment of a subject who fails in this futural orientation.[12]

If these have become, since the early twentieth century, markedly *psychoanalytic* assumptions, it is in *the theory of narcissism* that Leo Bersani finds something of an alien body inhabiting psychoanalytic thought. As Phillips writes, psychoanalysis "tends to treat" narcissism, with its emphasis on sameness rather than difference, as the enemy of becoming; he leaves open the possibility that other "tendencies" might inflect psychoanalytic thinking. Bersani's work actualizes one such inflection. In 1993, Bersani and Ulysse Dutoit ask, "might there be a type of narcissistic identification in our responses to art for which psychoanalytic theories of narcissism and psychoanalytic approaches to art have not been able to account?" (*AI* 160–61). Responding to this query, we conclude our study of homomonadology by exploring the concept of narcissism, which Bersani, having first dealt with the topic in his mid-1970s texts, persistently "recategorizes" in the five decades of his work's unfolding. The theory of narcissism opens up to an ontology of allness, a *speculative cosmology*. This account of being can be articulated in the Leibnizian terms that we have been exploring in this study: a postpsychoanalytic understanding of narcissism, such as Bersani's, posits a subject that at once approximates, asymptotically, nothingness (the incorporeal monad) and entails all in its image—that, in other words, contains "at once less and infinitely more than [what we call] individuality" (*TT* 84). The recategorizations this chapter threads in Bersani suggest an ethics in which we, through speculative work and everyday practice, seek the world through "an expansive rather than a self-enclosing narcissism" (*C* 80).

One of the reasons behind Bersani's persistent ambivalence about psychoanalysis, particularly its Laplanchean mode, is its constitutive *anthropocentrism*: the traumatized temporality of *Nachträglichkeit*, which precipitates translation, offers a model of becoming unique to the human. If this is the grounding assumption of psychoanalytic theory, it echoes a number of other philosophical discourses of the Western tradition: becoming-human emerges at the moment of a failure of instinctual satisfaction, of immediacy and presence, which after the fact is coded as a nonhuman—animal—capacity. This failure opens up a gap that sexuality, as a human-specific phenomenon, attempts to suture. Jean Laplanche writes in *Life and Death in Psychoanalysis* (1970): "From birth onward, insofar as this gap [*décalage*] subsists, there occurs a kind of *disqualification of the instinct*: the satisfaction of needs cannot pass through preestablished setups, that will emerge only gradually and according to the maturational rhythm, of the central nervous system, but satisfaction *must pass* from the beginning through intersubjectivity; i.e., *by way of another human, the mother*."[13] For Laplanche, it is always *a human call* that fascinates the subject into becoming, an assumption that Bersani, especially in his later, post-1980s work, wants to question.

One of the guises in which Bersani parries with Western thought's abiding anthropocentrism is the concept of narcissism as it develops in texts such as *A Future for Astyanax: Character and Desire in Literature*

(1976), *Homos* (1995), *Intimacies* (2008), and *Thoughts and Things* (2015). At the same time, the concept, moving toward something like a cosmology, suggests the *speculative* reach of Bersani's onto-ethics/aesthetics. In ways that we touched upon in our introduction, the tradition of speculative thought that culminates in Hegel has since Marx's critique been often deemed self-involved and, as its etymology would suggest, *narcissistic*. "One of the most persistent trends in modern philosophy since Descartes," as Hannah Arendt writes, ". . . has been an exclusive concern with the self, as distinguished from the soul or person or man in general, an attempt to reduce all experiences, with the world as well as with other human beings, to experiences between man and himself."[14] This dynamic has invited commentators to regard the Hegelian system, figured as something of modern thought's culmination, as organized around what Fredric Jameson calls "the narcissism of the Absolute": "We . . . search the whole world, and outer space, and end up only touching ourselves, only seeing our own face persist through multitudinous differences and forms of otherness. Never truly to encounter the not-I, to come face to face with radical otherness (or even worse, to find ourselves in an historical dynamic in which it is precisely difference and otherness which is relentlessly being stamped out): such is the dilemma of the Hegelian dialectic."[15] Hegel's system provides a privileged example of the way in which—as another contemporary Lutheran thinker writes—"modern subjectivity . . . assimilates to itself all otherness, all difference, everything over against me."[16] Hegelian thought, Oswald Bayer avers, is representative of "modern narcissism."[17]

In the theories that, with varied investments, Bayer, Schwanke, and Phillips paraphrase, "sameness" marks the evisceration of desire and—consequently—the human. This is because of these theories' grounding in the logic that remains hegemonic in our culture: the notion that it is *difference* that fuels all movement. For these theories, the narcissistic prioritization of the same reveals an inability to deal productively with our constitutive traumatization. "The problem with narcissism," as the Lacanian scholar Mari Ruti asserts, ". . . is that it prompts us to flee from any and all signs of this traumatizing otherness."[18] Narcissus refuses to acknowledge his woundedness by unknowability, an acknowledgment that, as a response to Echo's offer of love, would precipitate a journey of self-discovery. While we become-human when our trauma turns into an opportunity for the invention of newness, narcissism is marked by a deadening, dehumanizing sameness. Insisting with the self-sameness of the origin, the narcissist refuses to let time pass and renders the future impossible.

As we have observed in previous chapters, one of Bersani's consistent ambitions is to dislodge the ontology of trauma and lack as the unquestioned basis for ethics. One way he does this is by observing the dynamics of what we will call "speculative narcissism." The speculative mind, frozen in fascinated contemplation of its self, has at least since Luther exemplified the human pathology of refusing the other's solicitation as the very possibility of one's ethical movement in the world. Yet it is in the figure of the narcissist, enraptured by what he sees in the *speculum*, that Bersani finds something of a pressure point in the rigid body of contemporary onto-ethics. Attending to this point over some forty years, he wants to retrain this body in terms of—as Baruch Spinoza and Gilles Deleuze would say—what it can do. Such reinvention concerns the body's orientation toward sameness and difference. The contemporary theological texts we will sample indicate that it is not an accident that the term "clone" is shared by genetics and gay subcultures. In both cases, the clone, in its otherlessness and autoproduction, betrays our humanity. Yet it is this betrayal that Bersani has, in different ways, promoted as our first ethical demand. He frequently looks to gay subcultures for examples of how one can "betray the relational modes sanctified by the dominant culture" (*IRG* 60). We must, as he often writes, become *less* in order to be *more*; we must yield to centripetal self-impoverishment—relinquish our "humanist subjectivity"—to participate in a centrifugal self-scattering. In this scattering, what commentators from Lutherans to Lacanians consider the mortal paralysis of narcissistic fascination is reconfigured in terms of what Charles Baudelaire, in an anecdote we briefly discussed in chapter 3, calls "animal ecstasy." The fascination of this *ἔκστασις* exerts a dehumanizing—more appropriately perhaps, *a*humanizing—pull on the modern subject, thereby going against the grain of critical philosophy's anthropocentrism, which also the recent thinkers of "speculative realism" have, analogously to but differently from Bersani, sought to challenge.[19]

Homo-Narcissism

We find Bersani's earliest substantial engagement with the psychoanalytic theory of narcissism in *A Future for Astyanax*, and particularly its final chapter, "Persons in Pieces." As we observed in chapter 2, the early study as a whole constitutes his first attempt at outlining *modes of desiring*; in it Bersani comes to question the hegemony of a desire that is driven by difference and lack. In the final chapter, he observes two different forms of desire: in addition—but not in opposition—to the one based on difference, he locates a desire moved by sameness, a desire that becomes visible, as he writes, as "a union with the same" (*FA* 293). He identifies this mode with homosexual narcissism.

Bersani's argument in "Persons in Pieces" is based on a joint reading of, on the one hand, Jean Laplanche's analysis of Freud—this is the first substantial appearance of both in his work—and, on the other, two mid-1950s French erotic novels: Pauline Réage's (i.e., Anne Desclos) *The Story of O* (1954) and Jean de Berg's (Catherine Robbe-Grillet) *The Image* (1956). Initially, Réage's and Berg's novels exemplify the two ways in which, according to Laplanche, and Bersani after him, Freud understands the child's relation to the outside world: nonsexual mastery (found in *The Story of O*) and erotic sadism, derived from the pleasures of masochism (illustrated in Berg's text). Yet, having contrasted the approaches to otherness illustrated by the two novels, Bersani further complicates the argument by identifying two discrete modes within the violent but detached desire represented by Réage: apart from the cool sadism with which *O*'s men treat the women, he discerns a narcissistic, contemplative mode of pleasure in the attraction of the novel's male protagonist to an older man. This distinction between heterosexual, erotic sadism and nonsexual (or "homosexual"), aesthetic pleasure returns in a more explicit and elaborated form in his later work in the difference between self-shattering, whose inspiration we find in Laplanche's reading of Freud, and the dynamic Bersani comes to call "inaccurate replications" or, after Baudelaire (but also, we have suggested, Leibniz), "correspondence of forms."

Bersani notes the oddly "asexual" (*FA* 300) atmosphere of *The Story of O*'s tableaux of torture; in their elegant and "cool"—the word is repeated thrice (*FA* 299, 307, 308)—composition, the scenes of sadism appear to be informed by "a nonerotic imagination" (*FA* 300). The emotional distance of the executors of punishment from the suffering indicates their failure to be at all perturbed by the excitements of sadistic violence: the men approach the erotic scenes, as Réage writes, with "a certain attitude of detachment."[20] Turning to Freud's explanatory schema in "Instincts and Their Vicissitudes" (1915), "'A Child Is Being Beaten'" (1919), and "The Economic Problem of Masochism" (1924), Bersani suggests that the coolly detached masters of *The Story of O* exemplify what "Instincts and Their Vicissitudes" indicates is the child's initial, nonsexual relation to the world. But as Laplanche, in a move that will become important for Bersani (more so than to Laplanche himself), observes in *Life and Death in Psychoanalysis*, Freud vacillates about the primacy of nonsexual sadism—properly speaking, aggressiveness—in the subject's constitution. He originally postulates that the subject's initial orientation to others is that of control and mastery, and that aggressive impulses become eroticized only in the drive's subsequent vicissitudes: "A primary masochism, not derived from sadism," Freud writes, ". . . seems not to be met with."[21] Yet a footnote added in 1924 to "Instincts and Their Vicissitudes"[22] draws our attention to the ramifications of the force that, in *Beyond the Pleasure Principle* (1920), he calls *Todestrieb*, the death drive: the note directs us to "The Economic Problem of Masochism," where we find Freud speculating about the existence of a masochism prior to the stage of nonsexual sadism.[23] Freud seems to propose two forms of sadism that derive from the infant's earliest experiences: one of nonsexual aggressiveness, the other of torture in which the sadist seeks to re-experience his early masochistic jouissance. As Laplanche's reading indicates, Freud in fact prioritized the latter mode, suggesting that sadistic pleasures rest on a prior, masochistic jouissance: "the masochistic moment is first. The masochistic fantasy is fundamental, whereas the sadistic fantasy implies an identification with the suffering object; it is within the suffering position that the enjoyment lies."[24] As Bersani echoes in *A Future for Astyanax*: "We are erotically stimulated by someone else's pain because we identify with it, having already experienced pain as pleasure: that is, sadism is projected masochism" (*FA* 301). This form of *projected masochism* or *derived sadism* doesn't perturb O's men; they are not moved by the remembered excitements of masochistic—shattering—intensities from which sadistic pleasures derive.

If *The Story of O* demonstrates nonsexual mastery—the "cool" detachment of the observer from the scene of suffering—*The Image* describes the sadist's visceral identification with masochistic jouissance, an identification that reenacts the shattering mobilization of primary masochism. Berg's novel illustrates Freud's understanding of derived sadism in that in its scenes of punishment we find "both the sadist and the masochist experiencing excitement as a direct result of physical pain": "the sadist responds as if his body were being stimulated erotically, but what stimulates him (or her) are someone else's sensations" (*FA* 303). *The Image*'s male narrator is drawn into the spectacle of punishment by the scene's infectious jouissance; as the exemplary sadist, he thus illustrates "the Freudian suggestion that sadism is projected masochism. We can be excited by the pain of others because we have ourselves already experienced pain as sexually exciting" (*FA* 303). For Bersani, Berg demonstrates Laplanche's argument according to which "the sadist himself finds masochistic enjoyment in the pain he provokes in others through an identification with the suffering object."[25] The absence of the sexual, defined in these terms, from Réage's text indicates to Bersani that its violent scenes constitute a narrative whose choreography is interrupted neither by sexuality's absorptive intrusions nor by inassimilable otherness; in Berg's novel, on the other hand, sexuality becomes a force of otherness in its destabilization (which is also, simultaneously and aporetically, the constitution) of the enjoying subject. This observation concerning *The Image* marks the first appearance of the theory of *ébranlement* in Bersani. Already here, he seeks, as he puts it in a 1997 interview, "to move to a different relation to otherness, not one based in paranoid fascination but one that might use the masochistic element in the confrontation productively" (*IRG* 177). This work of realignment begins in *A Future for Astyanax*: with the help of Laplanche's reading of hominization in Freud, Bersani wants to think becoming-human in terms of a constitutive disorientation, of a shattered and scattered being whose pleasures are not dependent on the fascinations of cryptanalysis.

Yet, having illustrated the distinction between nonsexual and derived sadism with *The Story of O* and *The Image*, respectively, Bersani complicates the comparison: he proposes that O's nonsexual sadism bears within it *two forms* of disengagement. Bersani distinguishes the allure of spectacles of *difference* from an almost identical fascination with *sameness*, which nevertheless enables a crucially different form of self-absorption. O's heterosexual admirers are captured by her irresolvable difference, the dark continent of femininity; this form of attraction is exerted by the enigma of otherness. The enigma propels the subject onto a process of violent investigation: in a crucial passage, Réage's narrator describes René's persistent attempts "to understand the *raison d'être*, the truth which must have been lurking somewhere inside Jacqueline, under that golden skin, like the mechanism inside a crying doll."[26] Curiosity about the other impels the subject to take apart the object of his desire as a child would dismantle a mechanized toy in an effort to understand its principle of operation. Similar scenes abound in the Proustian world, Bersani's privileged example of a literary imagination enthralled by enigmatic otherness. As Bersani writes in *The Culture of Redemption* (1990), Proust gives us "a desire that exuberantly dismembers its objects" (*CR* 22). The fascinated lover of difference is captured by the promise of a truth hidden behind appearances, the truth whose discovery will necessitate the irreversible undoing (often in Proust, the assimilation) of the object.

In *A Future for Astyanax*, the obvious (and obviously ethical) counterpoint to the coolly violent responses elicited by such enigmatic difference is the self-shattering mobility of Berg's sadists. In comparison to the nonsexual mastery illustrated by *The Story of O*, their vertiginous pleasures disallow any effort to undo the other for epistemological gain. Thus, compared to Réage's men, Berg's subjects, shattered in their derived sadism, initially constitute ethical exemplars. Yet the argument in "Persons in Pieces" does not conclude here; rather, the essay's logic moves along a more involutive path, one on which Bersani is to continue in later decades. He contrasts the response of O's men, their coldness and cruelty, not only to the pleasures of self-shattering in Berg, but also, implicitly, to a form of desire that emerges in scenes of (male and female) homosexuality in Réage's novel. He identifies it in René's "nonsexual idolatry" of Sir Stephen (*FA* 293). Bersani calls O's lover's "fascinated worship" of the older man "'homosexuality'"—although, importantly, he puts the diagnosis in quotation marks (*FA* 295). This same-sex adoration constitutes a mode of relatedness that Bersani will identify as one of sameness, *correspondances*, and homoness.

It initially appears that Bersani sees in the two men's "homosexual" desire precisely the narcissistic object choice that Freud finds common in homosexual men. Such men, as Freud writes, "are plainly seeking *themselves* as a love-object, and are exhibiting a type of object-choice which must be termed 'narcissistic'";[27] likewise, René loves in Sir Stephen "an almost omnipotent version of [his] own identity" (*FA* 295). Yet Bersani also indicates that the men's narcissism is of a different order than—but not unrelated to—Freudian narcissism. He emphasizes the two men's absolute obedience to, and success in following, the protocols of heteronormative masculinity. Even with his "homosexuality," René perfectly fits into what Bersani identifies, in the larger structure of the novel, as "a kind of fantasy-blueprint of pure heterosexual desire, a mad dream of the 'ideal' resolution (especially by men) of Oedipal conflicts" (*FA* 293). The "purity" of heterosexuality comes from its having rendered (sexual) difference absolute: the other can be desired only as a constitutive lack on this side of difference, and consequently the object to be annihilated.

Yet this model entails not only the ossification of sexual difference into two incompatible realms, but also the transparency of one's "own" sex to oneself, its readiness for narcissistic recognition. As Bersani writes, "the post-Oedipal heterosexual male may no longer find any mystery of sexual identity in himself or in other men" (*FA* 293). As a paradigm of difference, cold heterosexuality may enable a desire not driven by what it can understand as difference. Because René, O's successfully oedipalized male subject, cannot conceive of any real difference between himself and other men (nor within himself), his "fascinated worship" of Sir Stephen must, to the system of hetero-desire, register as desire for the same and, hence, not as a form of desire at all. His "untroubled nonsexual adoration of an ideal version of the self" gives us "a 'homosexuality' so profound that it can dispense with sexual desire" (*FA* 295). For Bersani, René's fascination with the older man escapes the annihilative drive that marks the fascinations of difference because *it tempts the subject with nothing that he does not already, in some form, have.* The subject of homo-narcissistic desire is drawn not by the other's enigma but by the repetition, perhaps enhancement, of a familiar form. The homo-narcissist's relation to his or her object of desire is not driven by the kind of enigmatic otherness that we arguably find in Proust. Rather, Sir Stephen is "worshiped without curiosity": "René, unlike a Proustian lover, isn't trying to penetrate the secret of someone else's mysteriously different 'formula' for sexual excitement" (*FA* 294). Instead, we find in his desire a desire for sameness.

In "Persons in Pieces," we find emerging, then, two concepts that Bersani elaborates in his subsequent work: that of *shattering*—exemplified by *The Image*'s projected masochism—and that of *sameness* or *correspondences*, in the form of René's homo-narcissism in *The Story of O*. *A Future for Astyanax*'s final chapter anticipates, in other words, a move that becomes more obvious in Bersani's later work: from *ébranlement* to *correspondances*. In order to highlight this shift, the above reading—let us now confess—inverts the chronology of the theoretical narrative in "Persons in Pieces." In the chapter, Bersani moves from noting René's attraction to Sir Stephen in *The Story of O* to a consideration of Réage's male subjects' "cool" torturing of their female victims to accentuating the "shattering" involved in the derived sadism of *The Image*. The story's narrative ordering—where we shift, paradigmatically, from lesser details to the climactic dénouement—suggests Bersani's prioritization of what he finds in *The Image* as the solution to the ethical dilemma of the annihilation of otherness in desire. Whereas Bersani ends his theoretical narrative with the ethical importance of *ébranlement*, we have scrambled this line of argumentation, moving from shattering/derived sadism to the kind of worship of sameness that we find in René's "homosexuality," that is, his "nonsexual adoration" of Sir Stephen. We do this to anticipate the shift that Bersani undertakes in his subsequent work, one by which *ébranlement* is deprioritized in order to investigate the ramifications of the sameness—the homo-attraction—an example of which we find between René and the older man.

The sameness that binds the two men is of a peculiar order. Sir Stephen is not René's doppelgänger. There is nothing of the *unheimlich* terror and aggressiveness with which, according to psychoanalysis, the subject meets its specular other. The older man is not an apparition of the repressed, nor an imago promising bodily coordination and wholeness the subject, its body in pieces, finds in the mirror. Rather, René's "calm contemplation" of his recognizable form in the outside world suggests a nonegoic or, as Bersani often puts it, *impersonal* mode of narcissism. In this form of narcissistic love of self, the subject, rather than finding his specular double in the world, is drawn by similitudes and co-incidences between the self and the other. This dynamic is characterized by the appeal of sameness, but one whose narcissism doesn't rely on the terroristic appearance of one's murderous doubles.

Bersani becomes interested in homo-narcissism because it differs from modes of desire that are fueled by lack. We've noted his grappling with the implications of conceptualizations of desire where the subject's movement in the world is premised on an effort to regain that which has been radically lost to it, the most prominent example of which Bersani finds in Proust and, in the philosophical field, in Walter Benjamin. As we observed in chapter 2, *A Future for Astyanax* includes the first explicit engagement with divergent practices of desire, engagement that, as much as it is informed by the aesthetic texts Bersani reads, also bears the traces of his early encounter with Deleuzean philosophy. It is in the same book that he tentatively suggests that desire marked by lacking and difference—desire where being is *found wanting*—should not monopolize the subject's relations to its others, to the world. René's "nonsexual adoration" of Sir Stephen constitutes another form of desiring, one not seeking what Bersani comes to call "differential otherness" (*TT* 4).[28] His homo-narcissism becomes an early example of desiring movement that is not premised on want.

Chariot Allegory

For Bersani, the Proustian search begins with what Laplanche would suggest are the "enigmatic" solicitations that the infant receives from its originary human other, the primary caretaker, who unwittingly addresses the child sexually, seducing it from need to desire. While hominizing, via sexualization, the little animal, the enigmatic signifier promises to yield the missing information that would complete the subject's knowledge of himself. In this model, desire is driven by the (al)lure of such messages whose truth, as the subject thinks, others willfully obfuscate. Bersani writes in *Baudelaire and Freud* (1977) that the Proustian-psychoanalytic subject—which embodies our culture's hegemonic postulations about being and becoming—emerges through, and remains in the grip of, "fascinating and intoxicating spectacles of otherness" (*BF* 110). Nonsexual sadism, exemplified in *The Story of O*, is where the subject "coolly" eviscerates the other in order to uncover and then assimilate her secrets. In projected masochism, on the other hand, the subject is drawn into the vortex of desire, pulled apart in the jouissance of *ébranlement*'s repetition. While one of these ways of approaching the other is ethically preferable, both are grounded in modes of desire where the other fascinates the subject with that which the latter primordially lacks. While nonsexual sadism promotes the object's exenteration by an investigator-subject, in shattering the object and the subject come together in a catastrophic dénouement.

But there may be, as Bersani discerns already in 1976, another way of moving in the world, one that does not depend on sadism, whether that be the cold cruelty of torture or the eager witnessing of suffering that reactivates the subject's masochistic pleasures. This nonsadistic orientation is exemplified in René's fascination with Sir Stephen. The older man has nothing that the younger would *want*; instead, he offers René a *likeness*. But more: if sexuality, as a human-specific way of being in the world, names the subject's capture by the other's enigmatic solicitations, René's attraction to Sir Stephen is not, properly speaking, sexual. His is an "untroubled nonsexual adoration" (*FA* 295). Twenty years later, in *Homos*, Bersani speaks of André Gide's work in the same terms. "Gidean homosexuality is strangely undemanding," he writes of Michel, the protagonist of Gide's *The Immoralist* (1902). ". . . It is, so to speak, homosexuality without sexuality, desire that is satisfied just by the proximity of the other" (*H* 121). Bersani seeks to extricate homo-attractions from sexuality because, for him, like for Foucault, sexuality is contaminated by its role in the constitution of the modern subject. If Bersani becomes increasingly interested in the connectedness that he first observes between the two men in "Persons in Pieces," this is because the narcissistic attraction of like to like is not filtered through the sexual, psychological self. Instead, René's contemplation of the older man is an example of "pleasures of self-absorption in which the self is erased" (*AI* 207), of homo-narcissism.

The work of "reinvent[ing] the relational possibilities of narcissism" (*I* 76) continues in *Intimacies*, whose argument should be situated in the framework that begins to emerge in "Persons in Pieces."[29] In his collaboration with Phillips, Bersani turns to Plato's *Phaedrus*, particularly to the chariot allegory in Socrates's second speech. Contesting the notion (first articulated by Phaedrus, who recounts Lysias's speech, and then by Socrates himself) that it is better for the lover to prefer the calculative reason of a nonlover over the lover's passion, the palinode presents love as a mode of remembering the soul's pre-embodiment past. According to the myth, before their descent to earth, souls travel in a god's chariot in the heavens, where "abides the very being with which true knowledge is concerned; the colourless, formless, intangible essence, visible only to the mind, the pilot of the soul." Once on earth, the soul obscurely recalls what it has seen. No earthly poet will ever sing fully of the heavens to which the immortal gods ascend, yet all have varied degrees of access to "the recollection of those things our soul once saw while following God."[30] "Every human soul," Bersani writes, "remains in touch, through memory, with the god it followed" (*I* 79).

What we have in the allegory is a version of the Platonic theory of Forms: all have witnessed incorporeal perfection in heaven; our earthly ambition is to recall "beauty, wisdom, goodness, and the like" when prompted by various embodied objects. The experience of love is elicited by the lover's more or less obfuscated memory; the lover is a subject "who, when he sees the beauty of earth, is transported with the recollection of the true beauty."[31] Our earthly "love experience restores to us, below the conscious level, the memory of primal scenes from the soul's ancient past. Love causes the soul to take flight, thus resuming its original heavenly activity."[32]

Bersani connects Socrates's allegory to Freud's famous observation, in *Three Essays on the Theory of Sexuality* (1905), about object-love: that "[t]he finding of an object is in fact a refinding of it."[33] "Love, which we like to think of as a discovery," he writes, "is inseparable from memory" (*I* 72), for Freud the memory of the infant's satiety at the mother's breast. On the one hand, there is a "profound continuity" between the Freudian and Socratic accounts of love: in *Phaedrus*, as in the *Three Essays*, "love is a phenomenon of memory, and an instance of narcissistic fascination" (*I* 80). *Phaedrus* provides a myth that psychoanalysis rearticulates: love is self-love, indeed "narcissistic extravagance" (*I* 76). On the other hand, however, Socrates's "is a form of narcissism that the psychoanalytic version of narcissism, which it appears to resemble, makes it difficult for us to understand" (*I* 80). Socratic narcissism needs to be distinguished from "the specularity of a personal narcissism" (*I* 82), where sameness, in the form of one's doppelgänger or clone, evokes uncanny terror. The Socratic self is not the being we find in the Lacanian mirror, the ideal ego whose appearance the disorganized being of infancy meets first with jubilation and then with aggressiveness. One may propose, rather, that the subject that Bersani locates in Socrates's theory of love inhabits the *Leibnizian mirror*. Leibniz frequently describes monads as mirrors that reflect the world more or less adequately, according to their singular perspective. This facility is enabled by the world's connectedness: "since everything is connected because of the plenitude of the world, and since each body acts on every other body, more or less, in proportion to its distance, and is itself affected by the other through reaction, it follows that each monad is a living mirror or a mirror endowed with internal action, which represents the universe from its own point of view and is as ordered as the universe itself."[34] Unlike the Lacanian mirror that allows the egoic subject's distinction from its *Umwelt*, Leibniz's monadic mirrors contain the plenum in its (distorted) totality as indistinguishable from the subject.

The account of (self-)love that Bersani finds in *Phaedrus* repeats his earlier argument, in "Persons in Pieces," about René's homo-narcissistic "worship" of Sir Stephen. As much as the older man's sameness captures René, the Socratic subject is drawn to forms—human and otherwise—in which it recognizes remains of its heavenly companions. But whereas the Socratic narcissist orients itself vertically to pre-embodiment Forms, Bersani's reading of Plato is inflected through the onto-ethics/aesthetics of another thinker that has exerted a crucial influence on his work. We should, that is, detect in the commentary on *Phaedrus* in *Intimacies* echoes of Baudelaire's theory of "idealization," which Bersani elaborates in *The Culture of Redemption* and which we explored in chapter 3. Both Bersani and Baudelaire propose an ontology in which beings aspire toward their ideals, to what Irwin Edman, in his commentary on Plato, calls "the remembered eternities of beauty."[35] Yet the beauty that interests Bersani and Baudelaire differs from the Platonic Forms of eternal perfection. Rather, as is often noted in commentaries on Baudelaire, idealization's movement of becoming is *horizontal* rather than *vertical*: rather than an orientation to a transcendent world of Forms, idealization constitutes a continual drift of related forms toward each other in an immanent aesthetic field. A logic of singularity guides this movement: as Baudelaire writes, "each individual has his ideal."[36] Johann Kaspar Lavater's aesthetic theory, mapping correspondences between body parts, hues, colors—and so forth—that art should actualize, constitutes an attempt to codify these idealities. This aspect of Baudelairean aesthetics can be traced to Plato, too: in *Phaedrus*, Socrates proposes that "[e]very one chooses his love from the ranks of beauty according to his character."[37] In Plato's myth, beauty's "ranks" are ordered in pre-embodiment heaven: because we have shared god's chariot with other souls, on earth we recognize our fellow travelers, whose vague memory renders them appealing to us.

As we noted in chapter 3, the task of "Boundaries of Time and Being: Benjamin, Baudelaire, Nietzsche" is to glean from Baudelaire an aesthetic theory that, although contributing to Walter Benjamin's onto-ethics/aesthetics, would escape what for Bersani are the redemptive implications of Benjaminian philosophy. Redemptive philosophies, such as Benjamin's, imagine a world in terms of a puzzle that solicits our interpretive desire when some of its pieces have gone missing. Like the Lacanian *objet petit a*, the primordially lost pieces instigate our wanting: their promise is seen in objects that necessarily confuse, as Lacan would say, the object-cause of desire with objects of desire. This mode of desire determines psychoanalytic ontology: Bersani claims that Lacan "promot[es] . . . castration from an Oedipal fantasy to the meta-genital status of a lost plenitude of being" (*IRG* 54). Laplanche and Proust articulate versions of this ontology. In Baudelaire, we find something else: the mode of re-collection that guides the Baudelairean artist's work is premised on an economy where what is being re-membered is not lacking or lost but—as Bersani increasingly frequently puts it in his later work—exists in a *virtual* form.[38] Idealization aims at the remembered forms of singularity, an allness that we have called monadic.

Cosmic Narcissus

As Adam Phillips writes, classical psychoanalytic theory figures narcissistic pathology as "an attempt to stop time by killing desire."[39] Locked into narcissism's repetitions—which, rather than the freshness of difference, offer but the sickroom air of sameness—we refuse "development." A narcissist *par excellence*, the homosexual refuses to relinquish the mother's gaze (or voice) and, internalizing it, looks for in others only repetitions of his past self. This, as Phillips suggests, preempts futurity's promise of difference and development—it is where time comes to an end. It is in narcissism, its atemporality, that we most immediately find figured the futureless queerness that quilts the symbolic order's dialectical logic.[40]

Beginning with his encounter with Laplanchean psychoanalysis in "Persons in Pieces," Bersani's project has been increasingly focused on rethinking the seeming nonmovement that narcissism constitutes. The ethical options that emerge in the early analysis of Freud, Laplanche, Réage, and Berg seem to consist of nonsexual aggression and derived sadism: one either undoes the other with the coolness of Réage's sadists or pleasurably identifies with the world's annihilation. Yet, whether the violence is self-shattering or nonsexual, ecstatic or cool-headed, the world is still devastated in the self's search for pleasure. Hence, when Bersani and Dutoit ask in *Caravaggio's Secrets* (1998), and then *Arts of Impoverishment: Beckett, Rothko, Resnais* (1993), whether it is possible to imagine "a *non*sadistic relation to external reality" (*CS* 69), "a nonsadistic type of movement" (*AI* 147), they are remembering the analysis in "Persons in Pieces." The query returns at the opening of *Thoughts and Things*: "Is there a nonsadistic type of movement?" Bersani quotes himself (*TT* 1). The question persists not least because it productively troubles the ethical value of *ébranlement*. If the autonomous ego—the site of the subject's authority over and distance from the world—is constituted by being ecstatically undone, it loses its capacity for the kind of aggressive control that Réage's men exercise, instead becoming the masochistically ravished being whose examples we find in *The Image*. This argument has been well received particularly since its explicit queering in "Is the Rectum a Grave?" (1987). Its success, however, has obfuscated Bersani's *consistent ambivalence* about the dynamic it promotes. It has remained infrequently noted that Bersani is not only a thinker of the ethical potential of solipsism and masochism—of "the antisocial"—but also, always, a speculative ontologist who wants us to find ways of training ourselves in other modes of being-in-the-world than self-annihilation.

The problem with projected masochism, as the mechanism of *ébranlement*, is that it depends on our continual access to scenes of the other's suffering. We seek "spectacle[s] of the other person's commotion" (*FrB* 42), where we can be infected, once again, by the remembered intensities of our unraveling. "If erotic stimulation depends on the perceived or fantasized commotion of others," Bersani writes, "it becomes reasonable to put others into a state of maximal commotion" (*FrB* 42). Since we are thoroughly familiar with, indeed well trained in, such pleasures, can we meet the world otherwise than through sadistic intensities? If we are to do so, we must come up with "a convincing theory of nonmimetic sexuality," one that "could account for sexual excitement in terms no longer dependent on the fantasy-representations of the excitement of others."[41] This is no easy task, for such a project would need to counteract "the massive training which we receive in the art of mimetic stimulation."[42] To imagine other, possibly nonsadistic pleasures, Bersani does not turn to scenes of nonviolence; rather, he explores, for example, the thrilling visual narratives of war and hunting in ancient Assyrian palace reliefs. We discussed the analyses of *The Forms of Violence: Narrative in Assyrian Art and Modern Culture* (1985) already in chapter 1. As Bersani and Dutoit note, the reliefs' depictions of conquest and death offer pleasures immediately recognizable to subjects with our training in mimetic desire. We enjoy in them the kind of carnage that, according to the theory of derived sadism, makes us tremble with the originary intensity of our becoming-human. Yet Bersani and Dutoit also locate another mode of soliciting the viewer in the reliefs: apart from their "highly narrativized art," where the spectator's attention is compelled by violently climaxing sequences of images, the sculptors have devised "extraordinarily ingenious strategies for diverting our attention from the stories thus emphasized" (*FV* 9). In addition to the thrill offered by the reliefs' brutalizing action, a "centrifugal" repetition of forms—a spear is extended in a line that draws a bar in cage; a horse's hoof is replicated in the figure of a leaf; the side of a ladder is positioned next to an arm in such a way that a triangle emerges from the background, repeated elsewhere; and so on—enables a disengagement from narrative violence. Supplementing the stories of conquest and pillage, the latter techniques seduce us to abandon the narratives' fascinating violence for the less intense enjoyment of aesthetic repetitions.

In identifying these two modes of pleasure in Assyrian art, Bersani and Dutoit are implicitly instructed by the reading of *The Story of O* in "Persons in Pieces." René's contemplative and calm attraction to Sir Stephen—his homo-narcissistic pleasure—is enabled by the system of heterosexual difference, whether in the form of nonsexual mastery or projected masochism. In a strictly analogous manner, Bersani and Dutoit identify in the devastating violence of Assyrian representations a parasitic mode of connectedness, one that is thoroughly unfamiliar to an audience of our cultural training in the post-Freudian, modern West. Embedded in—or emerging from—the violent stories, the representations are organized such that they distract the spectator from his search for what Laplanche suggests are the pleasures of *ébranlement* in projected masochism. Promoting "perceptual moves which undo narrative organizations and prohibit a fascination with the violent stories of Assyrian history" (*FV* 14), the reliefs experiment with "nonsadistic movement." "The Assyrian sculptors," as Bersani writes, "show an exceptional willingness to deemphasize their subjects through various kinds of formal play; they continually invite us to move from narrative violence to the 'violence' of multiple contacts producing multiple forms" (*FrB* 70). It is here, in the unlikeliest of places, that he finds an experimentation with modes of pleasure other than that of derived sadism, itself a preferable ethical option to nonsexual aggressiveness.

As we noted in chapter 1, a parallel argument emerges—or the observations about Assyrian sculpture are recategorized—in *Caravaggio's Secrets*. As much as the reliefs offer us two modes of enjoyment, Caravaggio's art not only lures us with the sexiness of his models, but also solicits the viewer with a different spectatorial pleasure as its representations move "from the teasingly enigmatic eroticism of the portraits of boys to the nonsexual sensuality of physical contacts, extensions, and correspondences" (*IRG* 177). Bersani and Dutoit write that the latter form of "sensuality" in Caravaggio is "nonerotic" (*CS* 79). This is an argument whose embryonic form we have already seen: it echoes Bersani's comparison, in "Persons in Pieces," of the absorptive pleasures of derived sadism (in Berg) with the "nonerotic imagination" that informs René's "nonsexual adoration" of Sir Stephen in *The Story of O* (*FA* 300, 295). Already in *A Future for Astyanax*, Bersani begins to think of the ways in which the homo-narcissist is moved by "the milder sensual pleasure of discovering [his] inaccurate self-replications in the world, the aesthetically pleasing correspondences between the world and multiple partial aspects of [his] subjecthood."[43]

René, or the later Caravaggio, illustrates a mode of desiring different from the one that we moderns understand as "sexuality."

Thus we find the minor-key argument about homo-narcissism in "Persons in Pieces" recategorized in the analysis of Assyrian art in *The Forms of Violence*, of Caravaggio's sensuality in *Caravaggio's Secrets*, of Gide's homosexuality in *Homos*, and of Socratic love in *Intimacies*. It emerges, most recently, in the cosmological speculations of *Thoughts and Things*. Bersani begins the chapter "Far Out," perhaps the most "hyperbolic" or "fantastical" (*TT* 77, 89)—terms that may remind us of Bertrand Russell's bemused condemnation of Leibniz's metaphysics[44]—piece of writing he has ever produced, by referring to Lawrence Krauss's suggestion that our bodies contain atoms of far-off heavenly bodies, long ago extinguished: bearing the residue of exploded stars, we are, as Krauss puts it, "star children."[45] Krauss's argument about our bodies' recall of their remote celestial ancestry—"neural memories of our beginnings" (*TT* 80)—reminds Bersani of his own earlier speculations about narcissism. Prompted by speculative astronomy, he, for example, returns to his mythopoetic reading of *Phaedrus*. Referring to his discussion, in *Intimacies*, of the "kind of self-love," "a love for a different sameness" that he had observed in Socrates's story, he suggests that we regard the Platonic myth as a version of Krauss's observations: as much as the Socratic lover remembers the species to which he belonged in the heavens, "Krauss gives us a cosmic version of this identity of being" (*TT* 84). In this, we observe the most recent recategorization of the homo-narcissistic connectedness whose earliest examples emerge in *A Future for Astyanax*.

What compels Bersani in *Phaedrus* is in part the principle of reincarnation (παλινγενεσίᾳ, *palingenesía*) included in Plato's chariot allegory. If the lover chooses an object that "already belongs to the lover's type of being" (*I* 82), the beings that solicit one's desire may, because of this principle, include other forms than human.[46] *Phaedrus* offers an allegory for the constitution of what Bersani already in the 1990s calls "families" or "communit[ies] of forms" (*H* 121, *AI* 180)—an argument that can, again, be traced to its incipient form in the evocation of homo-narcissism in "Persons in Pieces." Each "family" expresses "a singular universal property distinct from the multiple particular individuals who embody it."[47] Such "metaphysical individuality," as "distinct from subjectivity," remains "indifferent to the human subject" (*CR* 82). The studies of Assyrian reliefs and Caravaggio's paintings echo the argument in tracking "perceptual orders that design some of the multitudinous relations between the human and the nonhuman" (*IRG* 87). To experience the ways in which the human extends "into other generations, other species, even into the inanimate" (*H* 147), we must unlearn our anthropocentric training; to actualize our homoness, we must betray humanity. Genet models for us the possibility, indeed the ethical necessity, of "the betrayal of all human ties, the attempted murder of humanity itself" (*H* 167). What makes us human is our boundedness to an identity; it is from these "human ties" that we must unbind (*dé-lier*) ourselves. To actualize its embeddedness in the world more fully, the subject must be *redeemed—erlöst*, as Nietzsche, and sometimes Laplanche, might say—from its monopolization by the human.

On Speculative Narcissism

In his effort to erode the anthropocentric frame that he sees organizing modern onto-ethics, Bersani turns not to the *non*human but to the *a*human. Rather than the categorial steadiness suggested by the prefix *non-*, *a-* moves the noun toward a verbal form, where the prefix, as the *Oxford English Dictionary* puts it, indicates a "motion onward or away from a position." "The ahuman"—rather, "to ahuman"—suggests a becoming that is an *a*vocation, a distractive call. We have referred to the solicitation of the enigmatic signifier similarly as an "avocation": the enigma with which the subject is called or caressed into hominization establishes a constitutive, and life-saving, distraction for the failed animal. Yet the process of *fourvoiement* precipitated by the call of otherness differs from the torture that Bersani has in mind. The psychoanalytic subject is distracted by a call from beyond the ontological divide between the self and the world, a divide whose constitution is simultaneous with the subject's emergence as a form of *response-ability*. Laplanche insists that this subject is never a monad, a being that would precede its centrifugal movement into the world; rather, the Freudian revolution replaces the idealist subject with one that becomes through its solicitation by preexistent otherness. In this, Laplanche repeats Marx's critique of speculative idealism: as much as Hegel posits a subject—a monad and a Robinson Crusoe—who never has to distract its gaze from its mirror, Freud fails his own revolution by relapsing, in his later work, to monadic assumptions about the subject (primary narcissism and the id of the second topography being the most obvious symptoms of Freud's error). Bersani, however, wants us to unlearn—to begin with, become conscious of—the onto-ethical habits affirmed by the psychoanalytic subject. Most notable among the hegemonic tendencies that inform our movement in the world are the postulations of anthropocentrism, enigmatic otherness, and the ontology of wanting being.

Going against the grain of the commonsense that we find in Marx and Laplanche, Bersani thinks the ahuman through "speculative narcissism."[48] This mode takes on the risks that modern thought has warned us against in its critique of speculative philosophy. The problem with the speculative orientation, we are often told, is that it assumes a world where there is nothing that is not in an *a priori* relation with the subject. Like the narcissist, the speculative philosopher, enraptured by his mirror image, ignores all true otherness: as Marx and Engels write, speculative thoughts have "grown out of the ether of your brain and not out of the material world."[49] In a way that influenced subsequent commentators, Marx complains about the disengagement of Hegelian idealism, the speculative subject's unresponsiveness to all solicitations of otherness. As it contemplates the world "enthroned in sublime solitude [*in erhabener Einsamkeit thronend*]," the Hegelian mind betrays the revolution that was supposed to have unseated all such imperious rulers.[50] Hegel's speculative self—as a convenient alibi for the bourgeois-idealist subject—not only discovers the world through solitary reflection, but also finds that the self and the world have always already coincided. "Consciousness," as Hegel boasts, "provides its own criterion from within itself, so that the investigation becomes a comparison of consciousness with itself."[51] If the world's otherness is posited always and only in terms of the self, the speculative subject appears in paralytic contemplation of the God's mirror that it presumes its self to be. The other can be apprehended only in the recognizable form of a specular inversion, a figment in the mirror that, as etymology suggests, conditions speculative thought's tortuous reflections. Johann Friedrich Pfaff reminds Hegel in a letter (to which Hegel's response has been lost): "*Speculation* comes from *speculum*, mirror, the thought that gazes at itself (that is reflected)."[52] Others have, implicitly or explicitly, echoed this observation in diagnosing in the Hegelian system what Jameson calls "the narcissism of the Absolute."[53] Arrested in contemplation of his own image, the abstract (disembodied, solipsistic) self of speculative thought fails to respond to the other's call and, instead, seeks the world's totalization (its totalitarianization, as we are further admonished) in the Absolute. Hubristically, Hegel's speculative subject, captured by his own mirror image, becomes impervious to all otherness, turns a deaf ear to the call that comes from the world outside.

It is not only the Marxist tradition that critiques speculative thought in these terms. If Marx finds that the speculative mind ignores worldly realities in its self-involvement, Luther deems philosophy an error when thinkers presume to be able to replace revelation with reason. "The speculative learning of the theologians is altogether worthless [*Speculativa scientia theologorum est simpliciter vana*]," he writes of Plato, Dionysus, and Bonaventure; a philosopher only "babbles" and "prattles [*nugatur*]" about being and nonbeing when he should humble himself in the face of God's mysterious grace.[54] Luther's objections to philosophy concern the prideful way in which the other's call—κλῆσις or *Berufung*—is disposed of. "Speculative theology belongs to the devil in hell" because the ostentatious monologue of baroque reasoning drowns out the call of creation.[55]

Following Luther, contemporary theologians continue to remind us of the folly of speculative thought: it is a prime example of the inward turning (*incurvatus in se*) that marks worldly indifference to God's solicitations. Human hubris assumes that we can reach divinity by reason, deducing its otherness from what we see in this world's mirrors. Yet God, as Oswald Bayer writes, "is not our mirror-image; God does not allow himself to be the object of human speculation [*Gott ist nicht unser Spiegelbild; er läßt sich also nicht spekulieren*]."[56] Heedless of Luther's warning, Western tradition proceeded on its speculative way, ending up with Hegelian idealism. Bayer outlines this development: "With great style, the Western concept of the movement of self-consciousness as a 'complete return of Mind to itself' reaches its apex in Hegel's thought. Even theologians have not been able to extricate themselves from the fascination of the thought of the speculative mind that is in love with its own mirror reflection [*der Faszination durch diesen spekulativen Geist, der in sein eigenes Spiegelbild verliebt ist*]."[57] The fallen mind is vulnerable to the fascinations of narcissistic thought, as much as, according to Freud, lack renders men susceptible to bewitchment by such mysterious, self-absorbed beings as narcissistic women (or felines and "large beasts of prey").[58] As "the devil's whore"—as Luther famously called philosophy—speculative thought captures the human in its trap with *fascination*, the paralyzing sorcery or witchcraft (from the Latin *fascināre* and *fascinum*) that leaves one in thrall of a malevolent other.[59] Fascinated, one is powerless to resist "the strange and unexpected forms of an approaching death," to turn away from the serpent's hypnotic gaze.[60]

As a narcissistic fascination, the speculative orientation proves not only "worthless," but also "sterile,"[61] for creation, as both Luther and genetics tell us, demands dualism and dialogue, not the sameness and monologue characteristic of the narcissistic self-replication. Unable to hear the other's call, the modern narcissist turns away from the possibility of love, from creation itself. "Creation," Johannes Schwanke writes, ". . . is not effected monologically but dialogically," a theological argument scientifically confirmed by "the free genetic exchange of information that forms the necessary presupposition for the fusion of two cells."[62] As a result of its fascinated paralysis, the speculative mind is unable to access the fecund cycle of newness. The modern subject, in his narcissism, refuses the ethicalness of ex-centricity, of being's grounding "outside himself, in another, in a stranger."[63] In such restatements of Luther's argument about human inwardness, contemporary theology exemplifies the hegemonic mode of modern onto-ethics, organized around an irrecuperable, constitutive difference ("the crushing, incomprehensible hiddenness of God").[64] In his prioritization of inscrutable otherness, Emmanuel Levinas's ethics provides a paradigmatic twentieth-century example of this tradition. For his part, Bersani locates versions of this mode of thought in Proust and psychoanalysis.[65] The Proustian subject approaches worldly objects in order to discover in them the solution to the riddle of his being. For Bersani, Proust's descriptions anticipate the theory of the enigmatic signifier, whose intrusion precipitates, in Laplanche's ontology, hominization's wayward career. The Laplanchean subject constitutes a vocation—more appropriately, we have suggested, an *a*vocation—where one follows, as in Luther, a distractive solicitation that comes from elsewhere. Emerging as a response to a call, this subject, much like the Proustian one, is characterized by "a paranoid fascination with the enigmatic signifier" (*CS* 95). This "paranoid fascination" bespeaks "our fascination with lack" (*CS* 99). It is this hegemony of *want* in modern thought that Bersani has sought to contest throughout his work.

In Bersani's work, the speculative narcissist emerges as an alternative to the modern subject of interiority and trauma. This subject is Réage's René, distracted from the pleasures of cool sadism by his contemplation of a familiar aesthetic form in Sir Stephen. The logic of his narcissism is repeated in the parasitic emergence of formal repetitions amidst the mesmerizing narratives of pillage and war in the Assyrian palace reliefs; it is further illustrated by the loving recognition of a shared, if unremembered, history that Plato allegorizes in *Phaedrus*. We suggested in our introduction that we find an antecedent for Bersani's narcissist in the speculative being of Hegel's philosophy. Bersani and Hegel, we further proposed, are related to one another through a mutual ancestor: Leibniz. Like the monadic being of Bersani's onto-ethics/aesthetics, Hegel's speculative proposition, as the highest mode of thought, unfolds according to strictly immanent determinations, its predicates having become intrinsic properties, essential to the grammatical subject. The speculative proposition gives us, as Jean-Luc Nancy writes, "the infinite self-relation of what is."[66] In an analogous way, Bersani's speculative narcissist is a being of "true singleness or individuality" (*FA* 181), one whose movement is not determined by lack but driven by an internal force. For Hegel, speculative propositions constitute conceptual thinking, characteristic of science; for Bersani, speculative self-unfolding belongs to the realm of *the aesthetic*. When Bersani observes this, he is not only speaking of what we habitually call "art"; rather, he proposes that "art" is merely one realm in which speculative becoming can take place, one mode of "the aesthetic." Other modes may include the shared chatter of friends or strangers, the anonymous intimacies of queer subcultures, and Freud's self-defeating theorizations of becoming-human.

On Animal Ecstasy

As a final illustration, we can return, like Bersani often does, to Baudelaire. In "The Painter of Modern Life," Baudelaire gives us a moment of speculative narcissism in recalling an artist-friend's childhood memory of watching his father dress. As the child observes the details of the half-naked man's body, the sight "penetrates" him as he engages in "the contemplation of form" that he will come to follow as his artistic vocation. He is drawn into a contemplative identification with the father, but a father whose human form disintegrates into an image rendered in the shading of pinks, yellows, and blues of the skin and veins.[67] This tableau is meant to illustrate the movement of "idealization" in painting, where the "model" is pulled apart across a network of correspondences. It is an example of an aesthetic *torquere*, where a figure's dissolution allows the artist to "remember" an ideal that has never existed, "the dazzling truth of its native harmony."[68] The child is responding, for the first time, to the calling of an artist, finding himself exercising a "mnemotechny of the beautiful."[69]

The child cannot turn away from the scene: "obsessed and possessed" by the sight of his father's undoing, he views the tableau with a "fixed and animally ecstatic gaze [*l'œil fixe et animalement extatique*]."[70] It is a gaze of identification, for it registers in the father the self that the artist will have become. Yet the child's narcissistic pleasure is nothing like a jubilant (mis)recognition of a cohesive bodily imago in the mirror. What we find here is not "the first capture by the image in which the first moment of the dialectic of identifications is sketched out," not a prototype for "the ineffable jouissance [the subject] finds in losing himself in the fascinating image."[71] The recognition of the self in the other does not establish the murderous dialectic theorized by Lacan. Rather than an uncanny doppelgänger, the child contemplates in the father-semblant a visual movement, the slightly nauseating sense of a body's dissolution into a purely aesthetic assemblage of lines and colors. In this movement, the model is twisted or queered (*torquere*), emerging correspondences enabling the re-membering of an unactualized ideal. Addressing a different example from Baudelaire, Bersani writes of this dynamic in *The Culture of Redemption*: "The correspondences through which objects complete themselves by connecting to related forms are always represented correspondences, correspondences perceived—or, perhaps more accurately, remembered—by a human subject" (*CR* 74). Implicating the (human) subject in the (nonhuman) world, the memory of correspondences constitutes "a going out of oneself, indeed an uncontrollable breakdown of the very boundaries of selfhood, which is also an exceptional self-expansion, a kind of celebration of the self-as-world, in short a narcissistic jouissance" (*CR* 74)—the jouissance of an ahuman call.

In exploring this jouissance of correspondences, Baudelaire becomes a theorist and practitioner of the speculative narcissism that Bersani has sought to clarify since his first encounter, in *A Future for Astyanax*, with psychoanalytic theory. The enthrallment of the child's "fixed" gaze in "The Painter of Modern Life" is identical to the "fascinated worship" with which René contemplates Sir Stephen in *The Story of O* (*FA* 295); the "animal ecstasy" in the boy's "penetration" by the father's image is a version of the "narcissistic fascination" that draws embodied beings to their likenesses in Plato's chariot allegory (*I* 80).[72] "Women are desired because they are different," Bersani observes of *The Story of O*, "but the stimulating lack in desire is perhaps no match for *the ecstatically calm contemplation of one's own self*, for a kind of self-effacement in the name of the self" (*FA* 295, emphasis added). Like René's in Réage, the child's gaze in Baudelaire, in its animalization—becoming-grotesque—becomes *ek-static*. "Ecstasy" is one of Bersani's keywords, something of a crypto-concept like "the monad." For him, the moving-out of the self that ecstasy names is not a movement toward the inscrutable, enigmatic other of modern onto-ethics. Rather, it constitutes an ecstasy of homomonadism, whose simultaneity of radical disconnect and universal concomitance places one at home in the world. It is not a scattering or dissemination, unless we designate these as "speculative" movements, ones that follow an internal principle.

The ecstasy of speculative narcissism gives us an alternative to Proustian desire, which, "eroticizing that which we are not, . . . saves us from the ecstasy of monadic self-containment" (*H* 141). Proust redemptively locates monadic beings in a network of relations produced by an economy of lack; the monad's solipsism is dissipated by the various solicitations and pastoral promises that distract being from its self-concentration. In Beckett and Genet, on the other hand, essences, indifferent to such seductions, remain enveloped by their narcissistic monadism; yet this is a nonrelatedness that, as Leslie Hill writes of *Murphy*, constitutes a "solipsistic ecstasy" and that Genet's narrator in *Funeral Rites* calls "that luminous monster who is exposed to the most splendid solitude, the one in whose presence I experience a kind of ecstasy."[73] If homomonadic solipsism is experienced ek-statically, it is a movement in which "[b]eing is transferred without being moved" (*FoB* 4). In supplementing "the ecstasy of monadic self-containment" with an "ecstatic oneness with the world" (*FoB* 172), Bersani evokes Leibniz's postulations of nonrelatedness and harmony. Leibniz writes: "it must be known that all things are *connected* in each one of the possible worlds: the universe, whatever it may be, is all of one piece, like an ocean: the least movement extends its effect there to any distance whatsoever, even though this effect become less perceptible in proportion to the distance."[74] While Russell sees in statements such as this one only dissembled monism, Bersani, encountering Leibnizian metaphysics through Proust, Deleuze, and (particularly) Beckett, is attracted to its challenge to think of ecstatic singularities, nonrelated and connected.[75]

For such Lutheran thinkers as Bayer, propositions about the "self-moving soul"[76] indicate the "fascination" that Western thought's speculative hubris continues to exert on us. Much like narcissistic women, cats, and large predators, the speculative subject allures us with the attraction of a faultlessly self-involved being. Perfecting the tendency of philosophy's *incurvatus in se*, Hegelian idealism, as Bayer continues, comes to exemplify "modern narcissism." The subject of the speculative proposition is a Narcissus, who, enraptured by its image, refuses the other's call. Like Narcissus, the speculative being, in the perfection of its self-determination

(*Selbstbestimmung*), hears nothing but its own internal voice (*Stimme*); having absorbed all possible predicates to its essence, it follows, undisturbed by otherness, nothing but its own destiny (*Bestimmung*).

When Bayer notes the "great style" in which modern thought's speculative excesses have been rendered—culminating in Hegel[77]—he evokes the familiar trope of the aesthete, more often than not a homo, who has turned to artful but sterile self-reproductions in order to escape the fecund terrors of difference that await for us in love. If this homoaesthete morphed into the clone after Stonewall, he models the possibility of an otherless reproduction. Whether in the laboratory or the Castro, the clone advertises the human hubris of the mad scientist who assumes to have solved the riddle of creation. In the process, he jeopardizes that which makes us human. The clone's efforts at self-stylization always go too far; striving for perfection, the clone risks, as the narrator of Rumaker's *A Day and a Night at the Baths* suggests, an uncanny loss of his human singularity, the affective interiority whose redemptive presence the heartbeat nevertheless reveals.

In his decade-long work of recategorizing the concept, Bersani suggests that, rather than dissociating homosexuality from narcissism, we reframe the question. There is, as he would say, another way to look at the issue (*CR* 189).[78] Much like Foucault in his essay on genealogical historiography, he proposes that there is nothing inevitable or inescapable in the way in which we have come to organize our onto-ethics. The epistemophilia, traumatism, and anthropocentrism that determine our habits of understanding our places in the world can be unlearned. We can train ourselves into speculative narcissism, a homomonadic self-relation that, in its "estheticizing movement" (*FrB* 11), may take the form of an "absolute narcissism [that] also opens a path onto the world, a world emptied of relations but where relationality has to be reinvented" (*H* 171). Yielding to "animal ecstasy," the speculative narcissist becomes less than human; yet this is "a lessness that allows [one] to reoccur, differently, everywhere" (*FoB* 9). In the spiraling movement of its unfolding, speculative narcissism betrays the developmental narratives that have often diagnosed in the homosexual an inability to move on from earlier stages of psychic maturation. What the homo-narcissist, uninterested in difference and seeking only self-relations, does to time in murdering desire is not unlike the destruction of the temporality of "perfectibility," whose influence Benjamin discerned in Hegelianism's and classical Marxism's normative models of becoming. The arrest of time that, as Phillips notes, is associated with narcissism may be as disruptively futural as the monadic "nowness" that Benjamin, synthesizing Leibniz and the Kabbalah, evokes in his theory of messianic becoming. In the crystal of the monad, "time . . . has come to a standstill," a stillness that intensively encompasses the past in its entirety.[79] While the monadic now is radically isolated from all other moments on the historical continuum, it simultaneously entails—as the Leibnizian logic of predication stipulates—all possible predicates in its essence. Like Bersani's homomonad, the speculative subject bets on the openness of the world it finds in its mirror.

Notes

Introduction

1. Kant, *Critique of Pure Reason*, Bxxx (117); *Kritik der reinen Vernunft*, 3.18. On the "rapturousness" of *Schwärmerei*, Kant writes: "[wer sie] bey wem [sie] sich die Zügellose phantasie mit Ideen des guten associirt: ein Enthusiast. Bey dem sie regellos ist: ein Träumer, (ist sie zugleich Zügellos, Überschwenglich), dazu auch der Schwärmer gehört" (*Gesammelte Schriften* 15.145, brackets in orig.; qtd. in Hinske, "Zur Verwendung der Wörter 'schwärmen,' 'Schwärmer,' 'Schwärmerei,' 'schwärmerisch' im Kontext von Kants Anthropologiekolleg," 78). For commentary on the term "*überschwenglich*" in Kant, see Palmquist, *Comprehensive Commentary on Kant's Religion Within the Bounds of Bare Reason*, 518.

2. Marx, "Contribution to the Critique of Hegel's Philosophy of Law," 181; "Zur Kritik der Hegelschen Rechtsphilosophie," 384.

3. Marx and Engels, *The Holy Family*, 125; *Die heilige Familie*, 137.

4. Bersani, Preface to the Second Edition, x–xi.

5. Ibid., xii.

6. Bersani, "Rigorously Speculating," 294.

7. See also *TT* 4; and "Rigorously Speculating," 283.

8. Bersani, Preface to the Second Edition, xi.

9. Laplanche, "Notes on Afterwardsness"; see also Laplanche, "The Freud Museum Seminar," 41–44; "Interview: Jean Laplanche Talks to Martin Stanton," 15–17; and "Time and the Other," 234–36.

10. Laplanche, "A Metapsychology Put to the Test of Anxiety," 81; "Une métapsychologie à lépreuve de l'angoisse," 706.

11. Laplanche, "Interview: Jean Laplanche Talks to Martin Stanton," 5.

12. Laplanche, "The Freud Museum Seminar," 55.

13. For Bersani's most explicit commentary on Deleuzean influences in his work, see "Rigorously Speculating," 289–91; and, concomitantly, *TT* 87–88n.

14. While Edward Said, too, reads "French theory" in the early 1970s, and has been called the first American critic to do so (see Radhakrishnan, *History, the*

Human, and the World Between, 119–20), the two thinkers' work unfolds along instructively different trajectories, whose respective shapes can be gauged in their early commentaries on Michel Foucault. In an essay originally published in 1982, Said's paradigmatic commitments compel his dismissal of the Foucauldian theory of power, which he nevertheless has the insight to call "Spinozist" ("Traveling Theory," 245). Bersani, on the other hand, is able to embrace Foucault in his introduction of the French thinker to English-speaking audiences with his 1977 review of *Surveiller et punir* and *La volonté de savoir* ("The Subject of Power," esp. 2–7). This embrace is at least partially enabled by his early engagement with Deleuze's work. On Said's paradigmatic (mis)reading of Foucault, see also Roach, *Friendship as a Way of Life*, 87.

15. Bersani refers to psychoanalytic theory in *Marcel Proust*, but his psychoanalysis is the one he finds in Proust scholarship. It is in *A Future for Astyanax* that he gives his first reference to Freud and Freud's soon-to-be influential French readers (Laplanche, Serge Leclaire, Jean-Bertrand Pontalis, Jacques Lacan, thinkers whose work was translated in the special *Yale French Studies* issue *French Freud: Structural Studies in Psychoanalysis* [ed. Mehlman, 1972]; see *FA* 9, 319n4). In ways that chapter 2 details, Laplanche's becomes the most important commentary on Freud for Bersani. For Bersani's first substantive discussions of Lacan, see *BF* 111–21, 144–45; and "The Subject of Power," 14–19. His references to Lacan, however, remain few and far between. In *The Freudian Body*, he suggests that the Freudian notion of the sexual has been "neutralized through a discourse inspired by structural linguistics" (*FrB* 64), an obvious reference to Lacanian theory. For some further commentary, see Bersani, "Rigorously Speculating," 287.

16. See also *FA* 8–9, 32. For a more recent account of Bersani's encounter with *Anti-Oedipus*, see "Rigorously Speculating," 290–91.

17. See also Bersani, "Rigorously Speculating," 289.

18. Bersani, Preface to the Second Edition, xix.

19. Bersani, "Rigorously Speculating," 294.

20. Hadot, "Philosophy, Exegesis, and Creative Mistakes," 75.

21. For recent reconsiderations of the question of ontology in contemporary theory, and particularly feminism, see Grosz, "Darwin and the Ontology of Life" and *The Nick of Time*; Haslanger, "Feminism in Metaphysics"; and Oksala, "Feministinen filosofia nykyisyyden ontologiana."

22. Castiglia, "Past Burning," 69.

23. Gilroy, *The Black Atlantic*, 32.

24. Badiou, *Pocket Pantheon*, 114.

25. Fuss, *Essentially Speaking*, 12.

26. On explorations of queerness and "debasement" influenced by Bersani's work, see Stockton, *Beautiful Bottom, Beautiful Shame*; and Scott, *Extravagant Abjection*.

27. See Lacan, "Kant with Sade"; and Bersani's discussion of Sade in *FrB* ch. 3; and Bersani and Dutoit, "Merde Alors."

28. Dewey, "Speculation," 568.

29. Schweppenhäuser, *Theodor W. Adorno*, 55; Gruner, "The Concept of Speculative Philosophy of History," 284.

30. Becker, "Spekulation," 1368; and Gasché, *The Tain of the Mirror*, 42.

31. Ebbersmeyer, "Spekulation," 1356; and Taminiaux, *Poetics, Speculation, and Judgment*.

32. Kant, *Critique of Pure Reason*, A634/B662 (585). On Kant and speculation, see Ebbersmeyer, "Spekulation," 1363–65.

33. See Meillassoux, *After Finitude*. Apart from Meillassoux, Steven Shaviro, Graham Harman, Iain Hamilton Grant, and Ray Brassier are most frequently identified as grounding figures in speculative realism. Shaviro's "Foreign Territory" and Rebekah Sheldon's "Form/Matter/Chora" provide useful (and, in Sheldon's case, critical) introductions to the field.

34. Hegel, *Science of Logic*, 25.

35. Hegel, *Phenomenology of Spirit*, §78 (49); *Phänomenologie des Geistes*, 72.

36. Hegel, *Phenomenology of Spirit*, §74 (47).

37. Verene, *Hegel's Absolute*, 15.

38. Hegel, *Phenomenology of Spirit*, §60 (37).

39. Ibid., §60 (37); *Phänomenologie des Geistes*, 57.

40. Marcuse, *Reason and Revolution*, 101.

41. Gasché, *The Tain of the Mirror*, 40, 48.

42. Marcuse, *Reason and Revolution*, 46.

43. Hegel, *Phenomenology of Spirit*, §58 (35); *Phänomenologie des Geistes*, 56.

44. Hegel writes: "material thinking [issues from] a contingent consciousness that is absorbed only in material stuff"; this mode "finds it hard work to lift the [thinking] self clear of such matter, and to be with itself alone" (*Phenomenology of Spirit*, §58 [35], brackets in trans.). The German original reads: "Jene Gewohnheit ist ein materielles Denken zu nennen, ein zufälliges Bewußtsein, das in den Stoff nur versenkt ist, welchem es daher sauer ankommt, aus der Materie zugleich sein Selbst rein herauszuheben und bei such zu sein" (*Phänomenologie des Geistes*, 56).

45. Meillassoux, *After Finitude*, 10–11.

46. Althusser, "Marxism and Humanism," 242.

47. For a subtle consideration of Deleuze's approach to Hegel, see D. W. Smith, *Essays on Deleuze*, ch. 4.

48. Grosz, *Volatile Bodies*, 222n1.

49. For an introduction to the question of "difference" in Hegelian thought, see Grier, ed. Bersani states his critique of the unquestioned reliance of our ethico-political imagination on dialectical difference most polemically in *Homos*.

50. Butler, *Subjects of Desire*, 18.

51. Hegel, *Science of Logic*, 540; *Wissenschaft der Logik*, 6.200. On Hegel's Leibniz, see Ingram, "Hegel and Leibniz on Individuation"; and Taylor, *Hegel*, 524–26.

52. For Marx and Engels's discussion of French and British materialisms, see *The Holy Family*, 126–32.

53. Butler, *Subjects of Desire*, 5.

54. Leibniz, "The Principles of Philosophy," §11 (214).

55. Hegel, *Science of Logic*, 56.

56. Russell, "Recent Work on the Philosophy of Leibniz," 399–400 and *A Critical Exposition of the Philosophy of Leibniz*, xvii; C. Wilson, *Leibniz's Metaphysics*, 2; Hacking, "What Mathematics Has Done to Some and Only Some Philosophers," 105.

57. Laplanche repeats this conceptualization in insisting on a "centripetal"—other-oriented—as opposed to a "centrifugal" view of the human subject: see Laplanche, "Masochism and the General Theory of Seduction," 211; "Seduction, Persecution, Revelation," 194–96; "Sublimation and/or Inspiration," 47; "The Theory of Seduction and the Problem of the Other," 664–65; "Time and the Other," 247; and "Transference," 225–26. Chapter 1 addresses Bersani's deployment of the concepts of "the centrifugal" and "the centripetal."

58. Marx, "Theses on Feuerbach," 4.

59. Marx, "Contribution to the Critique of Hegel's Philosophy of Law," 175.

60. Marx, "On the Jewish Question," 162; "Zur Judenfrage," 364.

61. Marx, *Grundrisse*, 83.

62. Miller, *History and Human Existence*, 235.

63. Derrida, "Introduction to 'The Origin of Geometry,'" 61. See also the proliferation of reference to monads in Derrida, *The Problem of Genesis in Husserl's Philosophy*; and "Speech and Phenomena," esp. ch. 3. For further discussion, see Kockelmans, *Edmund Husserl's Phenomenology*, 170–71; and MacDonald, "Husserl, the Monad and Immortality."

64. For references in Laplanche's work to the Leibnizian monad—discussed in chapter 2 below—see, for example, *Life and Death in Psychoanalysis*, 59, 70, and 72; *New Foundations for Psychoanalysis*, 23, 57, and 79; *The Unconscious and the Id*, 64; and *Essays on Otherness*, 81, 206, and 225.

65. Jameson, *Postmodernism*, 15.

66. Jameson, *The Political Unconscious*, 266.

67. Hacking, "What Mathematics Has Done to Some and Only Some Philosophers," 105.

68. On Benjamin's Leibniz, see esp. Schwebel, "Intensive Infinity." For further references, see chapter 4 below.

69. Adorno, *Minima Moralia*, §88 (135).

70. Qtd. in Ackerley and Gontarski, *The Grove Companion to Samuel Beckett*, 314.

71. In *Infidel Poetics: Riddles, Nightlife, Substance* (2009), Daniel Tiffany suggests a similar, Leibnizian-inflected map of twentieth-century thought. In developing a reading of "monadic communities which are at once inscrutable

and reflective, discontinuous and harmonious, solipsistic and expressive" (12), he briefly refers to Bersani's argument, in *Homos*, about an "anticommunal mode of connectedness" (*H* 10; qtd. also in Tiffany, *Infidel Poetics*, 13); yet, curiously, he does not explicitly note Bersani's frequent references to Leibnizian metaphysics. *The Essentialist Villain* might be modestly considered an elaboration of Tiffany's few sentences on Bersani in *Infidel Poetics*.

72. Laplanche, "The So-Called 'Death Drive,'" 458.

73. Malabou, *The Future of Hegel*, 185, 186.

74. Leibniz, *Correspondence with Arnaud*, 152.

75. Leibniz, "On the Method of Distinguishing Real from Imaginary Phenomena," 606.

76. Leibniz, *De Summa Rerum*, 23; see also Leibniz, "Logical-metaphysical principles," 51.

77. Leibniz, *New Essays on Human Understanding*, 56.

78. Mercer, *Leibniz's Metaphysics*, 4.

79. Leibniz is named in the early discussion of Deleuze's *Proust and Signs* (*BB* 235), and subsequently, again in reference to Deleuze, in *The Culture of Redemption* (*CR* 13). The philosopher gets a further, equally brief reference in Bersani's 1981 introduction to a reprint of Gustave Flaubert's novel *Madame Bovary* (xiv).

80. Derrida, *Of Grammatology*, 99.

81. Althusser, "On the Materialist Dialectic," 189.

82. For some critics whose commentaries on Bersani, while not mentioning Leibniz, nevertheless share a considerable deal with the reading developed here, see Dean, "Sex and the Aesthetics of Existence" and "What's the Point of Psychoanalytic Criticism?"; Glavey, "Leo Bersani and the Universe"; and Roach, *Friendship as a Way of Life*. Brinkema ("Rape and the Rectum") and ffrench ("Potential Not to Be") pick up on some of Bersani's Deleuzean resonances.

83. Bonaventure, *The Journey of the Mind to God*, ch. 3.

84. Bersani, "Rigorously Speculating," 289.

85. Hegel, *Phenomenology of Spirit*, §37 (21).

86. See Butler, *Subjects of Desire*; and Roth, *Knowing and History*.

87. See Malabou, *The Future of Hegel*; and Nancy, *The Speculative Remark*, 16–18, 29, 89. See also Nancy, *Hegel*.

88. Bersani, "Rigorously Speculating," 289.

89. Proust, *Remembrance of Things Past*, 1.369.

Chapter 1

1. On Deleuze's and Badiou's differing ontological investments, see Gillespie, "Neighborhood of Infinity"; Wahl, "The Subtractive"; and Peter Hallward's introductory volumes to the work of the two philosophers (*Out of This World*;

Badiou). On Nancy, see Devisch (*Jean-Luc Nancy and the Question of Community*), whose observation about Nancy's work—"It is a remarkable thing to be embarking on a first philosophy at the moment when the dirge for the end of metaphysics is sounding" (67)—we might use as commentary on Bersani's. Important here would also be to assess the work that has recently been linked to "the ontological turn," which Bersani's work predates with some decades.

2. Bersani does not explicitly refer to "Structure, Sign, and Play" in *Balzac to Beckett*, but the final sentence of the book's introduction, calling for "the pleasures of centrifugal play" (*BB* 23) in literary texts, resonates closely enough with the famous ending of Derrida's essay to be deemed an intentional echo.

3. Tournier, *Gemini*, 238.

4. Ibid., 237, 63.

5. Phillips, *Houdini's Box*, 23.

6. Russell, *A Critical Exposition of the Philosophy of Leibniz.*

7. See Leibniz, "Discourse on Metaphysics," §9 (42); and Letter to Pierre Dangicourt, 54.

8. Leibniz, "Principles of Nature and Grace, Based on Reason," §1 (207).

9. Blanchot, *The Book to Come*, 214–15.

10. White, *Marcel Proust*, 56; Barthes, *The Preparation of the Novel*, 296.

11. Beckett uses this term to describe his work, albeit in contradistinction not to Proust but to Joyce (qtd. in Tóibín, introduction, xiv). For Bersani's analogous reading of Joyce, see *CR* ch. 7.

12. Proust, *Remembrance of Things Past*, 2.655, 654. Already in his early essay "Contre Sainte-Beuve," Proust proposes that art dislodges a generality, a "common essence" from its varied objects: "from those impressions and others like it something common to them is liberated, something whose superiority to our everyday realities, even the realities of thought, and passion, and sentiment, we shall never be able to account for. Yet this superiority is so positive that it is almost the only thing we can never doubt. And when we recognise this thing, this common essence of our impressions, we feel a pleasure like no other pleasure, and while it stays with us we know that death is negligible" (79).

13. Derrida, "Structure, Sign, and Play in the Discourse of the Human Sciences," 279.

14. Ibid., 278.

15. Harland, *Beyond Superstructuralism*, 214.

16. Mikics, *Who Was Jacques Derrida?*, 60.

17. Kristeva, *Strangers to Ourselves*, 3, 29.

18. Ibid., 3. The signature term repeats: "Without a home, [the foreigner] disseminates": "multiplying masks and 'false selves' he is never completely true nor completely false" (8). On dissemination and the centrifugal, see also Kristeva, *Interviews*, 76. Kristeva's use of the "centrifugal" should also be traced to her engagement of Mikhail Bakhtin's work: Bakhtin identifies "the centripetal" with "monologism" and "monoglossia," and "the centrifugal" with "dialogism" and

"heteroglossia" (Bakhtin, *The Dialogic Imagination*, 270–73). For Kristeva's early discussion of Bakhtin, see *Desire in Language*, ch. 3.

19. Proust, *Remembrance of Things Past*, 1.331.

20. Deleuze, *Proust and Signs*, 41. Deleuze's suggestion of Proust's familiarity with Leibniz's philosophy (ibid., 188n2) is corroborated not only by the several occasions on which the philosopher is mentioned in *À la recherche* (*Remembrance of Things Past*, 1.1076, 1260; 2.278), but also the book's allusions to Leibniz's dictum of the existing universe's necessary status as "the best of all possible worlds" (1.619) and of "the universal and pre-established gravitation" or "harmony" that unites beings (1.897). The narrator, furthermore, offers us a recognizably monadological self-description: "my intelligence," Marcel proposes, "must be a uniform thing, perhaps indeed there exists but a single intelligence, in which everyone in the world participates, towards which each of us from the position of his own separate body turns his eyes, as in a theatre where, if everyone has his own separate seat, there in on the other hand but a single stage" (1.523–24). Adopting Leibniz's depiction of a monadic being that in its isolation nevertheless perceives the entire world from its specific viewpoint (see, for example, Leibniz, *Correspondence with Arnaud*, 133), Proust's narrator suggests that every being "part[akes] of the same special essence" (1.749), each expressing "the riches of the universal Mind" (1.518); he anthropomorphizes the indestructible monad by recasting it as "the eternal man" (2.1186). And, finally, Leibniz's radical understanding of predication—to which we'll return below—is reflected in the narrator's following description of "our substance": "we are not like buildings to which stories can be added from without, but like trees which draw from their own sap the knot that duly appears on their trunks, the spreading roof of their foliage" (1.811).

21. Deleuze, *Proust and Signs*, 43–44.

22. In *The Culture of Redemption* (1990), Bersani again speaks of Proust's "narrator's 'monadic' point of view" (*CR* 14). Even though his name largely disappears from Bersani's texts, Deleuze's onto-ethics, particularly in its Leibnizian dimensions, anonymously contributes to the work that proceeds in books such as *Forms of Being: Cinema, Aesthetics, Subjectivity* (2004). For example, Bersani and Dutoit's suggestion that the soldiers in Terrence Malick's *The Thin Red Line* "are individuated not as personalities but as perspectives on the world" (*FoB* 146) implicitly returns us to Bersani's early adoption, in *Balzac to Beckett* and *A Future for Astyanax*, of Deleuze's view of the Proustian essence as an individuating perspective incompletely expressed in the individual; the Proustian–Deleuzean distinction between individuality and the individual is strictly parallel to the one between "individuation and psychic individuality" (*FoB* 146).

23. Derrida, "Force and Signification," 19. Derrida's reference is to arguments such as the following from Leibniz's "Discourse on Metaphysics":

> [I]t is possible to find a geometric line whose notion is constant and uniform, following a certain rule, such that this line passes through all

> the points in the same order in which the hand had jotted them down.
>
> And if someone traced a continuous line which is sometimes straight, sometimes circular, and sometimes of another nature, it is possible to find a notion, or rule, or equation common to all the points of this line, in virtue of which these very changes must occur. For example, there is no face whose contours are not part of a geometric line and cannot be traced in one stroke by a certain regular movement. But, when a rule is extremely complex, what is in conformity with it passes for irregular.
>
> Thus, one can say, in whatever manner God might have created the world, it would always have been regular and in accordance with a certain general order. (§6 [39])

24. Derrida, "Force and Signification," 25.

25. "In Western and notably French thought," Derrida writes in *Of Grammatology*, "the dominant discourse—let us call it 'structuralism'—remains caught . . . within the metaphysics—logocentrism—which at the same time one claims rather precipitately to have 'gone beyond'" (99).

26. Derrida, "Cogito and the History of Madness," 57.

27. Boundas, "Ontology," 191; see also May, *Gilles Deleuze*, 13–25; and D. W. Smith, *Essays on Deleuze*, 275–76.

28. Deleuze, "Jean Hyppolite's *Logic and Existence*," 18.

29. Badiou, *Deleuze*, 20.

30. Bersani cites Blanchot already in his first encounter with Beckett 1966: see Bersani, "No Exit for Beckett," 267.

31. The most obvious of such allusions include Beckett's frequent descriptions of his characters' noncommunicative isolation in terms of monadic "windowlessness" (Beckett, *Murphy*, 109; *Watt*, 292; *Company*, 44–45) or "doorlessness" (Beckett, *The Unnamable*, 399); the characters' self-enclosed worlds partake in "the pre-established harmony" (Beckett, *Molloy*, 62) or, in *Watt*'s famous reformulation, of "a pre-established arbitrary" (276). On Beckett's monadology, see Ackerley, "Samuel Beckett and Science"; Dowd, *Abstract Machines*, esp. ch. 3; Fletcher, "Samuel Beckett and the Philosophers," 54–55; Mori, "Beckett's Windows and the Windowless Self," "Becoming Stone," and "'No Body Is at Rest'"; and the entry on Leibniz in Ackerley and Gontarski, *The Grove Companion to Samuel Beckett*.

32. Beckett, *Molloy*, 121.

33. Beckett, *Proust*, 65–66.

34. Blanchot, *The Book to Come*, 200.

35. Qtd. in Mercer, *Leibniz's Metaphysics*, 332, Mercer's translation and brackets.

36. Leibniz, *Correspondence with Arnaud*, 159–60, 228–29; "The Principles of Philosophy," §4–6 (213).

37. Leibniz, *Correspondence with Arnaud*, 233.

38. Qtd. in Mercer, *Leibniz's Metaphysics*, 332.

39. Deleuze, *Proust and Signs*, 162.

40. Ibid., 110.

41. Before *Arts of Impoverishment*, Bersani makes briefer returns to Beckett in *FrB* 7–9 and *CR* 168–71.

42. The term and its derivatives appear twelve times in the first chapter of *Arts of Impoverishment*. Leibniz's proper name is never mentioned. Leibniz is similarly missing from the list of Beckett's alleged philosophical sources ("St. Augustine, Dante, Descartes, Geulincx, Malebranche, Berkeley, Wittgenstein, etc., etc.") that Bersani gives us in a 1966 review article ("No Exit for Beckett," 262).

43. Beckett, "Three Dialogues with Georges Duthuit," 125.

44. Beckett, *The Unnamable*, 414.

45. Beckett, "Three Dialogues with Georges Duthuit," 103.

46. Beckett, *The Unnamable*, 291.

47. Ibid., 390.

48. Lovejoy, *The Great Chain of Being*, 80, 121.

49. Leibniz, "On the Radical Origination of Things," 487.

50. Beckett, *How It Is*, 140.

51. Qtd. in Lovejoy, *The Great Chain of Being*, 118.

52. Qtd. in Tóibín, introduction, xiv; Beckett, *Malone Dies*, 235.

53. Beckett, *Worstward Ho*, 106, 107.

54. Bersani, "No Exit for Beckett," 264, 267.

55. Blanchot, *The Space of Literature*, 26.

56. Blanchot, *The Book to Come*, 213.

57. Beckett, *Worstward Ho*, 89.

58. Blanchot, *The Book to Come*, 213.

59. Beckett, *Molloy*, 10.

60. Some key texts in these debates—texts that are sympathetic to the antiessentialist position but also cognizant of the danger of antiessentialism's hardening into the essentialization of essentialism—include Brennan, introduction (esp. 6–9); Fuss, *Essentially Speaking*; Riley, *"Am I That Name?"*; as well as Schor, introduction and "This Essentialism Which Is Not One." The most influential text for early queer theory in this tradition is, of course, Judith Butler's *Gender Trouble: Feminism and the Subversion of Identity* (1990).

61. Fuss, *Essentially Speaking*, 3.

62. Aristotle, *Metaphysica*, vi.4 (782).

63. Riley, *"Am I That Name?"* 111.

64. Russell, *A Critical Exposition of the Philosophy of Leibniz*, 13.

65. Leibniz, *Correspondence with Arnaud*, 233.

66. Ibid., 149.

67. Smith, *Essays on Deleuze*, 46.

68. Bersani inherits the non-Hegelian thrust also from Blanchot. As Joseph Libertson points out, the Blanchotian concept of "essential solitude" does not designate "[a]n interiority rooted in negativity. . . . Essential solitude or separation is . . . a moment indefinable by a classical ontology of identity and noncontradiction" (*Proximity*, 47). Essential solitude thus constitutes one way to think about "identities" whose self-sameness is not a reaction to, or a negation of, otherness. On Blanchot and Hegel, see also Critchley, "*Il y a*," 104–09; Gasché, *Of Minimal Things*, ch. 15; and Hill, *Blanchot*, 103–14, 121–24.

69. Bersani, "The Subject of Power," 12. Bersani notes this aspect of the Jamesian characters—their solitude and unrelatedness—already in 1960: see "The Narrator as Center in 'The Wings of a Dove,'" 143–44.

70. Russell, *A Critical Exposition of the Philosophy of Leibniz*, xvii; *A History of Western Philosophy*, 588, 590, 596. Russell considers the subject-predicate theory an almost universally applied error in the history of Western philosophy: according to him, Plato, Aristotle, Descartes, Spinoza, and Leibniz all mistakenly built their systems on the logic of predication, not noticing that "grammar and ordinary language have been shown to be bad guides to metaphysics" (*An Outline of Philosophy*, 195; see also Hylton, *Russell, Idealism, and the Emergence of Analytic Philosophy*, 154–55; and Winslade, "Russell's Theory of Relations," 83–85). For Russell, because the subject-predicate structure reduces external relations to predication, i.e., internal relations, it inevitably leads to idealist metaphysics—his major antagonist at the time when he wrote his Leibniz study. On Russell's turn-of-the-century critique of idealism, see Hylton, *Propositions, Functions, and Analysis*, ch. 1; and *Russell, Idealism, and the Emergence of Analytic Philosophy*.

71. Russell, *A Critical Exposition of the Philosophy of Leibniz*, 50.

72. Ibid. See also ibid., 59–60.

73. Blanchot, *The Work of Fire*, 283.

74. Blanchot, *The Space of Literature*, 22.

75. Hill, *Blanchot*, 112.

76. Blanchot, *Watt*, 276.

77. As Thomas Trezise argues, the thought of essential solitude—the isolation Bersani calls monadic—is "thoroughly constitutive of Beckett's *oeuvre*" (*Into the Breach*, 117).

78. Nietzsche, *Philosophy in the Tragic Age of the Greeks*, 48, 46.

79. Nietzsche, *The Birth of Tragedy*, 42.

80. Beckett, *The Unnamable*, 308, 376. For commentators who have connected Beckett to (Nietzsche's) Silenus, see Branigan, *Radio Beckett*, 148; and the entry for "birth" in Ackerley and Gontarski, *The Grove Companion to Samuel Beckett*. On Beckett and Schopenhauer, see Pothast, *The Metaphysical Vision*.

81. Deleuze, *Negotiations*, 143.

82. See Uexküll, *A Foray into the World of Animals and Humans*, 44–52; and Deleuze and Guattari, *A Thousand Plateaus*, 51, 257.

83. See Deleuze, "Immanence."

84. Proust, *Remembrance of Things Past*, 1.986.

85. Smith, *Essays on Deleuze*, 46–47.

86. Ibid., 47.

87. Leibniz, *Correspondence with Arnaud*, 109.

88. Agamben, *The Open*, 40.

89. On Uexküll's Leibnizianism, see Brier, "Cybersemiotics and Umweltlehre," 784, 785, 807; Buchanan, *Onto-Ethologies*, 23; Lassen, "Leibniz'sche Gedanken in der Uexküll'schen Umweltlehre"; Marcus, "On the Logical and Semiotic Status of Jakob von Uexküll's concept of Umwelt," 208; Sagan, "Umwelt after Uexküll," 21; and Winthrop-Young, "Bubbles and Webs," 242. Leibniz's and Uexküll's philosophies, write Undine Sellbach and Stephen Loo, assume an "uncanny proximity" ("Insects and Other Minute Perceptions in the Baroque House," 113).

90. Deleuze, *Negotiations*, 86.

91. Uexküll, *A Foray into the World of Animals and Humans*, 159–60. Like Uexküll, Leibniz illustrates the concomitance of noncommunicating entities with musical tropes: "it is like several bands of musicians or choirs separately taking up their parts and placed in such a way that they neither see nor hear one another, though they nevertheless, agree perfectly in following their notes, each one his own, in such a way that he who hears the whole finds in it a wonderful harmony much more surprising than if there were a connection between the performers" (*Correspondence with Arnaud*, 188).

92. Uexküll, *A Foray into the World of Animals and Humans*, 171ff.

93. Proust, *Remembrance of Things Past*, 2.899.

94. Deleuze and Guattari, *A Thousand Plateaus*, 314.

95. Deleuze, *Proust and Signs*, 175, 181, ellipsis in original.

96. Ibid., 161. In their assessment of the Proustian "literary machine" in *Anti-Oedipus*, Deleuze and Guattari similarly conjoin Leibniz and Uexküll: Proust's is a world a nonunified, nontotalized whole made of "aberrant paths of communication between noncommunicating vessels, transverse unities between elements that retain all their differences within their own particular boundaries" (42, 43). Although less persistently present than "the monad," the term "transversal"—which we leave unexplored here—constitutes one of Bersani's keywords or crypto-concepts.

97. Deleuze and Parnet, *Dialogues*, 7.

98. Butler, "*Geist ist Zeit*," 67.

99. Butler, *Subjects of Desire*, 216. Butler never relinquishes her claim about the universalizing heteronormativity of the Lacanian symbolic. She repeats this argument subsequently in, for example, *Gender Trouble*, ch. 2; *Bodies that Matter*, ch. 7; and *Antigone's Claim*. Deleuze, on the other hand, disappears almost completely from her subsequent work. If Butler's Hegelian-inflected work is paradigmatically incompatible with Deleuze's (see Tuhkanen, "Performativity and Becoming"), we

can discern the same radical divergence between her thought and Bersani's, given his early adoption of some characteristically Deleuzean propositions.

100. Butler, *Subjects of Desire*, 215.

101. Ibid.

102. Foucault, *The History of Sexuality*, vol. 1, 101; see also Foucault, "The End of the Monarchy of Sex," 218.

103. Faderman, *Surpassing the Love of Men*. Apart from Faderman's, see also Smith-Rosenberg's classic study of women's romantic friendships, "The Female World of Love and Ritual." The shift precipitated by the rise of sexology is further discussed in Somerville, *Queering the Color Line*, ch. 1; Terry, *An American Obsession*; and Tuhkanen, "Breeding (and) Reading." For discussions of the changing evaluations of male same-sex friendship, see Castiglia, "Same-Sex Friendships and the Rise of Modern Sexualities"; and Coviello, *Tomorrow's Parties*.

104. Foucault, "Friendship as a Way of Life," 138.

105. Foucault, *The History of Sexuality*, vol. 1, 101.

106. On iteration, see Derrida, *Limited Inc*. The modification of performativity through deconstructive philosophy takes place particularly in Butler's third book, *Bodies that Matter* (1993).

107. Butler, *Bodies That Matter*, 122.

108. Foucault, *The History of Sexuality*, vol. 1, 38.

109. This point—that first to emerge in discourses such as sexology are definitions of deviance, not the norm—has indeed been made by, for example, Katz, *The Invention of Heterosexuality*.

110. Elsewhere, Bersani identifies in moments when Freud takes "extraordinary speculative risk[s]" something he calls "the Proustian turn" (*FrB* 99), possibly a reference to the convoluted theory of desire we find in the opening of *Cities of the Plain*. At his most Proustian—which is to say, his most psychoanalytic—moments, Freud exhibits "a classificatory impotence" (*FrB* 102) that, if it weren't for his repeated, intense efforts, should make it impossible for psychoanalysis to become one of modernity's disciplinary discourses.

111. "*Betrayal is an ethical necessity*" opens the essay version of *Homos*'s concluding chapter: see Bersani, "The Gay Outlaw," 5. For some commentary on such opening lines, see *IRG* 192–93; and Royle, *In Memory of Jacques Derrida*, 113–14.

112. Connecting Bersani's discussions of Foucault and Mallarmé, we should note that *The Death of Stéphane Mallarmé* is preceded by a few years Bersani's first substantial encounter with Foucault's work in the review essay on *La volonté de savoir* and *Surveiller et punir*: see Bersani, "The Subject of Power." The phrase "psychic enigmas" indicates Bersani's critique of Jean Laplanche's psychoanalytic theory of subject constitution, which we'll consider in the next chapter.

113. Weeks, *Sexuality and Its Discontents*, 191, qtd. in *IRG* 13.

114. Weeks, *Sexuality and Its Discontents*, 191, qtd. in *IRG* 13.

115. See the description of this abandoned project in Davidson, "Ethics as Ascetics," 125.

116. Foucault, "Friendship as a Way of Life," 137.

117. Ibid.

118. While Bersani often cites his colleague's arguments concerning the rise of modern subjectivation in Cartesian epistemology and biopolitical discourses (including, importantly, psychoanalytic theory), his main interest lies in thinking with the texts of Foucault's "ethics" period. He uses the "genealogical" Foucault to diagnose the modern subject, but when he moves from description to prescription—when he shifts to the speculative work of imagining alternatives to our onto-ethical regime—he turns to the 1980s work. This is another way to indicate the differences between Bersani and Butler: while both are indebted to Foucault, important to their queer theories are texts from different stages of his oeuvre. In contrast to Bersani's, Butler's Foucault, as the final chapter of *Subjects of Desire* already makes clear, is the Foucault who in the 1970s sought not only to explore the shifts and breaks by which one historical episteme replaces another, but also to outline "the history of the present" (Foucault, *Discipline and Punish*, 31), a narrative of how we got where we are that may help us to move elsewhere. Bersani, too, sees the importance of Foucault's work in the way it enables us to think becoming; but the mode of becoming he is interested in is the one Foucault begun to delineate after he had abandoned, during the seven-year break, his original project of researching sexuality's history.

119. Foucault, *The History of Sexuality*, vol. 2, 253.

120. Davidson, "Ethics as Ascetics," 138.

121. Ibid., 129.

122. Ibid. On Hadot and Foucault, see also Davidson, "Spiritual Exercises and Ancient Philosophy," esp. 480–82. For Hadot's own commentary, see his "Reflections on the Idea of the 'Cultivation of the Self.'" Other classicists who influenced Foucault included Paul Veyne, Georges Dumézil, and Jean-Pierre Vernant (Davidson, "Ethics as Ascetics," 124).

123. Foucault, "Michel Foucault," 128.

124. Davidson, "Ethics as Ascetics," 137.

125. Dean makes this point in "The Antisocial Homosexual," 827. For a discussion of "the antisocial thesis," see Wiegman, "Sex and Negativity"; and the cluster of essays that also includes Dean's: Caserio et al., "The Antisocial Thesis in Queer Theory." For studies that move beyond queer theory's often simplistic reading of Bersani, see Dean, *Unlimited Intimacy*; Roach, *Friendship as a Way of Life*; and Rocco, *The Logic of the Lure*.

126. Genet, *Funeral Rites*, 249, qtd. in *H* 165, Returning to his reading of Genet a year after the publication of *Homos*, Bersani refers to self-identical subjects as "monads": "Each monad-like subject . . . feels obliged to arm itself against the difference embodied in other subjects equally determined to defend their 'integrity' against the Other" (*IRG* 43). Contradicting Bersani's otherwise consistent understanding of monadism as an ethical exigency, this formulation may evince the influence of Laplanche's psychoanalytic theory, where the "monad"

persistently marks the reduction of revolutionary otherness, enabled by Freud's original theory of seduction, to the more traditional ways of conceiving the self-other dialectic in philosophy. We will return to Laplanche's reading of monadology, and Bersani's reading of Laplanche, in the next chapter.

127. Bersani, "Learning to Escape," 65.

Chapter 2

1. Freud, *Introductory Lectures on Psychoanalysis*, 326.

2. Freud, "The Resistances to Psychoanalysis," 273.

3. Lacan calls Vienna, Freud's hometown, the site of "a revolution in knowledge of Copernican proportions" ("The Freudian Thing," 334); it was here that Freud discovered "the very truth" of "the self's radical eccentricity with respect to itself" ("The Instance of the Letter in the Unconscious," 435).

4. Laplanche, "The Unfinished Copernican Revolution," 59.

5. Ibid., 61.

6. We are here concerned with Bersani's single-authored books. Bersani and Dutoit's *The Forms of Violence: Narrative in Assyrian Art and Modern Culture* (1985) precedes the publication of *The Freudian Body* by a year; psychoanalysis figures centrally in the Dutoit collaboration too.

7. The intensity of the initial encounter is suggested by the fact that Bersani continues to engage its formulations in practically all of his subsequent work: for explicit references, see *FV* 33–39, 117–18; *FrB passim*; *CS* ch. 4; and *FoB* 37–39.

8. Laplanche, *Life and Death in Psychoanalysis*, 70.

9. Laplanche, "The Drive and Its Source-Object," 126, emphasis added.

10. Laplanche, "A Short Treatise on the Unconscious," 109; "Transference," 225.

11. Laplanche, "The Theory of Seduction and the Problem of the Other," 653.

12. Russell, *A History of Western Philosophy*, 129.

13. Fuss, *Essentially Speaking*, 7.

14. Heidegger, "The Origin of the Work of Art," 153–54.

15. Freud, *The Complete Letters of Sigmund Freud to William Fliess*, 264–67. Laplanche's *Essays on Otherness*, coupled with the interviews with Caruth and Stanton, provide good introductions to Laplanchean psychoanalysis. On Laplanche's early work, particularly in relation to Lacan's, see Fletcher, "The Letter in the Unconscious." For an overview of Laplanche's later, post-1985 work, see Fletcher, "Seduction and the Vicissitudes of Translation." For more general introductions, see Scarfone, *Laplanche*; and Fletcher and Ray, eds., *Seductions and Enigmas*. For a detailed reading of Freud that is influenced by Laplanche's work, see Fletcher, *Freud and the Scene of Trauma*.

16. Freud, *The Complete Letters of Sigmund Freud to William Fliess*, 264.

17. Fromm, *The Crisis of Psychoanalysis*, 32; Masson, *The Assault on Truth*. See Laplanche's (implicit or explicit) allusions to Masson's work: "The Drive and Its Source-Object," 127; *New Foundations for Psychoanalysis*, 122.

18. Freud, *Three Essays on the Theory of Sexuality*, 100n.

19. Ibid., 108.

20. Ibid.

21. Ibid., 96.

22. Ibid., 96n1.

23. Laplanche, "Seduction, Persecution, Revelation," 169. Arnold Davidson's by-now classic close reading of the *Three Essays* in "How to Do the History of Psychoanalysis" follows similar inconsistencies, which mark Freud's efforts to articulate the ramifications of his emerging, paradigm-shifting account of sexuality.

24. Laplanche, "Psychoanalysis, Time and Translation," 175. Rather than occurring, as Freud writes in the *Three Essays*, as the result of "accidental *external* contingencies" (108), seduction for Laplanche constitutes an *exigency*, a *fundamental anthropological situation*. With these terms, Laplanche designates the fact that seduction is "primal": "the primal is that element in the initial situation which is inevitable, which is beyond even the most general contingency" (*New Foundations for Psychoanalysis*, 89; see also Laplanche, "Exigency and Going-Astray"; "Interpretation between Determinism and Hermeneutics," 147; "Starting from the Fundamental Anthropological Situation"). Because of the human's premature birth and the need for an extended period of caretaking, "[i]t is *inevitable* that the mother should arouse pleasurable sensations [in the infant]; that possibility is inscribed in the situation and does not depend upon contingent factors" (*New Foundations for Psychoanalysis*, 121). Freud's mistake is that, rather than seeing seduction as "a basic human given," he "fails to extend precocious seduction to sexuality in general, limits its effects to the arousal of sensations in the genitals, and fails to note that arousal also occurs at the level of the erogeneity of the whole body, and especially at the level of oral and anal erogeneity" (121). Sexuality undergoes an unprecedented broadening in the theory of psychoanalysis: "sexuality would seem to include not only the small sector of genital activity, not only perversions or neuroses, but all of human activity" (*Life and Death in Psychoanalysis*, 25).

25. Laplanche, "The So-Called 'Death Drive,'" 456.

26. Laplanche, "Seduction, Persecution, Revelation," 169; see also "Interpretation between Determinism and Hermeneutics," 152–60.

27. On interhuman communication, see Laplanche, "The Drive and Its Source-Object," 132; "Interview: Jean Laplanche Talks to Martin Stanton," 10; "A Short Treatise on the Unconscious," 91n17.

28. Our hyphenated construction indicates that Laplanche's model of anthropogenesis agrees with what Gilles Deleuze and Félix Guattari would call "minoritarian" becoming. Beginning with a constitutive error, hominization must

be understood as errancy whose potentialities will not have been exhausted. (See Deleuze and Guattari, *Kafka*; *A Thousand Plateaus*, plateau 10.) If "[m]inoritarian authors are those who are foreigners in their own tongue" (Conley, "Minoritarian," 164), what we might call, with Laplanche, *enigmatics* is the human being's first tongue but also one in which she is perennially scrambling to find her bearings.

29. Laplanche, "The So-Called 'Death Drive,'" 464; see also "Psychoanalysis as Anti-Hermeneutics," 11; "A Short Treatise on the Unconscious," 89.

30. Laplanche proposes "compromised signifier" as a synonym for "enigmatic signifier," where "compromised" functions "in the dual sense that [the signifier] is *a* compromise, like the symptom, as well as being *compromised by the unconscious* of its originator." The sender of the message "*says* more than he consciously means" ("Interpretation between Determinism and Hermeneutics," 158).

31. For "riddle," see Freud, "The Sexual Enlightenment of Children," 176; "Zur sexuellen Aufklärung der Kinder," 163. For "puzzle," see Freud, *Three Essays on the Theory of Sexuality*, 123; *Drei Abhandlungen zur Sexualtheorie*, 108.

32. Freud, *Three Essays on the Theory of Sexuality*, 113; *Drei Abhandlungen zur Sexualtheorie*, 100.

33. Freud, "The Sexual Enlightenment of Children," 174; "Zur sexuellen Aufklärung der Kinder," 161.

34. Laplanche, "Time and the Other," 254–55n46.

35. Laplanche, "Kent Seminar," 23; see also "The Freud Museum Seminar," 57–58. Translating Laplanche before the consolidation of the English terminology, Richard Miller renders "*énigme*" as "puzzle": see Laplanche, "To Situate Sublimation," 19; *Problématiques III*, 106–07.

36. Laplanche, "Masochism and the General Theory of Seduction," 198.

37. Freud, *The Complete Letters of Sigmund Freud to William Fliess*, 265; *The Ego and the Id*, 378.

38. Laplanche, "Time and the Other," 241.

39. Laplanche, *The Unconscious and the Id*, 67.

40. Laplanche and Pontalis, "Fantasy and the Origins of Sexuality," 28.

41. Freud, *Introductory Lectures on Psychoanalysis*, 326.

42. Laplanche and Pontalis, *The Language of Psychoanalysis*, 337.

43. Ibid., 46.

44. Laplanche, *Life and Death in Psychoanalysis*, 59.

45. Laplanche and Pontalis, *The Language of Psychoanalysis*, 46.

46. Laplanche, *Life and Death in Psychoanalysis*, 70.

47. Laplanche and Pontalis, "Fantasy and the Origins of Sexuality," 16.

48. Laplanche and Pontalis, *The Language of Psychoanalysis*, 337–38, emphasis added.

49. Ibid., 256.

50. Laplanche, *Life and Death in Psychoanalysis*, 70.

51. For further discussion of primary narcissism in Freud, see Laplanche, *New Foundations for Psychoanalysis*, 68–81.

52. For a brief outline, see Ray, "Forming new knots," 53.

53. Proust, *Remembrance of Things Past*, 2.912.

54. Laplanche and Pontalis, *The Language of Psychoanalysis*, 256.

55. Laplanche, *Life and Death in Psychoanalysis*, 70; *New Foundations for Psychoanalysis*, 86.

56. Mercer, *Leibniz's Metaphysics*, 372.

57. Lovejoy, *The Great Chain of Being*, 144.

58. Russell, *A Critical Exposition of the Philosophy of Leibniz*, 97.

59. Bracken, "Berkeley, George," 447. On Leibniz's idealism, see also M. Wilson, "The Phenomenalisms of Leibniz and Berkeley"; Jolley, "Leibniz and Phenomenalism"; Rutherford, "Metaphysics," 144; Look, "Leibniz's Metaphysics," 102. On Leibniz's role in German Idealism, see Redding, *Continental Idealism*.

60. Laplanche, "The Drive and Its Source-Object," 128–29.

61. Jameson, *Postmodernism*, 15.

62. Marx, *Grundrisse*, 83; see also *Capital*, 1.169–70. On Marx and Defoe, see Harvey, *A Companion to Marx's* Capital, 43–44.

63. Adorno, "Letters to Walter Benjamin," 121.

64. "Since Copernicus, we have known that the earth is not the 'centre' of the universe," Althusser writes in "Freud and Lacan." "Since Marx, we have known that the human subject, the economic, political or philosophical ego is not the 'centre' of history—and even, in opposition to the Philosophers of the Enlightenment and to Hegel, that history has no 'centre' except in ideological misrecognition" (218).

65. Laplanche, "Seduction, Persecution, Revelation," 173.

66. Engels, "Socialism," 699.

67. Laplanche, "Sexuality and Attachment in Metapsychology," 35.

68. Laplanche, *Life and Death in Psychoanalysis*, 59; "Closing and Opening of the Dream," 181.

69. Laplanche, "The Unfinished Copernican Revolution," 72n.

70. Laplanche, *New Foundations for Psychoanalysis*, 75.

71. Although, particularly in his later work, Laplanche tends to posit the failure of the psychoanalytic revolution as part and parcel of the very movement of Freud's thought, his assessment remains more ambivalent than Bersani's, for whom the "collapse" of the psychoanalytic revolution is the result of an intrinsic failure or drift, not a recuperable wrong turn or misinvestment; for Bersani, that which renders the theory singular, and singularly useful, is also what necessitates its self-betrayal. Even though Laplanche at times implies that Freud's mistake should be regarded as a repetition of the originary, supplementary movement of going-astray in hominization, he sees in such counterrevolutionary moments "an

almost inevitable recoiling, which is not to be held against Freud, before the consequences of the priority of the other" ("Exigency and Going-Astray," 188, emphasis added). The fact that Freud's abandonment of the seduction hypothesis, as well as his failure to articulate it as a general theory, may have been prevented—it was only "almost inevitable"—suggests that it does not constitute a strict analogue to the moment of perversion that is primal in becoming-human.

72. Bersani, "The Other Freud."

73. Bersani, "The Subject of Power," 12.

74. Laplanche and Pontalis, *The Language of Psychoanalysis*, 256–57; *Vocabulaire de la psychanalyse*, 263.

75. Freud, *Introductory Lectures on Psychoanalysis*, 326.

76. Laplanche, "The Unfinished Copernican Revolution," 81.

77. See Bersani's references to *Anti-Oedipus* in *FA* 7, 8–9, 32; and his commentary on the importance of Deleuze and Guattari's book in Bersani, "Rigorously Speculating," 290–91.

78. Smith, *Essays on Deleuze*, 282; Grosz, *Volatile Bodies*, 222n1.

79. In the 1977 English-language edition of *Écrits: A Selection*, Alan Sheridan translates *l'agressivité* as *aggressivity*, while Bruce Fink's subsequent rendering is *aggressiveness*.

80. Freud, "Instincts and Their Vicissitudes," 125.

81. Laplanche, *Life and Death in Psychoanalysis*, 90.

82. Laplanche and Pontalis, *The Language of Psychoanalysis*, 401.

83. Laplanche, *Life and Death in Psychoanalysis*, 86.

84. Ibid., 89. Laplanche argues that Freud's conceptual pair of sadomasochism must be split into two, and masochism prioritized in the narrative of the human subject's constitution. The appeal of Laplanche's argument for Bersani issues in part from the fact that Deleuze proposes a similar redefinition to our understanding of sadomasochism. As Deleuze writes in "Coldness and Cruelty" (1967), we misunderstand the forces of sadism and masochism when we posit them, as Freud does, in a dialectical relation to one another. Masochism is a singular force; so is sadism. They do not need each other as counterparts to function; indeed, their binarization territorializes their singularity.

85. See *FrB* 39, 92; *I* 121; *IRG* 24–25, 174; *CR* 40–41. Bersani takes his argument from Laplanche, who writes: "self-preservation in man (his autonomous capacity to persist in being, what one might term his instinctual potentialities) is so precarious that it is sexuality which endlessly comes to make up for its deficiencies" (*The Unconscious and the Id*, 147).

86. Laplanche, *Life and Death in Psychoanalysis*, 91; *Vie et mort en psychanalyse*, 154.

87. Freud, *Three Essays on the Theory of Sexuality*, 120–26.

88. See Bersani and Dutoit, "Merde Alors," 25; and *FV* 39.

89. Bersani uses quotation marks to similar effect in speaking of Freud's postulation of "an 'original,' nonsexual sadism" (*BF* 79).

90. Laplanche, *Life and Death in Psychoanalysis*, 46.

91. Laplanche, *New Foundations for Psychoanalysis*, 128. We should note that Bersani's earlier work, even texts written before his encounter with psychoanalysis, uncannily anticipates Laplanchean language: already in *Balzac to Beckett* he writes of modernist texts that "[t]hey are enigmatic, but their enigmas are false or impenetrable ones" (*BB* 13), a description equally applicable to Laplanche's hominizing messages.

92. Suggesting that interhuman, enimatic communication is renewed in the cultural realm and the experience of art, Laplanche too refers to Mallarmé: see "Transference," 224.

93. I borrow this phrase from Dean, "Art as Symptom."

94. From the evocation of "luminous blindness" in Henry James (*FA* 136) to the claim, in *The Freudian Body*, that psychoanalysis and art experiment with "*disabled* consciousness" (*FrB* 6) to the suggestion, in the back cover of *Arts of Impoverishment*, that works of art "train us in a new mode of mobility" by "crippling" our perception, Bersani's work calls out for commentary from disability studies and crip theory. For an essay that begins this work, see Mollow, "Is Sex Disability?"

95. Proust, *Remembrance of Things Past*, 2.356, 2.587.

96. Ibid., 2.899; *À la recherche du temps perdu*, 4.132.

97. As the phrase suggest, it shares its epistemological orientation with other familiar modes of power-knowledge. Noting the incorporative ambitions of knowledge-production has become commonplace, for example, in postcolonial theory. Echoing a number of other critics, Édouard Glissant writes in *Poetics of Relation* (1990): "the verb *to understand* in the sense of 'to grasp' [*comprendre*] has a fearsome repressive meaning" in the context of twentieth-century globalization. He situates in the early century a shift in the practices of Western colonization after which "[u]nderstanding cultures . . . became more gratifying than discovering new lands" (26, brackets in trans.). It is in this context that we should read Bersani's critique of "textual imperialism" that aims at art's "mystifyingly intricate surfaces beyond which lie graspable meanings" (*DSM* 60): literary criticism shares with (neo)imperialist discourses and practices "the illusion that the ego can incorporate its environment. This illusion is ennobled and sublimated as the desire to understand, and we call the fruits of invasive appropriation 'knowledge'" (*CS* 70).

98. Forrester, *Truth Games*, 4.

99. On the law of "theoretico-genesis," see Laplanche, *Life and Death in Psychoanalysis*, 2, 9, 87; "The Unfinished Copernican Revolution," 81–82; *New Foundations for Psychoanalysis*, 167n22. What Laplanche has in mind here is analogous to what Shoshana Felman calls the "reading effect," the way in which

critical controversies uncannily repeat the dynamics internal to the literary texts in question. Such engagements constitute "a *repetition* of the scene dramatized in the text. The critical interpretation, in other words, not only elucidates the text but also reproduces it dramatically, unwittingly *participates in it*. . . . As a reading effect, this inadvertent 'acting out' is indeed uncanny: whichever way the reader turns, he can but be turned by the text, he can but *perform* it by *repeating* it" (Felman, "Turning the Screw of Interpretation," 101). This dynamic becomes visible, according to Laplanche and Bersani, in the way in which the Freudian text recapitulates the processes of becoming-human.

100. Laplanche, "The Unfinished Copernican Revolution," 72n.

101. Proust, "Contre Sainte-Beuve," 56; *Remembrance of Things Past*, 2.87.

102. Similarly, the "interpretative scramble" Maggie precipitates should perhaps evoke for us of the imperial project called "The Scramble for Africa," initiated by the European powers at the 1884–85 Berlin Conference, which, as the final pages of Chinua Achebe's *Things Fall Apart* (1959) suggest, relies as much on knowledge production by the colonialists (the guide the District Commissioner is writing) as on the physical coercion of conquest (Achebe, *Things Fall Apart*, 208–09).

103. Gaye, "I Want You."

104. Qtd. in Lovejoy, *The Great Chain of Being*, 60.

105. Hallward, *Out of This World*, 92. Elsewhere Hallward suggests that, given Deleuze's effort to escape all dialectical relations, to undo the hegemony of the Hegelian paradigm, the influence of his philosophy on postcolonial theory needs to be carefully scrutinized: see his *Absolutely Postcolonial*.

106. Hallward, *Out of This World*, 179n60.

107. Leibniz, "Logical-metaphysical principles," 50.

Chapter 3

1. Bersani, "The Other Freud," 48, 49.

2. Smith, *Essays on Deleuze*, 282.

3. *The Culture of Redemption* similarly includes chapters on writers whose works exemplify alternative modernities: see *CR* chs. 6 (on Herman Melville) and 8 (on Thomas Pynchon).

4. On Benjamin as a theorist of modern brooding, *Grübeln*, see Meyer-Sickendiek, *Tiefe*, 32–33, 46–49, 267–71, 277–87, 309–28; and Pensky, *Melancholic Dialectics*.

5. Benjamin, "The Storyteller," 162; "Der Erzähler," 465.

6. Benjamin, "The Work of Art in the Age of Its Technical Reproducibility," 254; "Das Kunstwerk im Zeitalter seiner technischen Reproduzierbarkeit," 477.

7. Benjamin, "The Work of Art in the Age of Its Technical Reproducibility," 253.

8. A good starting point for delving into the considerable literature on Benjamin's notion of "experience" is provided by Jay, *Songs of Experience*, ch. 8.

9. Benjamin, "On Some Motifs in Baudelaire," 316; see also "The Storyteller," 149.

10. Benjamin, "On Some Motifs in Baudelaire," 316; "Über einige Motive bei Baudelaire," 611.

11. Benjamin, "One-Way Street," 486.

12. Wolin, *Walter Benjamin*, 194, 31.

13. Ibid., 219.

14. Ibid., 225–26.

15. Ibid., 226, 227.

16. Bersani, "Death and Literary Authority," 865. Proust similarly becomes Benjaminian for Bersani: in the Proustian world, we find in art life's "annihilating salvation" (*CR* 11) or—Bersani culls the phrase from his encyclopedia article—"an annihilating and redemptive replication of experience" (*CR* 27).

17. The most important of Bersani's sources that include references to Leibniz—and which will be discussed below in detail—are the *Trauerspiel* study (Benjamin, *The Origin of German Tragic Drama*, 47–48, 92) and "On the Concept of History" (§17 [396]). Wolin, on whom Bersani relies, similarly discusses Benjamin's monadology at length.

18. As Françoise Meltzer writes, Benjamin "[c]anonized [Baudelaire] . . . as the father of modernity" (*Seeing Double*, 8). While Nietzsche's influence on Benjamin's work is less explicit than Baudelaire's, it has been analyzed by McFarland, *Constellation*; and Eiland, *Walter Benjamin*, 24–25, 43, 65. George Steiner suggests that Nietzsche's *The Birth of Tragedy* was one of Benjamin's models for his *Habilitationsschrift* (introduction, 12, see also 15). Bersani's point about Benjamin's widely accepted but mistaken reading of Baudelaire is also made in Singh, "Baudelaire without Benjamin."

19. Bersani, "Death and Literary Authority," 865–66.

20. Baudelaire, "The Salon of 1859," 229.

21. Nietzsche, *The Birth of Tragedy*, 26.

22. Habermas, "Walter Benjamin," 92.

23. Scholem, "Walter Benjamin and His Angel," 54. For an account of the debates surrounding Benjamin's influences, see Jennings, *Dialectical Images*, ch. 1.

24. Wolin, *Walter Benjamin*, 37, 286n7.

25. Scholem, *Walter Benjamin*, 41.

26. Scholem calls the eighteen theses on history Benjamin's "last datable writing" ("Walter Benjamin and His Angel," 85). On the composition and publication of the piece, see also Löwy, *Fire Alarm*, 17–21.

27. Benjamin, "On the Concept of History," §1 (389).

28. Habermas, "Walter Benjamin," 106.

29. Scholem, "Toward an Understanding of the Messianic Idea in Judaism," 3.

30. In ways that are not frequently recognized, Benjamin, in situating his theory of modernity in the Kabbalah of Galut, anticipates the more recent emphases on the diasporic dimension of Western modernity by such scholars as Enrique Dussel ("Eurocentrism and Modernity"), Walter Mignolo (*The Darker Side of the Renaissance*), and Robert F. Reid-Pharr (*Archives of Flesh*). Rather than locating the emergence of the modern in the Enlightenment, the French Revolution, or the upheavals around the Industrial Revolution and the rise of capitalism, Dussel, Mignolo, and Reid-Pharr trace it to the events of 1492, the moment that saw the exile of the Moors and the Jews from the Iberian peninsula, as well as the departure of Columbus on his expeditions—partially financed by the wealth confiscated from the expulsed populations (Shohat, *Taboo Memories, Diasporic Voices*, 209)—to the New World. In the tradition of Judaism that Scholem excavates, 1492 also precipitates apocalyptic messianism, which soon morphed from the narrative of the Israelites into full-fledged theory of being (Scholem, "The Messianic Idea in Kabbalism," 42–48). Especially after the disappointment of 1531—when the post-1492 Messianic prophecies failed to materialize (41–42)—the Kabbalah congealed into a cosmology: "by connecting the notions of Galut and redemption with the central question of the essence of the universe, [the mystics] managed to elaborate a system which transformed the exile of the people of Israel into an exile of the whole world, and the redemption of their people into a universal, cosmic redemption. . . . Galut was the condition of the universe as a whole, even of the deity" (43). In his philosophy, Benjamin articulates a version of this diasporic ontology, the proposition that "all being is in Galut" (45). On the relevance of diaspora theory to Bersani's work, see Tuhkanen, "Scattering Being."

31. Wolin, *Walter Benjamin*, 217.

32. Ibid., 227.

33. Meltzer, *Seeing Double*, 1.

34. Baudelaire, "The Painter of Modern Life," 48–49.

35. Benjamin, "On Some Motifs in Baudelaire," 333.

36. Baudelaire, "The Painter of Modern Life," 22.

37. Ibid.

38. Hiddleston, "Art and its representation," 143.

39. Baudelaire's original passage reads: "Modernity is that which is ephemeral, fugitive, contingent upon the occasion; it is half of art, whose other half is the eternal and unchangeable" ("The Painter of Modern Life," 32). J. A. Hiddleston similarly writes that, with the excess of examples with which Baudelaire seeks to illustrate the eternal aspect in art, we get "the sense of a vain proliferation,

a fall into time and number from which there seems no escape" ("Art and its representation," 143).

40. Hiddleston, "Art and its representation," 140.

41. Baudelaire, "The Salon of 1846," 84.

42. Ibid., 83.

43. Brix, "Modern Beauty versus Platonist Beauty."

44. Baudelaire, "The Painter of Modern Life," 22.

45. Baudelaire, "The Salon of 1846," 84.

46. Ibid., 84; "Le Salon de 1846," 456.

47. Baudelaire, "The Salon of 1859," 234–35. On Baudelaire's identification of memory with imagination, see ibid., 285.

48. Baudelaire, "The Salon of 1846," 84.

49. Brix, "Modern Beauty versus Platonist Beauty," 10.

50. Wilkinson, *The Dream of an Absolute Language*, 13.

51. Brix, "Modern Beauty versus Platonist Beauty," 6.

52. Baudelaire, "The Salon of 1846," 83.

53. Ibid., 42, 55, 71, 124.

54. Baudelaire, "Further Notes on Edgar Poe," 102–03.

55. Baudelaire, "The Painter of Modern Life," 22; "Le Peintre de la vie moderne," 685.

56. Leibniz, "The Principles of Philosophy," §11 (214).

57. Baudelaire, "The Salon of 1846," 127.

58. Baudelaire, "The Painter of Modern Life," 28, qtd. also in *CR* 71–72; "Le Peintre de la vie moderne," 691.

59. Baudelaire, "The Painter of Modern Life," 28.

60. Nietzsche, *The Case of Wagner*, 647.

61. Ibid.

62. Ansell Pearson, *How to Read Nietzsche*, 88–89.

63. Nietzsche, *The Birth of Tragedy*, 123.

64. Nietzsche, *Ecce Homo*, 732.

65. Benjamin, "The Life of Students," 43.

66. Benjamin, "The Storyteller," 147.

67. Ibid., 148.

68. Ibid.

69. Nietzsche, *The Birth of Tragedy*, 49.

70. See Bohrer, *Suddenness*, 115.

71. Nietzsche, *The Birth of Tragedy*, 99; *Die Geburt der Tragödie*, 132.

72. Nietzsche, *The Birth of Tragedy*, 36.

73. Baudelaire, "The Painter of Modern Life" 27, trans. modified. Norman Cameron translates Baudelaire's "ivre" as "*exhilarated*." For the original, see Baudelaire, "Le Peintre de la vie moderne," 690.

74. Baudelaire, "Edgar Allan Poe," 89; "Edgar Poe, sa vie et ses oeuvres," 315.

75. Nietzsche, *The Birth of Tragedy*, 36.

76. Baudelaire, "Further Notes on Edgar Poe," 108; Nietzsche, *The Birth of Tragedy*, 38.

77. Nietzsche, *The Birth of Tragedy*, 22.

78. Ibid., 45; *Die Geburt der Tragödie*, 63.

79. Nietzsche, *The Birth of Tragedy*, 45; *Die Geburt der Tragödie*, 62.

80. Nietzsche, *The Birth of Tragedy*, 35; *Die Geburt der Tragödie*, 49.

81. Nietzsche, *The Birth of Tragedy*, 48; *Die Geburt der Tragödie*, 66, qtd. also, with brackets, in *CR* 87.

82. Nietzsche, *The Birth of Tragedy*, 37.

83. Ibid., 65, 38; *Die Geburt der Tragödie*, 87, 53.

84. Nietzsche, *Ecce Homo*, 726. For Hegelian moments in *The Birth of Tragedy*, see particularly the discussion of art's "metaphysical comfort," its ability to "save" (*retten*) us from the horrors of life as it "nullifies" (*aufheben*) "appearances" (*Erscheinungen*) (59, 80). Walter Kaufmann speaks of the "fundamentally dialectical conception" of the study (*Nietzsche*, 392, see also 132–33).

85. Nietzsche, "David Strauss the Confessor and the Writer," 70.

86. Nietzsche, "On the Utility and Liability of History for Life," 142–43.

87. Ibid., 149; "Vom Nutzen und Nachteil der Historie für das Leben," 269.

88. Nietzsche, "On the Utility and Liability of History for Life," 147; "Vom Nutzen und Nachteil der Historie für das Leben," 266.

89. Marx, *The Economic and Philosophical Manuscripts of 1844*, 297; *Ökonomisch-philosophische Manuskripte aus dem Jahre 1844*, 536. For discussion of "orthodox" Marxism, see Miller, *History and Human Existence*, 103–24.

90. Nietzsche, "On the Utility and Liability of History for Life," 146.

91. Ibid., 160.

92. Deleuze, *Nietzsche and Philosophy*, 159.

93. Nietzsche, "On the Utility and Liability of History for Life," 94.

94. Foucauldian historiography entails, precisely, the cutting up of progressivist narratives: "I am completely opposed to a certain conception of history which takes for its model a kind of great continuous and homogenous evolution, a sort of great mythic life," Foucault announces in 1969. ". . . For the great mythology of change, evolution and the *perpetuum mobile* we must substitute a serious description of types of events and systems of transformation, and the establishment of series, and series of series" ("The Birth of a World," 66–67). In contradistinction to an "evolutionary" model, genealogical inquiry cuts our umbilical cord to an imagined past homogenous with the present. As Foucault continues in his program statement for Nietzschean historiography, "knowledge is not made for understanding; it is made for cutting" ("Nietzsche, Genealogy, History," 380), a proposition that we may compare to Lacan's advice to his analysts-in-training that, rather than offer the patient knowledge about himself, analysis should "cut"

his signifying chains, thereby enabling the emergence of alternate, unforeseen associations ("The Subversion of the Subject," 678).

95. Nietzsche, "On the Utility and Liability of History for Life," 94; "Vom Nutzen und Nachteil der Historie für das Leben," 218.

96. Nietzsche, *The Birth of Tragedy*, 72, 59–60; *Die Geburt der Tragödie*, 81.

97. Nietzsche, *The Birth of Tragedy*, 23, 60.

98. Ibid., 60.

99. Nietzsche, "Schopenhauer as Educator," 213.

100. Ibid., 213–14; "Schopenhauer als Erzieher," 326.

101. Nietzsche, "Schopenhauer as Educator," 234; "Schopenhauer als Erzieher," 345.

102. In *The Birth of Tragedy*, Nietzsche uses the same term to distinguish between lyrical and epic poetry. The latter is the more plastic, and hence Apollonian, of the two; the epic poet avoids the "pain and contradiction" that the lyricist experiences in the Dionysian frenzy of his art. Experiencing a "redemption in mere appearance [*Erlösung im Scheine*]" (49; *Die Geburt der Tragödie*, 67), the epic poet, he writes, "is protected against becoming one and fused with his figures [*er . . . gegen das Einswerden und Zusammenschmelzen mit seinen Gestalten geschützt ist*]" (*The Birth of Tragedy*, 50; *Die Geburt der Tragödie*, 68). Dionysian art, most notably music, demands the torture of becoming-one, of *zusammenschmelzen*, that for Bersani becomes synonymous with *ébranlement*.

103. Nietzsche, "Richard Wagner in Bayreuth," 328; 431.

104. Nietzsche, "Schopenhauer as Educator," 215; "Schopenhauer als Erzieher," 328.

105. Nietzsche, "Schopenhauer as Educator," 215.

106. Ibid., 216.

107. Deleuze, *Nietzsche and Philosophy*, 148.

108. Nietzsche, *The Birth of Tragedy*, 124; *Die Geburt der Tragödie*, 165, emphasis added.

109. Faber, introduction, xxvi.

110. De Man, "The Concept of Irony," 181.

111. Laplanche, "Interpretation between Determinism and Hermeneutics," 162.

112. Laplanche, "Transference," 227.

113. Laplanche, "Interpreting (with) Freud," 175.

114. Laplanche, "Intervention in a Debate between Daniel Widlöcher and Jacques-Alain Miller," 230, brackets in trans. Bersani, too, writes that "[i]n psychotherapy, errant speech is converted into stories" (*FrB* 102); this is one of the ways in which "the move from theory to practice can . . . be thought of as a flight from a specifically psychoanalytic type of thought" (*FrB* 4). As opposed to psychotherapy, analysis constitutes an undoing that is followed by the work of recomposition, a work that must be carried out not by the analyst but by the

analysand, a point that Freud makes in his self-criticism in the Irma dream. On Laplanche and "unbinding," see also Bersani, "Learning to Escape," 67–70.

115. Laplanche, "Time and the Other," 252; "Transference," 230, ellipsis in original.

116. Laplanche, "Time and the Other," 252, brackets in trans.

117. Ibid., 252, 253–54.

118. Mann, *The Magic Mountain*, 132, 127; *Der Zauberberg*, 205, 198.

119. Proust, *Remembrance of Things Past*, 1.172; *À la recherche du temps perdu*, 1.165–66, qtd. also, in Bersani and Dutoit's translation, in *CS* 67–68. For a condensed gloss on this scene, see Bersani and Dutoit, "Critical Reflections," 124.

120. The counterintuitive logic of being's appearance and becoming in Nietzsche and Baudelaire is perhaps suggested by what seems like an editorial oversight or oddly placed British colloquialism in the above sentence. What does it mean to be "different to oneself" (rather than the more idiomatic "different from oneself")? How does the relation between the self and the other asserted here differ from the one described in the phrase "identical to oneself"? If "different and identical to himself" indeed constitutes a grammatical error, the sentence may be a manifestation of "theoretico-genesis," of the way in which, according to Laplanche, thought recapitulates, as if obeying Haeckel's law, the difficulties and aporias of the operations it describes (hence, for example, Freud's self-betrayal, which repeats the unavoidable going-astray in hominization). The stuttering in the sentence may similarly symptomize what Bersani and Dutoit seek to describe.

Chapter 4

1. Luther, *Luther's Works*, 77.306, 28.46.

2. Ebeling, *Luther*, 120. On Luther's concept of calling, see also Weber, *Protestant Ethic and the Spirit of Capitalism*, esp. ch. 3; and Wingren, *Luther on Vocation*.

3. See Weber, *Protestant Ethic and the Spirit of Capitalism*, 155–63n3; on the significance of Luther's translations for the shift in the meaning of *Beruf/Berufung*, see also Frey, "*κλῆσις/Beruf*," 43–50. Weber's arguments about the consequences of Luther's theological breakthrough are anticipated by Karl Marx, for whom Luther revolts against external authority only to install an internal priest in the Christian ("Contribution to the Critique of Hegel's Philosophy of Law," 182); and Friedrich Engels, who sees in the Augustinian monk's refusal to support the peasant uprising of 1524–25 a prototype for the bourgeoisie's failure to carry out the revolution to its completion (*The Peasant War in Germany*, ch. 2).

4. Burroughs, *Tarzan of the Apes*, 106, 57.

5. Ibid., 32.

6. Ibid., ch. 16. In the concluding chapter to her *Manliness and Civilization* (1995), Bederman locates in Burroughs's novel an illustration of the "neurasthenic

paradox," whose convolutions, as she shows, had occupied nineteenth- and early twentieth-century thinkers of civilization. By the "neurasthenic paradox," Bederman names the tragic structure of civilizational becoming, where the susceptibility of Western subjects to education, once an advantage, inevitably leads to the emergence of a debilitating and effeminizing "nervousness" and, ultimately, to the civilization's degeneration. For a reading of *Tarzan of the Apes* that attends to the novel's thematization of calling and anthropobecoming, see Tuhkanen, "Grotesquely Becoming."

7. See "Fascination"; Beth, "Faszination."

8. Hamacher, "Uncalled," 74.

9. Laplanche and Pontalis, "Fantasy and the Origins of Sexuality," 18.

10. Laplanche, "To Situate Sublimation," 7.

11. Laplanchean psychoanalysis, we might further note, posits anthropogenesis as a radical process of occupation or *colonization*, the production or, as Frantz Fanon puts it in *The Wretched of the Earth*, "*fabricat*[*ion*]" of the subject in the process of its subjugation (2). If the psychoanalytic subject is drawn into becoming by the other's enigmatic call, the production of colonized subject begins, as Fanon indicates in his famous allegory, with a white child's solicitation of wonder and terror: "'Look, a Negro! . . . I'm frightened!'" (*Black Skin, White Masks*, 111–12). While Fanon, in the chapter "The Fact of Blackness," describes the inauthentic subjectivity of the colonized in the language of existentialism, the process of the subject's "fabrication" or "epidermalization" can also be understood in Laplanche's psychoanalytic terms. Indeed, here we arguably find the reason why psychoanalytically influenced contemporary theorists—most notably, Homi Bhabha (*The Location of Culture*) and Kobena Mercer ("Decolonisation and Disappointment")—have found Fanon's work on colonization immediately recognizable: for Fanon, as for psychoanalytic thought, subject-formation is synonymous with a *constitutive occupation*. Without addressing Fanon (or Bhabha or Mercer), Judith Butler's *The Psychic Life of Power* provides an introduction to these debates. For a critique that faults Fanon for the radicalness of his theory of colonization—for the seeming fact that Fanon doesn't allow any subjecthood beyond or before colonization—see Cooper, "Conflict and Connection," esp. 38–40.

12. For Foucault's use of the term, see *The Hermeneutics of the Subject*, 14; see also his description of Descartes in "The Ethics of the Concern of the Self," 294. For Bersani's discussion, see *IRG* 62, ch. 11; and *TT* 38, 46, 62.

13. The 2003 presentation ("Aggression, Gay Shame, and Almodóvar's Art" [*IRG* 63–82]) contains the first occurrence of the phrase "the aesthetic subject" in Bersani's work. The phrase may have been suggested to him by his participation in the conference and, subsequently, the collection *Aesthetic Subjects* (2000), ed. Matthews and McWhirter.

14. The Unnamable speaks of "this meaningless voice which prevents you from being nothing, just barely prevents you from being nothing and nowhere, just enough to keep alight this little yellow flame feebly darting from side to side,

panting, as if straining to tear itself from its wick, it should never have been lit, or it should never have been fed, or it should have been put out, put out, it should have been let go" (370–71). The chatter of Beckett's they should be compared and contrasted to the *Gerede* of They, which distracts Dasein from its search for authenticity in Heidegger.

15. Beckett, "Three Dialogues with Georges Duthuit," 124.

16. Ibid., 113, 112, 125.

17. Bersani and Dutoit do not mention Nietzsche in "Inhibited Reading," but turn to his work in the subsequent chapter, which tackles Mark Rothko's art. They find Nietzsche's *principium individuationis* operative in Rothko, whose paintings "striv[e] to represent, instead of difference, differentiality itself. To see Rothko's figures both dissolving and redesigning their own figured state (to see them lose and regain their visuality) is . . . to experience nonethically and nonpsychologically our own difference, to think of the individual as an ontological category prior to the constitution of an individual subject" (*AI* 141). The language here closely echoes that of "Boundaries of Time and Being": not only do both texts refer to Nietzsche's double redemption as a "two-way street" (*CR* 93; *AI* 140), but the description of Rothko's figures as "dissolving and redesigning their own figured state" repeats the operation of Nietzschean onto-aesthetics that Bersani characterizes as "a *figure dissolving its own figured state*" (*CR* 94). "Differentiality itself" emerges as another name for "the appearing of appearance," "initiating initiations," and "beginning of beginnings": "the *principle* of individuation in which all individual forms are grounded" (*CR* 99).

18. Mosès, *The Angel of History*, 114.

19. Foucault, "Nietzsche, Genealogy, History," 380, 369.

20. Benjamin, "On Language as Such and on the Language of Man," 71; "Über Sprache überhaupt und über die Sprache des Menschen," 153.

21. Beckett, *Waiting for Godot*, 73.

22. Laplanche and Pontalis, *Vocabulaire de la psychanalyse*, 263.

23. Beckett, "Assumption," 5.

24. Beckett, *The Unnamable*, 308, 376.

25. Hill, *Blanchot*, 112.

26. Morrison, *Sula*, 123.

27. Bersani, "No Exit for Beckett," 266.

28. Blanchot, *The Space of Literature*, esp. 19–34; *The Book to Come*, 210–17.

29. Bruns, *Maurice Blanchot*, 86.

30. The phrase "the fascinations of the imaginary" comes from Lacan, *The Seminar of Jacques Lacan, Book VII*, 199. For the term "lure" in Lacan, see Evans, *An Introductory Dictionary of Lacanian Psychoanalysis*, 104–05.

31. Lacan, *The Seminar of Jacques Lacan, Book I*, 87; *Le séminaire de Jacques Lacan, Livre I*, 102. Later in the same seminar, Lacan speaks of "the totality of the symbolic system in which the subject is called, in the full sense of the term, to

take up his place [*l'ensemble du système symbolique dans lequel le sujet est appelé, au sens plein du terme, à prendre sa place*]" (198; 223).

32. Beckett, *The Unnamable*, 383.

33. Ibid., 299.

34. In *The Culture of Redemption*, Bersani repeats himself as he, again, observes in Freud "modes of theoretical failure and even collapse . . . , the processes by which arguments are *at once* elaborated and disformulated" (*CR* 44, emphasis added).

35. The *at once* characterizes the mode of figuration that we appreciate as art: "Writing may begin to operate as the activity we call literature when, by a particular kind of replicative insistence . . . , it erodes its own statements and thereby blocks interpretation" (*FrB* 11). Elsewhere, speaking of his and Dutoit's studies of Assyrian art, Bersani defines the aesthetic as that which "simultaneously proposes and repudiates form; it is an enigmatic equivalence between formal elaborations and a continuous slippage of both sense and desiring intentionality away from any locatable forms" ("Rejoinder to Walter Benn Michaels," 163). We find this the defiguring of figuration in, for example, the "simultaneous emergence of form and erosion of boundaries" in Rothko (*AI* 122). Beckett's literary experimentations similarly describe "the linguistic 'I' that explodes the boundaries of a self at the instant of defining them" (*AI* 68). Evincing such simultaneity of appearing and dissolving, the Freudian text should be read as "a work of art," "the critical artistic text of our time" (*FrB* 5, 111–12).

The key phrase recurs elsewhere. In *Arts of Impoverishment*, Bersani and Dutoit note that in the psychoanalytic account of hominization "a coherent ego structure is *at once* posited and shattered" (*AI* 142, emphasis added); like Bersani does in "Boundaries of Time and Being," they connect this shattering to primary narcissism. In *The Culture of Redemption*, Bersani writes: "absolute narcissistic satisfaction *must coincide* with an explosion of the self's boundaries"; there is, consequently, an "implicit equivalence in Freud between primary narcissism and the *simultaneous* constitution and shattering of ego boundaries" (*CR* 73, emphases added). If we see, as Bersani proposes, "egoconstitution as identical to egoshattering" (*CR* 98), this identity is that of the temporal *at once* that we find in Beckettian figuration. A later chapter in *The Culture of Redemption* identifies a further example of such simultaneity in *Moby Dick*, where, as Bersani argues, we get an American history that "will take place in the space *at once* cluttered and blank where all imagined social bonds have been *simultaneously figured and dissolved*" (*CR* 149, emphases added). Malcolm Bowie suggests that the *at once* describes the style not only of the Freudian text, but also Bersani's own writing, which, as he observes, is characterized by "provocatively self-referring sentence[s]" that "make patterns" and "shatter them," "impose discipline" and "subvert it" ("Bersani on Proust," 28).

36. That this dynamic is not peculiar to Bersani, or his sources, is suggested by Bohrer, *Suddenness*.

37. Nietzsche, *The Birth of Tragedy*, 45; *Die Geburt der Tragödie*, 62.

38. On Benjamin's Nietzsche, see McFarland, *Constellation*; Pfotenhauer, "Benjamin und Nietzsche"; and Eiland, *Walter Benjamin*, 24–25, 43, 65.

39. Already in the early essay "The Life of Student" (1915 [1914–15]), he critiques progressivist ideals: "There is a view of history," the 22-year-old Benjamin writes, "that puts its faith in the infinite extent of time and thus concerns itself only with the speed, or lack of it, with which people and epochs advance along the path of progress. This corresponds to a certain absence of coherence and rigor in the demands it makes on the present" (37). The ideal of infinite "progress"—the Hegelian "perfectibility"—must be relinquished, Benjamin argues, if we are to think the present. In his later work, he consistently challenges the classical Marxist assumption of history's teleology according to which "capitalist production begets, with the inexorability of a natural process, its own negation" in the proletarian *Aufhebung* (Marx, *Capital*, 1.929). For Benjamin, such assertions, and the complacency they suggest, undo the possibility of politics. He insists, contra Marx, that "capitalism will not die a natural death" (*The Arcades Project*, X11a,3 [667]) but must be helped along its way to the grave. He wants to reconfigure such aspects of the Marxist dialectic by inflecting its *Werden* through the forces of history's disruption articulated in messianic philosophy.

40. Benjamin, *The Arcades Project*, N2,2 (460).

41. Benjamin, "On the Concept of History," §16 (396).

42. Ibid., §16 (396), §B (397).

43. As the editors of Benjamin's *Selected Writings* note, "*die kleine Pforte*" may be an allusion to "*die enge Pforte*," with which Luther renders the phrase from Matt. 7.13–14 (in English, "strait gate") in his German Bible (see the editors' notes in Benjamin, *Selected Writings*, 4.400n29).

44. For the most rigorous treatment of Leibnizian influences, most notably Cohen and Heimsoeth, in early Benjamin, see Schwebel, "Intensive Infinity"; for a study of Leibnizian influences in Benjamin and Heidegger, see Schwebel, "Monad and Time." On Benjamin and Leibniz, see also Engelhardt, "Der historische Gegenstand als Monade"; Fenves, *The Messianic Reduction*, 167–77, 281–82n2; Mosès, *The Angel of History*, 85–91; Wolin, *Walter Benjamin*, 96, 98–100, 125–26; and Zangenberg, "In the Midst of the Monad."

45. Benjamin, "The Concept of Criticism in German Romanticism," 146; *The Origin of German Tragic Drama*, 47–48. Mosès (*The Angel of History*, 85–86) incorrectly identifies the *Trauerspiel* study's prolegomena as the place where the term "monad" appears for the first time.

46. Schwebel, "Intensive Infinity," 589.

47. Tiedemann, "Dialectics at a Standstill," 940.

48. Benjamin, "On Language as Such and on the Language of Man," 71.

49. Ibid., 73; "The Work of Art in the Age of Its Technological Reproducibility," 254; "On Some Motifs in Baudelaire," 316.

50. Benjamin, "On Language as Such and on the Language of Man," 69, 65.

51. Ibid., 71; "Über Sprache überhaupt und über die Sprache des Menschen," 153. The German *Geschwätz* in Benjamin is alternatively translated as either "chatter" or "prattle." Benjamin draws the concept of *Geschwätz* partially from Kierkegaard: see Benjamin, *On the Origin of German Tragic Drama*, 233–34; and "On Language as Such and on the Language of Man," 71. On "chatter" (*snak*) in Kierkegaard, see Fenves, *"Chatter."*

52. Not surprisingly, Jacques Derrida criticizes Benjamin for his theological orientation. While his first substantive commentary on Benjamin, in "Force of Law" (1992), concerns another early text—"Critique of Violence" (1921)—his arguments can be applied to "On Language as Such," too. Derrida considers many of Benjamin's pronouncements "redoubtable" because they are premised on "the theory of the fall and of originary authenticity, the polarity between originary language and fallen language," that is, the tendencies that render Benjamin's thought, in Derrida's estimation, "too messianico-marxist or archeo-eschatalogical" ("Force of Law," 62). At least in his early work, Benjamin peddles the origin myths whose aporias deconstruction—as well as Lacanian and Laplanchean psychoanalysis—will unravel with the concept of *Nachträglichkeit.*

53. Tiffany, *Infidel Poetics*, 104n19.

54. Benjamin, *The Arcades Project*, N2,6 (461).

55. Benjamin, "On the Concept of History," §18 (396).

56. Ibid., §17 (396).

57. In the terms of Kabbalistic cosmology, the monadic moment, when history enters a "tremendous abbreviation," designates *zimzum*, the contraction of being before creation. On Luria's creation myth, see Scholem, *Kabbalah*, 129–35.

58. Nietzsche, *The Birth of Tragedy*, 22.

59. Ibid., 22n6.

60. Heine, "Songs of Creation," 356; "Schöpfunglieder," 445.

61. Freud, "On Narcissism," 79.

62. Ibid., 78.

63. But see Bersani's brief acknowledgment, two years later, of Sedgwick's *Tendencies*: *H* 193n49.

64. Sedgwick, *Tendencies*, xii.

65. Burroughs, *Tarzan of the Apes*, 32.

66. The essay includes the text of *AI* 55–77.

67. The translation of the essay, originally published in 1949, is reprinted, under the title of "Sociability," in the collection *On Individuality and Social Forms* (1971), from where we, following Bersani, cite the text.

68. Simmel, "Sociability," 128.

69. Foucault, "Friendship as a Way of Life," 138. For an extensive discussion of this aspect of Foucauldian ethics, one that also engages Bersani, see Roach, *Friendship as a Way of Life*.

70. See Pyyhtinen, *Simmel and "the Social,"* 39–49, 72–73, as well as chs. 5 and 7.

71. Benjamin, "On Language as Such and on the Language of Man," 72; "Über Sprache überhaupt und über die Sprache des Menschen," 154.

72. Marx, *Grundrisse*, 287; *Grundrisse der kritik der politischen Ökonomie*, 213.

73. Adorno, *Minima Moralia*, §97 (149).

74. Heidegger, *Being and Time*, §35 (159).

75. Harari, *Lacan's Four Fundamental Concepts of Psychoanalysis*, 29.

76. Luther, *Luther's Works*, 76.22; *D. Martin Luthers Werke*, 17.2.44.24.

77. See Laplanche, "Exigency and Going-Astray"; "Starting from the Fundamental Anthropological Situation."

78. Bersani and Dutoit, "Rohmer's Salon," 29.

79. Ibid.

80. Baldwin, *Giovanni's Room*, 283.

81. Ibid., 239, 267, 305.

82. Adorno, *Minima Moralia*, §42 (68); §42 (75).

83. On Adorno, homosexuality, and fascism, see Halle, "Between Marxism and Psychoanalysis"; Hewitt, *Political Inversions*; and Rycenga, "Queerly Amiss."

84. Horkheimer and Adorno, *Dialectic of Enlightenment*, 158.

85. Ibid., 112.

86. Adorno, *Minima Moralia*, §88 (135).

87. This is what Daniel Tiffany may have in mind when, in his extremely condensed discussion of Bersani in *Infidel Poetics*, he alludes to "the monadology of the bathhouse" (13). For commentary, influenced by Bersani's thought, on gay men's sexual subcultures, see Dean, *Unlimited Intimacy*. For further work that engages Leibniz (mainly by way of Benjamin) in an effort to conceptualize queer subcultural spaces, see Chisholm, *Queer Constellations*.

88. Simmel, *The Sociology of Georg Simmel*, 52; *Grundfragen der Soziologie*, 115. See the corresponding passage in "Soziologie der Geselligkeit," 11 ("Sociability," 136), where the term *Geschwätz* does not appear.

89. Simmel, "Sociability," 136.

90. Bersani, "Rigorously Speculating," 282.

91. Beckett, *Molloy*, 121.

Chapter 5

1. Lacan, *The Seminar of Jacques Lacan, Book VII*, 319; *Le séminaire de Jacques Lacan, Livre VII*, 368.

2. Schwanke, "Luther's Theology of Creation," 205.

3. Ibid. See also Schwanke, "The Indispensability of Theological Adscription in Biomedicine," esp. 213–15; and "Lebendige Kommunikation oder technische Reproduktion?" esp. 66.

4. Phillips, "Sameness Is All," 338, emphasis added.

5. Ibid., 340.

6. Meyer, "Warhol's Clones," 110. For a classic treatment of the gay clone, see Levine, *Gay Macho*. For a psychoanalytically oriented discussion, see Dean, "Sameness without Identity," 32–36.

7. Rumaker, *A Day and a Night at the Baths*, 41–42.

8. Adorno, *Minima Moralia*, §88 (135). Max Weber famously explores this argument in *Protestant Ethic and the Spirit of Capitalism* (1920). On the Lutheran notion of inwardness (which nevertheless must be distinguished from what Luther deemed the sinful condition of *incurvatus in se*), particularly in terms of Hegel's thought, see Mattes, "Georg W. F. Hegel," 50; and Rózsa, *Modern Individuality in Hegel's Practical Philosophy*, 234. On the establishment of modern "interiority" in another context, see Castiglia, *Interior States*.

9. See Gobineau, *Essai sur l'inégalité des races humaines*; and Young, *Colonial Desire*, 99–117.

10. See Bramen, *The Uses of Variety*.

11. Ong, *Orality and Literacy*.

12. Of course, the specter of sameness has been raised not only against queers: as an appellation for straight folk, the fag slang term "breeders" denotes the brainless, mechanical, and docile reproduction of the same, the endless repetition of identical days in lifeless suburbs. Breeders constitute the heterosexual counterparts to gay clones, something like inverse mirror images of what straight society sees when it looks at the clone: both are swallowed in their futureless sameness. Despite what one might initially think, the breeders' reproductive activity does not align them with the production of difference on which futurity relies. Whether gay or straight, sameness threatens (or amuses) us as an image of futurelessness; its uncanniness (or comedy) issues, at least partially, from its eugenic associations—its blurring the line of human and nonhuman reproduction.

13. Laplanche, *Life and Death in Psychoanalysis*, 60, last two emphases added; *Vie et mort en psychanalyse*, 103.

14. Arendt, *The Human Condition*, 254.

15. Jameson, *The Hegel Variations*, 131.

16. Bayer, "Hermeneutical theology," 144.

17. Bayer, "The Modern Narcissus," 304.

18. Ruti, *The Singularity of Being*, 178.

19. On the "ahuman," see Tuhkanen, "Grotesquely Becoming."

20. Réage, *The Story of O*, 80.

21. Freud, "Instincts and Their Vicissitudes," 125.

22. Ibid., 125n3.

23. Freud, "The Economic Problem of Masochism," 418–19.

24. Laplanche, *Life and Death in Psychoanalysis*, 91.

25. Laplanche, "Masochism and the General Theory of Seduction," 204.

26. Réage, *The Story of O*, 182.

27. Freud, "On Narcissism," 81.

28. See also *TT* 8, 33, 45, and 63; and Bersani, Preface to the Second Edition, xix.

29. We reserve for a future occasion the discussion of Joan Copjec's critique of Bersani's understanding of narcissism and sublimation: see Copjec, *Imagine There's No Woman*, ch 2.

30. Plato, *Phaedrus*, 247c (288), 249c (290).

31. Ibid., 246e (287), 249d (290).

32. Nicholson, *Plato's* Phaedrus, 177.

33. Freud, *Three Essays on the Theory of Sexuality*, 145.

34. Leibniz, "Principles of Nature and Grace," §3 (207).

35. Edman, Introduction, xxxvi.

36. Baudelaire, "The Salon of 1846," 84.

37. Plato, *Phaedrus*, 252d (294).

38. For a brief commentary on this term, see Bersani, "Rigorously Speculating," 281.

39. Phillips, "Sameness Is All," 338.

40. See Edelman, *No Future*.

41. Bersani and Dutoit, "Merde Alors," 26.

42. Ibid., 27.

43. Bersani, "Broken Connections," 414–15.

44. See Russell, "Recent Work on the Philosophy of Leibniz," 399–400; *A Critical Exposition of the Philosophy of Leibniz*, xvii.

45. Krauss, *A Universe from Nothing*, 17, qtd. in *TT* 77. Krauss echoes Carl Sagan's observation that all life on earth, including human bodies, "is made of star stuff," of atoms from collapsed stars ("Carl Sagan, Cosmos—Star Stuff," *YouTube*, 2 Mar. 2007, Web, 5 June, 2015).

46. See Plato, *Phaedrus*, 248c–249d (289–91).

47. Bersani, Preface to the Second Edition, xiv.

48. Speaking of "reason's abiding narcissism," Jason Wirth, too, uses the phrase "speculative narcissism." He deploys it to describe "the ego of reason," whose otherlessness and "self-love" he considers characteristic of modern philosophy (*The Conspiracy of Life*, 51). With the phrase, he restates the familiar critique of Hegelian "narcissism," which it is our project to develop beyond its simple dismissal.

49. Marx and Engels, *The Holy Family*, 59.

50. Marx, "Critique of the Hegelian Dialectic and Philosophy as a Whole," 328; "Kritik der Hegelschen Dialektik und Philosophie überhaupt," 569.

51. Hegel, *Phenomenology of Spirit*, §84 (53).

52. Qtd. in Nancy, *The Speculative Remark*, 188n22.

53. Jameson, *The Hegel Variations*, ch. 11.

54. Luther, *Luther's Works*, 54.112; *D. Martin Luthers Werke, Tischreden*, 1.302–03.

55. Luther, *Luther's Works*, 54.22.

56. Bayer, "The Modern Narcissus," 312; "Der neuzeitliche Narziß," 85.

57. Bayer, "The Modern Narcissus," 304; "Der neuzeitliche Narziß," 76. The importance of the term "speculation" is deemphasized in the English translation of Bayer's essay by the omission of the subsection title "*Spekulieren?*" (ibid., 76).

58. Freud, "On Narcissism," 82–83. James Strachey helps us make the connection here: "*Solche Frauen üben den größten Reiz auf die Männer aus*," Freud writes ("Zur Einführung des Narzißmus," 55); "Such women," Strachey translates, "have the greatest fascination for men."

59. Luther uses the term to describe an occult force (*fascinatione*), whose visitations—in the form of a neighborhood witch (*fascinatrice*)—he recalls from childhood (*Luther's Works*, 54.188; *D. Martin Luthers Werke, Tischreden*, 3.131; see also ibid., 3.602).

60. Proust, *Remembrance of Things Past*, 2.87.

61. Luther, *D. Martin Luthers Werke*, 5.319.23.

62. Schwanke, "The Indispensability of Theological Adscription in Biomedicine," 205.

63. Bayer, "The Modern Narcissus," 310.

64. Ibid., 311.

65. On Levinas's and Laplanche's shared onto-ethical investments, see Zupančič, "Sex, ontology, subjectivity," 200–01; and *Why Psychoanalysis?* 21–40.

66. Nancy, *Hegel*, 9.

67. Baudelaire, "The Painter of Modern Life," 28, trans. modified.

68. Baudelaire, "The Salon of 1846," 84.

69. Ibid., 83.

70. Baudelaire, "The Painter of Modern Life," 28; "Le Peintre de la vie moderne," 690.

71. Lacan, "Aggressiveness in Psychoanalysis," 91; Lacan and Cénac, "A Theoretical Introduction to the Function of Psychoanalysis in Criminology," 122.

72. The concept of "fascination" in Bersani's work, which we have occasionally evoked here, will require its own study, one that will contribute to the emerging field of what can be called "Fascination Studies." The grounding texts in this field include Abbas, "Dialectic of Deception"; Baumbach, *Literature and Fascination*; Degen, *Ästhetische Faszination*; Hahnemann and Weyand, eds., *Faszination*; Seeber, *Literarische Faszination in England um 1900*; Thys, *Fascinatie*; and Weingart, "Contact at a Distance."

73. Hill, *Beckett's Fiction*, 15; Genet, *Funeral Rites*, 161.

74. Leibniz, *Theodicy*, §9 (128).

75. For further references to "ecstasy" in Bersani, see, for example, *BF* 74–75; *FrB* 64; *CR* 38, 73, 74, 81, 86, 101, 145; and *FoB* 172, 176.

76. Hegel, *Science of Logic*, 56.

77. Bayer, "The Modern Narcissus," 304.

78. See also Kurnick, "Embarrassment and the Forms of Redemption," 62.

79. Benjamin, "On the Concept of History," §16 (396).

Works Cited

Abbas, Ackbar. "Dialectic of Deception." *Public Culture* 11.2 (1999): 347–63. *Highwire P.* Web. 4 July 2015.

Achebe, Chinua. *Things Fall Apart*. 1959. New York: Anchor, 1994. Print.

Ackerley, C. J. "Samuel Beckett and Science." *Companion to Samuel Beckett*. Ed. S. E. Gontarski. Oxford: Wiley-Blackwell, 2010. 143–63. Print.

Ackerley, C. J., and S. E. Gontarski. *The Grove Companion to Samuel Beckett: A Reader's Guide to His Works, Life, and Thought*. New York: Grove P, 2004. Print.

Adorno, Theodor W. "Letters to Walter Benjamin." *Aesthetics and Politics*. 1977. By Theodor W. Adorno, Walter Benjamin, Ernst Bloch, Bertolt Brecht, and Georg Lukács. London: Verso, 2007. 110–33. Print.

———. *Minima Moralia: Reflections from Damaged Life*. 1951. Trans. E. F. N. Jephcott. London: Verso, 2005. Print.

———. *Minima Moralia: Reflexionen aus dem beschädigten Leben*. 1951. *Gesammelte Schriften*. Vol. 4. Ed. Rolf Tiedemann. Frankfurt-am-Main: Suhrkamp, 1980. Print.

Agamben, Giorgio. *The Open: Man and Animal*. 2002. Trans. Kevin Attell. Stanford, CA: Stanford UP, 2004. Print.

Althusser, Louis. *For Marx*. 1965. Trans. Ben Brewster. London: Verso, 1996. Print.

———. "Freud and Lacan." *Lenin and Philosophy and Other Essays*. Trans. Ben Brewster. New York: Monthly Review P, 1971. 195–219. Print.

———. "Marxism and Humanism." 1963–65. *For Marx* 219–47.

———. "On the Materialist Dialectic: On the Unevenness of Origins." *For Marx* 161–217.

Ansell Pearson, Keith. *How to Read Nietzsche*. London: Granta, 2005. Print.

Arendt, Hannah. *The Human Condition*. 1958. 2nd ed. Chicago: U of Chicago P, 1998. Print.

Aristotle. *Metaphysica (Metaphysics)*. Trans. W. D. Ross. *The Basic Works of Aristotle*. Ed. Richard McKeon. 1941. New York: Modern Library, 2001. 681–926. Print.

Badiou, Alain. *Deleuze: The Clamor of Being*. 1997. Trans. Louise Burchill. Minneapolis: U of Minnesota P, 2000. Print.

———. *Pocket Pantheon: Figures of Postwar Philosophy*. 2008. Trans. David Macey. London: Verso, 2009. Print.

Bakhtin, Mikhail. *The Dialogic Imagination*. Ed. Michael Holquist. Trans. Caryl Emerson and Michael Holquist. 1981. Austin: U of Texas P, 1987. Print.

Baldwin, James. *Giovanni's Room*. 1956. *Early Novels and Stories*. New York: Library of America, 1998. 217–360. Print.

Barthes, Roland. *The Preparation of the Novel: Lecture Courses and Seminars at Collège de France (1978–1979 and 1979–1980)*. 2003. Ed. Nathalie Léger. Trans. Kate Briggs. New York: Columbia UP, 2011. Print.

Baudelaire, Charles. "Edgar Allan Poe: His Life and Works." 1856. *Painter* 69–92.

———. "Edgar Poe, sa vie et ses oeuvres." 1856. *Œuvres* 2.296–318.

———. "Further Notes on Edgar Poe." 1857. *Painter* 93–110.

———. *The Mirror of Art: Critical Studies*. Ed. and trans. Jonathan Mayne. Garden City: Doubleday Anchor, 1956. Print.

———. *Œuvres complètes*. 2 vols. Ed. Claude Pichois. Paris: Bibliothèque de la Pléiade, 1975–76. Print.

———. "The Painter of Modern Life." 1863. Trans. Norman Cameron. *The Essence of Laughter and Other Essays, Journals, and Letters*. Ed. Peter Quennell. New York: Meridion, 1956. 17–62. Print.

———. *The Painter of Modern Life and Other Essays*. Ed. and trans. Jonathan Mayne. London: Phaidon P, 1964. Print.

———. "Le Peintre de la vie moderne." 1863. *Œuvres* 2.683–724.

———. "Le Salon de 1846." 1846. *Œuvres* 2.415–96.

———. "The Salon of 1846." 1846. *Mirror* 38–130.

———. "The Salon of 1859." 1859. *Mirror* 220–304.

Baumbach, Sibylle. *Literature and Fascination*. New York: Palgrave Macmillan, 2015. Print.

Bayer, Oswald. "Hermeneutical theology." Trans. Gwen Griffith-Dickson. *Scottish Journal of Theology* 56.2 (2003): 131–47. *Cambridge Core*. Web. 24 Dec. 2016.

———. "The Modern Narcissus." 1993. Trans. Christine Helmer. *Lutheran Quarterly* 9 (1995): 301–13. Print.

———. "Der neuzeitliche Narziß." 1993. *Gott als Autor: Zu einer poietologischen Theologie*. Tübingen: Mohr Siebeck, 1999. 73–85. Print.

Becker, Werner. "Spekulation." *Handbuch Philosophischer Grundbegriffe*. Ed. Hermann Krings, Hans Michael Baumgartner, and Christoph Wild. 3 vols. Munich: Kösel, 1973–74. 3.1368–75. Print.

Beckett, Samuel. "Assumption." 1929. *The Complete Short Prose, 1929–1989*. Ed. S. E. Gontarski. New York: Grove P, 1995. 3–7. Print.

———. *Company*. 1980. *Nohow* 1–46.

———. *The Grove Centenary Edition*. Vol. 1: Novels. Ed. Paul Auster. New York: Grove P, 2006. Print.

———. *How It Is*. 1961. New York: Grove P, 1964. Print.

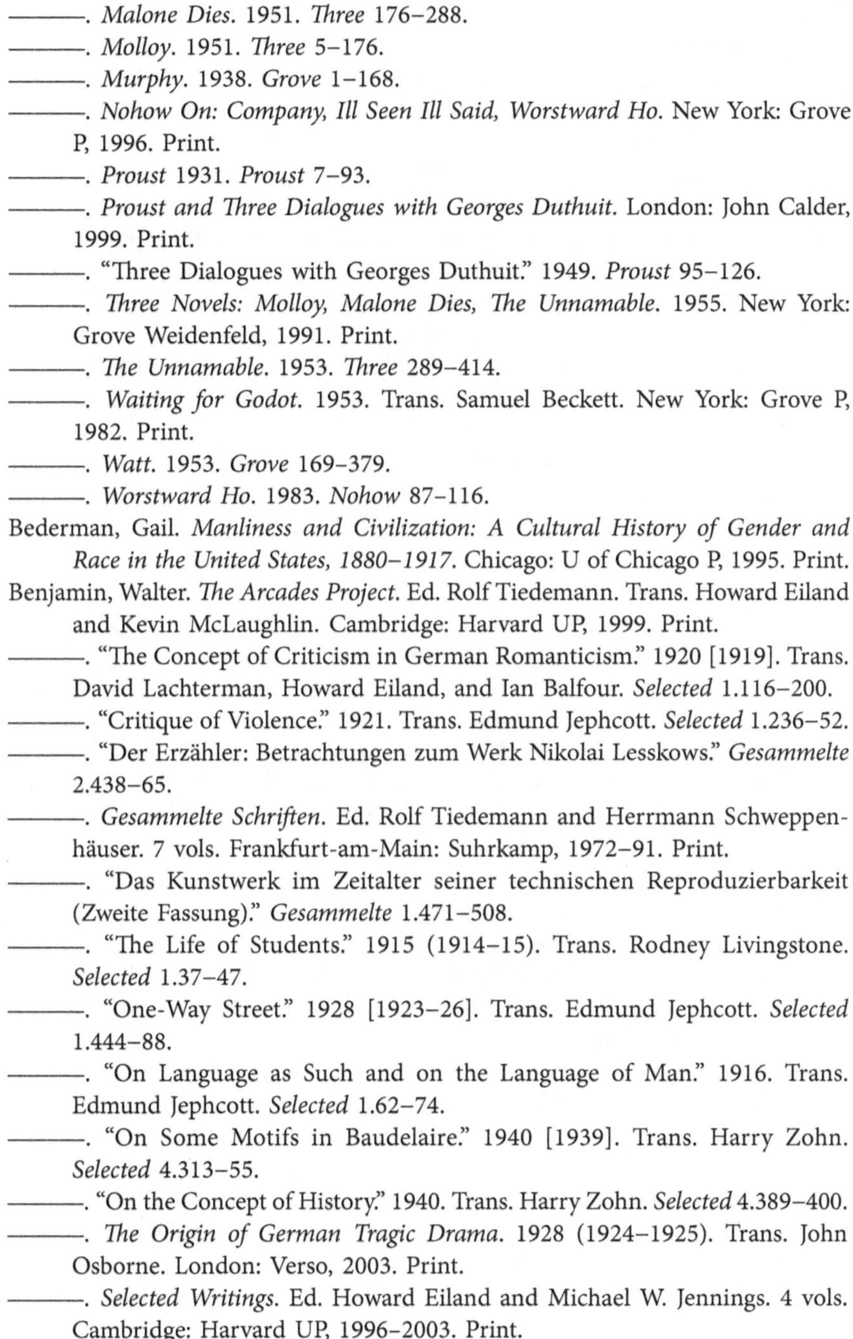

———. *Malone Dies*. 1951. *Three* 176–288.

———. *Molloy*. 1951. *Three* 5–176.

———. *Murphy*. 1938. *Grove* 1–168.

———. *Nohow On: Company, Ill Seen Ill Said, Worstward Ho*. New York: Grove P, 1996. Print.

———. *Proust* 1931. *Proust* 7–93.

———. *Proust and Three Dialogues with Georges Duthuit*. London: John Calder, 1999. Print.

———. "Three Dialogues with Georges Duthuit." 1949. *Proust* 95–126.

———. *Three Novels: Molloy, Malone Dies, The Unnamable*. 1955. New York: Grove Weidenfeld, 1991. Print.

———. *The Unnamable*. 1953. *Three* 289–414.

———. *Waiting for Godot*. 1953. Trans. Samuel Beckett. New York: Grove P, 1982. Print.

———. *Watt*. 1953. *Grove* 169–379.

———. *Worstward Ho*. 1983. *Nohow* 87–116.

Bederman, Gail. *Manliness and Civilization: A Cultural History of Gender and Race in the United States, 1880–1917*. Chicago: U of Chicago P, 1995. Print.

Benjamin, Walter. *The Arcades Project*. Ed. Rolf Tiedemann. Trans. Howard Eiland and Kevin McLaughlin. Cambridge: Harvard UP, 1999. Print.

———. "The Concept of Criticism in German Romanticism." 1920 [1919]. Trans. David Lachterman, Howard Eiland, and Ian Balfour. *Selected* 1.116–200.

———. "Critique of Violence." 1921. Trans. Edmund Jephcott. *Selected* 1.236–52.

———. "Der Erzähler: Betrachtungen zum Werk Nikolai Lesskows." *Gesammelte* 2.438–65.

———. *Gesammelte Schriften*. Ed. Rolf Tiedemann and Herrmann Schweppenhäuser. 7 vols. Frankfurt-am-Main: Suhrkamp, 1972–91. Print.

———. "Das Kunstwerk im Zeitalter seiner technischen Reproduzierbarkeit (Zweite Fassung)." *Gesammelte* 1.471–508.

———. "The Life of Students." 1915 (1914–15). Trans. Rodney Livingstone. *Selected* 1.37–47.

———. "One-Way Street." 1928 [1923–26]. Trans. Edmund Jephcott. *Selected* 1.444–88.

———. "On Language as Such and on the Language of Man." 1916. Trans. Edmund Jephcott. *Selected* 1.62–74.

———. "On Some Motifs in Baudelaire." 1940 [1939]. Trans. Harry Zohn. *Selected* 4.313–55.

———. "On the Concept of History." 1940. Trans. Harry Zohn. *Selected* 4.389–400.

———. *The Origin of German Tragic Drama*. 1928 (1924–1925). Trans. John Osborne. London: Verso, 2003. Print.

———. *Selected Writings*. Ed. Howard Eiland and Michael W. Jennings. 4 vols. Cambridge: Harvard UP, 1996–2003. Print.

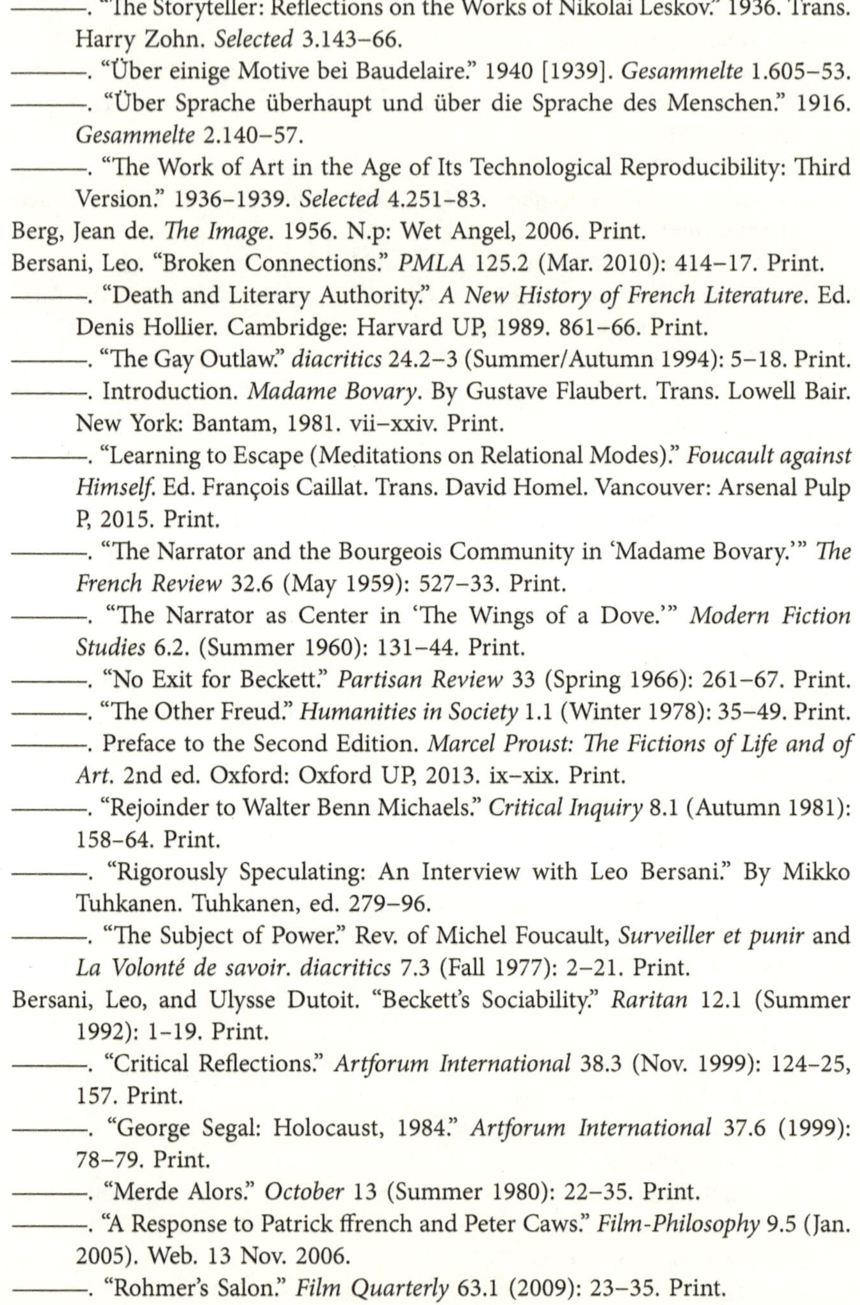

———. "The Storyteller: Reflections on the Works of Nikolai Leskov." 1936. Trans. Harry Zohn. *Selected* 3.143–66.

———. "Über einige Motive bei Baudelaire." 1940 [1939]. *Gesammelte* 1.605–53.

———. "Über Sprache überhaupt und über die Sprache des Menschen." 1916. *Gesammelte* 2.140–57.

———. "The Work of Art in the Age of Its Technological Reproducibility: Third Version." 1936–1939. *Selected* 4.251–83.

Berg, Jean de. *The Image*. 1956. N.p: Wet Angel, 2006. Print.

Bersani, Leo. "Broken Connections." *PMLA* 125.2 (Mar. 2010): 414–17. Print.

———. "Death and Literary Authority." *A New History of French Literature*. Ed. Denis Hollier. Cambridge: Harvard UP, 1989. 861–66. Print.

———. "The Gay Outlaw." *diacritics* 24.2–3 (Summer/Autumn 1994): 5–18. Print.

———. Introduction. *Madame Bovary*. By Gustave Flaubert. Trans. Lowell Bair. New York: Bantam, 1981. vii–xxiv. Print.

———. "Learning to Escape (Meditations on Relational Modes)." *Foucault against Himself*. Ed. François Caillat. Trans. David Homel. Vancouver: Arsenal Pulp P, 2015. Print.

———. "The Narrator and the Bourgeois Community in 'Madame Bovary.'" *The French Review* 32.6 (May 1959): 527–33. Print.

———. "The Narrator as Center in 'The Wings of a Dove.'" *Modern Fiction Studies* 6.2. (Summer 1960): 131–44. Print.

———. "No Exit for Beckett." *Partisan Review* 33 (Spring 1966): 261–67. Print.

———. "The Other Freud." *Humanities in Society* 1.1 (Winter 1978): 35–49. Print.

———. Preface to the Second Edition. *Marcel Proust: The Fictions of Life and of Art*. 2nd ed. Oxford: Oxford UP, 2013. ix–xix. Print.

———. "Rejoinder to Walter Benn Michaels." *Critical Inquiry* 8.1 (Autumn 1981): 158–64. Print.

———. "Rigorously Speculating: An Interview with Leo Bersani." By Mikko Tuhkanen. Tuhkanen, ed. 279–96.

———. "The Subject of Power." Rev. of Michel Foucault, *Surveiller et punir* and *La Volonté de savoir*. *diacritics* 7.3 (Fall 1977): 2–21. Print.

Bersani, Leo, and Ulysse Dutoit. "Beckett's Sociability." *Raritan* 12.1 (Summer 1992): 1–19. Print.

———. "Critical Reflections." *Artforum International* 38.3 (Nov. 1999): 124–25, 157. Print.

———. "George Segal: Holocaust, 1984." *Artforum International* 37.6 (1999): 78–79. Print.

———. "Merde Alors." *October* 13 (Summer 1980): 22–35. Print.

———. "A Response to Patrick ffrench and Peter Caws." *Film-Philosophy* 9.5 (Jan. 2005). Web. 13 Nov. 2006.

———. "Rohmer's Salon." *Film Quarterly* 63.1 (2009): 23–35. Print.

Beth, Karl. "Faszination." *Handwörterbuch des deutschen Aberglaubens*. Ed. Eduard Hoffman-Krayer and Hanns Bächtold-Stäubli. 10 vols. Berlin: de Guyter, 1987. 2.1263–65. Print.

Bhabha, Homi K. *The Location of Culture*. 1994. New York: Routledge, 1995. Print.

Blanchot, Maurice. *The Book to Come*. 1959. Trans. Charlotte Mandell. Stanford, CA: Stanford UP, 2003. Print.

———. *The Space of Literature*. 1955. Trans. Ann Smock. Lincoln: U of Nebraska P, 1982. Print.

———. *The Work of Fire*. 1949. Trans. Charlotte Mandell. Stanford, CA: Stanford UP, 1995. Print.

Bohrer, Karl Heinz. *Suddenness: On the Moment of Aesthetic Appearance*. 1981. Trans. Ruth Crowley. New York: Columbia UP, 1994. Print.

Bonaventure, St. *The Journey of the Mind to God*. Ed. Stephen F. Brown. Trans. Philotheus Boehner. Indianapolis: Hackett, 1993. Print.

Boundas, Constantin V. "Ontology." Parr 191–92.

Bowie, Malcolm. "Bersani on Proust." *Oxford Literary Review* 20.1–2 (1999): 23–32. Print.

Bracken, Harry M. "Berkeley, George." *The Columbia History of Western Philosophy*. Ed. Richard H. Popkin. 445–52. New York: MJF, 1999. Print.

Bramen, Carrie Tirado. *The Uses of Variety: Modern Americanism and the Quest for National Distinctiveness*. Cambridge, MA: Harvard UP, 2000. Print.

Branigan, Kevin. *Radio Beckett: Musicality in the Radio Plays of Samuel Beckett*. New York: Peter Lang, 2008. Print.

Breé, Germaine. *The World of Marcel Proust*. Boston: Houghton Mifflin, 1966. Print.

Brennan, Teresa. Introduction. *Between Feminism and Psychoanalysis*. Ed. Brennan. London: Routledge, 1989. 1–23. Print.

Brier, Søren. "Cybersemiotics and Umweltlehre." *Semiotica* 134 (July 2001): 779–814. Print.

Brinkema, Eugenie. "Rape and the Rectum: Bersani, Deleuze, Noé." *Camera Obscura* 58 20.1 (2005): 33–57. Print.

Brix, Michel. "Modern Beauty versus Platonist Beauty." Trans. Tony Campbell. *Baudelaire and the Poetics of Modernity*. Ed. Patricia A. Ward. Baltimore, MD: Johns Hopkins UP, 2004. 1–14. Print.

Bruns, Gerald L. *Maurice Blanchot: The Refusal of Philosophy*. 1997. Baltimore, MD: Johns Hopkins UP, 2005. Print.

Buchanan, Brett. *Onto-Ethologies: The Animal Environments of Uexküll, Heidegger, Merleau-Ponty, and Deleuze*. Albany, NY: State U of New York P, 2008. Print.

Burroughs, Edgar Rice. *Tarzan of the Apes*. 1912. New York: Ballantine, 1990. Print.

Butler, Judith. *Antigone's Claim: Kinship between Life and Death*. New York: Columbia UP, 2000. Print.

———. *Bodies that Matter: On the Discursive Limits of "Sex."* New York: Routledge, 1993. Print.

———. "*Geist ist Zeit*: French Interpretations of Hegel's Absolute." *Berkshire Review* (Sep. 1985): 66–80. Print.

———. *Gender Trouble: Feminism and the Subversion of Identity*. New York: Routledge, 1990. Print.

———. *The Psychic Life of Power: Theories in Subjection*. Stanford, CA: Stanford UP, 1997. Print.

———. *Subjects of Desire: Hegelian Reflections in Twentieth-Century France*. 1987. New York: Columbia UP, 1999. Print.

Caserio, Robert L., et al. "The Antisocial Thesis in Queer Theory." *PMLA* 121.3 (May 2006): 819–36. Print.

Castiglia, Christopher. *Interior States: Institutional Consciousness and the Inner Life of Democracy in the Antebellum United States*. Durham: Duke UP, 2008. Print.

———. "Past Burning: The (Post-)Traumatic Memories of (Post-)Queer Theory." *States of Emergency: The Object of American Studies*. Ed. Russ Castronovo and Susan Gillman. Chapel Hill: U of North Carolina P, 2009. 69–87. Print.

———. "Same-Sex Friendships and the Rise of Modern Sexualities." *The Cambridge History of Gay and Lesbian Literature*. Ed. E. L. McCallum and Mikko Tuhkanen. Cambridge: Cambridge UP, 2014. 288–304. Print.

Chisholm, Dianne. *Queer Constellations: Subcultural Space in the Wake of the City*. Minneapolis: U of Minnesota P, 2005. Print.

Conley, Verena. "Minoritarian." Parr 164–65.

Cooper, Frederick. "Conflict and Connection: Rethinking Colonial African History." 1994. *The Decolonization Reader*. Ed. James D. Le Sueur. New York: Routledge, 2003. 23–44. Print.

Copjec, Joan. *Imagine There's No Woman: Ethics and Sublimation*. Cambridge: MIT P, 2002. Print.

Coviello, Peter. *Tomorrow's Parties: Sex and the Untimely in Nineteenth-Century America*. New York: New York UP, 213. Print.

Critchley, Simon. "*Il y a*—A Dying Stronger than Death (Blanchot with Levinas)." *Oxford Literary Review* 15.1–2 (1993): 81–131. Print.

Davidson, Arnold I. "Ethics as Ascetics: Foucault, the History of Ethics, and Ancient Thought." *The Cambridge Companion to Foucault*. Ed. Gary Gutting. New York: Cambridge UP, 1994. 115–40. Print.

———. "How to Do the History of Psychoanalysis: A Reading of Freud's *Three Essays on the Theory of Sexuality*." *The Trial(s) of Psychoanalysis*. Ed. Françoise Meltzer. Chicago: U of Chicago P, 1988. 39–64. Print.

———. "Spiritual Exercises and Ancient Philosophy: An Introduction to Pierre Hadot." *Critical Inquiry* 16.3 (Spring 1990): 475–82. *JSTOR*. Web. 20 July 2017.

Dean, Tim. "The Antisocial Homosexual." *PMLA* 121.3 (May 2006): 826–28. Print.

———. "Art as Symptom: Žižek and the Ethics of Psychoanalytic Criticism." *diacritics* 32.2 (Summer 2002): 21–41. Print.

———. "Sameness without Identity." *Umbr(a): A Journal of the Unconscious* (2002): 25-41. Print.

———. "Sex and the Aesthetics of Existence." *PMLA* 125.2 (March 2010): 387–92. Print.

———. *Unlimited Intimacy: Reflections on the Subculture of Barebacking*. Chicago: U of Chicago P, 2009. Print.

———. "What's the Point of Psychoanalytic Criticism?" *Oxford Literary Review* 20.1–2 (1998): 143–71. Print.

Degen, Andreas. *Ästhetische Faszination: Die Geschichte einer Denkfigur vor ihrem Begriff*. Berlin: Walter de Gruyter, 2017. Print.

Deleuze, Gilles. *Bergsonism*. 1966. Trans. Hugh Tomlinson and Barbara Habberjam. 1988. New York: Zone, 1997. Print.

———. "Coldness and Cruelty." 1967. *Masochism*. By Gilles Deleuze and Leopold von Sacher-Masoch. Trans. Jean McNeil. New York: Zone, 1991. 7–138. Print.

———. "Immanence: A Life." 1995. *Pure Immanence: Essays on A Life*. Trans. Anne Boyman. New York: Zone, 2001. 25–33. Print.

———. "Jean Hyppolite's *Logic and Existence*." 1954. *Desert Islands and Other Texts, 1953–1974*. Ed. David Lapoujade. Trans. Michael Taormina. Los Angeles and New York: Semiotext(e), 2004. 15–18. Print.

———. *Negotiations, 1972–1990*. 1990. Trans. Martin Joughin. New York: Columbia UP, 1995. Print.

———. *Nietzsche and Philosophy*. 1962. Trans. Hugh Tomlinson. New York: Columbia UP, 1983. Print.

———. *Proust and Signs*. 1964. Trans. Richard Howard. Minneapolis: U of Minnesota P, 2000. Print.

Deleuze, Gilles, and Félix Guattari. *Anti-Oedipus*. 1972. Trans. Robert Hurley, Mark Seem, and Helen R. Lane. 1977. Minneapolis: U of Minnesota P, 1998. Print.

———. *Kafka: Toward a Minor Literature*. 1975. Trans. Dana Polan. 1986. Minneapolis: U of Minnesota P, 2000. Print.

———. *A Thousand Plateaus: Capitalism and Schizophrenia*. 1980. Trans. Brian Massumi. Minneapolis: U of Minnesota P, 1987. Print.

Deleuze, Gilles, and Claire Parnet. *Dialogues*. Trans. Hugh Tomlinson and Barbara Habberjam. New York: Columbia UP, 1987. Print.

De Man, Paul. "The Concept of Irony." *Aesthetic Ideology*. Ed. Andrzej Warminksi. Minneapolis: U of Minnesota P, 1996. 163–84. Print.

Derrida, Jacques. "Cogito and the History of Madness." *Writing* 31–63.

———. "Force and Signification." 1963. *Writing* 3–30.

———. "Force of Law: The 'Mystical Foundation of Authority.'" 1992 [1989–90]. Trans. Mary Quaintance. *Deconstruction and the Possibility of Justice*. Ed.

Drucilla Cornell, Michael Rosenfield, and David Gray Carlson. New York: Routledge, 1992. 3–67. Print.

———. "Introduction to 'The Origin of Geometry.'" *Edmund Husserl's* Origin of Geometry: *An Introduction*. 1962. Trans. John P. Leavey, Jr. 1978. Lincoln: U of Nebraska P, 1989. 23–153. Print.

———. *Limited Inc*. Trans. Samuel Weber and Jeffrey Mehlman. Evanston, IL: Northwestern UP, 1988. Print.

———. *Of Grammatology*. 1967. Trans. Gayatri Chakravorty Spivak. Baltimore: Johns Hopkins UP, 1998. Print.

———. *The Problem of Genesis in Husserl's Philosophy*. 1990. Trans. Marian Hobson. Chicago: U of Chicago P, 2003. Print.

———. "Speech and Phenomena: Introduction to the Problem of Signs in Husserl's Phenomenology." *Speech and Phenomena and Other Essays on Husserl's Theory of Signs*. 1967. Trans. David B. Allison. 1973. Evanston: Northwestern UP, 1984. 1–104. Print.

———. "Structure, Sign, and Play in the Discourse of the Human Sciences." *Writing* 278–93.

———. *Writing and Difference*. 1967. Trans. Alan Bass. Chicago: U of Chicago P, 1978. Print.

Devisch, Ignaas. *Jean-Luc Nancy and the Question of Community*. London: Bloomsbury, 2013. Print.

Dewey, John. "Speculation." *Dictionary of Philosophy and Psychology*. Ed. James Mark Baldwin. 3 vols. New York: Macmillan, 1911. 2.568. Print.

Dowd, Garin. *Abstract Machines: Samuel Beckett and Philosophy and Deleuze and Guattari*. Amsterdam: Rodopi, 2007. Print.

Dussel, Enrique. "Eurocentrism and Modernity (Introduction to the Frankfurt Lectures)." *boundary 2* 20.3 (Autumn 1993): 65–76. Print.

Ebbersmeyer, Sabrina. "Spekulation." *Historisches Wörterbuch der Philosophie*. Ed. Joachim Ritter, Karlfried Gründer, and Gottfried Gabriel. 13 vols. Basel: Schwabe, 1971–2007. 9.1355–72. Print.

Ebeling, Gerhard. *Luther: An Introduction to His Thought*. 1964. Trans. R. A. Wilson. Philadelphia: Fortress P, 1970. Print.

Edelman, Lee. *No Future: Queer Theory and the Death Drive*. Durham, NC: Duke UP, 2004. Print.

Edman, Irwin. Introduction. Plato, *Works* xi–xlviii.

Eiland, Howard. *Walter Benjamin: A Critical Life*. Cambridge: Harvard UP, 2014. Print.

Engelhardt, Hartmut. "Der historische Gegenstand als Monade." *Materialien zu Benjamins "Über den Begriff der Geschichte": Beiträge und Interpretationen*. Ed. Peter Bulthaup. Frankfurt am Main: Suhrkamp, 1975. 292–317. Print.

Engels, Friedrich. *The Peasant War in Germany*. 1850. Marx and Engels, *Collected* 10.397–482.

———. "Socialism: Utopian and Scientific." 1880/1892. *The Marx-Engels Reader*. 2nd ed. Ed. Robert C. Tucker. New York: W. W. Norton, 1978. 683–717. Print.

Evans, Dylan. *An Introductory Dictionary of Lacanian Psychoanalysis*. London: Routledge, 1996. Print.

Faber, Marion. Introduction. Nietzsche, *Human* ix–xxvii.

Fademan, Lillian. *Surpassing the Love of Men: Romantic Friendship and Love Between Women from the Renaissance to the Present*. New York: William Morrow, 1981. Print.

Fanon, Frantz. *Black Skin, White Masks*. 1952. Trans. Charles Lam Markmann. New York: Grove P, 1982. Print.

———. *The Wretched of the Earth*. 1961. Trans. Richard Philcox. New York: Grove P, 2004. Print.

"Fascination." *Encyclopedia of Occultism and Parapsychology: A Compendium of Information on the Occult Sciences, Magic, Demonology, Superstitions, Spiritism, Mysticism, Metaphysics, Physical Science, and Parapsychology, with Biographical and Bibliographical Notes and Comprehensive Indexes*. 2nd ed. Ed. Leslie A. Shepard. 3 vols. Detroit: Gale, 1984. 1.454–56. Print.

Felman, Shoshana. "Turning the Screw of Interpretation." *Literature and Psychoanalysis: The Question of Reading: Otherwise*. 1982. Ed. Shoshana Felman. Baltimore, MD: Johns Hopkins UP, 1989. 94–207. Print.

Fenves, Peter. *"Chatter": Language and History in Kierkegaard*. Stanford, CA: Stanford UP, 1993. Print.

———. *The Messianic Reduction: Walter Benjamin and the Shape of Time*. Stanford, CA: Stanford UP, 2011. Print.

Ffrench, Patrick. "Potential Not to Be: Bersani and Dutoit's Forms of Being." *Film-Philosophy* 9.3 (Jan. 2005): n.p. Web. 13 Nov. 2006.

Fletcher, John. *Freud and the Scene of Trauma*. New York: Fordham UP, 2013. Print.

———. "The Letter in the Unconscious: The Enigmatic Signifier in the Work of Jean Laplanche." Fletcher and Stanton, 93–120.

———. "Samuel Beckett and the Philosophers." *Comparative Literature* 17.1 (Winter 1965): 43–56. Print.

———. "Seduction and the Vicissitudes of Translation: The Work of Jean Laplanche." *Psychoanalytic Quarterly* 76.4 (2007): 1241–91. Print.

Fletcher, John, and Martin Stanton, eds. *Jean Laplanche: Seduction, Translation, Drives: A Dossier*. Trans. Martin Stanton. London: Institute of Contemporary Arts, 1992. Print.

Fletcher, John, and Nicholas Ray, eds. *Seductions and Enigmas: Cultural Readings with Laplanche*. London: Lawrence & Wishart, 2014. Print.

Forrester, John. *Truth Games: Lies, Money, and Psychoanalysis*. Cambridge, MA: Harvard UP, 1997. Print.

Foucault, Michel. "The Birth of a World." 1969. Trans. John Johnston. *Foucault Live* 65–67.

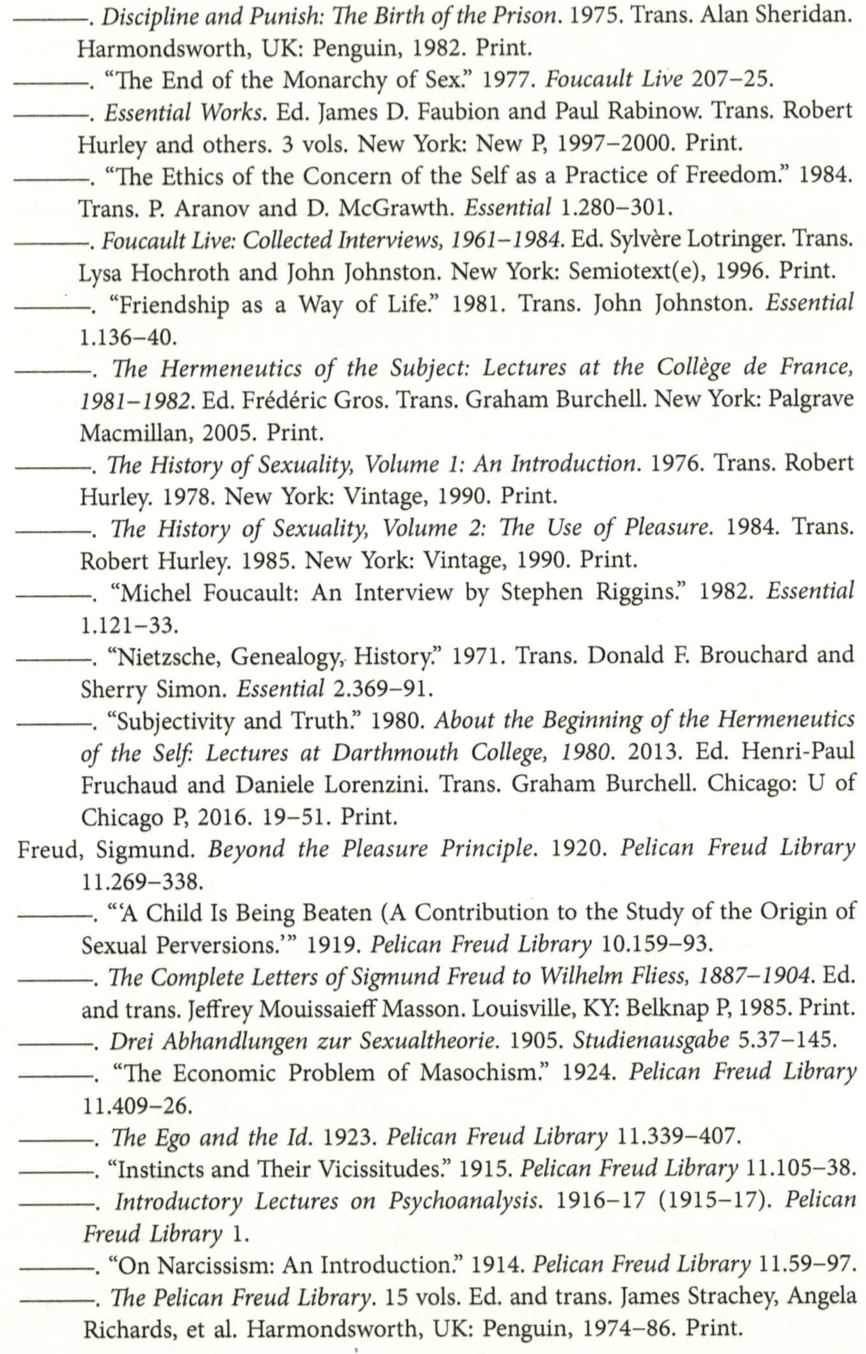

———. *Discipline and Punish: The Birth of the Prison*. 1975. Trans. Alan Sheridan. Harmondsworth, UK: Penguin, 1982. Print.

———. "The End of the Monarchy of Sex." 1977. *Foucault Live* 207–25.

———. *Essential Works*. Ed. James D. Faubion and Paul Rabinow. Trans. Robert Hurley and others. 3 vols. New York: New P, 1997–2000. Print.

———. "The Ethics of the Concern of the Self as a Practice of Freedom." 1984. Trans. P. Aranov and D. McGrawth. *Essential* 1.280–301.

———. *Foucault Live: Collected Interviews, 1961–1984*. Ed. Sylvère Lotringer. Trans. Lysa Hochroth and John Johnston. New York: Semiotext(e), 1996. Print.

———. "Friendship as a Way of Life." 1981. Trans. John Johnston. *Essential* 1.136–40.

———. *The Hermeneutics of the Subject: Lectures at the Collège de France, 1981–1982*. Ed. Frédéric Gros. Trans. Graham Burchell. New York: Palgrave Macmillan, 2005. Print.

———. *The History of Sexuality, Volume 1: An Introduction*. 1976. Trans. Robert Hurley. 1978. New York: Vintage, 1990. Print.

———. *The History of Sexuality, Volume 2: The Use of Pleasure*. 1984. Trans. Robert Hurley. 1985. New York: Vintage, 1990. Print.

———. "Michel Foucault: An Interview by Stephen Riggins." 1982. *Essential* 1.121–33.

———. "Nietzsche, Genealogy, History." 1971. Trans. Donald F. Brouchard and Sherry Simon. *Essential* 2.369–91.

———. "Subjectivity and Truth." 1980. *About the Beginning of the Hermeneutics of the Self: Lectures at Darthmouth College, 1980*. 2013. Ed. Henri-Paul Fruchaud and Daniele Lorenzini. Trans. Graham Burchell. Chicago: U of Chicago P, 2016. 19–51. Print.

Freud, Sigmund. *Beyond the Pleasure Principle*. 1920. *Pelican Freud Library* 11.269–338.

———. "'A Child Is Being Beaten (A Contribution to the Study of the Origin of Sexual Perversions.'" 1919. *Pelican Freud Library* 10.159–93.

———. *The Complete Letters of Sigmund Freud to Wilhelm Fliess, 1887–1904*. Ed. and trans. Jeffrey Mouissaieff Masson. Louisville, KY: Belknap P, 1985. Print.

———. *Drei Abhandlungen zur Sexualtheorie*. 1905. *Studienausgabe* 5.37–145.

———. "The Economic Problem of Masochism." 1924. *Pelican Freud Library* 11.409–26.

———. *The Ego and the Id*. 1923. *Pelican Freud Library* 11.339–407.

———. "Instincts and Their Vicissitudes." 1915. *Pelican Freud Library* 11.105–38.

———. *Introductory Lectures on Psychoanalysis*. 1916–17 (1915–17). *Pelican Freud Library* 1.

———. "On Narcissism: An Introduction." 1914. *Pelican Freud Library* 11.59–97.

———. *The Pelican Freud Library*. 15 vols. Ed. and trans. James Strachey, Angela Richards, et al. Harmondsworth, UK: Penguin, 1974–86. Print.

———. "The Resistances to Psychoanalysis." 1925 (1924). *Pelican Freud Library* 15.261–75.

———. "The Sexual Enlightenment of Children (An Open Letter to Dr. M. Fürst)." 1907. *Pelican Freud Library* 7.171–81.

———. *Studienausgabe*. Ed. Alexander Mitscherlich, Angela Richards, and James Strachey. 10 vols. Tübingen: S. Fischer, 1969. Print.

———. *Three Essays on the Theory of Sexuality*. 1905. *Pelican Freud Library* 7.31–169.

———. "Zur Einführung des Narzißmus." 1914. *Studienausgabe* 3.37–68.

———. "Zur sexuellen Aufklärung der Kinder." 1906 (1905). *Studienausgabe* 5.159–68.

Frey, Christiane. "*κλῆσις/Beruf*: Luther, Weber, Agamben." *New German Critique* 105 35.3 (Fall 2008): 35–56. Print.

Fromm, Erich. *The Crisis of Psychoanalysis*. New York: Holt, Rinehard, Winston, 1970. Print.

Fuss, Diana. *Essentially Speaking: Feminism, Nature, and Difference*. New York: Routldge, 1989. Print.

Gasché, Rodolphe. *Of Minimal Things: Studies in the Notion of Relation*. Stanford, CA: Stanford UP, 1999. Print.

———. *The Tain of the Mirror: Derrida and the Philosophy of Reflection*. Cambridge, MA: Harvard UP, 1988. Print.

Gaye, Marvin. "I Want You." *I Want You*. 1976. Motown, 1998. CD.

Genet, Jean. *Funeral Rites*. 1953. Trans. Bernard Frechtman. New York: Grove P, 1969. Print.

Gillespie, Sam. "Neighborhood of Infinity: On Badiou's *Deleuze: The Clamor of Being*." *Umbr(a): A Journal of the Unconscious* (2001): 91–106. Print.

Gilroy, Paul. *The Black Atlantic: Modernity and Double Consciousness*. Cambridge, MA: Harvard UP, 1993. Print.

Glavey, Brian. "Leo Bersani and the Universe." Rev. of Leo Bersani, *Is the Rectum a Grave? and Other Essays*. *Criticism* 52.2 (Spring 2010): 317–23. Print.

Glissant, Édouard. *Poetics of Relation*. 1990. Trans. Betsy Wing. 1997. Ann Arbor: U of Michigan P, 2000. Print.

Gobineau, Arthur de. *Essai sur l'inégalité des races humaines*. 1835–1855. 6 vols. *Les classiques des sciences sociales*. Université du Québec à Chicoutimi. Web. 23 Nov. 2013.

Grier, Philip T., ed. *Identity and Difference: Studies in Hegel's Logic, Philosophy of Spirit, and Politics*. Albany, NY: State U of New York P, 2007. Print.

Grosz, Elizabeth. "Darwin and the Ontology of Life." *Time Travels: Feminism, Nature, Power*. Durham: Duke UP, 2005. 35–42. Print.

———. *The Nick of Time: Politics, Evolution, and the Untimely*. Durham, NC: Duke UP, 2004. Print.

———. *Volatile Bodies: Toward a Corporeal Feminism*. Bloomington: Indiana UP, 1994. Print.

Gruner, Rolf. "The Concept of Speculative Philosophy of History." *Metaphilosophy* 3.4 (Oct. 1972): 283–300. *JStor*. Web. 25 Jan. 2017.

Habermas, Jürgen. "Walter Benjamin: Consciousness-Raising or Rescuing Critique." Trans. Frederick G. Lawrence. G. Smith, 90–128.

Hacking, Ian. "What Mathematics Has Done to Some and Only Some Philosophers." *Proceedings of the British Academy* 103 (2000): 83–138. *British Academy*. Web. 19 Jan. 2017. http://www.britac.ac.uk/pubs/proc/files/103p083.pdf

Hadot, Pierre. *Philosophy as a Way of Life: Spiritual Exercises from Socrates to Foucault*. Ed. Arnold I. Davidson. Trans. Michael Chase. Malden, UK: Blackwell, 1995. Print.

———. "Philosophy, Exegesis, and Creative Mistakes." *Philosophy* 71–78.

———. "Reflections on the Idea of the 'Cultivation of the Self.'" *Philosophy* 206–13.

Hahnemann, Andy, and Björn Weyand, eds. *Faszination: Historische Konjunkturen und heuristische Tragweite eines Begriffs*. Frankfurt-am-Main: Peter Lang, 2009. Print.

Halle, Randall. "Between Marxism and Psychoanalysis: Antifascism and Antihomosexuality in the Frankfurt School." *Journal of Homosexuality* 29 (1995): 295–317. Print.

Hallward, Peter. *Absolutely Postcolonial: Writing between the Singular and the Specific*. Manchester: Manchester UP, 2001. Print.

———. *Badiou: A Subject to Truth*. Minneapolis: U of Minnesota P, 2003. Print.

———. *Out of This World: Deleuze and the Philosophy of Creation*. London: Verso, 2006. Print.

Hamacher, Werner. "Uncalled: A Commentary on Kafka's 'The Test.'" *Reading Ronell*. Ed. Diane Davis. Urbana and Chicago: U of Illinois P, 2009. 74–93. Print.

Harari, Robert. *Lacan's Four Fundamental Concepts of Psychoanalysis: An Introduction*. Trans. Judith Filc. New York: Other P, 2004. Print.

Harland, Richard. *Beyond Superstructuralism: The Syntagmatic Side of Language*. London: Routledge, 1993. Print.

Harvey, David. *A Companion to Marx's* Capital. London: Verso, 2010. Print.

Haslanger, Sally. "Feminism in Metaphysics: Negotiating the Natural." *The Cambridge Companion to Feminism in Philosophy*. Ed. Miranda Fricker and Jennifer Hornsby. Cambridge: Cambridge UP, 2000. 107–26. Print.

Hegel, Georg Wilhelm Friedrich. *Phänomenologie des Geistes*. 1807. *Werke* 3.

———. *Phenomenology of Spirit*. 1807. Trans. A. V. Miller. Oxford: Oxford UP, 1977. Print.

———. *The Science of Logic*. 1812–16 (1808–16). Trans. A. V. Miller. New York: Humanities P, 1976. Print.

———. *Werke*. Ed. Eva Moldenhauer and Karl Markus Michel. 20 vols. Frankfurt-am-Main: Suhrkamp, 1969–71. Print.

———. *Wissenschaft der Logik*. 1812–16 (1808–16). *Werke* 5 and 6.

Heidegger, Martin. *Being and Time*. Trans. Joan Stambaugh. Albany, NY: State U of New York P, 1996. Print.

———. "The Origin of the Work of Art." Trans. Albert Hofstadter. *Basic Writings*. Ed. David Farrell Krell. New York: Harper & Row, 1977. 143–87. Print.

Heine, Heinrich. "Schöpfungslieder." 1844. *Gesammelte Werke*. Vol. 1. 2nd ed. Berlin: Aufbau, 1956. 442–45. Print.

———. "Songs of Creation." 1844. *The Complete Poems of Heinrich Heine*. Trans. Hal Draper. Boston: Suhrkamp/Insel, 1982. 354–56. Print.

Hewitt, Andrew. *Political Inversions: Homosexuality, Fascism, and the Modernist Imaginary*. Stanford, CA: Stanford UP, 1996. Print.

Hiddleston, J. A. "Art and its representation." *The Cambridge Companion to Baudelaire*. Ed. Rosemary Lloyd. Cambridge: Cambridge UP, 2005. 130–44. Print.

Hill, Leslie. *Beckett's Fiction: In Different Words*. Cambridge: Cambridge UP, 1990. Print.

———. *Blanchot: Extreme Contemporary*. London: Routledge, 1997. Print.

Hinske, Norbert. "Zur Verwendung der Wörter 'schwärmen,' 'Schwärmer,' 'Schwärmerei,' 'schwärmerisch' im Kontext von Kants Anthropologiekolleg: Eine Konkordanz." *Aufklärung* 3.1 (1988): 73–81. *JStor*. Web. 8 Apr. 2017.

Horkheimer, Max, and Theodor W. Adorno. *Dialectic of Enlightenment: Philosophical Fragments*. 1947. Ed. Gunzelin Schmid Noerr. Trans. Edmund Jephcott. Stanford, CA: Stanford UP, 2002. Print.

Husserl, Edmund. *Cartesian Meditations: An Introduction to Phenomenology*. 1931 (1929). Trans. Dorion Cairns. Dordrecht: Kluwer, 1995. Print.

Hylton, Peter. *Propositions, Functions, and Analysis: Selected Essays on Russell's Philosophy*. Oxford: Oxford UP, 2005. Print.

———. *Russell, Idealism, and the Emergence of Analytic Philosophy*. Oxford: Clarendon P, 1990. Print.

Ingram, David. "Hegel and Leibniz on Individuation." *Kant-Studien* 76 (1985): 420–35. Print.

Jameson, Fredric. *The Hegel Variations: On the* Phenomenology of Spirit. London: Verso, 2010. Print.

———. *The Political Unconscious: Narrative as a Socially Symbolic Act*. 1981. Ithaca, NY: Cornell UP, 1986. Print.

———. *Postmodernism, or The Cultural Logic of Late Capitalism*. 1991. Durham, NC: Duke UP, 1997. Print.

Jay, Martin. *Songs of Experience: Modern American and European Variations on a Universal Theme*. Berkeley, CA: U of California P, 2005. Print.

Jennings, Michael. *Dialectical Images: Walter Benjamin's Theory of Literary Criticism*. Ithaca, NY: Cornell UP, 1987. Print.

Jolley, Nicholas. "Leibniz and Phenomenalism." *Studia Leibnitiana* 18.1 (1986): 38–51. Print.

Kant, Immanuel. *Critique of Pure Reason*. 1781/1787. Trans. Paul Guyer and Allen Wood. 1998. New York: Cambridge UP, 2000. Print.

———. *Gesammelte Schriften*. 29 vols. Berlin: Walter de Gruyter, 1900– . Print.

———. *Kritik der reinen Vernunft*. 1781/1787. *Gesammelte Schriften* 3–4.

Katz, Jonathan Ned. *The Invention of Heterosexuality*. New York: Dutton, 1995. Print.

Kaufmann, Walter. *Nietzsche: Philosopher, Psychologist, Antichrist*. 4th Ed. Princeton, NJ: Princeton UP, 1974. Print.

Kockelmans, Joseph J. *Edmund Husserl's Phenomenology*. West Lafayette: Purdue UP, 1994. Print.

Krauss, Lawrence M. *A Universe from Nothing: Why There Is Something Rather than Nothing*. New York: Free P, 2012. Print.

Kristeva, Julia. *Desire in Language: A Semiotic Approach to Literature and Art*. Ed. Leon S. Roudiez. Trans. Thomas Gora, Alice Jardin, and Leon S. Roudiez. New York: Columbia UP, 1980. Print.

———. *Interviews*. Ed. Ross Mitchell Guberman. New York: Columbia UP, 1996. Print.

———. *Strangers to Ourselves*. Trans. Leon S. Roudiez. New York: Columbia UP, 1991. Print.

Kurnick, David. "Embarrassment and the Forms of Redemption." Tuhkanen, ed. 55–67.

Lacan, Jacques. "Aggressiveness in Psychoanalysis." *Écrits* 82–101.

———. "Aggressivity in Psychoanalysis." *Écrits: A Selection*. 1966. Trans. Alan Sheridan. New York: W. W. Norton, 1977. 8–29. Print.

———. *Écrits*. 1966. Trans. Bruce Fink with Héloïse Fink and Russell Grigg. New York: W. W. Norton, 2006. Print.

———. "The Freudian Thing, or the Meaning of the Return to Freud in Psychoanalysis." 1956 (1955). *Écrits* 334–63.

———. "The Instance of the Letter in the Unconscious, or Reason Since Freud." 1957. *Écrits* 412–41.

———. "Kant with Sade." 1963 (1962). *Écrits* 645–68.

———. *Le séminaire de Jacques Lacan, Livre I: Les écrits technique de Freud*. Ed. Jacques Alain-Miller. Paris: Seuil, 1975. Print.

———. *Le séminaire de Jacques Lacan, Livre VII: L'éthique de la psychanalyse 1959–1960*. Ed. Jacques-Alain Miller. Paris: Seuil, 1986. Print.

———. *The Seminar of Jacques Lacan, Book I: Freud's Papers on Technique 1953–1954*. 1975. Ed. Jacques-Alain Miller. Trans. John Forrester. New York: W. W. Norton, 1991. Print.

———. *The Seminar of Jacques Lacan, Book VII: The Ethics of Psychoanalysis 1959–1960*. 1986. Ed. Jacques-Alain Miller. Trans. Dennis Porter. New York: W. W. Norton, 1992. Print.

———. "The Subversion of the Subject and the Dialectic of Desire in the Freudian Unconscious." 1960. *Écrits* 671–702.

Lacan, Jacques and Michel Cénac. "A Theoretical Introduction to the Function of Psychoanalysis in Criminology." 1951 (1950). Lacan, *Écrits: First Complete* 102–22.

Laplanche, Jean. "Closing and Opening of the Dream: Must Chapter VII Be Rewritten?" 2000. Trans. Mira Reinberg and Thomas Pepper. *Dreams of Interpretation: A Century Down the Royal Road.* Ed. Catherine Liu, John Mowitt, and Thomas Pepper. Minneapolis: U of Minnesota P, 2007. 177–96. Print.

———. "The Drive and Its Source-Object: Its Fate in the Transference." Trans. Leslie Hill. *Essays* 117–32.

———. *Essays on Otherness.* Ed. John Fletcher. Oxon: Routledge, 1999. Print.

———. "Exigency and Going-Astray." 1993. Trans. Nicholas Ray. *Psychoanalysis, Culture & Society* 11 (2006): 185–89. Print.

———. *Freud and the* Sexual: *Essays 2000–2006.* Ed. John Fletcher. Trans. John Fletcher, Jonathan House, Nicholas Ray. n.p.: International Psychoanalytic Books, 2011. Print.

———. "The Freud Museum Seminar: 3 May 1990." Fletcher and Stanton 41–63.

———. "Interpretation between Determinism and Hermeneutics: a Restatement of the Problem." Trans. Philip Slotkin, rev. Jean Laplanche. *Essays* 138–65.

———. "Interpreting (with) Freud." 1968. Trans. Nicholas Ray. *Psychoanalysis, Culture & Society* 11 (2006): 171–84. Print.

———. "Intervention in a Debate between Daniel Widlöcher and Jacques-Alain Miller: 'The Future of Psychoanalysis.'" 2005. *Freud* 229–34.

———. "Interview: Jean Laplanche Talks to Martin Stanton." Fletcher and Stanton 3–18.

———. "An Interview with Jean Laplanche." By Cathy Caruth. *Postmodern Culture* 11.2 (Jan. 2001): n. pag. Web. 1 Mar. 2012.

———. "Kent Seminar: 1 May 1990." Fletcher and Stanton 21–40.

———. *Life and Death in Psychoanalysis.* 1970. Trans. Jeffrey Mehlman. 1976. Baltimore: Johns Hopkins UP, 1985. Print.

———. "Masochism and the General Theory of Seduction." Trans. Luke Thurston. *Essays* 197–213.

———. "Une métapsychologie à lépreuve de l'angoisse." *Psychoanalyse à l'Université* 4 (1979): 709–36. Print.

———. "A Metapsychology Put to the Test of Anxiety." *International Journal of Psycho-Analysis* 62 (1981): 81–89. Print.

———. *New Foundations for Psychoanalysis.* 1987. Trans. David Macey. Oxford: Blackwell, 1989. Print.

———. "Notes on Afterwardsness." *Essays* 260–65.

———. *Problématiques III: La sublimation.* 1980. Paris: Quadrige/Presses Universitaires de France, 1998. Print.

———. "Psychoanalysis as Anti-Hermeneutics." Trans. Luke Thurston. *Radical Philosophy* 79 (Sep./Oct. 1996): 7–12. Print.

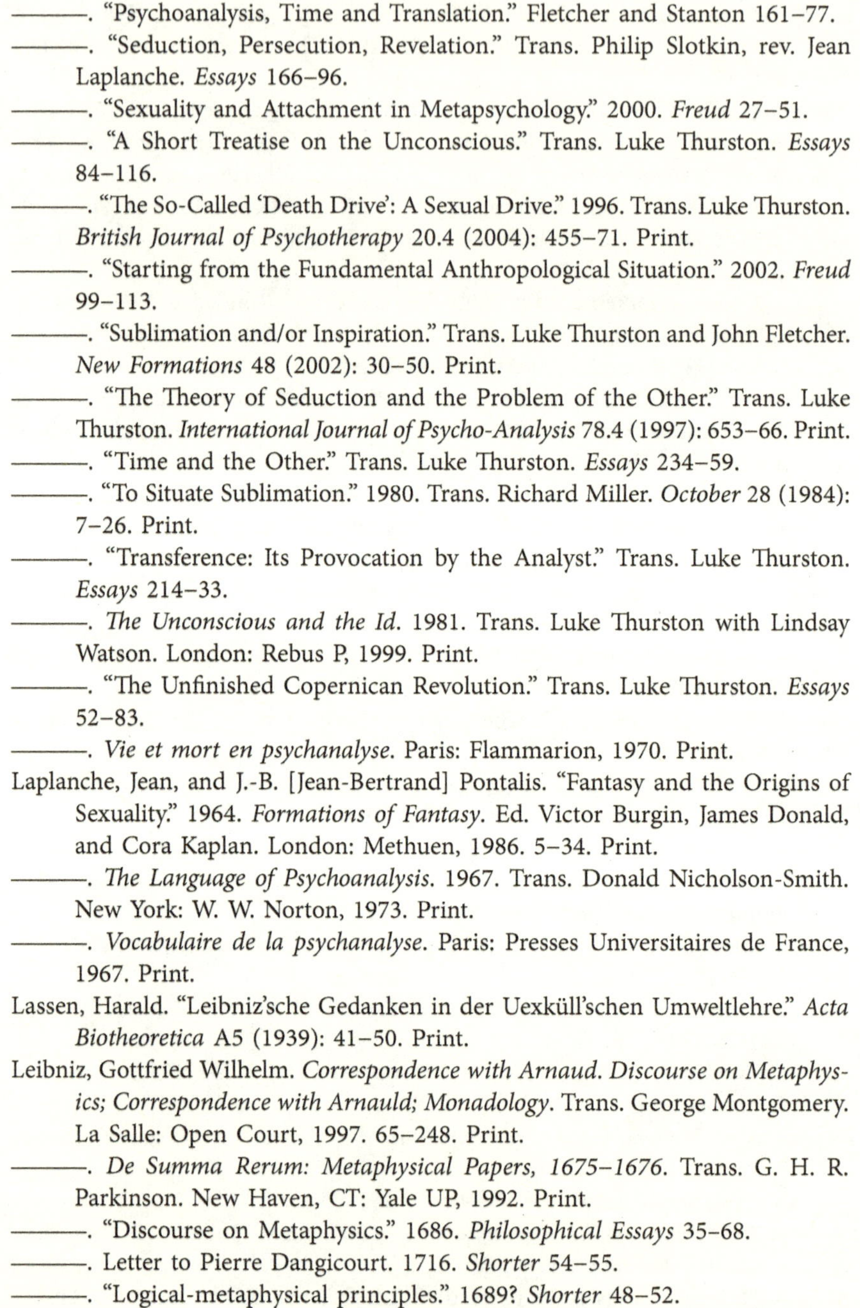

———. "Psychoanalysis, Time and Translation." Fletcher and Stanton 161–77.

———. "Seduction, Persecution, Revelation." Trans. Philip Slotkin, rev. Jean Laplanche. *Essays* 166–96.

———. "Sexuality and Attachment in Metapsychology." 2000. *Freud* 27–51.

———. "A Short Treatise on the Unconscious." Trans. Luke Thurston. *Essays* 84–116.

———. "The So-Called 'Death Drive': A Sexual Drive." 1996. Trans. Luke Thurston. *British Journal of Psychotherapy* 20.4 (2004): 455–71. Print.

———. "Starting from the Fundamental Anthropological Situation." 2002. *Freud* 99–113.

———. "Sublimation and/or Inspiration." Trans. Luke Thurston and John Fletcher. *New Formations* 48 (2002): 30–50. Print.

———. "The Theory of Seduction and the Problem of the Other." Trans. Luke Thurston. *International Journal of Psycho-Analysis* 78.4 (1997): 653–66. Print.

———. "Time and the Other." Trans. Luke Thurston. *Essays* 234–59.

———. "To Situate Sublimation." 1980. Trans. Richard Miller. *October* 28 (1984): 7–26. Print.

———. "Transference: Its Provocation by the Analyst." Trans. Luke Thurston. *Essays* 214–33.

———. *The Unconscious and the Id*. 1981. Trans. Luke Thurston with Lindsay Watson. London: Rebus P, 1999. Print.

———. "The Unfinished Copernican Revolution." Trans. Luke Thurston. *Essays* 52–83.

———. *Vie et mort en psychanalyse*. Paris: Flammarion, 1970. Print.

Laplanche, Jean, and J.-B. [Jean-Bertrand] Pontalis. "Fantasy and the Origins of Sexuality." 1964. *Formations of Fantasy*. Ed. Victor Burgin, James Donald, and Cora Kaplan. London: Methuen, 1986. 5–34. Print.

———. *The Language of Psychoanalysis*. 1967. Trans. Donald Nicholson-Smith. New York: W. W. Norton, 1973. Print.

———. *Vocabulaire de la psychanalyse*. Paris: Presses Universitaires de France, 1967. Print.

Lassen, Harald. "Leibniz'sche Gedanken in der Uexküll'schen Umweltlehre." *Acta Biotheoretica* A5 (1939): 41–50. Print.

Leibniz, Gottfried Wilhelm. *Correspondence with Arnaud. Discourse on Metaphysics; Correspondence with Arnauld; Monadology*. Trans. George Montgomery. La Salle: Open Court, 1997. 65–248. Print.

———. *De Summa Rerum: Metaphysical Papers, 1675–1676*. Trans. G. H. R. Parkinson. New Haven, CT: Yale UP, 1992. Print.

———. "Discourse on Metaphysics." 1686. *Philosophical Essays* 35–68.

———. Letter to Pierre Dangicourt. 1716. *Shorter* 54–55.

———. "Logical-metaphysical principles." 1689? *Shorter* 48–52.

———. *New Essays on Human Understanding.* 1690. Ed. and trans. Peter Remnant and Jonathan Bennett. Cambridge: Cambridge UP, 2003. Print.

———. "On the Method of Distinguishing Real from Imaginary Phenomena." *Philosophical Papers and Letters.* 2 vols. Ed. and trans. Leroy E. Loemker. Chicago: U of Chicago P, 1956. 2.602–07. Print.

———. "On the Radical Origination of Things." 1697. *Philosophical Papers and Letters.* 2nd ed. Ed. and trans. Leroy E. Loemker. Dordrecht: Springer, 1976. 486–91. Print.

———. *Philosophical Essays.* Ed. and trans. Roger Ariew and Daniel Garber. Indianapolis: Hackett, 1989. Print.

———. "Principles of Nature and Grace, Based on Reason." 1714. *Philosophical Essays* 206–13.

———. "The Principles of Philosophy, or, the Monadology." 1714. *Philosophical Essays* 213–25.

———. *The Shorter Leibniz Texts.* Ed. and trans. Lloyd Strickland. London: Continuum, 2006. Print.

———. *Theodicy: Essays on the Goodness of God, the Freedom of Man, and the Origin of Evil.* Ed. Austin Farrer. Trans. E. M. Huggard. New Haven, CT: Yale UP, 1952. Print.

Levine, Martin P. *Gay Macho: The Life and Death of the Homosexual Clone.* New York: New York UP, 1998. Print.

Libertson, Joseph. *Proximity: Levinas, Blanchot, Bataille and Communication.* The Hague: Martinus Nijhoff, 1982. Print.

Look, Brandon C. "Leibniz's Metaphysics: The Path to the Monadology." *The Continuum Companion to Leibniz.* Ed. Brandon C. Look. London: Continuum, 2011. 89–109. Print.

Lovejoy, Arthur O. *The Great Chain of Being: A Study of the History of an Idea.* 1936. New York: Harper, 1960. Print.

Löwy, Michael. *Fire Alarm: Reading Walter Benjamin's "On the Concept of History."* 2001. Trans. Chris Turner. London: Verso, 2005. Print.

Luther, Martin. *D. Martin Luthers Werke: Kritische Gesamtausgabe.* 121 vols. Weimar: Herrmann Böhlau, 1883–2009. Print.

———. *Luther's Works.* 79 vols. General ed. Jaroslav Pelikan and Helmut T. Lehmann. Philadelphia: Concordia P, 1955–2016. Print.

MacDonald, Paul. "Husserl, the Monad and Immortality." *Indo-Pacific Journal of Phenomenology.* 7.2 (Sept. 2007): 1–18. Web. 7 Apr. 2012.

Malabou, Catherine. *The Future of Hegel: Plasticity, Temporality, and Dialectic.* 1996. Trans. Lisbeth During. London: Routledge, 2005. Print.

Mann, Thomas. *The Magic Mountain.* 1924. Trans. John E. Woods. New York: Vintage, 1996. Print.

———. *Der Zauberberg.* 1924. Frankfurt-am-Main: Fischer, 2002. Print.

Marcus, Solomon. "On the Logical and Semiotic Status of Jakob von Uexküll's concept of Umwelt." *Semiotica* 134 (July 2001): 201–10. Print.

Marcuse, Herbert. *Reason and Revolution: Hegel and the Rise of Social Theory*. 1941. London and Henley: Routledge, 1986. Print.

Marx, Karl. *Capital: A Critique of Political Economy*. Trans. Ben Fowkes and David Fernbach. 3 vols. London: Penguin, 1990–91. Print.

———. "Contribution to the Critique of Hegel's Philosophy of Law: Introduction." 1844 (1843–44). Marx and Engels, *Collected* 3.175–87.

———. "Critique of the Hegelian Dialectic and Philosophy as a Whole." 1844. Marx and Engels, *Collected* 3.326–46.

———. *The Economic and Philosophic Manuscripts of 1844*. Marx and Engels, *Collected* 3.229–346.

———. *Grundrisse der kritik der politischen Ökonomie*. 1939 (1857–58). Marx and Engels, *Werke* 42.47–768.

———. *Grundrisse: Foundations of the Critique of Political Economy (Rough Draft)*. 1939. Trans. Martin Nicolaus. London: Penguin, 1993. Print.

———. "Kritik der Hegelschen Dialektik und Philosophie überhaupt." 1844. Marx and Engels, *Werke* 40.568–88.

———. *Ökonomisch-philosophische Manuskripte aus dem Jahre 1844*. Marx and Engels, *Werke* 40.465–588.

———. "On the Jewish Question." 1844 (1843). Marx and Engels, *Collected* 3.146–74.

———. "Theses on Feuerbach." 1888 (1845). Marx and Engels, *Collected* 5.3–5.

———. "Zur Judenfrage." 1844 (1843). Marx and Engels, *Werke* 1.347–77.

———. "Zur Kritik der Hegelschen Rechtsphilosophie: Einleitung." 1844 (1843). Marx and Engels, *Werke* 1.378–91.

Marx, Karl and Friedrich Engels. *Collected Works*. 50 vols. New York: International Publishers, 1975–2004. Print.

———. *Die heilige Familie, oder der Kritik der kritischen Kritik: Gegen Bruno Bauer und Konsorten*. 1845 (1844). *Werke* 2.3–223.

———. *The Holy Family, or Critique of Critical Criticism: Against Bruno Bauer and Company*. 1845 (1844). *Collected* 4.3–211.

———. *Werke*. 43 vols. Berlin: Karl Dietz, 1959–1990. Print.

Masson, Jeffrey Moussaieff. *The Assault on Truth: Freud's Suppression of the Seduction Theory*. New York: Farrar, Straus and Giroux, 1984.

Mattes, Mark. "Georg W. F. Hegel (1770–1831)." *Nineteenth-Century Lutheran Theologians*. Ed. Matthew L. Becker. Göttingen: Vandenhoeck & Ruprecht, 2016. 41–66. Print.

Matthews, Pamela, and David McWhirter, eds. *Aesthetic Subjects*. Minneapolis: U of Minnesota P, 2000. Print.

May, Todd. *Gilles Deleuze: An Introduction*. Cambridge: Cambridge UP, 2005. Print.

McFarland, James. *Constellation: Friedrich Nietzsche and Walter Benjamin in the Now-Time of History*. New York: Fordham UP, 2013. Print.

Mehlman, Jeffrey, ed. *French Freud: Structural Studies in Psychoanalysis*. Spec. issue of *Yale French Studies* 48 (1972). *JSTOR*. Web. 22 July 2014.

Meillassoux, Quentin. *After Finitude: An Essay on the Necessity of Contingency*. 2006. Trans. Ray Brassier. London: Bloomsbury, 2009. Print.

Meltzer, Françoise. *Seeing Double: Baudelaire's Modernity*. Chicago: U of Chicago P, 2011. Print.

Mercer, Christia. *Leibniz's Metaphysics: Its Origins and Development*. Cambridge: Cambridge UP, 2001. Print.

Mercer, Kobena. "Decolonisation and Disappointment: Reading Fanon's Sexual Politics." *The Fact of Blackness: Frantz Fanon and Visual Representation*. Ed. Alan Read. London: Institute of Contemporary Arts, 1996. 114–31. Print.

Meyer, Richard. "Warhol's Clones." *Negotiating Lesbian and Gay Subjects*. Ed. Monica Dorenkamp and Richard Henke. New York: Routledge, 1995. 93–122. Print.

Meyer-Sickendiek, Burkhard. *Tiefe: Über die Faszination des Grübelns*. Paderborn and Munich: Wilhelm Fink, 2010. Print.

Mignolo, Walter D. *The Darker Side of the Renaissance: Literacy, Territoriality, and Colonization*. 2nd ed. Ann Arbor: U of Michigan P, 2003. Print.

Mikics, David. *Who Was Jacques Derrida?: An Intellectual Biography*. New Haven, CT: Yale UP, 2009. Print.

Miller, James. *History and Human Existence: From Marx to Merleau-Ponty*. Berkeley, CA: U of California P, 1979. Print.

Mollow, Anna. "Is Sex Disability? Queer Theory and the Death Drive." *Sex and Disability*. Ed. Robert McRuer and Anna Mollow. Durham: Duke UP, 2012. 285–312. Print.

Mori, Naoya. "Beckett's Windows and the Windowless Self." *After Beckett/D'après Beckett*. Ed. Anthony Uhlmann, Sjef Houppermans, and Bruno Clément. Amsterdam: Rodopi, 2004. 357–70. Print.

———. "Becoming Stone: A Leibnizian Reading of Beckett's Fiction." *Samuel Beckett Today* 19 (2008): 201–10. Print.

———. "'No Body Is at Rest': The Legacy of Leibniz's Force in Beckett's Oeuvre." *Beckett at 100: Revolving It All*. Ed. Linda Ben-Zvi and Angela Moorjani. Oxford: Oxford UP, 2008. 107–20. Print.

Morrison, Toni. *Sula*. 1973. New York: Alfred A. Knopf, 1994. Print.

Mosès, Stéphane. *The Angel of History: Rosenzweig, Benjamin, Scholem*. 1992. Trans. Barbara Harshav. Stanford, CA: Stanford UP, 2009. Print.

Nancy, Jean-Luc. *Hegel: The Restlessness of the Negative*. 1997. Trans. Jason Smith and Steven Miller. Minneapolis: U of Minnesota P, 2002. Print.

———. *The Speculative Remark: (One of Hegel's Bon Mots)*. 1973. Trans. Céline Surprenant. Stanford, CA: Stanford UP, 2001. Print.

Nicholson, Graeme. *Plato's* Phaedrus*: The Philosophy of Love*. West Lafayette, IN: Purdue UP, 1999. Print.

Nietzsche, Friedrich. *Basic Writings of Nietzsche*. Ed. and trans. Walter Kaufmann. New York: Modern Library, 2000. Print.

———. *The Birth of Tragedy*. 1872/1886. *Basic* 1–144.

———. *The Case of Wagner*. 1888. *Basic* 601–53.

———. "David Strauss the Confessor and the Writer." 1873. *Unfashionable* 3–81.

———. *Ecce Homo*. 1908 [1888]. *Basic* 655–791.

———. *Die Geburt der Tragödie oder Griechentum und Pessimismus*. 1872/1886. *Sämtliche Werke in zwölf Bänden*. Vol. 1. Stuttgart: Alfred Kröner, 1964. 27–191. Print.

———. *Human, All Too Human: A Book for Free Spirits*. 1878/1886. Trans. Marion Faber with Stephen Lehmann. Lincoln: U of Nebraska P, 1986. Print.

———. "On the Utility and Liability of History for Life." 1874. *Unfashionable* 83–167.

———. *Philosophy in the Tragic Age of the Greeks*. 1873. Trans. Marianne Cowan. Chicago: Henry Regnery, 1962. Print.

———. "Richard Wagner in Bayreuth." 1876. *Unfashionable* 257–331.

———. "Richard Wagner in Bayreuth." 1876. *Unzeitgemäße Betrachtungen*. *Zeno.org: Meine Bibliothek*. Web. 6 Mar. 2015.

———. "Schopenhauer als Erzieher." 1874. *Unzeitgemäße Betrachtungen*. *Zeno.org: Meine Bibliothek*. Web. 6 Mar. 2015.

———. "Schopenhauer as Educator." 1874. *Unfashionable* 169–255.

———. *Unfashionable Observations*. Trans. Richard T. Gray. Stanford, CA: Stanford UP, 1995. Print.

———. "Vom Nutzen und Nachteil der Historie für das Leben." *Zeno.org: Meine Bibliothek*. 1874. Web. 6 Mar. 2015.

Oksala, Johanna. "Feministinen filosofia nykyisyyden ontologiana." *Feministinen filosofia*. Ed. Oksala and Laura Werner. Helsinki: Gaudeamus, 2005. 156–205. Print.

Ong, Walter J. *Orality and Literacy: The Technologization of the Word*. 1982. London: Routledge, 1991. Print.

Palmquist, Stephen R. *Comprehensive Commentary on Kant's Religion Within the Bounds of Bare Reason*. Chichester, UK: Wiley-Blackwell, 2016. Print.

Parr, Adrian, ed. *The Deleuze Dictionary*. New York: Columbia UP, 2005. Print.

Pensky, Max. *Melancholy Dialectics: Walter Benjamin and the Play of Mourning*. Amherst: U of Massachusetts P, 1993. Print.

Pfotenhauer, Helmut. "Benjamin und Nietzsche." *"Links hatte noch alles sich zu enträseln": Walter Benjamin im Kontext*. Ed. Burkhardt Lindner. Frankfurt-am-Main: Syndikat, 1978. 100–26. Print.

Phillips, Adam. *Houdini's Box: The Art of Escape*. 2001. New York: Vintage, 2002. Print.

———. "Sameness Is All." *Promises, Promises: Essays on Literature and Psychoanalysis*. London: Faber and Faber, 2000. 334–41. Print.

Plato. *Phaedrus*. *Works* 263–329.

———. *The Works of Plato*. Ed. Irwin Edman. Trans. Benjamin Jowett. New York: Modern Library, 1956. Print.

Pothast, Ulrich. *The Metaphysical Vision: Arthur Schopenhauer's Philosophy of Art and Life and Samuel Beckett's Own Way to Make Use of It*. New York: Peter Lang, 2008. Print.

Proust, Marcel. *À la recherche du temps perdu*. 1913–27. 4 vols. Ed. Jean-Yves Tadié. Paris: Gallimard, 1987–89. Print.

———. "Contre Sainte-Beuve." *On Art and Literature, 1896–1919*. Trans. Sylvia Townsend Warner. New York: Meridian, 1958. 17–276. Print.

———. *Remembrance of Things Past*. 2 vols. Trans. C. K. Scott Moncrieff and Stephen Hudson. London: Wordsworth, 2006. Print.

Pyyhtinen, Olli. *Simmel and "the Social."* Houndmills: Palgrave Macmillan, 2010. Print.

Radhakrishnan, R. *History, the Human, and the World Between*. Durham, NC: Duke UP, 2008. Print.

Ray, Nicholas. "Forming new knots: Jean Laplanche, 1924–2012." *Radical Philosophy* 174 (July–Aug. 2012): 53–56. Web. 5 Mar. 2017. <https://www.radicalphilosophy.com/wp-content/files_mf/rp174_obituary_nicholas_ray_jeanlaplanche.pdf>

Réage, Pauline. *The Story of O*. 1954. Trans. Sabine d'Estrée. 1965. New York: Ballantine, 1973. Print.

Redding, Paul. *Continental Idealism: Leibniz to Nietzsche*. London: Routledge, 2009. Print.

Reid-Pharr, Robert F. *Archives of Flesh: African America, Spain, and Post-Humanist Critique*. New York: New York UP, 2016. Print.

Riley, Denise. *"Am I That Name?": Feminism and the Category of "Women" in History*. Minneapolis: U of Minnesota P, 1988. Print.

Roach, Tom. *Friendship as a Way of Life: Foucault, AIDS, and the Politics of Shared Estrangement*. Albany, NY: State U of New York P, 2012. Print.

Rocco, John Paul. *The Logic of the Lure*. Chicago: U of Chicago P, 2002. Print.

Roth, Michael S. *Knowing and History: Appropriations of Hegel in Twentieth-Century France*. Ithaca, NY: Cornell UP, 1988. Print.

Royle, Nicholas. *In Memory of Jacques Derrida*. Edinburgh: Edinburgh UP, 2009. Print.

Rózsa, Erzsébet. *Modern Individuality in Hegel's Practical Philosophy*. Trans. Tamás Nyirkos. Leiden: Brill, 2012. Print.

Rumaker, Michael. *A Day and a Night at the Baths*. Bolinas, CA: Grey Fox P, 1979. Print.

Russell, Bertrand. *A Critical Exposition of the Philosophy of Leibniz*. 1900. London: Routledge, 1992. Print.

———. *A History of Western Philosophy and Its Connection with Political and Social Circumstances from the Earliest Times to the Present Day*. New York: Simon and Schuster, 1945. Print.

———. *An Outline of Philosophy*. 1927. London: Routledge, 2001. Print.

———. "Recent Work on the Philosophy of Leibniz." 1903. *Leibniz: A Collection of Critical Essays*. Ed. Harry G. Frankfurt. Garden City, NY: Anchor, 1972. 365–400. Print.

Rutherford, Donald. "Metaphysics: The Late Period." *The Cambridge Companion to Leibniz*. Ed. Nicholas Jolley. Cambridge: Cambridge UP, 1995. 124–75. Print.

Ruti, Mari. *The Singularity of Being: Lacan and the Immortal Within*. New York: Fordham UP, 2012. Print.

Rycenga, Jennifer. "Queerly Amiss: Sexuality and the Logic of Adorno's Dialectics." *Adorno: A Critical Reader*. Ed. Nigel Gibson and Andrew Rubin. Malden, UK: Blackwell, 2002. 361–78. Print.

Sagan, Dorion. "Umwelt after Uexküll." Introduction. Uexküll 1–34.

Said, Edward W. "Traveling Theory." 1982. *The World, the Text, and the Critic*. Cambridge, MA: Harvard UP, 1983. 226–47. Print.

Scarfone, Dominique. *Laplanche: An Introduction*. Trans. Dorothée Bonnigal-Katz. New York: Unconscious in Translation, 2015. Print.

Scholem, Gershom. *Kabbalah*. 1974. New York: Meridian, 1978. Print.

———. "The Messianic Idea in Kabbalism." 1958. Trans. Moses Hadas. *Messianic* 37–48.

———. *The Messianic Idea in Judaism and Other Essays in Jewish Spirituality*. 1971. New York: Schocken, 1995. Print.

———. "Toward an Understanding of the Messianic Idea in Judaism." 1959. Trans. Michael A. Meyer. *Messianic* 1–36.

———. 'Walter Benjamin and His Angel." 1972. Trans. Werner Dannhauser. G. Smith 51–89.

———. *Walter Benjamin: The Story of a Friendship*. 1975. Trans. Harry Zohn. New York: New York Review Books, 1981. Print.

Schor, Naomi. Introduction. Schor and Weed, vii–xix.

———. "This Essentialism Which Is Not One: Coming to Grips with Irigaray." Schor and Weed, 40–62.

Schor, Naomi, and Elizabeth Weed, eds. *The Essential Difference*. Bloomington and Indianapolis: Indiana UP, 1994. Print.

Schwanke, Johannes. "The Indispensability of Theological Adscription in Biomedicine: An Answer to Peter Dabrock from a Lutheran Perspective." *Christian Bioethics* 16.2 (2010): 203–17. *Oxford Academic*. Web. 23 Feb. 2016.

———. "Lebendige Kommunikation oder technische Reproduktion? Schöpfungsverständnis in Luthers Großer Genesisvorlesung (1535–45)." *Schöpfungsglaube—von der Bioethik herausgefordert*. Ed. Friedrich-Otto Scharbau. Erlangen: Martin-Luther-Verlag, 2001. 47–67. Print.

———. "Luther's Theology of Creation." *The Oxford Handbook of Martin Luther's Theology*. Ed. Robert Kolb, Irene Dingel, and L'ubomír Batka. Oxford: Oxford UP, 2014. 201–11. Print.

Schwebel, Paula L. "Intensive Infinity: Walter Benjamin's Reception of Leibniz and Its Sources." *MLN* 127.3 (Apr. 2012): 589–610. Print.

———. "Monad and Time: Reading Leibniz with Heidegger and Benjamin." *Sparks Will Fly: Benjamin and Heidegger*. Ed. Andrew Benjamin and Dimitri Vardoulakis, eds. Albany, NY: State U of New York P, 2016. 123–44. Print.

Schweppenhäuser, Gerhard. *Theodor W. Adorno: An Introduction*. Trans. James Rolleston. Durham, NC: Duke UP, 2009. Print.

Scott, Darieck. *Extravagant Abjection: Blackness, Power, and Sexuality in the African American Literary Imagination*. New York: New York UP, 2010. Print.

Sedgwick, Eve Kosofsky. *Tendencies*. Durham, NC: Duke UP, 1993. Print.

Seeber, Hans Ulrich. *Literarische Faszination in England um 1900*. Heidelberg: Universitätverlag Winter, 2012. Print.

Sellbach, Undine, and Stephen Loo. "Insects and Other Minute Perceptions in the Baroque House." *Deleuze and the Non/Human*. Ed. Jon Roffe and Hannah Stark, eds. London: Palgrave Macmillan, 2015. 103–21. Print.

Shaviro, Steven. "Foreign Territory: The Promises and Perils of Speculative Realism." *Genealogies of Speculation: Materialism and Subjectivity since Structuralism*. Ed. Armen Avanessian and Suhail Malik. London: Bloomsbury, 2016. 29–40. Print.

Sheldon, Rebekah. "Form/Matter/Chora: Object Oriented Ontology and Feminist New Materialism." *The Nonhuman Turn*. Ed. Richard Grusin. Minneapolis: U of Minnesota P, 2015. 193–222. Print.

Shohat, Ella. *Taboo Memories, Diasporic Voices*. Durham, NC: Duke UP, 2006. Print.

Simmel, Georg. *Grundfragen der Soziologie: Individuum und Gesellschaft*. 1917. *Gesamtausgabe*. Vol. 16. Ed. Gregor Fitzi and Otthein Rammstedt. Frankfurt-am-Main: Suhrkamp, 1999. 59–149. Print.

———. "Sociability." 1910. Trans. Everett C. Hughes. *On Individuality and Social Forms: Selected Writings*. Ed. Donald N. Levine. Chicago: Chicago UP, 1971. 127–40. Print.

———. *The Sociology of Georg Simmel*. Ed. and trans. Kurt H. Wolff. New York: Free P, 1950. Print.

———. "Soziologie der Geselligkeit." 1910. *Verhandlungen des 1. Deutschen Soziologientages*. Ed. Deutsche Gesellschaft für Sociolozie. Frankfurt-am-Main: Sauer und Auvermann, 1969. 1–16. Print.

Singh, Sonam. "Baudelaire without Benjamin: Contingency, History, Modernity." *Comparative Literature* 64.4 (Fall 2012): 407–28. Print

Smith, Daniel W. *Essays on Deleuze*. Edinburgh: Edinburgh UP, 2012. Print.

Smith, Gary, ed. *On Walter Benjamin: Essays and Recollections*. Cambridge, MA: MIT P, 1988. Print.

Smith-Rosenberg, Carroll. "The Female World of Love and Ritual: Relations Between Women in Nineteenth-Century America." 1975. *Disorderly Conduct: Visions of Gender in Victorian America*. New York: Oxford UP, 1985. 53–76. Print.

Somerville, Siobhan B. *Queering the Color Line: Race and the Invention of Homosexuality in American Culture*. Durham, NC: Duke UP, 2000. Print.

Steiner, George. Introduction. Benjamin, *Origin* 7–24.

Stockton, Kathryn Bond. *Beautiful Bottom, Beautiful Shame: Where "Black" Meets "Queer."* Durham, NC: Duke UP, 2006. Print.

Taminiaux, Jacques. *Poetics, Speculation, and Judgment: The Shadow of the Work of Art from Kant to Phenomenology*. Trans. Michael Gendre. Albany, NY: State U of New York P, 1993. Print.

Taylor, Charles. *Hegel*. 1975. Cambrige: Cambridge UP, 2005. Print.

Terry, Jennifer. *An American Obsession: Science, Medicine, and Homosexuality in Modern Society*. Chicago: U of Chicago P, 1999. Print.

Thys, Michale. *Fascinatie: Een fenomenologisch-psychoanalytische verkenning van het onmenselijke*. Amsterdam: Boom, 2006. Print.

Tiedemann, Rolf. "Dialectics at a Standstill: Approaches to the Passagen-Werk." Trans. Gary Smith and André Lefevere. Benjamin, *Arcades* 929–45.

Tiffany, Daniel. *Infidel Poetics: Riddles, Nightlife, Substance*. Chicago: U of Chicago P, 2009. Print.

Tóibín, Colm. Introduction. Beckett, *Grove* ix–xvi.

Tournier, Michel. *Gemini*. 1974. Trans. Anne Carter. Baltimore: Johns Hopkins UP, 1998. Print.

Trezise, Thomas. *Into the Breach: Samuel Beckett and the Ends of Literature*. Princeton, NJ: Princeton UP, 1990. Print.

Tuhkanen, Mikko. "Breeding (and) Reading: Lesbian Knowledge, Eugenic Discipline, and *The Children's Hour*," *Modern Fiction Studies* 48.4 (Winter 2002): 1001–40. Print.

———. "Grotesquely Becoming: *Tarzan*'s Queer Hominization." *diacritics* 44.1 (2016): 28–58. Print.

———. "Performativity and Becoming." *Cultural Critique* 72 (Spring 2009): 1–35. Print.

———. "Scattering Being: Leo Bersani and Diasporic Modernity." *CR: The Centennial Review* 13.3 (2013): 53–88. Print.

Tuhkanen, Mikko, ed. *Leo Bersani: Queer Theory and Beyond*. Albany, NY: State U of New York P, 2014. Print.

Uexküll, Jakob von. *A Foray into the World of Animals and Humans: With a Theory of Meaning*. 1934. Trans. Joseph D. O'Neil. Minneapolis: U of Minnesota P, 2010. Print.

Verene, Donald Phillip. *Hegel's Absolute: An Introduction to Reading the* Phenomenology of Spirit. Albany, NY: State U of New York P, 2007. Print.

Wahl, François. "The Subtractive." Preface. Alain Badiou, *Conditions*. 1992. Trans. Steven Corcoran. London: Continuum, 2008. viii–xliv. Print.

Weber, Max. *The Protestant Ethic and the Spirit of Capitalism*. 1920. Trans. Talcott Parsons. 1930. London: Routledge, 2001. Print.

Weeks, Jeffrey. *Sexuality and Its Discontents: Meanings, Myths, and Modern Sexualities*. London: Routledge and Kegan Paul, 1985. Print.

Weingart, Brigitte. "Contact at a Distance: The Topology of Fascination." *Rethinking Emotion: Interiority and Exteriority in Premodern, Modern, and Contemporary Thought*. Ed. Rüdiger Campe and Julia Weber. Berlin: De Gruyter, 2014. 72–100. Print.

White, Edmund. *Marcel Proust*. New York: Lipper/Viking, 1999. Print.

Wiegman, Robyn. "Sex and Negativity; or, What Queer Theory Has for You." Rev. of Lauren Berlant and Lee Edelman, *Sex, or the Unbearable*. *Cultural Critique* 95 (Winter 2017): 219–43. *Project Muse*. Web. 19 July 2017.

Wilkinson, Lynn Rosellen. *The Dream of an Absolute Language: Emanuel Swedenborg and French Literary Culture*. Albany, NY: State U of New York P, 1996. Print.

Wilson, Catherine. *Leibniz's Metaphysics: A Historical and Comparative Study*. Princeton: Princeton UP, 1989. Print.

Wilson, Margaret D. "The Phenomenalisms of Leibniz and Berkeley." *Essays on the Philosophy of George Berkeley*. Ed. E. Sosa. Dordrecht: D. Reidel. 3–22. Print.

Wingren, Gustaf. *Luther on Vocation*. 1942. Trans. Carl C. Rasmussen. Eugene: Wipf & Stock, 2004. Print.

Winslade, William J. "Russell's Theory of Relations." *Essays on Bertrand Russell*. Ed. E. D. Klemke. Urbana: U of Illinois P, 1970. 81–101. Print.

Winthrop-Young, Geoffrey. "Bubbles and Webs: A Backdoor Stroll through the Readings of Uexküll." Afterword. Uexküll 209–43.

Wirth, Jason M. *The Conspiracy of Life: Meditations on Schelling and His Time*. Albany, NY: State U of New York P, 2003. Print.

Wolin, Richard. *Walter Benjamin: An Aesthetic of Redemption*. New York: Columbia UP, 1982. Print.

Young, Robert J. C. *Colonial Desire: Hybridity in Theory, Culture and Race*. 1995. London: Routledge, 1996. Print.

Zangenberg, Mikkel Bruun. "In the Midst of the Monad: Reflections on Auratic Alignments of the Everyday in Leibniz and Benjamin." *Actualities of Aura: Twelve Studies of Walter Benjamin*. Ed. Dag Petersson and Erik Steinskog. Svanesund, Sweden: Nordic Summer UP, 2005. 170–95. Print.

Zupančič, Alenka. "Sex, ontology, subjectivity: In conversation with Alenka Zupančič." By Randall Terada. *Psychoanalysis, Culture and Society* 20 (2015): 192–206. Web. 5 Aug. 2016. doi: 10.1057/pcs.2015.16

———. *Why Psychoanalysis? Three Interventions*. Aarhus: Aarhus Universitetsforlag/ Nordisk Sommeruniversitet Press, 2008. Print.

Index

Adamic language, 132, 140
Adorno, Theodor, 16–17, 68, 143, 149
the aesthetic: Bersani on, 19–20; as beyond sexuality, 122; Dionysian/Apollonian dynamics, 103–6, 109–10, 112
"afterwardsness," 4, 6, 48, 135
Agamben, Giorgio, 43
ahuman, 167–68
AIDS, 8, 9
Althusser, Louis, 13, 68, 193n46
analysis: Laplanche on, 113–14; vs. psychotherapy, 201–2n114; as redemptive, 118
Anaximander, 18
animal ecstasy, 171–75
annihilating desire. *See* desire
anthropogenesis, 73, 121, 191–92n28, 203n11
antiessentialism, 36, 47
antinatalism, 40, 43, 126
Arendt, Hannah, 151
Aristotle, 15, 35, 37, 59, 186n70
Arnauld, Antoine, 37
Artaud, Antonin, 38
Arts of Impoverishment: Beckett, Rothko, Resnais (Bersani and Dutoit): and Beckett's aesthetics of failure, 125–26; Bersanian shift in, toward sociability, 124–25; and centrifugality of Resnais's cinema, 55; modernity in, 87; monadology, in 32–34; narcissism and psychoanalysis in, 150; and queering, 137
Arts of Impoverishment: Beckett, Rothko, Resnais (with Bersani), monadology in, 38
ascesis, 51, 52, 144–45
Assyrian art, 54–56, 164–65
at once mode, 205n35
avocation, 121, 167, 170

Badiou, Alain, 7, 23, 30, 181n1
Bakhtin, Mikhail, 182–83n18
Baldwin, James, 142–43
Balzac, Honoré de, 27, 31, 48
Balzac to Beckett: Center and Circumference in French Fiction (Bersani), 31; centrifugality in, 24, 26–29; and centrifugal queer theory, 48–50; monadology in, 30–32; overview of, 23–24; shift to centripetality in, 31
Barthes, Roland, on Proust, 25
Baudelaire, Charles, 19, 38, 53, 91, 93–101, 162, 171–73
Baudelaire and Freud (Bersani): monadology in, 38; and psychoanalytic theory, 58
Bayer, Oswald, 151, 169, 173–74
beauty, 96–99, 162

Beckett, Samuel: aesthetic of, vs. Proust's, 25–26; aesthetics of impoverishment, 33–34, 40, 41, 45, 124, 126; antinatalism, 43; and becoming-human, 122–23, 137–38; and centripetality, 31, 45; and "chattering," 141–42; "cult of failure," 49; and ethics of failure, 135–36; and failure, 125–26; and Genet, 49–50; Leibnizian orientation of works, 32–33, 39–40, 60; monadology in works by, 31, 37, 124, 128, 173, 184n31, 186n77; and nonrelationality, 17, 38–39; on Proust, 32; and the Unnamable, 126–27, 203–4n14

becoming-human: Beckett's vs. Laplanche's theories of, 122–23; Laplanche on, 150; as queering, 137

Benjamin, Walter, 16, 88–93, 102, 123, 130–32, 140, 162, 198n30, 206n39, 207n52

Bergson, Henri, 18, 30, 33, 40

Berkeley, George, 67, 68, 185n42

Bersani, Leo: on the aesthetic, 19–20; on Benjamin, 92; Benjamin's influence on, 142; and "circular mobility," 2–3; Deleuze's influence on, 5–6; Derrida's influence on, 28; essentialism of works by, 1–8; on French modernist literature, 25–34; on Freud, 10, 61; on Freudian realism, 68–69; Freud's influence on, 4–5; on Godard, 41–43; on James, 79–81; on jouissance, 9, 73; and Laplanche, 58, 60–61, 70–72, 74; and monadology, 17–18, 38, 61; ontology of, 7–8, 17; and the other, 82–83; on primary narcissism, 69; on Proust, 3, 26; Proust's influence on, 4–5; and queer theory, 25, 35, 45, 48–54, 137; on "recategorization," 3–6, 9–10, 21, 25, 45, 128, 138, 150, 165, 166, 174; on relationality, 17; speculativeness of works by, 1, 8–21; and "spiral model," 4; works: *Arts of Impoverishment: Beckett, Rothko, Resnais* (with Dutoit), 32–34, 38, 55, 87, 124–26, 137, 150; *Balzac to Beckett: Center and Circumference in French Fiction*, 4, 6, 23–24, 26–29, 30–32, 48–49; *Baudelaire and Freud*, 6, 38, 58; *Caravaggio's Secrets*, 19; *Caravaggio's Secrets* (with Dutoit), 54–55, 114–17, 165–66; *The Culture of Redemption*, 2, 3, 27, 87–112, 134–35, 172, 183n22; *The Death of Stéphane Mallarmé*, 2, 75–81; *Forms of Being: Cinema, Aesthetics, Subjectivity* (with Dutoit), 55; *The Forms of Violence* (with Dutoit), 54, 164–65; *The Freudian Body: Psychoanalysis and Art*, 10, 19, 129; *A Future for Astyanax: Character and Desire in Literature*, 6, 38, 58, 70, 141, 152–58; *Homos*, 45, 48–49, 159; "Is the Rectum a Grave?," 8–9, 51, 141; *Is the Rectum a Grave?*, 143–44; *Marcel Proust: The Fictions of Life and of Art*, 2, 3, 6; "The Other Freud," 86; *Thoughts and Things*, 4, 18, 41–43, 166. *See also* specific works

Bersanian onto-ethics/aesthetics, 19–20, 23; as both Proustian and Beckettian, 26; in *The Culture of Redemption* (Bersani), 91; of impoverishment, 40; and monadology, 60; Nietzsche's influence on, 103; as Proustian-Deleuzean and Beckettian-Blanchotian, 33–34

betrayal, 50, 166–67
The Birth of Tragedy (Nietzsche), 133–34
Blanchot, Maurice: and centripetal withdrawal, 45; on essential solitude, 39, 126
Bodies That Matter (Butler), 188n106
Bonaventure, 19
Boundas, Constantin, 30
Bowie, Malcolm, 205n35
Brée, Germaine, 2–3
"breeders," 209n12
Brix, Michel, 96, 98
Bruno, Giordano, 33
Burroughs, Edgar Rice, 120, 202–3n6
Butler, Judith, 18, 32; antiessentialism of, 47; and feminist antiessentialism, 36; and Foucault, 46–47, 189n118; on performativity, 46; performativity concept, 25, 48, 51, 56; on speculative metaphysics, 14–15; works: *Bodies That Matter*, 188n106; *Gender Trouble: Feminism and the Subversion of Identity*, 36, 46, 185n60; *The Psychic Life of Power*, 203n11; *Subjects of Desire: Hegelian Reflections in Twentieth-Century France*, 46, 187–88n99

callings. *See* vocations
Caravaggio's Secrets (Bersani and Dutoit): and centrifugality, 54–55; and desire, 165–66; and Proust's buttercup scene, 115–17; and psychoanalytic theory, 114–15
Cartesian moment, 121–22, 149
Castiglia, Christopher, 7
centrifugality: in *Balzac to Beckett: Center and Circumference in French Fiction* (Bersani), 24, 26–29; in Bersani's thought, 54–55; defined, 180n57; and Derrida, 28; in *The Forms of Violence* (Bersani and Dutoit), 54, 164–65; in Foucault's thought, 48; of French modernist literature, 45; in Proust's works, 28–29, 41; of queer theory, 45, 48; and relationality, 56; of Resnais's cinema, 55
centripetality: and Beckett, 31, 45; and Blanchot, 45; defined, 180n57; Deleuze on, 44–45; as essentialist, 35; in Godard's films, 41–42, 55; in Proust's works, 28–29; and sexuality, 24, 55; shift to, in *Balzac to Beckett: Center and Circumference in French Fiction* (Bersani), 31; and sociability, 124, 140. *See also* monadology
chariot allegory, 159–162, 166, 172
"chattering," 140–1446. *See also* sociability
Christianity, 109
"circular mobility," 2–3. *See also* recategorization
cloning, 148–49, 152, 174
Cooper, Dennis, 115, 137
correlationism, 11
correspondences, 96–98, 117, 118, 157, 172
Critique of Pure Reason (Kant), 1–2
cruising, 143–44
The Culture of Redemption (Bersani): and Baudelaire, 91, 93–101; and Benjaminian thought, 88–93; centrifugality of psychoanalytic theory, 27; and correspondences, 172; and modern alienation, 87–88; modernity in, 87; and monadism of Proustian narrator, 183n22; and Nietzsche, 91, 93, 101–12; and the Unnamable, 134–35

Darwin, Charles, 17

Davidson, Arnold, 52–53
A Day and a Night at the Baths (Rumaker), 149, 174
death drive, 71, 154
The Death of Stéphane Mallarmé (Bersani): and enigmatic signifiers, 78–81; and ethics of otherness, 75–80
de Beauvoir, Simone, 36
deconstruction, 48
Deleuze, Gilles: on centripetal withdrawal, 44–45; influence of, on Bersani, 5–6; on monadology, 17, 29; on Nietzsche, 108; and the other, 82; on Proust, 29, 30, 43–44; on the tick, 40; works: *Anti-Oedipus: Capitalism and Schizophrenia*, 5–6
Derrida, Jacques, 6, 8, 183–84n23; on Benjamin, 207n52; *différance*, 149; influence of, on Bersani, 28; "iteration" concept, 47; on monadology, 16; works: "Force and Signification," 29–30; *Of Grammatology*, 23–24, 26–27; "Structure, Sign, and Play in the Discourse of Human Sciences," 23–24, 26–27
Descartes, René, 2, 14, 22, 37
desire, 70–71, 77, 79–83, 147; and *Caravaggio's Secrets* (Bersani and Dutoit), 165–66; death of, 151; modes of, 152–53
Dewey, John, 10–11
difference, 149, 152, 155
Dionysian/Apollonian dynamics, 103–6, 109–10, 112, 130, 201n102
the drive, 98
dualism, 94–95, 103–6, 170
Duns Scotus, 38
Duthuit, Georges, 32–33
Dutoit, Ulysse: on relationality, 17; works: *Arts of Impoverishment: Beckett, Rothko, Resnais* (with Bersani), 32–34, 38, 55, 87, 124–26, 137, 150; *Caravaggio's Secrets* (with Bersani), 54–55, 114–17, 165–66; *Forms of Being: Cinema, Aesthetics, Subjectivity* (with Bersani), 55; *The Forms of Violence* (with Bersani), 54, 164–65
Dyer, Richard, 51, 52

ébranlement: and Baudelaire's aesthetic, 100–101; and Freud's work, 21; and hominizing masochism, 73; and recategorization, 9; and self-loss, 51. *See also* "shattering"
ecstasy, 172–73
Edman, Irwin, 162
The Ego and the Id (Freud), 65
"empty time," 129–130
Engels, Friedrich, 2, 14, 22, 68
enigmatic signifiers, 78–81, 115–16, 117, 136–37, 192n30; and hominization, 159; vocations as, 120–21
essence. *See* essentialism; monadology
essentialism: of Bersani's works, 1–8; centripetality of, 35; critical views of, 7; and the eternal, 95–96; Leibniz on, 32; and queer theory, 35; and speculative thought, 12–13
"essential solitude," 39, 126, 186n68, 186n77
the eternal, 95–96
evolutionary Marxism, 108

Faderman, Lillian, 47
failure, ethics of, 33, 125, 135–36
Fanon, Frantz, 203n11
Felman, Shoshana, 195–96n99
feminist theory, 35–36
Feuerbach, Ludwig, 15
Fichte, Johann Gottlieb, 46, 68
Finnegan's Wake (Joyce), 78

Flaubert, Gustave, 27, 34
Fliess, Wilhelm, 62, 64
Forms of Being: Cinema, Aesthetics, Subjectivity (Bersani and Dutoit), 55
The Forms of Violence (Bersani and Dutoit), and centrifugality, 54, 164–65
Forrester, John, 77
Foucault, Michel: and aesthetics of existence, 52–53; Butler's view of, 46–47; Butler's vs. Bersani's view of, 189n118; on centrifugality, 48; and "confessional" psychology, 79; and dialectic, 108; on historiography, 200–201n94; and homosexuality, 47, 52; and interiority, 149; and queer theory, 46–48; and relationality, 56; Said's vs. Bersani's view of, 178n14; on sexuality, 55; and singularity of moments, 123–24
free association, 113
French modernist literature, 25–34, 45
Freud, Sigmund: Bersani on, 61; influence of, on Bersani, 4–5; Laplanche on, 4; on masochism, 72–73; on nonsexual sadism, 153–54; on object-love, 160–61; on primary masochism, 8–9, 154; on primary narcissism, 66, 134; "realism" of, 68–69; seduction theory, 59–60, 62–66, 193–94n71; speculativeness of works by, 10; as speculative thinker, 21; works: *Civilization and Its Discontents*, 3; *The Ego and the Id*, 65; *Introductory Lectures on Psychoanalysis*, 57; *Three Essays on the Theory of Sexuality*, 62, 64, 160–61. *See also* psychoanalytic theory
The Freudian Body: Psychoanalysis and Art (Bersani), 129
Fromm, Erich, 62
fugues, 27–28, 43–44
Fuss, Diana, 8, 35, 59
A Future for Astyanax: Character and Desire in Literature (Bersani): "chattering" in, 141; desire in, 70; monadology in, 38; and narcissism, 152–58; and psychoanalytic theory, 58

Gasché, Rodolphe, 12
Gaye, Marvin, 81–82
gay macho culture, 51
Gender Trouble: Feminism and the Subversion of Identity (Butler), 36, 46
Genet, Jean, 25, 49–51, 56, 167
German Idealism, 11
Gide, André, 159
Gilroy, Paul, 7
Giovanni's Room (Baldwin), 142–43
Glissant, Édouard, 79, 195n97
Gobineau, Arthur de, 149
Godard, Jean-Luc, 55; Bersani on, 41–43; centripetality in films by, 41–42; and Proust, 41
The Golden Bowl (James), 79–81
The Great Chain of Being (Lovejoy), 33
Grosz, Elizabeth, 13, 71
Guattari, Félix, 71; works: *Anti-Oedipus: Capitalism and Schizophrenia*, 5–6

Habermas, Jürgen, 92
Hacking, Ian, 16
Hadot, Pierre, 7, 21, 53
Hallward, Peter, 82
Harland, Richard, 28
Hartmann, Eduard von, 108
Hegel, G.W.F.: Butler's synthesis of, 46; on consciousness, 168; and monadology, 14, 20; and narcissism, 151; Nietzsche, on, 107–8; on

Hegel, G.W.F. *(continued)*
speculation, 2, 11–13; works: *Phenomenology*, 14; *Science of Logic*, 11, 14, 15
Heidegger, Martin, 61, 69, 119, 140
Heine, Heinrich, 133, 134
Hill, Leslie, 173
hominization, 72–73, 136, 159, 191–92n28
homomonadology, defined, 24
Homos (Bersani), 45, 48–49, 159
homosexuality: and "chattering," 142–43; and "cloning," 148–49, 152; and Foucault, 47, 52; and gay macho culture, 51; and monadism, 143; and narcissism, 158; and Proustian thought, 49; and *The Story of O* (Réage), 156–58. *See also* queer theory
Husserl, Edmund, 16

Idealism, 22, 66–69, 81
idealization, 96–101, 161–62
The Image (Berg), 153, 154–57, 163
impoverishment, principle of, 33–34, 40, 53, 145
individuation. *See* monadology
interiority, 149
Intimate Strangers (film), 145
"Is the Rectum a Grave?" (Bersani): and ascesis, 51; and "chattering," 141; speculative orientation of, 8–9
Is the Rectum a Grave? (Bersani), sociability in, 143–44
"iteration" concept, 47

James, Henry, 38, 79–81, 141–42
Jameson, Frederic, 16, 83, 151, 168
jouissance, 128–29; and the aesthetic, 19; and Baudelaire's aesthetic, 99; Bersani on, 9, 73; of correspondences, 172; and Freud's primary masochism, 8–9; in *The Image* (Berg), 154–55
Joyce, James, 78

Kabbalism, 198n30, 207n57
Kant, Immanuel: on speculation, 1–2, 11; works: *Critique of Pure Reason*, 1–2, 11
Kaufman, Walter, 117, 133
Klein, Melanie, 72
Krauss, Lawrence, 18, 166
Kristeva, Julia, 28, 60, 182–83n18

Lacan, Jacques, 5, 9, 46–47, 75, 82, 127, 161, 162, 178n15
language, 140. *See also* "chattering"
The Language of Psychoanalysis (Laplanche and Pontalis), 66–67
Laplanche, Jean, 57; on analysis, 113–14; on becoming-human, 150; and Bersani, 60–61, 70–72, 74; and *ébranlement*, 9; and enigmatic signifiers, 78–80; on enigma vs. riddle, 64; on Freud, 4; on Freud's seduction theory, 62–66; influence of, on Bersani, 58; and Leibnizian philosophy, 67; on monadism, 66; on monadology, 16; on the other, 59; on primary narcissism, 65, 66, 69; and recategorization, 3; rejection of monadology, 58–61; and relationality, 58–59; on sexuality, 73, 191n24; on "spiral model," 4; on vocations, 120–21; works: *The Language of Psychoanalysis* (with Pontalis), 66–67; *Life and Death in Psychoanalysis*, 58–59
Lavater, Johann Kaspar, 96, 162
Leconte, Patrice, 145
Leibniz, Gottfried Wilhelm, 14, 183–84n23, 187n91; and Benjaminian

thought, 90; on connectedness, 173; on essences, 32; on mirrors, 161; monadology of, 24–25, 36–37, 42–43, 67, 83; and Proust, 183n20; works: *Monadology*, 15
Levinas, Emmanuel, 30, 36, 170
Libertson, Joseph, 186n68
Life and Death in Psychoanalysis (Laplanche), 58–59
Linneaus, Carl, 17
literary criticism, 75–78
love, 161
Lovejoy, Arthur, 67; *The Great Chain of Being*, 33–34
Luther, Martin, 11, 22, 119, 143, 147, 169

Malabou, Catherine, 17, 20
Malebranche, Nicolas, 2, 14
Mallarmé, Stéphane, 43, 75–81
Mann, Thomas, 114
Marcuse, Herbert, 12
Marx, Karl, 83, 140; and monadology, 15–16, 20, 68; on speculation, 1–2
masochism, 8–9, 72–73, 115–16, 153–55, 164, 194n84. *See also* primary masochism
Masson, Jeffrey, 62
Meillassoux, Quentin, 11
Meltzer, Françoise, 93–94
Mercer, Christia, 67
messianism, 198n30
Meyer, Richard, 148–49
Mikics, David, 28
Miller, James, 16
mirrors, 161
modernity: in *Arts of Impoverishment: Beckett, Rothko, Resnais* (Bersani and Dutoit), 87; Benjamin's understanding of, 88; in *The Culture of Redemption* (Bersani), 87–88; and interiority, 149; and monadism, 143; Nietzsche's critique of, 102–3; and ontology of lack, 86. See also *The Culture of Redemption* (Bersani)
monadic time, 130–34
monadism, 189–190n126; and homosexuality, 143; impoverishment of, 145; Laplanche on, 66; and modernity, 143; postulate of, 67; and primary narcissism, 74–75; of Proustian narrator, 183n22
monadology: in *Arts of Impoverishment: Beckett, Rothko, Resnais* (Bersani and Dutoit), 32–34; in *Balzac to Beckett: Center and Circumference in French Fiction* (Bersani), 30–32; in Beckett's work, 31, 37; and Benjaminian thought, 90, 130–32; in Bersani's works, 17–18, 38, 61; and Blanchot's "essential solitude," 39; Deleuze on, 29; and Hegel, 14, 20; Laplanchean, 16, 58–61; in Leibnizian thought, 24–25, 36–37, 42–43, 83; and Marx, 15–16, 20; and mirrors, 161; in modern thought, 16–17; and psychoanalytic theory, 61, 75–82; and relationality, 42–43; Russell on, 38–39; and speculative thought, 15
Muriel (film), 55

Nachträglichkeit. See "afterwardsness"
Nancy, Jean-Luc, 20, 23, 171
narcissism, 22, 65–67, 68; atemporality of, 163; and cloning, 148–49; and desire, 153; and *A Future for Astyanax: Character and Desire in Literature* (Bersani), 152–58; and homosexuality, 158; and love, 161; and the other, 148, 151; primary, 65, 66, 68, 69, 70–75,

narcissism *(continued)*
134; and psychoanalytic theory, 149–150; and relationality, 160; speculative, 152, 167–174, 210n48; and speculative cosmology, 150–51; and *The Story of O* (Réage), 156–57
Nietzsche, Friedrich, 38, 40, 43, 49–50, 91, 93, 101–12, 130; works: *The Birth of Tragedy*, 133–34, 201n102
nonsexual sadism, 74
"now-time," 123

object-love, 160–61
Ong, Walter, 149
ontology: of Bersani, 7–8, 17; as critical target, 7
the other: and Baudelaire's aesthetic, 99–100; in Bersanian thought, 82–83; and Deleuze, 82; ethics of, 75–80; Laplanche on, 59; and narcissism, 148, 151; and the self, 168–69; and *The Story of O* (Réage), 155
"The Other Freud" (Bersani), 86

paradigmatic differences, 6–7
Passion (film), 41
pastoral narratives, 86
Pearson, Keith Ansell, 101–2
performativity, 46, 47–48, 49–51
personality, 127
Pfaff, Johann Friedrich, 168
Phaedrus (Plato), 160–61, 162, 166
Phillips, Adam, 24, 148, 149, 163, 174–75
Plato, 52, 59, 71, 169; chariot allegory, 159–162, 166, 172; works: *Phaedrus*, 160–61, 162, 166, 170
Platonic Forms, 96–97, 103, 160–62
Plotinus, 52
Poe, Edgar Allan, 104
Pontalis, Jean-Bertrand, 65, 66, 69, 121
predicates, 12–13, 35–36
primary masochism, 8–9, 74, 154. *See also* masochism
primary narcissism, 65, 66, 68, 69, 70–75, 128, 134
Proust, Marcel, 182n12; aesthetic of, vs. Beckett's, 25–26; Bersani on, 3, 26; Brée on, 2–3; and centrifugality/centripetality, 28–29, 41; Deleuze on, 29, 30, 43–44; and Godard, 41; and homosexuality, 49; influence of, on Bersani, 4–5; and Leibnizian philosophy, 183n20; as psychoanalytic novelist, 3; works: *À la recherche du temps perdu*, 3
The Psychic Life of Power (Butler), 203n11
psychoanalytic theory: and *Baudelaire and Freud* (Bersani), 6; and Bersani's work, 58; and *Caravaggio's Secrets* (Bersani and Dutoit), 114–15; and "chattering," 140–41; as Copernican revolution, 57–58; *ébranlement* of, 21; and *A Future for Astyanax: Character and Desire in Literature* (Bersani), 6; and monadology, 61, 75–82; and narcissism, 149–150; and Proust's works, 3; and redemption, 118; and sexuality, 60. *See also* Freud, Sigmund

queerness, 137
queer theory: antisocial mode of, 25; centrifugality of, 45, 48; and essentialism, 35; and Foucault, 46–48; and recategorization, 45. *See also* homosexuality

recategorization: Bersani on, 3–6, 9–10, 21, 25, 45, 128, 138, 150, 165, 166, 174; defined, 3, 4; and

ébranlement, 9–10; and queer theory, 45; and "spiral model," 4
redemption: and analysis, 118; Nietzsche's critique of, 101–13; terminology, 89; two movements of, 117–18
relationality: Bersani on, 17; and centrifugality, 56; in Laplanche's thought, 58–59; and monadology, 42–43; and narcissism, 160. *See also* sociability
Resnais, Alain, 55
reverse discourse, 47, 49
Rimbaud, Arthur, 38
Robinson Crusoe (Defoe), 67–68
Rothko, Mark, 204n17
Rousset, Jean, 29
Rubin, Gayle, 36
Rumaker, Michael, 149, 174
Russell, Bertrand, 16, 24–25, 36, 38–39, 42, 59, 67, 126, 166, 173, 186n70
Ruti, Mari, 151

Sade, Marquis de, and *ébranlement*, 9, 73
sadism, 72–73, 153–58, 159, 194n84
Said, Edward, 177–78n14
sameness. *See* correspondences
Scenario (film), 41
Scholem, Gershom, 89, 92, 93
Schopenhauer, Arthur, 40
Schwanke, Johannes, 148, 170
Schwebel, Paula, 131
Schweppenhäuser, Gerhard, 11
Sedgwick, Eve Kosofsky, 137
seduction theory, 59–60, 62–66, 193–94n71
Seneca, 52, 53
sexual abuse, 62–63
sexuality: the aesthetic as "beyond," 122; and becoming-human, 137; and centripetality, 24, 55; and *ébranlement*, 9–10; Laplanche on, 73, 191n24; in psychoanalytic thought, 60. *See also* seduction theory
"shattering," 9, 58, 73, 98–99, 106, 111, 117, 124, 129, 157, 205n35. See also *ébranlement*
Simmel, Georg, 20, 124, 138–39, 144
singularity. *See* monadology
Smith, Daniel W., 16, 37, 42, 68, 71, 86
sociability: in *Arts of Impoverishment: Beckett, Rothko, Resnais* (Bersani and Dutoit), 124–25; and centripetality, 124, 140; and "chattering," 141, 142, 145–46; in *Is the Rectum a Grave?* (Bersani), 143–44; in Simmel's thought, 138–39, 144. *See also* "chattering"; relationality
speculative astronomy, 18–19
speculative cosmology, and narcissism, 150–51
speculative idealism, 167
speculative narcissism, 152, 167–174, 210n48
speculativeness: of Bersani's works, 1, 8–21; and essentialism, 12–13; of Freud's work, 10, 21; Hegel on, 2, 11–13; of "Is the Rectum a Grave?" (Bersani), 8–9; Kant on, 1–2, 11; Marx on, 1–2; and monadology, 15; and "predicates," 12–13; theologians on, 169
speculative realism, 11, 13
Spencer, Herbert, 82
Spinoza, Baruch, 2, 13, 27
"spiral model": and "circular mobility," 2–3; Laplanche on, 4; recategorization as, 3
Stendahl, 27, 48

The Story of O (Réage), 153, 154, 155–58, 159–160, 161, 163, 165, 172
storytelling, 88, 103
Strachey, James, 64
structuralism, 29–30
Subjects of Desire: Hegelian Reflections in Twentieth-Century France (Butler), 46
Swedenborg, Emanuel, 97

Tarzan of the Apes (Burroughs), 120
temporality: "empty time," 129–130; monadic time, 130–34; and shift from psychoanalytic to aesthetic subject, 124; and the Unnamable, 128
Thoughts and Things (Bersani), 41–43, 166
Three Essays on the Theory of Sexuality (Freud), 62, 64, 160–61
the tick, 40
Tiedemann, Rolf, 131
Tiffany, Daniel, 132, 180–81n71
Tournier, Michel, 24
traumatic repetition, 3–4
Trezise, Thomas, 186n77

Uexküll, Jakob von, 40, 43–44
Ulysses (Joyce), 78
the Unnamable, 126–28, 134–35, 203–4n14
unrelatedness. *See* monadology

vitalism, 40
vocations, 119–120; as enigmatic signifiers, 120–21

Weber, Max, 119–120
Weeks, Jeffrey, 51–52
Wirth, Jason, 210n48
Wolin, Richard, 89, 92, 93

www.ingramcontent.com/pod-product-compliance
Lightning Source LLC
LaVergne TN
LVHW090807070826
844660LV00022B/1101

* 9 7 8 1 4 3 8 4 6 9 6 6 9 *